Rust Belt Resistance

Rust Belt Resistance

How a Small Community Took On Big Oil and Won

Perry Bush

The Kent State University Press
Kent, Ohio

Library of Congress Catalog Card Number 2011047790
ISBN 978-1-60635-117-8
Manufactured in the United States of America

Library of Congress Cataloging-in-Publication Data
Bush, Perry, 1959–
Rust belt resistance : how a small community took on big oil and won / Perry Bush.
p. cm.
Includes bibliographical references and index.
ISBN 978-1-60635-117-8 (hardcover : alk. paper) ∞
1. Lima (Ohio)—Economic policy—Decision making. 2. Petroleum—Refining—Ohio—Lima. 3. British Petroleum Company. 4. Corporate power—Ohio—Lima. I. Title.
HC108.L427B87 2012
338.7'66550977142—dc23

2011047790

16 15 14 13 12 5 4 3 2 1

For Elysia

Who has hung in there with me

Contents

Acknowledgments

This book took shape over a productive period of sabbatical release time, together with more summers of research and writing than I care to remember. In the process I have become deeply indebted, intellectually and otherwise, to several friends and colleagues. If any good results from this book, it ought to accrue to them. In return I can at least give these good people the small pleasure of seeing their names in print here.

A whole group of people provided a steady foundation of support at Bluffton University. Foremost among these have been my academic deans, John Kampen and Sally Weaver Sommer, who approved my sabbatical plans and in many other ways facilitated the completion of this project. I was also the grateful recipient of the financial assistance provided by a grant from the Bluffton University Research Center. Jim Harder took time out of his busy schedule as Bluffton's president to read and critique a chapter. Jeff Gundy and Hamid Rafizadeh read the entire manuscript, offering page after page of valuable critical suggestions. I likewise benefited immensely from the encouragement and insights of other Bluffton faculty colleagues as well as friends off campus: Jim Satterwhite, Andy Chappell-Dick, Rory Stauber, Gerald Mast, Lamar Nisly, Susan Streeter Carpenter, Hans Houshower, and J. Denny Weaver. In particular I want to thank Lamar Nisly for his constant encouragement on this project in our late night runs through the streets of Bluffton. George Lehman and Hamid Rafizadeh, of Bluffton's Division of Business Studies, did their best to teach this social historian something of the worldview and approaches of their discipline. If I proved a poor student it is no fault of theirs. I am indebted to Mary Jean Johnson and her staff at Bluffton University's Mussleman Library, who aided this project in a great many ways, particularly to reference librarians Paul Weaver, Kathleen

Aufderhaar, Carrie Phillips, Karyl Crawford, and Audra Hammond. Brenda Groman and Steve Rodabaugh were a continual help in troubleshooting my many computer problems. This research was also aided immensely by the dedicated labor of a team of student research assistants, who, over the years, spent endless hours at the copy machine, transcribed interviews, hunted down citations, and helped with many other thankless tasks. So I want to express my appreciation to Adam Criblez, Cortland Schoenherr, Matt Francis, Norma Flores, Erin Miller, Andrea Buckner, Bill Freil, Joel Koerner, Jacob Kovach, Brendan Haggerty, Jon Vanhouwe, Liz Bretz, Katy Hamann, Brent Householder, and Nadin-Sarah Salkic.

I was encouraged and recharged at key points by fruitful conversations with friends off campus: Ray Person of Ohio Northern University, David Koeller of North Park University, Steve Tripp of Grand Valley State University, and Bill Trollinger of the University of Dayton. Joel Tarr of Carnegie Mellon University was kind enough to read and critique the entire manuscript, sharing with me in this manner something of his decades of expertise in the history of urban infrastructures. Especially in the earlier stages of this undertaking, my thinking on the power and role of corporate mechanisms in American life was greatly stimulated by Greg Coleridge and his colleagues with the project on Corporations, Law, and Democracy of the American Friends Service Committee.

In completing the research for this book, I made, of course, a great many trips into Lima. This project could not have been completed without the ready cooperation and invaluable assistance of key people there. Foremost among these has been the honorable David Berger, mayor of the City of Lima, who shared with me significant papers and his memories, oral and written, of his city's engagement with British Petroleum. Judy Gilbert was similarly generous in allowing me access to some of her personal papers. Anna Selfridge of the Allen County, Ohio, Historical Society led me to old papers and photographs and in other ways greatly deepened my grasp of something of Lima's earlier history. In like ways I was aided by the staff at the Ohio Historical Center in Columbus. A great many of the photographs that illustrate this story came from the files of the *Lima News,* especially through the kind intervention of photo editor Craig Orosz, and WLIO-TV Lima, with the able assistance of Jeff Fitzgerald.

I would not have been able to trace this story had not many busy people graciously shared hours of their time in oral interviews. While space does not allow me to list them all here, I would be remiss in not thanking by name David Berger of Lima and Judy Gilbert and James Schaefer of BP, for their interviews were especially lengthy and spread over several days. In addition, I need to express my appreciation to a senior BP executive who preferred to remain unnamed but whose insights measurably deepened my grasp of the internal decision-making process at British Petroleum.

I am delighted that Kent State University Press agreed to publish this book. I need to extend my thanks to its first-rate editorial and production staff; its director, Will Underwood; its managing editor, Mary Young; and especially its acquisitions editor, Joyce Harrison, for the warm and professional way she initially cultivated the manuscript and then eased its way to publication.

Finally, I need to mention a few dear ones who contributed to this project both in overt and in less obvious ways. My father, Fred Bush, read the entire manuscript and kept pushing me to see it through to the end. My brother Preston Bush was a similar indefatigable source of encouragement. This book has been in construction through many of the teenage years of Kerry and Jackson Bush and through much of the childhood of Cassidy Bush, yet they all endured its presence patiently and with good humor. Their mother, Elysia Caldwell Bush, has likewise been close witness to this book's long gestation. More than that: she has shared in the many trials and the uncertain pleasures of life with me for more than a quarter of a century. It is enough to just say here that I am supremely and inexpressibly grateful. This book is for her.

Chapter 1

"Local Communities Are No Match for Industrial Corporations"

Lima, the county seat of Allen County, is a weathered industrial city of about forty thousand people, set against the flat and prosperous farmlands of northwest Ohio. It still possesses a certain charm. Local people can boast of a set of nearly new schools, a few grand old boulevards where the city's early industrialists once lived, and wide, tree-lined streets with some of the cheapest housing of any similar place in America. Nonetheless, the city seems haunted by the question of whether, when its financial magnates left, they might have taken its best days with them. Even as fierce a defender as its longtime mayor remembers that when he first drove into Lima as a young man, his first impressions were of a beaten-down old city that "hadn't taken very good care of itself." Three decades later Lima's face still seems worn and gray, especially when compared with the tracts of comfortable housing developments on its edges. Lima's urban thoroughfares are pockmarked with vacant lots and its most memorable physical characteristics are the number of railroad crossings that nearly barricade off its downtown. In fact, one cannot enter Lima without being reminded of the constant physical presence of trains. The city's heart consists of two massive hospitals, some public buildings and a varied collection of small restaurants and businesses spread over about eight blocks, and a business district tenaciously holding on against the attractions of the malls in the suburbs west of town. It is the kind of town perennially described by outside journalists with words like "blue-collar" and "gritty."[1]

Lima is also an island in every sense except the strictly geographic. In the spring and summer, it is an urban island amidst limitless green fields of corn and soybeans. Economically and demographically, it remains an island of working-class sensibilities surrounded on all sides by middle-class suburbia. These are the

The Lima refinery in the foreground, with downtown Lima behind. *Photo courtesy of the* Lima News.

Main entrance gate, BP Lima Refinery, mid-1990s. *Photo courtesy of the* Lima News.

"townships" that remain politically separate from the city while fully dependent on its services. The city is a political island as well, though one has to dig a bit deeper to fully see this. As the national left-leaning journal the *Nation* informed readers in 1996, Lima was "a rock-ribbed Republican bastion, a town that still brags of going for Goldwater in 1964." In fact, that claim isn't true; Lima went for Johnson that year by a small margin. Even so, conservative political instincts still run deep across Allen County and have been reinforced for decades by the city's newspaper, the *Lima News,* which for a generation now has served as a faithful, steady fount of libertarian free-market ideology. On the other hand, amidst the vast sea of Republican governments that dominate northwest Ohio, Lima's residents have, for more than two decades, retained enough blue-collar roots to regularly elect a feisty and progressive Democrat as their mayor. Not surprisingly, the city's newspaper and its mayor have generally locked horns, except for one short period, the greatest crisis in the city's modern history, when they joined in an unlikely but effective partnership.[2]

Lima is an island in another way, too, one that can be fully appreciated only by traveling south on Main Street from the business district, over the Ottawa River, past increasingly ramshackle homes to stand on a railway overpass. There to the west, just south of the city limits, unfolds a truly alien world. It is a scene that could be lifted from a futuristic movie: huge sculpted scaffolds of pipes emerging from fields of asphalt, dozens of valves emitting steam, blue flames flaring into the sky, all tended by a uniformed army in hard hats. The functionaries of this world speak in a whole different vocabulary, conversing knowledgeably of matters like the *cat cracker, alkylation, throughput,* and BPDs. At night the place burns with the glitter of a thousand orange lights while the machinery throbs on relentlessly. Local people tell the story of a visitor to the city who was once staying in a motel west of town. He woke up in the middle of the night, saw an immense orange glow on the southern horizon, and immediately concluded that half the city was on fire. Only after he had jumped into his car and driven to the

The Lima refinery at night, mid-1990s. *Photo courtesy of the* Lima News.

south edge of town did he realize that Lima was not on fire. It was only another normal working night at the city's oil refinery.[3]

Perhaps it is the immensity of the place, along with its bizarre panorama, that has secured for the refinery such a prominent place in both the local economy and the city's very identity. It is the largest single taxpayer in the county, the biggest single consumer of local water and electricity, and, with a payroll of upwards of $31 million, one of the largest local employers. But there is more to it than that. The plant has operated continually since the days of John D. Rockefeller, more than a century ago. Succeeding generations of local people have worked there, often generations of the same families, and most of them have lived and spent their salaries in the Lima community. Through such ties, the plant has so deeply cemented itself into the unspoken consciousness of the city as to become something close to iconic. "It's one of foundations of the city," a refinery staffer observed. "It's like it's in peoples' blood or something . . . you're always aware of its presence." A drawing of an oil derrick and the "eternal flame" of the refinery dominates the city's flag.[4]

Finally, the very presence of the city's refinery means that Lima stands out as an island of possibility in the larger landscape of deindustrializing America. For many similar communities around the world, this has become a relatively bleak and barren terrain. By all standard logic of the era—and especially by the intentions of British Petroleum (BP), the longtime owner of Lima's refinery—the sprawling facility on the south edge of town should no longer exist. In the mid-1990s, over the anguished but seemingly futile protests of local people, BP decided that the plant no longer fit into its current corporate profile and moved to shut it down. At that time, BP was one of the most powerful and wealthy corporations in the world, and Lima had already been so staggered by successive waves of plant closings that it had come to symbolize the national economic dislocation of the "rust belt." The refinery—and, to some degree, the larger Lima region—stood poised to join a hundred other such locales already carelessly discarded onto the industrial scrap heap. Yet Lima's refinery did not close. It continues to pump out oil and generate wealth, to the benefit of both its corporate owner and the regional economy. It does so because of the strenuous efforts of a range of dedicated people, both inside and outside the plant gates, who were determined to secure for themselves a different future than the one dictated by BP. The story of how they succeeded reveals previously hidden possibilities in an era of deindustrialization. What if corporate decisions are not immutable and absolute? What if communities can still imagine themselves, at least to some degree, as masters of their own fates?

"Birth certificates and death sentences to entire communities"

Part of what makes the encounter between BP and Lima such a compelling story is that both entities were struggling against forces and economic calculations larger than themselves. Throughout the United States, large corporations, responding to an intensely competitive economic environment, sought to close down outdated industrial plants. The reasons behind such closures came as small consolation to the stricken communities these corporations left behind, however. As historian Stanley Buder has recently observed, corporate America underwent a signal period of restructuring through the 1980s. Marked by a series of leveraged buyouts and hostile takeovers, this restructuring may have ultimately strengthened the business sector, but in the interim it meant profound uncertainty for corporate heads. The "clear message had been sent out" to business CEOs: either "act boldly or lose your job." A revolution in corporate governance, beginning about the same time, fed the new ruthless search for profits. Faced with the prospect of hostile takeovers by a newly emerging class of corporate raiders, CEOs faced a stark choice. As summarized by corporate theorist Marjorie Kelly, they had to either "start wringing every dime from operations (sending jobs overseas, selling off weak divisions, laying off thousands), or be taken over by someone who would." One study of corporate heads of Fortune 500 firms from 1996 to 2000 explored what happened when stock analysts downgraded their recommendations about purchasing company stock by just one grade, from "buy" to "hold": within six months, almost half of the top executives of such companies had lost their jobs.[5]

Oil companies in particular faced an intensely competitive economic environment, where their ability—or inability—to function at the point of greatest efficiencies could spell the difference between a successful year or a disastrous one. The oil industry has always suffered from extremely high overhead; as business scholar Geoffrey Jones noted, "the investments required to develop an oil field or build a refinery were extremely large" and "entailed high fixed costs. As a result, small variations in price or in output had a relatively powerful effect on profits." This was a particularly worrisome trend for big oil executives in the 1980s, when they faced a sudden and unexpected drop in oil prices because of the global "oil glut." It was in this context that BP began to consider reducing its refining capacity and ultimately set events in motion that would lead to its decision to close its Lima facility. Reporting on the plant closings by international oil companies in the 1990s, journalists noted that it was no longer enough for big oil executives to merely report sumptuous profits; they had to worry about the extent of their profit margins, whether their efficiencies were at peak, and whether investment in a specific plant would produce an even higher rate of return if applied elsewhere.[6]

Civic leaders faced with plant closings had to sort through their own set of grim calculations. At first glance, it was not clear why the Lima region's future should be any different from that of hundreds of similar communities, whose municipal leaders had discovered their relative powerlessness when the reigning corporate partner had decided to close up local operations and move elsewhere. Between 1962 and 1982 alone, the country witnessed the closure of more than one hundred thousand manufacturing firms, each employing more than nineteen workers, a full fifth of them in the five states of the old industrial Midwest. From 1979 to 1986, this region had suffered a 19.3 percent decline in manufacturing employment, losing nearly 950,000 full-time manufacturing jobs. These job losses originated in a variety of complex underlying economic factors (see chapter 4 for greater detail). By the 1970s, many U.S. corporations faced increased overseas competition and rapidly declining profits. Plant closings therefore seemed, on their face, a natural and inevitable end to the industrial life cycle. Corporate managers quickly moved to pin the blame on an overpaid, unproductive workforce and aging, obsolete equipment. "Yet the closing of an obsolete mill," one analyst has summarized recently, "was often the direct result of management's failure to modernize or their active decision to invest somewhere else." Technological innovations, such as the computer and communications revolution and containerized shipping, facilitated the decisions of corporate managers to shift their production elsewhere, to low union areas in the American South or, even better, overseas, wherever the prevailing wages were lowest and the hand of governmental regulation the lightest.[7]

Cities like Lima also face a marked disadvantage in corporate economic decisions because of the privileged place of capital in U.S. corporate law and history. By the later twentieth century, U.S. corporations had been working the legal system for at least a century, successfully attaining a whole range of new powers. In fact, they have become something akin to a new kind of legal entity altogether. In the first one hundred years following ratification of the U.S. Constitution, American courts wrestled with two different readings of the essential nature of corporations. One view held that the corporation was an artificial being, a creation only of laws for specific purposes, and thus could be readily restricted—or even dissolved—by the popular will. The other view held that corporations were "natural entities," real beings with a separate existence deserving of basic rights. Understandably enough, corporate leaders strongly favored the latter view, and thus, as legal scholar James Willard Hurst has noted, through much of the nineteenth century, corporations approached federal court under the "odd fictions" that they were citizens.

This latter interpretation of the nature of corporations was given great weight by two key legal decisions, which together facilitated the rise to dominance of great corporations in the late nineteenth and early twentieth centuries. The first of these was the *Santa Clara* decision of 1886, in which the U.S. Supreme Court issued the bizarre but foundational legal opinion establishing in law the fiction that corporations were real persons, deserving of every protection as natural beings under the Fourteenth Amendment. This amendment had been ratified in 1868, primarily to clarify the status of recently freed slaves, thus establishing the normative definition of U.S. citizenship. Corporate lawyers quickly used the *Santa Clara* ruling to induce courts to strike down hundreds of laws regulating corporations and in other ways restricting their autonomy as real persons. In the first half-century following the *Santa Clara* ruling, noted Supreme Court Justice Hugo Black in 1938, more than 50 percent of the cases invoking it did so in order to extend the rights of corporations; less than a half of 1 percent of the cases involved the issue of racial justice. In recent decades, corporations have used the decision to appropriate many of the other constitutional protections commonly awarded living human citizens under the Bill of Rights. In the *Bellotti* case of 1978, for example, the Massachusetts Supreme Court struck down a law restricting corporate political advertising because of the basic American right to free speech.[8]

The second watershed legal decision solidifying corporate power came in 1919. In *Dodge v. Ford,* the Michigan Supreme Court ruled in 1919 that a corporation existed primarily to enrich its shareholders, that this was its essential purpose. Hence a corporate action aimed at any other end—to, say, soften the effect of plant closings on its partner communities—became essentially untenable. Technically, these or any other expressions of corporate social responsibility were illegal. In the emerging political and economic climate of the Reagan-Bush decades, when paeans to the virtues of the unrestricted free market reverberated with near-religious conviction, new devotees of this view did not shrink from such expressions of corporate social irresponsibility. Instead, they celebrated them. "The one and only . . . social responsibility of business," the Nobel Prize–winning economist and free-market apostle Milton Friedman proclaimed, is to "increase its profits."[9]

In the sphere of corporate law, corporations have thus come to possess capacities that are nearly cosmic. They are persons entitled to every right that real U.S. citizens enjoy, yet at the same time they are something like superpersons. They are immortal; they cannot be killed. They may legally be persons but they can officially feel no human emotions like guilt or shame. While on the one hand, they can devour one another, on the other, if its suits their interest, they can break apart like amoebas into constituent parts, which all have the same privileges as the mother body. They can disband themselves in one location and then suddenly rematerialize states or oceans away. By the 1930s, the legal powers accumulated by large business enterprises seemed so all-encompassing that New Deal theorist Adolf Berle could only conclude that "the rise of the modern corporation has brought about [such] a concentration of economic power that it can compete on equal terms with the modern state."[10]

Against this awesome array of corporate powers, individual communities labor to safeguard their own interests under a variety of marked disadvantages. Their powers are weak compared to those of state or national governments. Faced with a harmful decision from a large corporation, therefore, the immediate municipal response of many local governments is to enlist the help of a governor or senator. Yet if such officials are disengaged, or if the corporation in question has better means of influencing them, what then? Corporate decisions to come and go are especially fraught with danger for individual communities. In their desperation to woo new businesses, officials from competing cities often vie with each other in offering inducements to corporations, such as reduced property taxes. Given the dependence of local governments on property taxes, civic leaders must tread carefully around their corporate partners in whatever they do, especially in light of the increased mobility of the multinational corporation. If a corporation, aggravated by local actions, decides to pack up and move away, its decision levies a body blow to the community, weakening its ability to finance its schools and other basic services. Corporate mobility places city officials at a profound practical disadvantage as well. Their need for corporations, and for the jobs and taxes they bring, is so palpable, and the impact of losing them so harsh, that civic leaders of all stripes usually find themselves predisposed to corporate needs and generally willing to do almost anything to avoid the aura of a "negative business climate."[11]

For the repercussions of plant closings are severe. Numerous studies have documented the social, economic, and psychological effects of unemployment, especially on people who have long held steady jobs. Common among these are high blood pressure and other stress-related health problems, difficulties often exacerbated by the fact that, at least until full implementation of the new health care reform law, when Americans lose their jobs they often lose their accompanying health benefits. Other signs of social trauma—increased rates of alcohol and drug abuse, domestic violence, mental health problems, and even suicides—likewise follow lost jobs and reduced incomes. Industrial communities experience their own set of interrelated crises connected to a loss of tax income, ranging from a decline in the quality of local schools to increased demands for public assistance. In other words, as the stricken city's income declines, the demands on it increase. Moreover, the loss of one type of job, especially high-paying manufacturing sector jobs, tends to accelerate the loss of others. The U.S.

Chamber of Commerce estimates that for every three manufacturing jobs lost, a community loses two service-sector jobs. In this manner, the job losses from plant closings can have a kind of multiplier effect. As one political scientist has summarized it, "Private corporations have acquired the power to issue birth certificates and death sentences to entire communities."[12]

The loss of a major local employer can evoke a range of responses from urban officials, responses that have been classified by scholars. Some officials seem unable to respond effectively, instead taking a "bystander" role, in which they mostly just wring their hands and emit sympathetic sounds to the press while passively waiting for the market to make the necessary adjustments. Given the possible repercussions from plant closures described above, however, many stir themselves into frenzied action despite the many handicaps they face. Some adopt a moderate but still fundamentally reactive posture, allowing the corporation to retain control of major decisions but doing what they can—through job retraining programs, for instance—to "offset" some of the destructive impacts of those decisions. Other municipal leaders take a more proactive stance, strongly contesting such corporate decisions even at the risk of upsetting the ostensibly harmonious business climate. Often these activist officials are those with close ties to unions and other community groups, as opposed to area businesses. They use the local legal structure to forestall plant closings, file eminent domain or other lawsuits, and try to pass laws restricting corporate autonomy, as well as working with community groups in local management buyout schemes. Yet activist leaders are often handicapped because they generally lack the requisite staff, technical and financial expertise, and other resources—not to mention the political and economic power—to compete in the high-stakes terrain of large corporations. Not surprisingly, therefore, the record of success for such activist responses has been a poor one. In sum, there seems little ground to question the consensus recently reached in a noted new study of the North American rust belt: "Local communities," Steven High concluded, "are no match for industrial corporations."[13]

In early autumn 1996, however, an informal and ideological diverse coalition of local people in Lima, Ohio, set out to test this conventional academic wisdom. They had no choice, for the decision was thrust upon them. After eight months of dutifully trying to sell the local refinery—indeed, after repeatedly assuring local people that the plant remained an excellent facility and a buyer would certainly appear—BP suddenly announced that the sale had failed and that the company intended to demolish the plant. Given the refinery's central role in the regional economy, area leaders from Lima's mayor on down quickly concluded that they would not accept BP's decision without a fight. The odds against their success could not have been higher. British Petroleum was, at that time, the world's second-largest oil company and one of the richest and most powerful such business enterprises in the world. It employed close to 100,000 people in more than one hundred different countries and reaped in gross profits of upwards of $170 billion annually. Lima, on the other hand, stood so battered and bruised by two decades of successive waves of plant closings that, to many people, this last threat seemed something like the end.[14]

Yet city officials sensed an opening, for BP—on the surface, at least—seemed ready to rebut the critics asserting that a corporation in its essence could have no sense of social conscience. In some ways this was not a new development. As early as the 1920s, in reaction to an increasing public perception of business leaders as senseless, predatory monopolists, corporate executives had already sought to cultivate a benevolent public image of their companies. The corporate campaign for social responsibility had ebbed and flowed over the decades but had noticeably accelerated in the 1990s in reaction to worldwide antiglobalization protests. Moreover, in this corporate movement to present themselves as sensitive and responsible public citizens, BP especially seemed to be leading the way. The task seemed especially close to the heart of BP's chief executive, a diminutive, hard-driving Brit named John Browne. Like other oil company executives, Browne was an ambitious and sometimes ruthless workaholic. Unlike many of them, however, he exhibited a polish and sophistication that perfectly suited the global leadership he desired for his company. He was a graduate of Cambridge and Stanford who collected art and frequented the ballet and opera. Browne spoke eloquently, expressing big and expansive thoughts. He insisted that his company's sense of responsibility was rooted in "hard-headed business logic," but in his speeches he increasingly stressed the kinds of social responsibilities that BP owed the world. Late in the decade he even began to position his company, rhetorically at least, at the forefront of the struggle against global warming. "If we're going to win back public acceptance and trust," he instructed his fellow corporate executives, "we have to be progressive."[15]

In the Lima metropolitan region in the mid-1990s, local people presented Browne with a perfect opportunity to put such fine words into practice. The ensuing confrontation between an aging and economically battered industrial city on the one hand and a powerful global corporation on the other would reveal a lot: about the real extent of the corporate social conscience, about the core issue of corporate personhood, and even about the extent of real agency left to industrial communities.

Yet—to borrow an old and appropriate Lima metaphor—to fully follow the story, one has to travel way up the tracks: before BP entered Lima, and before Lima's emergence as a national poster child of the rust belt. One has to travel back in time to the city's great golden age, when Lima made a fine living from bedrock industrial enterprises like steel and steam, and then extend the reach of historical memory back even further. For Lima is a city whose modern history both begins and ends with oil.

Chapter 2

Oil Town

In May 1885, after weeks of drilling, oil came shooting upward out of a hole along a riverbank in downtown Lima. By all accounts, the oil was nasty stuff. Black, greasy, and smelling strongly of sulfur, it turned the dust of the drill site into a sticky mess. Vast globs of it coated the tepid surface of the river for some distance. Local people discovered that the oil stuck to everything, ruined their clothes, and sickened their farm animals, but no matter. They greeted it with joy. Crowds thronged the drill site, scooping it into small bottles which they waved around like trophies and later on passed down to their descendents like sacred family heirlooms.

For half a century, the people in and around the growing town of Lima had busied themselves with wringing a living from their farms and businesses, never realizing the black resource that lay deep beneath their feet. Their town had grown well enough without it; they did not need it. Moreover, at least until the late 1850s, they would not have known what to do with it if they had found it. By the 1880s, however, in the emerging economic climate of America's Gilded Age, the oil bubbling out of the ground at Hog Creek seemed to herald the coming of a whole new day. For the town at large, it promised to draw to Lima a number of manufacturing concerns that could anchor its economic well-being for generations to come. For the ordinary citizen, it promised steady jobs, good wages, and all the other elements of the emerging working-class dream. And for a few plucky entrepreneurs with skill and daring, the oil was the foundation on which great fortunes could be built. No wonder news of its discovery sent civic boosters into a kind of ecstatic delirium.

In the event, Lima's oil indeed brought fortunes—but it also brought darker consequences that the boosters could not yet envision. The oil drew into town a set of mighty players from the outside who irrevocably attached Lima's prospects to decisions made far away. No community exists in total isolation; to some degree, perhaps, this development was unavoidable. But in an era resounding with hymns of praise to the self-made man, and with individuals resolutely marching into the future as confident architects of their own fates, these new realities could prove discomfiting.

"The land is first rate, and I think will be in a place of business"

The land that eventually took shape politically as Allen County, Ohio, with Lima as its county seat, was located in the new state's last frontier region, its northwest corner. Statehood had come to Ohio in 1803. By 1833, the state's eastern and southern regions had begun to bear physical testimony to a growing number of busy and energetic people. In thirty years, Ohio's white population had risen from 45,000 to nearly a million inhabitants. Forests had given way to cornfields, rude cabins had been replaced by solid farmhouses, and along the many navigable waterways lacing the region, steamboats traveled, both with and against the currents, bringing yet more people and goods to now bustling cities like Cleveland, Cincinnati, and the new state capital in Columbus.[1]

Northwestern Ohio had seen little of this activity, however, principally because much of it lay within the confines of the Great Black Swamp. The last residue of the glacier melt that had remained at the end of the last ice age, the swamp was a fearful place for most Europeans, and had effectively functioned to limit their conquest and settlement for a century. For early pioneers, the swamp was nearly impassable. Its canopy of hardwood trees allowed only a dim light to sift down to the forest floor, much of which was covered by water. Foolhardy adventurers who entered the swamp watched their horses flounder shoulder-deep in mud, as did U.S. Army troops hurrying northward to reinforce Fort Meigs in the war of 1812. Even corduroy roads constructed of felled trees disappeared deep into the ooze. Pioneers also feared the damp, insect-infected air of the swamp, which brought with it the uncontrollable shakes of the "ague" (later identified as malaria). Not even the Indians had attempted to live in the swamp, instead preferring, as did later whites, to construct their villages on the swamp's edges or on the high banks of the rivers draining it, the Auglaize and the Maumee. Even so, by 1830, with the Indians mostly vanquished and sent westward, the pressure of white land hunger had mounted to a point where the forces of agrarian conquest gathered. Armed with axes and plows, new armies of pioneers had begun to push up against the southern outskirts of the swamp and prepare for the final assault. The state legislature passed an act, effective in

1820, "to erect fourteen counties" in the region, one of which was "to be known by the name of Allen." Gripped by one last epidemic of "Ohio Fever," thousands of farmers and aspiring farmers began to filter through the forests to the very edge of the Great Black Swamp, and then beyond.[2]

One of the pioneers purchasing a claim at the area land office in Piqua, Ohio, was Christopher Wood, a fifty-two-year-old veteran of the Kentucky and Ohio Indian wars. With two sons and a son-in-law, Wood spent two weeks cutting his way from Piqua through roughly a hundred miles of forest and reached the Shawnee settlement in April 1824. After obtaining seed for their crops, the men traveled north for two more days to a pleasant stream called Sugar Creek, and began the long, exacting process of carving a farm and homestead from raw wilderness. Shortly afterward, other families undertook similar journeys to the same vicinity, though widely dispersed at first. In 1826, for example, the two Wood sons, out hunting five miles south of their homestead along Hog Creek, followed the sound of a chopping axe and stumbled onto Samuel McClure, working next to his completed cabin. McClure had been living there for eight months but it was the first time that either pioneer had laid eyes on the other.[3]

Within five years, encountering new neighbors in the woods became more common; the waterlogged barrier of the swamp was ten or so miles north and the good land around Sugar and Hog creeks proved increasingly attractive. By the fall of 1830, with upwards of seventy local pioneers in the area, the time had come to set up a more formal mechanism of local government. Early in 1831, the judges of the common pleas court, acting at the direction of the state legislature, designated a slate of county officials, including the first county commissioners and Wood as "town director," and charged them to "cause a town to be laid out at some suitable point" which "shall be, and will remain the permanent seat of justice of Allen County." Accordingly, one spring day in 1831, Wood selected a small clearing a few hundred yards north of Hog Creek and drove a wooden stake into the ground. That would be, he decided, the site of the town square, and the center of the 160-acre town plot that the legislature had stipulated. The prospects seemed to augur well for future growth. "I have bought 250 acres on Hog River" five miles from Lima, wrote a new settler named Griffith John that October. "The land is first rate, and I think will be in a place of business."[4]

It fell to Wood, as town director, "to give said town a name," but in the event he had help. One evening when several local settlers had gathered at a cabin, they suddenly decided to settle the matter. Each person present dropped a suggested name into a hat. The informal paper ballots were taken out, one by one, discussed, and discarded. The last name to be pulled from the hat, Lima, was accepted; the other suggestions were never recorded. Some local arguing ensued afterward about who had come up with the name. More interesting today, perhaps, is the question of why pioneer families deep in the Ohio woods would think to name their new town after the capital city of Peru. The choice is less bizarre than it first appears, perhaps, simply because *Lima* was a word familiar in their daily lives. Given the settlers' proximity to the swamp and the prevalence of mosquitoes and malaria, quinine, the common medical antidote to malaria, was a staple in the community. Since quinine hailed from Peru, Lima may well have been listed as the point of origin on numerous barrels about the settlement. Sturdily independent pioneers would insist on placing their own particular stamp on the name, however, rejecting the Spanish pronunciation of "Leemah" and instead calling the town "Lye-ma" (as in the bean).[5]

Though it was not officially incorporated until 1842, the small village grew steadily. Within two decades, the work of thousands of axes had cleared away about a quarter of the county's forest cover. Lured by the promise of free land in exchange for their labor, new settlers drove into the swamp itself. There they began the long, sweaty process of draining and ditching that would render the seven thousand square miles of the Great Black Swamp—with all its wildflowers and mosses, its trickling rivulets and dark fetid pools, its mosquitoes, and its innumerable mysteries—into flat, malleable, and immensely rich farmland. Already by 1870, two neighboring counties to the north and west of Allen, Putnam and Van Wert counties, were laced with more than a thousand miles of ditches. Today farmers in northwestern Ohio work a layer of soil that rests over a huge complex of sluice pipes, three feet down, forty feet apart, mile after mile after mile, the most heavily drained land, locals claim, this side of Holland. By the end of the century, the swamp was little more than a fading memory, and lends its name today only to such matters as local art festivals and children's soccer leagues.[6]

While it still lived, the swamp both inhibited and stimulated Lima's growth. On the one hand, its proximity rendered Lima an unhealthy place to live. In addition, townspeople sometimes found it difficult to secure a firm foundation for their buildings or to dig dry root cellars. Travel to the north and west was difficult. On the other hand, its location allowed Lima to emerge as the key market town of the Black Swamp area, and provided the town with a valuable and plentiful commodity to exploit. Lima's life was first fueled by lumber. Area forests and the swamp itself were thick with oaks, walnuts, ash trees, and hickories, for which local entrepreneurs discovered a real demand in places south and east. A dozen water-powered sawmills sprang up in town, where hundreds labored to manufacture both raw planks and finished goods, such as wagons and their various parts, tool handles, window sashes, and, later, thousands of gun stocks for Union armies.[7]

This kind of economic activity drew the key linchpin of economic growth in the nineteenth century: railroads. In 1845, to the city's misfortune, the Miami and Erie Canal missed Lima, passing instead through the town of Delphos, fourteen miles to the west. Locals worried that with this kind of advantage, and with the poor roads outside of Lima, Delphos would soon outstrip their own town and become the bustling city of the region. Nine years later, however, the Ohio & Indiana Railroad arrived in town, connecting Lima with a number of important commercial centers.

The burgeoning small town of Lima built from this economic base. Its social and economic world radiated outward from the public square, which functioned in the rural Midwest as village greens did in New England. Up until the Civil War, the local militia drilled on the square. During the antebellum years, the town seemed to have been little shaken by the political debates that roiled the country, but when the call to arms came in 1861, Allen County young men dutifully reported to the recruiting offices. Nearly two thousand men from the county enlisted in a number of Union regiments, most prominently the 20th, the 99th, and the 118th Ohio. Many did not come home again. Once they were mustered and drilled, soldiers in these units were quickly plunged into heavy fighting in the western theater of the Civil War, struggling in places like Shiloh, Chattanooga, and Sherman's series of battles at the gates of Atlanta. The troops of the 99th Ohio Infantry suffered particularly heavy casualties when the Confederate general John Breckenridge assaulted the Union right on the third day of the Battle of Stone's River and paid another heavy price in lives twenty months later in the smoking woods along Chickamauga Creek.[8]

The chattering of telegraph wires in the wake of such terrible encounters surely would have sent much heartache filtering back to Ohio homesteads, a sadness that still echoes in an obscure document or two. Take, for instance, the reminiscences of Mrs. M. L. Hunter. In 1917, as another war raged in Europe, she set down on paper what she saw and experienced in Lima's downtown public square in April 1865, as the Civil War came to a close. "All turned out to celebrate the homecoming of the boys," she recalled. People had soaked balls of candlewick in turpentine and strung them across the square; when lit, they blazed like lighting. A torchlight procession careened around the square to the sounds of bands playing and cannons firing. "People ran with blanched cheeks" in the excitement. Then "when everything was at its height . . . someone mounted a store box and said: 'Lincoln is shot.' It seemed in a twinkling of an eye flags were lowered at half-mast; bells tolled; all festivities stopped; crepe bought; tears poured like rain; flags draped in black, and I can still feel a shade of sadness when I think of that night. Lots of copper heads were there, and when they recklessly said they were glad, were promptly knocked down by some boys in blue." Very soon the square was deemed "unsafe for women and children . . . A deep gloom settled over the town for days afterwards."[9]

In the years immediately after the war, the current of Lima's social life largely returned to its prewar channels, with a few new twists. As in prewar years, once again the major engine of Lima's transformation was economic. Historians of American industrialization have fully explained the basic economic shift sweeping through Gilded Age America. On a national level, the United States was moving from light industry (e.g., textiles, grain milling, lumber) to heavy industry (e.g., machinery, steel, oil). Many factors contributed to this shift, including the development of new rationalized administrative and management practices, pioneered by the railroads, that paved the way for the rise of larger corporate enterprises, and a new ability, thanks to the Bessemer furnace process, to replace iron structures (like building girders, railroad tracks, and locomotives) with ones of cheaper, lighter, and more durable steel. Since telegraph lines accompanied the racing expansion of railroad tracks, the nation soon acquired an extensive, reliable transportation and communications infrastructure, which by itself facilitated the development of mass markets for goods. Larger financial houses, like Morgan & Company, arose to bankroll such larger operations, particularly in their marketing of stocks and their purchasing of corporate bonds. Finally and perhaps most importantly, many of these changes were literally fueled by the development of cheaper and more reliable sources of power: coal-driven steam engines and later electricity.[10]

Larger cities possessed a number of inherent advantages that perfectly situated them to ride such developments to immense urban expansion. Mass immigration to these cities offered manufacturers a large and cheap labor supply. As railroad centers, big cities could readily import and distribute the raw materials the rising industrialists needed. Moreover, the regional nature of capitalization in this era often meant that larger population centers could supply the necessary levels of finance required by bigger industrial operations. As a result, historians relate, the population of the nation's urban centers shot up to unprecedented heights during the Gilded Age. The populations of New York City and Philadelphia doubled and tripled, while Chicago's passed the million mark, making it the nation's second-largest metropolis. Smaller cities also proved themselves able to translate their economic resources into means for growth, and it should come as no surprise that Lima harnessed the same factors in expanding its own economic base. Before the Civil War, it had deftly used the resources it had—water-driven sawmills to process abundant local lumber—to transform itself into a thriving small town. Now, in the 1870s, Lima's manufacturers, along with their rivals elsewhere, increasingly turned to steam power, fueled by coal and especially the new resource of natural gas. Gas had some drawbacks: it was highly flammable and sometimes hard to control, and building the complex piping needed to deliver it required a high initial investment. Still, it presented a number of advantages over waterpower and coal. As one local historian recognized, "It afforded clean and very hot heat." By 1870, of the thirty-nine sawmills in Allen County, all but one ran by steam. In addition, county manufacturers used steam power in two cabinet shops, a flax mill, a foundry, a woolen mill, and a paper mill.[11]

The town's railroad network was also expanding. The Cincinnati, Hamilton, and Dayton Railroad located its repair shops in Lima, employing 130 men, while both the Dayton & Michigan and the Lake Erie and Western railroads not only did likewise but also elected to place their roundhouses there. This expansion not only attracted manufacturing operations but also brought additional businesses and jobs. Some industries arose to service the trains themselves. In 1869, five local entrepreneurs had pulled together a new business primarily to produce sawmills and farm machinery, but they soon recognized that there were bigger profits with the railroads. In 1879, reincorporated as the Lima Machine Works, the plant began to lay the basis for what would emerge as one of Lima's foundational industries when it completed three entire locomotives at the bidding of a logging firm. There would be more. Altogether, the city found itself in a virtuous cycle that would replicate itself again and again for much of the next eighty years: resources brought industries, industries brought jobs, jobs brought labor, and the city's labor and resources attracted still more industries. By 1880 Lima's population stood at 7,500 people, more than triple its 1860 level, and further growth seemed highly likely. By the 1880s, in fact, much of the country, and especially what was emerging as the industrial Midwest, seemed bewildered and dizzied by the economic success that had come upon them unawares.[12]

In February 1885, the most aggressive and ambitious of Lima's entrepreneurs, Benjamin Faurot, quietly began a drilling operation on the grounds of his paper mill on the west bank of Hog Creek. Ironically, Faurot's team of drillers began boring into the cold winter earth scarcely a mile from where the old frontiersman Christopher Wood had, fifty-four years before, hammered down a wooden stake to officially begin settlement of what would become the city of Lima. Faurot's objectives were more prosaic, however: his paper mill needed a more reliable source of power. Like other Lima businessmen, he had watched, with avid interest and some envy, the tremendous economic boom enjoyed by Lima's rival city of Findlay, forty miles north, which had resulted from its discovery of a large pool of natural gas deep beneath it. Faurot hoped his drilling team would likewise tap into natural gas, or, failing that, into a more reliable supply of water. With 7,500 people, Lima was already water-deficient, and obtained most of its water from wells. Faurot was a private man and tried to avoid publicity, but as the drilling proceeded through March and April, local newspapers began to comment briefly but almost daily on his progress. Early in May, one paper disclosed that Faurot's drillers were sure to hit gas within twenty-five feet. Then on the evening of May 9, 1885, the paper instead reported to readers that "about noon today, an oil vein was struck in the well at the paper mill. It is dark, crude oil, and was struck at the depth of 1,255 feet. They are still boring."[13]

"Our city is still in a furore of excitement"

Oil was scarcely a new or unseen substance in 1885, either in the greater United States or in the rural Midwest. Seneca Indians in western Pennsylvania were well familiar with it, commonly using it as a liniment or as an addition to body paint. Sensing possible profits, canny settlers there later bottled and marketed it as a medicinal aid called "Seneca Oil." Scattered Ohio farmers likewise had occasionally come across errant pools of petroleum seeping into their fields; they saw it only as a nuisance. Ohio pioneers drilling a salt well on the Muskingum River in 1819 had struck oil and abandoned the site. Ten years later, a businessman had tried to sell oil oozing from a Kentucky well, but could find no market for the stuff. If Americans wanted light or lubricant, they commonly turned to whale oil, which Yankee whalers in New Bedford and Nantucket kept in abundant supply.[14]

By the late 1850s, however, the New England fleets had nearly obliterated the great Atlantic whale herds. This economic context gave birth to the country's first great oil boom in western Pennsylvania in 1859. When chemical analysis of a barrel of Pennsylvania oil indicated that it could indeed function as lighting fuel, a group of entrepreneurs called the Pennsylvania Rock Oil Company sent a thirty-eight-year-old railroad conductor named Edwin Drake to western Pennsylvania to find more oil and somehow get it to market. He poked around in western Pennsylvania long enough to identify what looked like a promising spot, and hired a crew of German and Irish immigrants to begin drilling there. In September 1859, they found what they were looking for, prompting the *New York Tribune* to proclaim, "Subterranean Fountain of Oil Discovered." The rush was on. Even as the nation grappled with civil war, thousands poured into the Allegheny foothills to flood newly created cities like Oil City and Pithole, and tens of thousands more came after the war ended with Robert E. Lee's surrender at Appomattox. They were preachers, clerks, and farm boys dreaming of a different future than following a mule under a hot sun; they were gamblers, adventurers, and deserters, cutthroats, thieves, and ne'er-do-wells of every description. (Among the latter was a drunken actor and future assassin named John Wilkes Booth, who brawled his way through the oil region in 1864, spouting hot Confederate sentiments, before heading toward his appointment with Mr. Lincoln.)[15]

Fortunes were made in western Pennsylvania and many more lost, as refiners fought the producers with monopolies and cartels, before, in the late 1870s, nearly all concerned came face to face with what appeared as an incontrovertible fact: Pennsylvania's great oil fields were drying up and no more were to be found elsewhere. In 1885, the same year that Faurot began drilling in Lima, Pennsylvania's state geologist warned that the nation's oil boom was merely "a temporary and vanishing phenomenon—one which young men will live to see come to its natural end." The budding young American oil industry had come, it seemed, to a sudden demise. Faurot's oil strike along Hog Creek changed all that, however. From 1885 until the Spindletop gusher blew in Texas in 1901, the epicenter of the American oil industry would be Lima, Ohio.[16]

As the first entrepreneur on the scene, Benjamin Faurot suddenly had a potential fortune dumped right into his lap, and if anyone in Lima was capable of maximizing its possibilities, it was he. For much of his life, Faurot had seemed the local archetype of the American success myth, the poor boy made good, Lima's own answer to the rise of a Rockefeller or an Andrew Carnegie. Faurot was a farm boy from nearby Kenton whose father had pulled him out of school at age seven because he needed his son's labor. As a teen he labored as a teamster, hauling gravel in neighboring Hardin County; he then moved to Lima with the arrival of the railroads in the early 1850s because he sensed the opportunities they brought. Faurot found work managing a livery stable, and when the Civil War erupted, he somehow wangled a government contract to supply horses and mules to the Union army. In four years as an army contractor he made his first fortune, and began to search for ways to parley it into more. With the war's end, Faurot helped incorporate what became the Lima National Bank, and by 1880 was its president. In 1870 he bought the Lima Paper Mills Company to manufacture egg cases out of straw board (an early variant of cardboard), a venture that proved immensely successful. At one point this company was one of the largest employers in Lima, and with its profits Faurot branched out still further. Soon after the completion of the city's first streetcar system in 1878, he bought the whole enterprise, and two years later embarked upon his greatest venture yet: he purchased an entire city block along the public square and transformed it into the magnificent "Faurot Block." When completed in 1882, the block stood five stories tall with an ornate façade, and housed eight stores, dozens of offices, Faurot's Lima National Bank, a music hall, and—its crown jewel—a glittering opera house, commissioned and owned by Faurot himself. In 1885, Faurot was fifty-five years old, short of stature, supremely self-confident, and comfortably rich. He was a devout Methodist who did not drink or smoke, and now God had apparently blessed him with black oil spurting up out of the ground at his paper mill. Here was his chance to rise to even greater heights—to play on the same field, perhaps, as a Jay Gould or a Rockefeller.[17]

Once the strike happened, the news spread quickly. Faurot's grandson immediately mounted his pet pony and rode home, brandishing a bottle filled with

Lima entrepreneur Benjamin C. Faurot; undated photo but clearly from the later Gilded Age. *Photo courtesy of the collections of the Allen County, Ohio, Historical Society.*

petroleum and shouting, "We found oil!" The public square quivered with the news, as storeowners and customers clustered in doorways going over the few known details. The drilling site itself drew crowds like a magnet, so many that Faurot's drillers were forced to construct a tall fence to keep people away from the well's mouth. Even so, enough people got through in the two days after the initial strike that hundreds displayed samples of the oil in small bottles, which they waved around like trophies. Daily the drill bored deeper, the volume of oil increased, and the town's frenzy grew. For local citizens, the climax may have come ten days after the initial find, when Faurot's experts determined they needed to "shoot" the well to increase and steady the flow. This meant dropping a metal "go-devil" down the well shaft to set off a nitroglycerin charge at its base. Altogether the display finally gave the assembled crowds something worthwhile to watch. Nobody felt the explosion, but suddenly they could observe men running from the mouth of the well and then a column of oil shooting up seventy-five feet into the air, covering the surface of Hog Creek with oil for a distance of several blocks. Soon Faurot's well—a small one, by later standards—was filling about twenty-five barrels a day, and nobody could dispute the summary by a Lima newspaper: "Our city is still in a furore [*sic*] of excitement over the discovery of oil at the paper mills," it declared, "and the progress of the work with all the attendant benefits to our city is the principal theme of conversation about the streets."[18]

Ohio oil astonished a great many people, not least the nation's geologists, who had, it turned out, forecast the end of the nation's oil reserves somewhat prematurely. If more oil was to be found anywhere, they expected it in hilly regions like Pennsylvania, not the flat, converted swampland of northwestern Ohio. Within a month of the first strike, Ohio's state geologist, the esteemed Edward Orton, actually visited the site in person, expressing his own surprise. Even more delightful from a driller's point of view was that this oil burbled up from comparatively shallow depths, 1,500 feet as compared with depths of 3,000 feet or more in Pennsylvania. It would not take a great capital investment to get at it. Very soon the nation's oilmen were consulting railroad ticket agents about fares to Lima, and all sorts of newcomers began arriving in town. Only one day after Faurot's first strike, a local woman later remembered, groups of strangers had already appeared in town and stood around discussing the leasing or purchase of nearby farmland. By late summer 1885, drillers had punctured the crust of area topsoil with over 250 wells, and another great oil boom was under way.[19]

Of the many new partnerships and oil firms formed in the Lima oil fields during the memorable summer of 1885, Faurot's Trenton Rock Oil Company

Ground zero of the Lima oil boom: Faurot's first oil derrick along the Ottawa River, with his straw board factory in the background, probably late 1880s. *Photo courtesy of the collections of the Allen County, Ohio, Historical Society.*

was among the first. The entrepreneur immediately realized what kind of gift he had in hand, and formed a partnership with two other Lima businessmen to exploit the resource properly. One of them made a quick trip to the Pennsylvania fields to learn what he could about the oil business. Reliable sources there told him that oil fields generally ran from northeast to southwest, and soon agents from Faurot's new company fanned out northeast of Lima to buy up land rights, the first in the field to do so.[20]

Yet Faurot's firm and those of his competitors soon stumbled across a hard truth of the oil business that their Pennsylvania contacts could have revealed or that Faurot himself might have learned from manufacturing paperboard. As Adam Smith had prophesied and the history of almost every emerging industry had largely confirmed, after the initial burst of manufacturing success, one could expect a dramatic collapse of prices. This same dynamic had injected an aura of desperation into the Pennsylvania oil fields that had lasted for twenty years. Making money from Ohio oil was easy at first. Everyone wanted to do it, and nearly everyone did. In 1886, three miles east of Lima, a veteran driller from the Pennsylvania fields—an amiable, guilt-stricken Christian named Samuel M.

Scenes from the Lima oil boom: oil field workers getting ready to "shoot" a well. The man holding the can is pouring nitroglycerine into a shell. The worker at the far back right is examining a "go-devil," while those in the right foreground relax on a huge bellows. *Photo courtesy of the collections of the Allen County, Ohio, Historical Society.*

Jones—tapped into Ohio's first great oil well, the Tunget well. It quickly brought forth six hundred barrels of oil a day, and this well was merely one of many. By the next year, upwards of twenty separate oil companies were operating in the immediate vicinity of Lima, and overproduction had sent oil prices plunging from forty cents per barrel to fifteen. Even at this low price, drilling was still profitable, because the oil's shallow location kept the costs of extracting it even lower than the price. Nobody knew how much lower the price would drop, however, and, as in Pennsylvania, the continuing flood of new drillers guaranteed that the industry would remain subject to great instability.[21]

More than anything else, perhaps, it was this climate of instability that later induced Faurot's partners to make their big—as it turned out, monumentally big—mistake, for they had begun to operate in a climate that would extract a high cost from even small errors in judgment. The news of the great Ohio oil strike had rippled far and wide in the small circles of American oilmen, and soon tingled the ears of the biggest oil firm of them all. Within a year after Faurot's big find, the long arm of Standard Oil suddenly shot out like a tentacle toward Lima, Ohio, and then pulled its swollen body closer to the prize.

"We did not understand the art of competition, and so we surrendered (sold out) to the Standard"

Of course John D. Rockefeller had watched developments in northwest Ohio with a quiet but intense interest. As Rockefeller began his rise to universal acclaim as an industrial titan, the world was discussing the alarming new theory about the survival of the fittest put forward by biologist Charles Darwin in his *On the Origin of Species*. To the growing number of academics who dared to take what Darwin wrote about biology and apply it to social science, the emerging set of captains of industry appeared, by dint of their own success, as a set of supermen, humankind's shining lights who had been naturally selected by their own innate abilities to rise and to rule. If ever there was an ideal laboratory for testing out the fanciful theories of the new social Darwinists, it would have been the intense, dog-eat-dog capitalist jungle of the Pennsylvania oil fields, and by the late 1870s, the figure of John D. Rockefeller towered over it like a colossus.

For two decades, a war had raged in the Pennsylvania fields between the drillers and producers of oil on the one hand and the refiners on the other. From the beginning, Rockefeller had led the refiners. He abhorred the speculative, greedy, get-rich-quick attitude of the drillers, and particularly their refusal to discipline and order their industry to keep up prices. Their world was characterized, he believed, by "chaos and disorder, waste and incompetence, competition at its worst." For this reason, he had steadfastly refused to let his new company, Standard Oil, enter the field of production. As late as 1880, the company owned only four oil-producing properties, and most Standard employees had never even seen a well. Instead, Rockefeller coaxed, manipulated, and then forced his fellow processers of oil to obtain a stranglehold on the transport and refining of their commodity. The producers counterattacked against the cartels Rockefeller had stapled together, forcing other railroads to give them cheaper rates, and trying to stand together to limit production and force a rise in prices. Suspecting their discipline could not last, however, Rockefeller patiently waited them out, counting on the fact that one producer or another would surely undermine the others by pumping out more oil into a saturated market, leading to its collapse. As the cards fell according to plan, Standard began to devour its rival refiners, concentrating the power and wealth of the industry into a single entity. Rockefeller rejoiced in this concentration of power; in his mind, it was simply the way of the future. Someone would have to dominate the field in order to best use the resources that God had provided, and it might as well be him. As a person, he was reserved to the point of chilliness—"that bloodless Baptist bookkeeper" was one of the milder descriptions of him by the Pennsylvania oil crowd—and avoided involvement in politics, civic affairs, or even country clubs. He dropped his natural diffidence only when receiving great financial news, at which point he would clap his hands, laugh aloud, and shout his joy to the world. "I'm bound to be rich," he cried at one such exultant moment, "*bound to be rich!*"[22]

By the mid-1880s, Rockefeller was very rich indeed, but a fundamental insecurity gnawed deep in the vitals of his empire: Standard Oil's wealth and power could cow rivals and buy entire legislatures—but it could not alter geological realities. By this point, Standard Oil consisted of a towering structure of refining apparatus resting on a dwindling base of supply. Pennsylvania's oil was drying up; oilmen there had to drill ever deeper, almost to the point where costs of extraction exceeded the price. One expert assured John D. Archbold, a Rockefeller lieutenant, that the chances of finding another such bonanza were one in a hundred. Archbold was convinced. Told in 1885 that small amounts of oil had been found in Oklahoma Territory, he replied skeptically, "Are you crazy, man?" "Why I'll drink every gallon of oil produced west of the Mississippi!" Quietly he began to sell some of his Standard stock. Other Standard chiefs shared Archbold's alarm. At one executive committee meeting in the early 1880s, a few suggested that Standard leave the oil business altogether and make money in a more trustworthy enterprise. The CEO remained undeterred, however; pointing skyward, Rockefeller intoned, "The Lord will provide."[23]

Thus, it would not have been hard for Rockefeller, soon thereafter, to see the hand of Providence in the new flow of oil along Lima's Hog Creek. Within a year of hearing the news and assessing the situation, Standard began to move in. Rockefeller arrived in northwest Ohio having made one of the great strategic decisions in the history of his company. It was time, he told his chiefs, to integrate the firm vertically as well as horizontally. They needed to free themselves from their insecure reliance on the speculative chaos of the producers; they needed their own, exclusive sources of supply. It was time, he told them, to enter into the shaky realm of oil production. Amounting as it did to an abrupt change in direction for the corporation—which had, in fact, been fighting the producers for decades—the decision occasioned a sharp and prolonged debate among Standard's executives, one that dragged on for years. At every executive committee meeting, as Rockefeller proposed leasing more and more Ohio land, a conservative faction of board members firmly opposed him. In his memoirs, Rockefeller remembered that they "held up their hands in holy terror." Finally, the chief executive had had enough. He offered to underwrite the acquisition of more land out of his own pocket, if need be, but whether or not the company came along, he made it clear that he was going ahead. The executives quietly backed down, and within two years, Standard had become the largest producer of crude oil in the world.[24]

Rockefeller's biographers highlight this decisive moment both as a turning point in the history of Standard Oil and as a quintessential example of Rockefeller's business genius. However interpreted, the decision had a critical impact on the history of the Ohio oil fields, and it changed the town of Lima forever. Having decided to enter production, Rockefeller sent his agents fanning out across Lima and the developing oil fields to the southwest and (especially) the northeast, buying land or long-term leases on huge tracts. Any driller who hit oil was soon approached on the spot with an offer. Standard invested millions in properties, storage tanks, and pipelines. In fact, it formed its own pipeline company, Buckeye Pipeline, which crisscrossed the oil fields with a network of pipes. Soon they extended through oil rush Ohio boomtowns like Cygnet and Bowling Green as far as Toledo in order to bring back oil to Standard's central collection point of Lima. There it accumulated in "tank farms," row upon row of gigantic storage tanks the company constructed in former cornfields south of Lima, awaiting processing and a higher price.[25]

Standard also moved in short order to process the oil. Rockefeller decided, for the present at least, to center production in Lima, a decision that undercut the refining capacities and economic base of both Cleveland and Pittsburgh (within a decade Standard had phased out its Cleveland refinery), but occasioned great joy in Allen County. Standard agents began negotiating with a local farmer, James Hover, for a 193-acre field he owned (then planted in navy beans) south of Lima. The process was intricate; if nothing else, it indicated that even as far back as a century ago, corporations already had begun playing off one community against the next. Two other communities, Toledo and Findlay, Ohio, were competing for the refinery and were thought to be in the lead for it. Frank Rockefeller, John D.'s brother, headed a Standard team that came to Lima and toured various possible sites. The team finally determined that Hover's bean field really would be ideal, but this presented a new problem: Hover had already signed a long-term lease with Faurot's firm, the Trenton Rock Oil Company. Even though Trenton was a competitor of Standard Oil, its leaders could not stand to see the refinery lost for Lima and gave the go-ahead to Hover to cancel their lease. Hover signed a contract with Standard's refinery, only to discover that the original lease-holding company would not cancel the Trenton lease unless paid $10,000 in cash—and in 1886, this was a fortune. Aware that Hover badly wanted the refinery for Lima, Frank Rockefeller knew how to apply the squeeze. "Mr. Hover," he said in a helpful manner, "although I have a valid agreement with you, I will not see you held up in this manner. I will call everything off, and we will locate our refinery either at Findlay or Toledo." Hover took the cue accordingly, and responded, as would a thousand mayors around the world over the next century, with the only move possible: he scratched for concessions. After hurried negotiations of his own, the farmer managed to cut down the lease-holding company's penalty for canceling the deal to $5,000, a loss that he himself swallowed. Standard had accomplished everything neatly. Later, Rockefeller even magnanimously shared Hover's loss by presenting him with a personal check for $2,500, thus assuring happy feelings all around.[26]

As the man whose sacrifice had obtained a major business for his city, Hover later had a municipal park named after him. More immediately, Lima got its refinery. In September 1886, workmen waded into Hover's beans and began digging. The field soon turned to mud in the fall rains; laborers later claimed they grew three inches in height every day from the heavy clay that stuck to their boots. But by that December, having constructed two brick pump houses, a machine shop, a storehouse-office, and twenty-six-hundred-barrel crude "stills," operations were under way. Before long the complex sprawled over what would ultimately be more than five hundred acres and served as an economic anchor not only for the emerging community of South Lima but for the region as a whole. For the next eighty-five years the city would enjoy a mutually satisfactory relationship with Standard Oil, even though the refinery never directly bore the corporation's name. When Rockefeller officially launched the refinery, he had begun to realize that somehow his name had already come to serve in the public mind as the epitome of the rapacious monopolist. As Progressive Era muckrakers like Ida Tarbell and Upton Sinclair launched exposés of corporate malfeasance, it would not do, corporate officials determined, to overemphasize the name of Standard Oil. Instead, Lima's new industry was officially incorporated in December 1886 as the Solar Refinery Company.[27]

Standard had delayed coming to Ohio for about a year, but when it did arrive at the Lima fields it did so in force, an entrance that must have occasioned deep alarm among other area oil producers. Some companies, resigning themselves to the inevitable, soon began negotiating with Standard agents; state geologist Edward Orton later reported that Standard swiftly bought out "scores" of the smaller firms. Others, however, prepared to resist the oncoming storm of market competition presented by the behemoth. At least two other refineries in the vicinity of Lima tried to compete with Standard's Solar works. One of them spread over eighty acres, making it less than half the size of Solar. Both of these competitors failed within twenty years.[28]

More astute oilmen tried to beat Standard at its own game. In 1887, several independent producers (including the veteran driller Sam Jones), alarmed over the falling price of oil and also casting a worried eye over their shoulders at the approach of Standard Oil into the Lima fields, united to form a larger enterprise called the Ohio Oil Company. They quickly set about expanding their leases, and achieved some notice in Lima business circles as a force to be reckoned with. In the end, however, their major achievement was merely to force Rockefeller to up his price. Standard bought them out in 1889 for more than half a million dollars. Others had fared worse in their conflicts with Rockefeller: the deal made the principals wealthy men. Still, in later years Jones wistfully wished that he and his partners had fought Standard longer. They knew the business better than anyone, he thought, and had had a chance to "capture the Ohio field." Yet "we did not understand the art of competition, and so we surrendered (sold out) to the Standard." (Nevertheless, the best years of Samuel Jones's career were yet to come. Expanding his already considerable fortune by his invention and patenting of an oil-drilling device, Jones shortly afterward married a Toledo socialite and moved to her city in 1894, where he quickly surfaced as a powerful local manufacturer with a deep and solicitous concern for his workers. Three years later, the combined popularity of Jones's evangelical Christianity, republican politics, and socialist ideals brought about his election as mayor of Toledo. Revered by Toledo's poor as "Golden Rule" Jones, he would hold this position until his death in 1904, emerging as one of the great radical reform mayors of the Progressive Era.)[29]

In Lima, nearly the only player that mattered was Standard Oil, which by 1890 stood in complete command of the field. Only one problem remained. Prices of Ohio oil had fallen rapidly not only because of overproduction but also because of a characteristic of Lima oil that had been apparent to everyone the minute Faurot's drillers blew it to the surface in 1885: its smell. In the words of one local newspaper, "The chief fault with the Ohio stuff is that it smells like a stack of polecats and is only worth forty cents on the barrel." Pennsylvania competitors noted its high sulfur content and immediately ridiculed it as "skunk oil." Ohio oilmen soon discovered that the smell remained even after subjecting their crude to the usual practice of cleansing it with sulfuric acid. Detailed chemical explanations aside, perhaps in a weird way the stink was the belated revenge of Ohio's disappearing swamp. These were years when the most common household use for petroleum was as lamp oil. It did not take a business genius to discern that millions of American housewives would be unlikely to take to a product whose principal effects were to blacken their lamp chimneys and leave their parlors smelling something like the sour effluvium of the Great Black Swamp.[30]

Local scouts for Standard Oil had immediately brought the problem to the attention of the big boss, but Rockefeller elected to move his company into the Lima fields despite it. What his detractors derided as his cold fish exterior may have been merely the poker face of a master gambler. In effect, in his rapid acquisition of the vast bulk of the physical and financial capital of the Ohio oil fields, Rockefeller was betting a major fortune that he could somehow find a way to remove the sulfur from the millions of barrels of oil accumulating in Standard's "tank farm" in South Lima. Maybe it was his faith in Providence that enabled him to take such risks so serenely. "It seemed to us impossible," he later wrote in his memoirs, "that this great product had come to the surface to be wasted and thrown away; so we went on experimenting with every process to utilize it, in spite of the protests of the conservatives in the Board." In the meantime, Rockefeller would do what he could to help the Lord further bless Standard Oil, instructing his agents to follow the lead of other Ohio oil producers and market the oil as industrial fuel. Individual homeowners might object to the smell, but large manufacturing complexes were less likely to possess such sensibilities. To develop the market, Standard men gave away thousands of barrels of Ohio oil as free samples and sold the oil at a loss. By 1891 Standard had cornered 70 percent of the fuel oil market but had lost more than $1 million in doing so. As a stopgap measure, the strategy of marketing the Ohio oil as fuel oil seemed a failure, intensifying the pressure on Standard to find a way of removing the sulfur from its mounting reservoir.[31]

Rockefeller placed this problem in the capable hands of a cranky German scientist named Herman Frasch, who had immigrated to the United States following the Civil War. The stocky Frasch could be a terror to work with: he was vain and had a choleric temper. Contemporaries called him the Wild Dutchman—but probably not to his face. Volatile or not, he also was, as one historian commented, "probably the only trained petroleum chemist in the United States."

Rockefeller installed him at Lima's Solar Refinery in 1886 and told him to focus his energies on the sulfur problem. Rockefeller's biographers have nearly universally lauded him as an excellent judge of character, a man with an uncanny knack for selecting the right lieutenants. In this instance, Standard's chief seemed to have chosen correctly; in most ways, Frasch was the right man for the job. Following two years of careful experimentation, he validated Rockefeller's confidence by figuring out a way of removing the sulfur. Put simply, Frasch processed the oil through a "sweetening still" which redistilled the oil in a satisfactory manner. This was no minor achievement. In so doing, he saved Standard's considerable investment in Ohio oil, saved Ohio's oil boom, and may even have saved the United States' fledgling oil industry. Whatever the deficiencies of Frasch's persona and temper, they were a long way removed from the immediate environs of John D. Rockefeller and seemed to matter little to the high command.[32]

Yet Frasch did harbor an ambition that had escaped Rockefeller's purview, an oversight that might have ruined Standard's entire fortunes in Ohio and instead allowed the vast wealth of the Lima fields to fall to an Ohio producer, particularly to Faurot's old Trenton Rock Oil Company, one of the few independent Ohio firms remaining beyond Standard's grasp. Perhaps Frasch merely wanted his due, spurred by his considerable ego. Perhaps he entertained private dreams of sharing more equitably in the financial windfall so conspicuously enjoyed by Standard's upper echelon. Whatever the reason, once he had cracked the sulfur problem, he privately approached executives of the Trenton Company with a tempting offer. If they would build a refinery to process this new, more refined, and much more saleable oil, and if they would award him a half-share in the venture, he would leave Standard, taking the patents of his refining process to Trenton, and together they would enter realms of wealth beyond their wildest dreams. The great fortune promised by Ohio oil now lay at the doorstep of a local Lima company.[33]

Trenton company executives deliberated and then—incredibly—flatly rejected Frasch's offer. In his own bitter financial downfall in later years, perhaps Benjamin Faurot took some solace in the fact that while he had made many mistakes, he was in no way responsible for that error; frustrated by the slow return of his oil investment and wanting other empires to conquer, Faurot had sold his interest in Trenton the previous year. Remaining Trenton executives had no such excuse. Three decades later, a former Trenton executive, George Waldorf, confessed to a local historian what had happened. In an effort to broaden its financial base, the firm had formed a partnership with a Pennsylvania oil company. Now, when presented with Frasch's offer, the new partners were suspicious. They did not know Frasch, they did not trust smelly Ohio oil, and, for that matter, they did not quite trust their Lima partners. They were not ready for any wild ventures with a nutty German scientist.[34]

In retrospect, admitted Waldorf, rejecting Frasch's offer had been a great mistake. Indeed, the move now appears as one of the most colossally foolish business decisions in Ohio's, if not in the nation's, history. Frasch took his patents back to Standard, presumably saying nothing to his superiors about his private business dealings, and the rest of the story followed a path that might have been scripted by the Standard public relations staff. On October 13, 1888, an excited Standard official wired Rockefeller with wonderful news: "We are pleased to inform you that by experimenting with the Frasch process we have succeeded in producing a merchantable oil." Immediately, the price of Lima crude jumped from fifteen cents a barrel to a dollar a barrel. For the next fifteen years, Frasch's patents alone (now owned by Standard) reaped in millions of dollars. The scientist's breakthrough removed any lingering corporate hesitation, and from then on Rockefeller sent the machinery of his corporation steaming full throttle across the midwestern countryside. Hungering for ever-greater tracts of land, he wired Archbold, "Buy all you can get." One executive remembered the big boss standing before a map of the Ohio fields. "You'd better take this," he said, pointing to one area of the map. Then, hands brushing across another area, he added, "Take all this." Pointing to yet another spot on the map, Rockefeller instructed his subordinate, "Don't miss this." The company soon owned oil rights to hundreds of thousands of acres, tracts of land bigger than entire counties, ranging from New York State to West Virginia to Indiana. By 1891, Standard owned a majority of the Lima fields, and long before the turn of the century—remarkable for a firm that until six years earlier had avoided any involvement in oil production—it was refining 95 percent of the nation's oil. The converted swampland of northwest Ohio had functioned, in sum, as midwife in the emergence of America's first great monopoly.[35]

Maybe the full weight of Standard Oil would have crushed Trenton Rock Oil Company anyway, even without Frasch's inventions; by 1891, Standard had sunk $32 million into Ohio oil, an amount that no competitor could even approach. (With Frasch's process in hand, it was able to realize a profit of 13 percent on this investment.) Maybe Standard was simply fated to dominate the industry. On the other hand, maybe not: with the considerable millions brought by Frasch's patents, and as the only company able to transform Ohio crude into a saleable lamp oil, Trenton just might have been able to give Standard a fight. As matters stood, Trenton proceeded to lose a great amount of money, and sold its holdings to a Standard subsidiary in 1899.[36]

"Our city is fast approaching her most prosperous era"

As in any boom, there had been winners and losers in the Ohio oil strike. As in the California gold rush, where some of great riches were made not by prospectors but by the merchants who sold them supplies, one of the biggest winners in Ohio's oil boom was the burgeoning small city of Lima. Oil, of course, quickly emerged as a mainstay of the regional economy. Shortly before the turn of the century, the Lima oil fields were producing 21 million barrels of oil annually, and Lima oil had helped to power the Chicago World's Fair of 1893. By 1900, Standard's Solar Refinery Company employed upwards of four hundred men, most of whom lived and spent their wages locally. Beyond them, the massive infusion of energy and capital from the oil boom led the city into a golden age. The huge Lima oil industry also attracted others, as satellite industries arose to serve the oilmen. There were enterprises that manufactured well-drilling implements, and another that churned out items like "sucker rods." One local entrepreneur saw an opening for a plumbing contracting business, which not only provided the oilmen with items like well casings and fittings but also contracted with individual homeowners to bring natural gas lines into their residences. Oil was stored in barrels, and Lima soon saw the establishment of its own small cooperage industry to provide them. When processed, oil was shipped away in special railroad cars, and at least four firms moved to Lima to construct tank cars. One of them by itself required the labor of eighty-six workers.[37]

Ten years after the start of the oil boom: looking south from the Ottawa River to a Lima landscape dotted with oil derricks, April 1895. *Photo courtesy of the collections of the Allen County, Ohio, Historical Society.*

This kind of manufacturing energy built on the foundation of existing industrial enterprises in the city and then served to attract others. Once again, oil was key. Often, city boosters discovered happily, natural deposits of oil were accompanied by nearby pools of natural gas. In 1886, industrialists created the North West Ohio Natural Gas Company to exploit it. A year later, the city streets of Lima were illuminated by natural gas. The ready availability of cheap gas as an effective fuel for steam engines in turn facilitated the development of a wide variety of manufacturing interests. By the turn of the century, Lima workers were producing everything from shoes to hats, hoe handles to horse carriages, railroad ties to railroad cars to entire locomotives. Like laborers, merchants saw opportunities in Lima's boom and arrived at the city in droves. In just two years, from 1888 to 1890, Lima's downtown expanded from forty-five to fifty-six retail blocks, where shoppers could obtain a wealth of locally made goods, including a decent, Lima-made, five-cent cigar. This economic explosion wrought a parallel demographic spurt, as the city experienced the greatest era of population growth in its history. From 7,500 residents in 1880, Lima's population had tripled to 21,000 by 1900.[38]

The new residents of the growing blue-collar city soon discovered what later generations of citizens came to know as well: that, particularly for working people, Lima held out the promise that arduous labor could bring a passably rewarding life. There was no doubt that the city's manufacturers demanded hard work. Laborers at the Solar Refinery, for example, were set to two shifts: a ten-and-a-half-hour day shift or a thirteen-and-a-half-hour night shift. When, once each month, the shifts changed, workers could look forward to either working a numbing twenty-four hours in a row, or enjoying a single, monthly twenty-four-hour period all to themselves. Not only were the hours long, but work at the refinery was hot and dangerous. Cleaners who entered Frasch's huge "sweetening stills" to chip away the metallic by-products sometimes worked in veritable ovens, with temperatures reaching 140 degrees. Even with protective clothing, they suffered burns, and men all over the plant found that the dust there caused ugly skin rashes. Laborers who worked with the common copper oxide compound watched their hair and beards turn green.[39]

Depending on their position, refinery workers could expect to receive fifteen to seventeen cents an hour for such labor; skilled laborers, such as bricklayers, made up to a quarter an hour. Elsewhere in the city, most workers could expect to labor ten hours a days and six days a week for an average of $473 a year, or about $9 a week. If one's spouse made a bit extra by bringing in boarders or doing piecework at home, working families could scrape by in modest comfort. In 1895, an entire five-room house could be purchased for around $800 or rented for six dollars a month. These lodgings were not princely. In 1887, the city completed its first water system, but even ten years later it brought running water only to the homes of the wealthy; working people turned to cisterns or wells, and headed to outhouses. But still, a workingman's family could find small pockets of comfort. The women could choose from a whole array of social activities centered in Lima's many churches. Victorian culture lifted its restrictions—and dress hemlines, which crept above ankles—to allow them to join in the new craze for bicycling, which swept across the country in the "gay 90s." Crowds also thronged the Faurot Driving Park to watch either local boys or touring professionals race each other at breakneck speed.[40]

The many efforts of entrepreneur Faurot also eased the city's physical expansion when, in 1887, he harnessed the very streets of his city to the marvelous new wonder of electricity. He had already constructed a small electric power station to power the lights of his opera house. Now he added a small steam engine and a primitive sixty-horsepower generator and attached it to his streetcar line. On the morning of the Fourth of July, 1887, the motormen of the Lima Street Railway, Motor & Power Company started electric trolley service down Main Street. Suddenly it was possible to live in one part of the city and reach a place of employment elsewhere, simply by boarding a streetcar and hurtling along the streets of Lima at speeds that approached twenty miles per hour. In particular, the electric railway both facilitated the growth and development of neighborhoods marked by social class and served to integrate them into the larger city. By the 1890s, one coherent blue-collar neighborhood was clearly identifiable north of the Pennsylvania Railroad tracks in the Old North End, while another strong, growing working-class neighborhood had begun to come together in the shadows of the refinery and railroad repair shops of South Lima. Now Faurot's electric railway helped to tie this neighborhood to the city of Lima.[41]

For their part, members of Lima's wealthy elite—men like Faurot, Dr. Samuel Baxter, and a wealthy financier and future U.S senator named Calvin Brice—preferred to live among the cultured ladies and gentlemen of their own class, constructing rows of elegant, palatial homes on West Market Street. This stretch (where the Allen County Museum and the Lima Public Library now stand) included one particularly handsome cluster of homes so grandiose it became known as the "golden block." But the progress and glory of their city shone beyond the golden block. Already by 1889, when the wealth of the oil fields was just beginning to permeate Lima, the inhabitants of these homes—together with their assorted maids and butlers, their grocers and draymen, and the hordes of dirty men who scurried back and forth across their rail yards and factories—certainly would have agreed with the assessment of the *Allen County Democrat.* "Our city," the paper proclaimed, "is fast approaching her most prosperous era."[42]

"She is now the Greatest Oil City of the United States"

Perhaps in the halcyon days of the 1890s, Ohio's oil boom seemed likely to last forever, but, like all booms, it came to an end. Oil production of the Lima fields peaked at 25 million barrels in 1896, and it ebbed sharply thereafter. As the oil-consuming public would rediscover time and time again to its immense regret, oil was like bison or redwood trees; it was an exhaustible resource. Ohio's oil had given the region a great run, but it, too, could last only so long. By 1925, oil derricks could pump only two million barrels out of the entire Lima field from Toledo southwestward, and, soon after, as in Pennsylvania, the costs of extracting the oil came to exceed the price it brought. The excitement had vanished long before. When the immense oil fields of Texas gushed out at Spindletop in 1901, the nation's oilmen had a new boom to work, and quickly focused their attentions westward. From then on, Lima would need to settle down and make a more routine living.[43]

Yet Lima's oil had left the city a marvelous heritage from which to build. Oil had made Lima into a city and also had laid a foundation that made future growth easier. The city's moment as the center of Rockefeller's dreams had been brief. Barely two years after the incorporation of the Solar Refinery in 1886, the high command at Standard had made another strategic decision: it would base its great refining apparatus not in a small city like Lima but nearer to a megalopolis. By May 1889, Standard had launched the construction of a stunningly huge refinery at Whiting, Indiana, at the base of Lake Michigan. When completed two years later, this new works could process upwards of 36,000 barrels of crude per day. Seventeen miles from Chicago, the Whiting refinery took full advantage of that city's tremendous railroad and shipping network, and soon came to function as the nerve center for Standard Oil in the entire valley of the Mississippi. It was left to the Solar works at Lima to simply serve as a lesser outpost of the Standard empire—an assignment that, in the end, suited Lima just fine, for the nation's thirst for oil would only increase in the coming years. Up until about 1913, the primary function of nearly all refineries, Solar included, had been to produce kerosene for heat and light. Gasoline had been an unneeded by-product in the refining process, so useless that Solar workers commonly disposed of it by dumping it into Hog Creek. The sudden advent of the internal combustion engine and the Model-T Ford changed that equation, and as the nation's demand for gasoline soared, the Solar Refinery found a profitable and reasonably secure future, which it could share with its nearby city. Cheap local oil and an extensive supply of natural gas would assure Lima's own growth as a manufacturing center for an indefinite time to come. Perhaps the Lima *Republican Gazette* could be forgiven its bit of editorial excess in 1903 when it characterized its city as, "She is now the Greatest Oil City of the United States."[44]

Even so, for more thoughtful local residents—if they cared to probe that far—an uncomfortable lesson and a couple of discomfiting questions hovered at the edge of all their confidence and optimism. The sad fall of Benjamin Faurot might serve as a worrisome parable for the fate of his city. At one time, Faurot's star had seemed destined for the rarified realm of a Rockefeller or a Carnegie, but his descent had come fast and hard. Not long after his team of drillers had inaugurated Ohio's oil boom on his paper mill property in 1885, Faurot concluded that neither paperboard nor even oil was sufficient grist for his ambitions. The real money was in railroads and land. He sold his interest in the Trenton firm, sold his paper mill, and used the proceeds to buy his own railway. Initially he planned to extend it from Columbus to well into Michigan, and then connect it with a ferry line across Lake Michigan to Milwaukee. The original vision sought in this manner to connect the coalfields of Appalachia to the upper Midwest, distributing the coal in that region, but Faurot soon cast his eyes further afield and conceived of a yet greater glory. The diminutive entrepreneur entered into negotiations with the government of Mexico and acquired a vast chunk of that country, 2.7 million acres, rich with minerals, along the southern border of New Mexico. He would, he decided, run a railroad into his new private reserve and colonize it with Mormons. After that, who could say what would emerge: his own state, his own country, a veritable Faurotopia?[45]

By this point in the early 1890s, however, Faurot had seriously overextended himself, and his many creditors had begun to gather like wolves. One by one, he began to cash in his assets in an increasingly desperate attempt to keep the Mexican venture afloat. This was a process that induced a run on his own Lima National Bank and thus accelerated Faurot's financial collapse. Personal tragedies compounded his troubles: his wife died in 1895, shortly followed by one of his two daughters and his son-in-law. His remaining and now widowed daughter was "forced to turn her home into a rooming house" before the bank foreclosed on it, evicting her; shortly thereafter, she and her father would watch her own three grown sons, Faurot's grandsons, succumb, one by one, to tuberculosis.

For his part, Faurot fought back. Although his railroad never reached Milwaukee, by 1899 Faurot had completed a chunk of it and rode it triumphantly from Lima to Defiance, Ohio. For Faurot this was a supremely happy moment. He blustered, scrabbled, and shot off hot words of remonstrance to his financial persecutors. You are engaged, he wrote one creditor, in "one of the most damnable conspiracies that was ever perpetrated upon any set of men on earth." Yet such rearguard actions just delayed his oncoming and truly bitter end. Once again, Faurot's creditors gathered and, one by one, seized his remaining assets: his Lima street railway, his electric power plant, his seven-hundred-acre farm south of Lima, and his own splendid home along Market Street. Now dabbling in Lima real estate, the Rockefeller interests dispassionately took the Faurot block and his magnificent opera house. When in 1903 the once-formidable businessman sent in an application to be the city's postmaster, contemporaries began to realize the extent of his fall. A visiting reporter found him, in the words of a later historian, truly a "pathetic figure," arriving by buggy promptly at nine every morning to his one remaining office in the old Faurot block, spending the day in fruitless schemes to recover his fortune.[46]

When Lima's old titan of industry suddenly died in Sandusky in the fall of 1904, citizens overdid themselves with celebration, lavishing upon Faurot in death the praise and honor they had denied him in life. They brought his body back to Lima and laid it there in state for a day. Huge crowds attended his funeral and his interment at stately Woodlawn Cemetery—another of the many Lima enterprises that the living Faurot had once planned and promoted. Later on, city leaders planted his name on an elementary school and on the city's great, sweeping public park. Yet all the commemoration obscured the valuable lesson that the rise and fall of a Ben Faurot might have provided for any who cared to look. Fortunes, his story indicated, could float in like the rising tide, but they could also ebb away just as easily and unexpectedly. So far, to Lima, fortune had mostly just come. The city built ever upward in a happy cycle: resources brought industries, which brought jobs, which brought people and more industries. But what would happen on some sad day far into the future, when the process just might conceivably reverse itself? What resources could the city turn to, what strategies could it employ, on the day when that should happen?[47]

Chapter 3

Rust Belt

Late in 1965, the members of Lima's city council decided the city needed its own official flag and solicited possible designs through a citywide contest. The winning entry came from Shirley Barr of Lakewood Avenue. In return for $100 prize money and a brief moment of local fame, Mrs. Barr offered her city a white flag with red and blue borders and "Lima, Ohio" inscribed in bold, large letters across the top. Beneath the writing lay a shield with twelve gold stars across the top, to represent the twelve original townships in the county, and "1831" at the bottom in memory of the city's founding date. But the flag's center captured the city's heritage best. Between the stars and the date Mrs. Barr had drawn the silhouettes of two factories belching smoke, vivid reminders of the economic base that had sustained the city for a century. And in between the two factories, Mrs. Barr sketched in the unmistakable girders and flicking gas flame of an oil derrick.[1]

Given what the refinery had come to mean to Lima, it is no wonder that Mrs. Barr's design hit home so conclusively with the city council members. In 1965 the refinery remained the old cornerstone industry of a growing and prosperous manufacturing city. Thanks to the refinery and the other industries it had attracted, Lima looked forward to a future that still seemed to gleam as brightly as the flames atop the refinery's smokestacks. Certainly the city had problems yet to solve. Municipal expansion, for example, would require moving beyond the city limits, requiring Lima to come to grips with the politically explosive issue of annexation. Equally vexing was the fact that most of Lima's people of color had yet to share in the prosperity that the city promised its citizens. By 1965, they had begun to loudly and relentlessly demand full admittance to that good life, and city officials were about to discover what further delays on this promise might cost.

Even so, the aura of seemingly permanent prosperity saturating the area gave city leaders confidence that Lima had the resources to deal with these problems and many others. It was a small but key city in the mighty economic heartland of the nation, the industrial Midwest, a region where bedrock industries such as steel, oil, and auto manufacturing had anchored the nation's wealth and provided a decent living for hardworking Americans for several generations already. Through the 1960s, every economic indicator suggested to both corporate officials and the region's myriad blue-collar workers that the basis for their prosperity would extend indefinitely into the future.

As it turned out, the events of the next three decades would render Mrs. Barr's drawing even more appropriate as a symbol for Lima than anyone could have known in 1965. Thirty years after city officials enshrined an oil derrick on the city's flag to symbolize its economic prosperity, the refinery would be the last of Lima's traditional industries left standing. No longer would the city's future seem bright with the promise of indefinite prosperity. By 1995, increasingly, area residents were concluding that hard work was no guarantor of economic security for themselves or their children. In cascading numbers they would desert Lima for wealthier suburbs on its outskirts, or for sunnier regions farther away, where booming economies and long "help wanted" columns offered opportunities that their hometown no longer held out. Lima would join other old smokestack cities—Youngstown, Flint, Homestead—as emblematic of an industrial era whose day had come and gone. Like those other cities, its name would evoke images of shuttered plant gates, environmental scars, and long, gray, deserted streets. The fact that these economic calamities may have been visited on such cities by decisions made elsewhere was, in some ways, beside the point. They would come to represent a new and sad chapter in the history of the American Midwest: its transformation from industrial heartland to a wasteland of postindustrial decay, a new dust bowl, a rust bowl.[2]

"Your city makes everything from locomotives to buttermilk"

Part of the reason that the sudden waves of deindustrialization would hit the American Midwest with the particular cultural and psychic shock they did was because they were so unexpected. Like other industrial centers, Lima had quickly become accustomed to prosperity and the changes it brought. In the first half of the twentieth century, the city was specifically enriched by two major currents, one economic and one demographic, that would change the course of its subsequent history. Economically, it secured its immediate financial future in the transportation industry, particularly locomotive and then automobile manufacture. Demographically, its population and culture were immeasurably enhanced—though not without tension—by the arrival of several thousand new African American citizens from the rural South.

The man who brought the locomotive industry to Lima was a rumpled Michigan lumberman named Ephraim Shay, who had come to town in 1878 looking for a more efficient means of hauling logs to his sawmill. Soon he contracted with a new local firm, the Lima Machine Works, to build a steam-powered, geared locomotive of his own design that could maneuver the steep grades and sharp curves of the forests of northern Michigan. The stout little engine proved such a success that within three years orders were pouring in from logging outfits around the country eager to replace horsepower with new steam railroad technology. By 1890, the Lima Machine Works was employing a workforce of 150 men and producing five Shay locomotives a month. By 1900, the firm had supplied more than five hundred Shays to lumbermen around the country, and demand had escalated to a point where orders "could not be filled within six months of receipt."[3]

Executives of the Lima Machine Works soon realized that a golden future beckoned, and responded accordingly. Since their facility on East Market Street could not meet the increased demand, in 1902 they purchased the facilities of the old Lima Car Works, near the Solar Refinery off Main Street in South Lima, and expanded them dramatically. Ultimately, the new plant would encompass sixteen major buildings spread over sixty acres, including a steel foundry, a furnace, a carpenter shop, and separate shops for constructing boilers and wooden patterns. The plant's centerpiece was a huge erecting hangar for assembling the massive locomotives, a six-story building so massive that workers came to call it "the cathedral." The company itself underwent various transmutations, finally emerging, after an injection of New York financing in 1916, as the Lima Locomotive Works (LLW).[4]

The new managers quickly moved to expand production. As the demand for Shays faded in the early 1920s, the firm's chief mechanical engineer, Will Woodard, began to toy with new possibilities. A brilliant and creative engineer and a true devotee of the cult of steam, Woodward began to sketch out a design for a new locomotive that maximized its power. "I am going to see that steam lasts as long as possible," he told his son, "and have fun doing it." Soon he developed an improved, two-cylinder steam locomotive, based on a theory of "abundant speed at steam," an idea neatly summarized for marketing purposes in a term he called "superpower." Lima executives numbered the new engine 1, classed A-1, and in February 1925 sent it out for an introductory lap around the nation's tracks to demonstrate the capabilities of superpower. Able to produce more than twice as much horsepower than existing engines while using 20 percent less fuel, the new A-1 met with rave reviews, quickly becoming, as one historian noted, "one of the most influential locomotives in the history of steam power." New orders flooded in to Lima from around the country. Instantly identifiable by their diamond-shaped nameplate with its cast-iron insignia reading "Lima Locomotive Works, Incorporated," Lima engines quickly gained a sterling reputation in the field as some of the finest available, and for more than three decades the LLW held a consistent market share as the nation's third-largest manufacturer of locomotives. In 1928, the firm expanded its expertise further, creating a Shovel and Crane Division for the manufacture of steam-powered shovels, cranes, and the like.[5]

As had happened in the oil boom, when the establishment of one industry functioned to lure in others, the locomotive plant attracted satellite industries of its own. In 1907, Lima Machine Works chiefs heard of plans for a new steel foundry, initially set to locate in Indiana, and invited it to Lima instead, promising a ready market for the steel and iron castings needed in locomotive construction. Local businessmen sweetened the offer with $10,000 to assist in the move, and in September 1907, Ohio Steel opened its foundry on a tract of industrial property adjacent to the locomotive works. Its profits buoyed the success of the locomotive works, while the infusion of government contracts pouring in during World War I allowed Ohio Steel to eventually emerge into one of the key steel rolling mills in the country.[6]

Meanwhile, as the sprawling industrial complex on Lima's south side expanded dramatically, the city's downtown and north side likewise continued to grow. In 1907, the state of Ohio constructed Lima State Hospital for the incarceration of the criminally insane in rural farmland north of downtown, a move that would eventually spawn the establishment of a larger complex of related corrections facilities. It was also on the city's north side that numbers of area women began to enter the industrial economy in the only major local industry willing to hire them: the Diesel-Wemmer Cigar Works. Like many Lima establishments, Diesel-Wemmer had humble beginnings. It traced its roots back to 1884, when a young German immigrant, Henry Diesel, began rolling cigars in his home on Jackson Street in Lima. He found such a ready market that he expanded operations and two years later took in two partners, brothers named Wemmer, who pushed sales further. By the turn of the century, the Diesel-Wemmer partnership was successful enough to construct a large building on North Main Street, next to the Pennsylvania Railroad tracks, and then to begin to expand operations into nearby small towns in the Ohio countryside. In the ten years from 1906 to 1916, the budding firm established seventeen branch factories within a twenty-mile radius of Lima, and employed more than four thousand people to roll cigars, most of them female.[7]

Very early on, local industrialists began to learn a basic lesson about the Lima workforce that would characterize it for generations: Lima's workers would work long and hard but expected basic fairness and decency. When they failed to receive justice from their employers, they would resist. Locomotive workers regularly struck for issues ranging from wages to the degree of supervisory oversight they received: in 1889, when the company imported scabs, and again in 1903, when management responded with a pay increase of fifteen cents an hour. Even so, new industries arrived—Superior Coach, which constructed school buses and funeral coaches, and Gro-Cord Rubber, which produced rubber shoe soles—while older industries boomed. In 1926, a Lima Locomotive Works executive recited impressive figures for the Lima Chamber of Commerce: oil prices were rising, steel production expanding, local housing construction was up substantially, and, with orders pouring in for the new A-1 superpower engines, employment at the locomotive works had doubled from six hundred to fourteen hundred workers over the previous six months. Overall, employment rose steadily at a number of Lima industries through the spring of 1929, and as late as 1931, the city's manufacturing capacity so impressed a visiting railroad executive that he observed to a crowd of businessmen, "Your city makes everything from locomotives to buttermilk."[8]

For a century, the golden opportunities of America had attracted the energies and talents of millions of new immigrants; it was as deeply an American story as that of the Pilgrims on Plymouth Rock. The same dynamics emerged in Lima and intensified in the late 1930s. With Europe at war and the nation's industrial engines gradually accelerating once again, a new and assertive black community emerged in the city. Its birth was due in no small part to the efforts of Ohio Steel chief John Galvin, whose plant was expanding with the onset of war contracts. Galvin, needing workers, surmised that black labor would work as well as white, and sent his recruiters into the African American communities of the rural South, promising steady work at decent wages and the means to obtain it. Word of Galvin's offer attracted black southerners like a magnet; a particularly large contingent came to Lima from the region around Hurtsboro and Florence, Alabama. With their rail fare and expenses covered by their new employer, hundreds of African Americans from Alabama, Mississippi, and elsewhere across the South began arriving in Lima on the B&O Railroad and immediately reporting for work at Ohio Steel at wages above 72 cents an hour.[9]

These waves of new arrivals soon coalesced into a strong African American community on Lima's south side. Rufus Williamson arrived in Lima with his family in 1936; at the time, he later recalled, there were only four houses standing on the land beyond the complex of the locomotive works, steel plant, and oil refinery, farmland so inviting that his father actually farmed stretches of it with a homemade tractor he had fashioned from an old car, growing corn and some sugar cane. With the onset of World War II and the intensification of black migration, however, the vacant farmland on Lima's southern edge began to fill with houses, a process that soon intensified with the wartime housing shortage. In 1943, the steel company threw up a supposedly temporary housing development near Eighth Street and Reese Avenue as a stopgap measure. In the spirit of the times, they called it Victory Village. Williamson moved there and watched the new migrants roll in, "all southern—they brought them in by the truck loads and truck loads." The new arrivals found it cramped and overcrowded—not much of a victory at all. Newly arrived from Mississippi, Red Parker realized the village "wasn't the best in the world but it was better than what I had left from," and at least provided a place to call home while war wages beckoned.[10]

Yet there was another, less pleasant reason why the African American community expanded so rapidly on Lima's south side. New migrants may have left the South behind, but they still recognized in Lima the familiar ugly face of Jim Crow. When he arrived in Lima from Georgia in 1924 at about age eighteen, Eldridge "Bubba" Fields quickly saw that "there was prejudice here then, a lot of prejudice. We were segregated here." Ohio Steel would hire them, but the locomotive works would not, and their opportunities with the railroads were restricted to the traditional roles of bellhop and Pullman care service or to manual labor jobs in the roundhouse or on track maintenance. Residential segregation intensified as the flood of black migrants increased. Buses would not stop for African Americans north of the Pennsylvania Railroad tracks, and blacks avoided the entire north end of town at night for fear of being attacked. Adults found themselves barred from restaurants, stores, and restrooms, and confined to the balcony in Lima's movie houses. One of the few real differences from the South seemed to be that the Jim Crow signs were missing in Lima. "You'd go into a restaurant and you'd wait and you'd wait," a woman remembered, "and you'd sit, and all of a sudden it dawns on you: they're not waiting on me. They'd just kind of walk around you like you weren't there." The talented African American contralto Marian Anderson came to Lima in 1940 for a special concert at South High School. Anderson at that time was a glittering star with a national following, but when she stayed in the Argonne Hotel downtown, she had her meals brought to her room on a tray, because she was not allowed in the hotel's dining room.[11]

Even in this separate racial world imposed by de facto segregation, local African Americans came to share with white workers two persistent characteristics of Lima's working classes. First of all, they learned that economic success was possible in Lima but demanded hard labor. Coming from a sharecropping family in rural Georgia, Fields was no stranger to heavy work, but he still was not quite ready for what he encountered when he signed on with Ohio Steel and went to work as a "chain hooker," loading railcars with iron castings on their way to Ohio Steel. "You worked in them days," he recalled, in labor that was "dirty! Rough! Rough! Hard work! . . . chippers and hammers running all day long. You couldn't hear nobody talking." In the late 1930s, the company reduced Fields's working shift from twelve hours a day to eight. As a lye vat attendant earning fifty cents an hour at the Nickel Plate Railroad, James Ward spent his day dipping locomotive parts into bubbling lye to remove the grease from them. The dripping lye burned holes in his clothes. Pete McDaniel hired on as a "chipper" with Ohio Steel, blasting excess metal off hot castings with an air hammer. The job plunged him into an inferno of dirt, noise, and stink, where the air was so thickened with particles following the pouring of a cast that sometimes he could not see a fellow worker standing a few feet away.[12]

Second, like other Lima workers, the city's new black residents quickly recognized injustice and agitated against it. More often than not in Lima, they were led in their protests by an Ohio-born African American activist named Furl Williams. Williams had been raised in rural Paulding County, thirty miles away, where his grandfather had arrived two generations before, escaping slavery with the help of the Underground Railroad. In the 1920s, he and his siblings naturally gravitated toward the big city. "This was a real adventure, to come from down there in the country to Lima," he remembered; they would sit in the black sections of theaters and catch the latest movies. In 1937, at age thirty, Williams moved to Lima for good, hiring on as a chipper with Ohio Steel for thirty-six cents an hour. There he found the work so hot and dirty that, in the days before the company installed a shower room, at the end of the workday "you couldn't tell the whites from the blacks. They all looked alike." Before long, Ohio Steel farmed Williams out to the locomotive works across the street to chip excess metal from engine wheels, and it was

Furl Williams, Lima politician and activist for labor and racial justice, late in life, late 1980s. *Photo courtesy of the collections of the Allen County, Ohio, Historical Society.*

at Lima Locomotive that Williams learned some basic principles of organizing. When he discovered that a fellow white worker was receiving fifteen cents more an hour than he was for the same work, he laid his tools down immediately and went to talk to the management about it. He quickly saw his wages raised that fifteen cents, and soon he was talking union.[13]

In 1941, the United Auto Workers organized Ohio Steel and Williams found himself appointed to the grievance committee, then elected chair of the bargaining committee. He discovered that these positions provided a platform from which he could push hard for justice in a number of areas. When he discovered that management was trying to eliminate a number of women workers, he fought for them, filing grievance after grievance on their behalf. When in 1945 the company then targeted Williams and fired him on a trumped-up pretext, upwards of 2,400 fellow workers shut the plant down for two weeks, refusing to return to work until management rehired him. And when Rufus Williamson landed a job as a lathe operator with Ohio Steel because of his obvious ability, and white operators shut down their machines in protest, Williams was central in negotiating a settlement that ultimately helped African Americans to begin to leave the realm of chippers and lye vat attendants and join the ranks of skilled labor.[14]

Most significantly, in the late 1930s and through the war years, Williams and an emerging cohort of local black activists in the newly formed Lima chapter of the National Association for the Advancement of Colored People (NAACP) began to slowly grind away at the massive glacial edifice of Jim Crow Lima. It was only in response to agitation by Williams and other NAACP activists that in 1948 local officials finally allowed blacks to swim one day a week at the Schoonover pool. Williams integrated other facilities on his own. He once walked into a local restaurant on South Main Street to buy a sandwich but suddenly decided that this time he would not take the sandwich to go. When employees asked him to leave and threatened to call the police when he would not, Williams—by then president of the union local at Ohio Steel—offered to make the call himself. Two policemen showed up and fined the restaurant $25 while Williams enjoyed his sandwich inside. Meanwhile, civic activist Letitia Dalton formed a local organization called the Hy-Ho Club to ease the path of many young blacks into college and extended the campaign against segregation on a number of other fronts. She pressured Lima's Episcopal church into accepting her as its first African American member and organized a youth civic group, the Junior League, to proceed along the same lines. One member, an African American teenager named Nathzollo Gurley, recalled that Dalton focused the league's sights on a popular local franchise of the hamburger chain called Kewpees, which would serve blacks only from the outside takeout window. Dalton told her charges "to go to Kewpee's to petition to come inside and eat." But Kewpees would not abandon its racist policy because of a little petition. The owner told them bluntly, "I don't care if I get your money. I don't need your pennies; you are not coming into my establishment." To young Gurley, the bitterness of the experience must have sunk deep. Her father tried to comfort her as best he could. "It was only because of the color of your skin and nothing else," he soothed, "just let it go, because one person is not going to change the whole thing."[15]

In the early 1940s, small winds of change began to blow, emanating from the great social convulsion of war. As in most other places around the country, and particularly the nation's industrial areas, to Lima the coming of World War II brought heartbreak to scattered individual families but mostly it meant economic boom. Already by June 1941, contracts from the European war and the United States' mobilization for war triggered headlines in the *Lima News*. "Employment Hits High Figure as Plants Hum Busily Day and Night," proclaimed the paper, detailing how employment levels at the city's four largest industries—Lima Locomotive Works, Westinghouse, Ohio Steel, and Superior Coach—had risen to total more than six thousand workers. But this was only the beginning. Six months later, in the frantic rush of nationwide mobilization following Japan's attack on Pearl Harbor, both local employment and production levels began soaring ever higher, regularly shattering city records nearly every time officials stopped to measure them. In the first eleven months of 1942, they reported, job placements in area defense industries increased 223 percent over the same period for 1941, but it still was not enough. In August 1943, a special Lima Emergency Committee, staffed by representatives from management and labor, launched a drive to recruit seven thousand more war workers, a figure that would raise the industrial employment total at area factories to more than twenty-five thousand. The following March, the state manpower director listed Lima as "one of the three most critical labor areas" in Ohio. So desperate were Ohio manufacturers to fill their labor needs that, like their colleagues elsewhere in the country, they finally resorted to hiring people they had written off for decades as unfit for the industrial workplace. "One-Fourth of Lima's War Workers Are Women," headlined the *Lima News* in 1943. With the level of female employment in Lima industrial facilities up 45 percent by that January, the men at the locomotive works or Ohio Steel could glance around the shop floor and see plenty of local representatives of the national "Rosie the Riveter" archetype. Nor was that precedent the only one broken by the war: the level of African American employment at Lima's industrial firms rose by 41 percent in the same period.[16]

Like those of other American communities, Lima's citizens navigated the regimen of ration books, jumped to the whistles of the civil defense officials, and obediently cut their lights during blackouts. The bigger crisis concerned housing. With defense workers in critical supply and special committees strenuously wooing more, the crucial question became where to put them. Victory Village, with its 140 separate units, daycare and community centers, and recreation room, helped a lot. As its payroll swelled from 900 to 2,500 workers, Ohio Steel took measures on its own, purchasing another tract of land on the south side, where it installed 1,000 mobile homes to help house its labor force. Residential construction also stepped in as the city's population skyrocketed to ever-greater highs, from 44,000 in 1941, to 50,000 in 1942, to an estimated 54,000 a year later.[17]

Lima industrialists desperately needed labor because the infusion of war contracts nearly overwhelmed them with work. In the five years from 1939 to 1944, Westinghouse, now producing most of the generators the Army Air Corps used in its bombers, nearly quadrupled its workforce, from 1,400 to 5,800 women and men. Ohio Steel packed a huge variety of military materiel onto train cars heading away from Lima: rolling mills rolls for armor plates on tanks and ships, fragmentation bombs, gun base parts, and cannon mountings of all kinds. At three different times during the war years, the company received the Army-Navy "'E' for Excellence" award for its key role in developing cast breech rings. A key aspect of a gun's firing mechanism, breech rings had previously been made of forged steel, a process requiring a tremendous amount of machining before they were functional. After much experimentation in 1941, Ohio Steel workers succeeded in casting breech rings, thereby saving the war effort millions of dollars in labor and machinery. Meanwhile, workers at Lima Locomotive pushed themselves to new levels of frenzied activity because of the war orders flooding in. On the last day of December 1944, workers paused briefly in the great erecting hangar for speeches and applause commemorating their completion of their 306th locomotive that year, two-thirds of them ordered by the U.S. government and shipped around the world for the war effort. In the same week, their comrades in the Shovel and Crane Division stopped to celebrate the completion of their 500th crane that year, a machine that two workers named the "Axis Grave Digger." Early in the war, the locomotive works had received a contract to build tanks as well, and Lima's own version of the military-industrial complex in the south rim of the city expanded still further in 1942, when a General Motors (GM) subsidiary located there won a contract to modify and process military vehicles, especially tanks. Within a year, more than 4,000 men and women were engaged in the task, and by the war's end nearly 100,000 combat vehicles had passed through the facility.[18]

On a Sunday afternoon in mid-July 1943, fifty thousand area residents jammed Lima's downtown for what the papers correctly called the "greatest military display" in the county's history. Designed to kick off a $700,000 campaign to build two bombers that would be named for the city and county, the parade really was an impressive display of military muscle by any yardstick. Military bands played,

The Lima Locomotive Works about 1945. *Photo courtesy of the collections of the Allen County, Ohio, Historical Society.*

officials waved from convertibles, half-tracks and cannon ground their way by, and the spectators thrilled to the parade's highlight: thirty-two of the massive thirty-one-ton Sherman tanks recently completed by the Lima Locomotive Works, adorned by pretty girls waving regally to the crowds. Already, by midway through the war, local citizens had a lot to celebrate. With a unanimity of purpose that temporarily eased racial and class tensions, they had thrown themselves into helping to relieve their country's crisis by achieving an unprecedented level of industrial production. They had unselfishly labored hard for the national good, and, as a happy consequence of the demands of war, also pushed their own community to new heights of economic and demographic growth.[19]

The war years did spell the final doom for the old days of steam, however. By the late 1930s, most of the nation's train towns were already living on borrowed time. The golden age of American railroading ended right about the time of World War I, with passenger usage declining relatively rapidly after its peak in 1916. Thanks to a team of engineers at Ford Motor Company and their 1914 perfection of the moving assembly line, the joys of automobile travel rapidly passed from the exclusive realm of the rich into the reach of the masses. Within two years, people were buying Fords at the rate of half a million cars a year, and the frenzy would only escalate as the price fell further; by 1925, a new Model T sold for a grand total of $260. Competition from the commercial airline industry would not provide the final blow to mass use of railroad passenger service until after World War II, but already by the 1920s the attractions of the family car were eating away at the profits of the nation's passenger trains like a fast-growing cancer. Meanwhile, the ease of shipping goods by semi trucks on the emerging highway system and of moving petroleum products through a network of pipelines was rapidly undermining railroad freight traffic. Railroads could barely keep pace with these developments during the boom times of the 1920s, and with the onset of the Great Depression the nation's major railroad lines abandoned thousands of miles of track every year. Attached to steam power with near-religious devotion, the Lima Locomotive Works belatedly embraced new diesel technology in 1947, but by then the plant was so far behind its industry rivals that in 1950 it dropped locomotive production altogether and tried to make a profit by producing shovels and cranes instead. In May 1949, Lima Locomotive rolled its last engine off the line, a steam-powered, piston-driven Berkshire locomotive. From the firm's foundation in 1879 until September 1949, the company had constructed 7,752 locomotives. Now it was all over.[20]

Yet the passing of Lima's era as a train town did not bring its great economic boom to a sudden end; history does not move in neat and predictable cycles of boom and bust. "In opposition to a simple, unidirectional story of political and economic stability followed by decline," write Jefferson Cowie and Joseph Heathcott, the real story of both industrialization and deindustrialization is found in a history "characterized by unevenness, fits and starts, and regional variance." Even as local residents mourned the loss of a prosperous era rooted in locomotive construction, they found themselves fortunately situated to take advantage of the next great wave in transportation technology, one that would extend their boom period further into the future.[21]

"You could go anyplace in this town and get a good-paying factory job"

While the automotive revolution had been transforming the nation for decades, it was just after World War II that automobile and other large industrial corporations registered their greatest impact on the economic possibilities for America's working classes. At the end of World War II, with nearly every other major nation devastated by the war, the military and economic might of the United States had mounted to a point where public opinion leaders casually began to refer to an upcoming "American century." American corporations dominated the world's finances, and American manufactured goods flooded the globe. The United States held over half of the world's usable productive capacity, and, if American corporations could reach industrial peace with organized labor, they stood to reap profits beyond their dreams. In effect, beginning with the war's end, American corporate management offered workers what numerous social scientists refer to as the great postwar "social contract." If workers would refrain from strikes and other confrontations, their employers would share their profits with them in a more equitable manner. Moreover, following the path laid out by the New and Fair deals, the federal government would expand the "social wage," defined by economists Barry Bluestone and Bennett Harrison as "the amalgam of benefits, workplace protections and legal rights that acts to increase the social security of the working class."[22]

It was a deal that postwar developments had rendered labor ripe to accept. The political tide had begun to turn against organized labor with the restrictions on labor militancy written into law by the Taft-Hartley Act of 1948, and the red baiting of labor leaders that people like Senator Joe McCarthy developed into an art form. The backlash blunted the growth of organized labor and led to the ascent of more conservative labor leaders like George Meany, head of the AFL-CIO, who focused on consolidating labor's gains rather than pushing for new ones. Moreover and best of all, the deal did seem to work. Through about 1973, average real wages rose steadily in America, levels of economic inequality eased, and blue-collar Americans increasingly began to internalize the package of material and personal expectations—things like a decent home, health care benefits, and college education for their children—that previously had been the province of a wealthy, white-collar elite.[23]

This postwar social contract between big business and big labor also augured good fortune for the particular communities where industries chose to locate. Given its geographic proximity to Detroit, the industrial Midwest reemerged after the war as the nation's automobile heartland. It also strengthened its manufacturing capacities in satellite industries, many of which came to form a close association with one or another midwestern city: in Ohio, for example, rubber with Akron, glass with Toledo, and ball bearings with Canton. Following the construction of the nation's interstate highway system in the late 1950s, automobile assembly plants extended southward from Detroit, particularly along I-65 in Indiana and I-75 through northwest Ohio.[24]

In June 1955, a decade before bulldozers cleared the way for the new Interstate 75 two miles east of Lima's downtown, local residents awoke to an electrifying headline in the *Lima News*, "Ford to Build Giant Lima Plant." Soon girders rose for what would be a truly massive industrial facility: 950,000 square feet of building spread over a twenty-seven-acre tract of land located in rural Bath Township, less than a mile east of the Lima city limits. Within three years, more than four thousand autoworkers would be scrambling over the assembly of engines for new Ford automobiles, the fourth such facility that the automaker had constructed since the end of the war. Later that same year, the refinery, still bearing the name of Rockefeller's flagship company Sohio, from Standard Oil of Ohio, announced that it would break ground for a sister plant for the manufacture of different industrial chemicals. In subsequent additions over the years, the Sohio chemical plant would spread farther south of town, into what was then the woodlots and rolling farmland of Shawnee Township. The fact that both the new Ford plant and the new Sohio chemical plant, along with the old Sohio refinery, were technically outside city limits did not seem to occasion much alarm to Lima city leaders at the time. With the local economy booming and most of the housing capacity for the incoming waves of new workers remaining inside city limits—in 1950 Bath could not boast six thousand people nor Shawnee many more than three thousand—Lima officials could rest assured that the new jobs would redound to the benefit of the county in general and the city of Lima in particular.[25]

From 1960 to 1980, the Ford engine plant would remain the largest single employer in the county, but Lima was also able to follow the lead of many other cities in the country and secure a foothold in the burgeoning defense industry, which expanded dramatically through the 1950s as the cold war deepened. After World War II, the U.S. Defense Department had allowed the old tank plant to lapse into hibernation, and sold many of its old tanks to midwestern farmers, who used them for grain storage bins. With the outbreak of hostilities in Korea, however, activity once again began to swirl around the old defense facilities south of Lima; by 1951, twenty-seven hundred people labored there, preparing or modifying tanks. Already by 1951, Lima had fully remobilized to do its part in the cold war. The old locomotive works, now constructing cranes and other building equipment as the Baldwin-Lima-Hamilton Corporation, devoted nearly 50 percent of its output that year to contracts for the Defense Department, while defense work constituted 70 percent of the total output at Westinghouse. Ohio Steel was also awash in defense contracts again, as were the new Ex-Cello Corporation, which built jet engine parts; Superior Coach, which turned out five hundred buses and ambulances for the federal government; and North Star Woolen Mills, which spun out thousands of woolen blankets for the army and navy.[26]

Increasingly, the new workers drawn to Lima followed patterns set during World War II and filed into the ranks of organized labor. "Lima was a pretty strong union town in the late to mid-1940s," Williams recalled. By 1974, one labor leader estimated that 15,000 of the 53,000 people working in the county, or nearly 30 percent, were members of one union or another, 9,000 with the

United Auto Workers (UAW) alone, and 3,500 with the Teamsters. Local union members mostly conducted their relationships with their employers amicably and without violence, but, as in the years before the war, when corporate management pushed, labor would push back. Labor militancy in and around Lima climaxed in the 1950s, with regular wildcat strikes at places like Superior Coach and Ex-Cello—where workers struck twenty-five times in 1954 alone—and longer, union-organized strikes elsewhere. In mid-October 1955, nearly 2,000 union members walked out of the Westinghouse plant, in solidarity with a national work stoppage, and did not return until the following March. Westinghouse retaliated with a back-to-work campaign, waving cash advances in front of laborers willing to cross picket lines. Striking workers forcibly confronted their workmates who did so, however, and tensions percolated at a full boil. A smaller but equally lengthy strike occurred simultaneously at Gro-Cord, a local rubber factory, where 96 percent of determined union members left the plant and the UAW surrounded the factory with 250 picketers. Similar strikes roiled the Ex-Cello Corporation for seven weeks in 1955 and fifteen weeks in 1958.[27]

Meanwhile, the political opinions of many of the city's residents increasingly began to work at variance with those of its local newspaper. Since the late 1920s, the *Lima News* had been owned by a local family and, in the words of a *Business Week* reporter in 1958, had been regarded around northwestern Ohio as "one of the finest smaller city newspapers in the state." The *Lima News* had held close to a mainstream Republican editorial line for national and international matters but locally had been a strong booster of civic activities and institutions. In 1956, however, it had been bought by the newspaper magnate Raymond Hoiles as the eleventh paper in his chain, and it immediately began preaching the far-right libertarianism of its owner. This meant that, among other positions, the newspaper now firmly opposed public libraries and schools as manifestations of "socialism" and exhibited a fierce hatred of organized labor. "Everything possible had been done to alienate every single group in this town since Hoiles took over," recalled a local business owner. When the *Lima News* opposed a local bond issue supporting public libraries, claiming that the bond would move Lima closer "to socialism, communism, collectivism or whatever you want to call it," an outraged Lima community proceeded to pass the bond issue by the largest margin in the city's history. Hoiles was undaunted. When *Lima News* employees, then members of the American Newspaper Guild, went on strike in 1957, he imported strikebreakers to destroy the action.[28]

Despite such setbacks, however, labor's real power was evident not in strikes but in the day-by-day, year-by-year economic advances made of Lima residents. Local newspapers told the story. "Ford Workers Earn Record Wages," trumpeted the *Lima News* in 1961; "Average Allen Worker Chalking Up Gains," another headline read. In 1958, a reporter from the *Toledo Blade* featured Lima as a busy, prosperous community of 55,000, with new schools, a falling crime rate, a new library in planning, and thirty-five new industrial plants that had arrived in the previous eight years alone. In 1966, the city's population hit 57,000 people, growing at a faster rate than the county as a whole, partly because of its physical expansion. In 1960–61, Lima annexed two large subdivisions on its western and northern edges, part of an overall strategy to break through the residential areas on the city's outskirts and gain more land for industrial expansion. For their part, residents of these districts were glad to join the city because of the lower sewer and water rates that annexation promised.[29]

As ever, economic success in Lima required hard and demanding labor, day after day. Union bargaining power and the intervention of prolabor politicians had provided workers with decent wages, paid vacations, and unemployment and retirement insurance, but none of the benefits could help workers escape from the monotony of assembly-line production. It is an easy error to romanticize the hard physical labor that factory work involved. The New Jersey autoworkers studied by Ruth Milkman, for example, "yearned to escape" the "relentless and dehumanizing rhythms" of the assembly line and the "daily humiliations" of working for GM. "We're constantly working to cut monotony and keep productivity up," admitted a Lima UAW leader in 1974, "and we still don't have any final answers on that."[30]

Lima remained a blue-collar town. As late as 1974, only 11 percent of the city's adult population had finished more than a year of college. Yet more than half of residents had graduated from high school and could look forward to the tangible rewards that factory labor offered working people in Lima in the 1950s and 1960s: modest but decent homes of their own on shaded, tree-lined streets, networks of nearby family and friends, and education and a secure future for their children. Lima's industries demanded hard work, but paid far better than the salaries many local college grads garnered by teaching school. Through the early 1970s, at least, plenty of local manufacturing jobs remained available—well-paying jobs that communities could be built upon. Clarence Roller, for example, grew up in rural Bath Township in the years following World War II and then was drafted into the military. When he returned home from Vietnam in 1969, he went around to Lima's various employers putting in applications. "I think everyone was hiring," he recalled. Within days, both the chemical plant and Ford Motor Company had offered him jobs. Roller signed on in an entry-level position at the refinery, primarily because they had called him back first. Nobody from his graduating class at Bath High School had run into any trouble finding local work. "When I got out of school, you could go anyplace in this town and get a good-paying factory job," recalled one laid-off Lima machinist in the early 1980s. "You could take your pick." The only remaining major social task would be to admit to the good life an important group of Lima citizens who had been left out.[31]

"You are down, we have our foot on your neck"

Like those of many American cities, Lima's economic fortunes in the postwar era could not be separated from its halting efforts to deal with its racial problems and the structural injustices they had spawned. The great boom of the postwar years had not been equitably shared. For most of Lima's African Americans, going home after work or school meant heading for the south side of town, and the south side meant poverty. Their opportunities for better housing remained limited, partly because of racist realtor practices, and partly because of the quiet racism that permeated the city as a whole. People of color found that landlords routinely refused to rent property to them, and their options to buy homes of their own were likewise restricted. For decades, realtors refused to show homes to blacks outside Lima's two black neighborhoods, and African Americans had difficulty financing such purchases anyway. Many blamed local banks, which usually denied them loans; the bankers, in turn, blamed the sellers, who overpriced property for black buyers. Either way, the effect was the same. Melvin Woodard, for example, arrived with his wife and family in Lima in 1964 to take up the pastorate of Second Baptist Church. Woodard was an educated, polished man, a respected pastor and military veteran, but he soon discovered that realtors would show him homes only on Lima's south side, or in the small black neighborhood west of downtown. When Woodard explored by himself and found homes for sale in other areas, realtors insisted they just could not line up a proper time to show him those homes. The new pastor persisted, however, and finally found a realtor willing to sell him a pretty little house in Lima's north end. Shortly afterward, the realtor called Woodard in some anxiety, desperate to sell him a different home: his phone had been buzzing with calls from angry whites, all threatening to pull their own listings from him unless he cancelled the deal. Even an accomplished and acknowledged local black leader like union activist Furl Williams had difficulty buying a house in Lima. He failed three times before finally becoming a homeowner, including once because no local bank would finance his purchase of a home outside the south side and another time when the seller reneged on the sale because of pressure from neighboring whites.[32]

With African Americans confined to limited neighborhoods because of white racism in the housing market, the south side, particularly from Tenth to Eighteenth streets, deteriorated into a ghetto in the years after World War II.

Victory Village on Lima's south side in 1958, two decades after the migration of thousands of African Americans from the Deep South to Lima. *Photo courtesy of the collections of the Allen County, Ohio, Historical Society.*

During the war, Ohio Steel had built trailers to house its black war workers, but the company reclaimed the trailers at the war's end and offered their old tenants no help in resettling. Many bought lots and built what homes they could outside the city limits in rural Perry Township. They lived in shacks built from old sheet metal, scrap wood, and wooden crates, and without water or sewage lines, since those amenities stopped at the city limits. When Alberta Shurelds left Mississippi in 1953 and joined her family on Lima's south side, she was shocked to discover that their home in the supposedly affluent North lacked indoor plumbing, and the family had to buy water from street vendors. Already by the late 1950s, Lima's black leaders routinely referred to the south side as "the worst Negro ghetto in the United States," an assessment that did not change even as much of the rest of the region rode the tides of industrial prosperity. When the director of the U.S. Civil Rights Commission visited Lima in 1971, he was astounded at the rows of shacks lining the south end. "I saw these kinds of structures in Georgia in the 1930s," he declared, "but I didn't expect to find anything like these in Ohio."[33]

Nevertheless, there was a certain vitality and vibrancy to Lima's south side, thanks in great part to the creativity and resourcefulness of the people who made it home. Local entrepreneur Rufus Williamson, who had begun to make a good deal of money as a south side businessman, remembered it fondly. "When you'd come out of bars you could hear the music and people laughing and cars would be parked along the streets, both sides of the street would just be full of cars," he recalled. "The town was just alive." But it was also a town stunted and warped by racism, and in the early 1950s, the objects of Jim Crow began to push more forcefully against the edges of their confinement. In the early 1960s, led by a new activist named David Powell, the Lima NAACP pushed the campaign. A lawsuit brought down the "Negroes Only" cordons at the Ranger Theater downtown. When an official of the Baldwin-Lima-Hamilton Corporation told Powell in 1964 that it would not hire blacks, the NAACP promptly filed suit, triggering the federal government to withdraw a $2 million contract from the corporation. Powell worked through local unions to gain black admittance to the skilled trades. By 1971, he and the NAACP had managed to open these skilled trades to 173 successful applicants, and NAACP pressure was likewise central in the hiring of 17 African American schoolteachers by the Lima City Schools. Activists also focused on the hiring of African Americans at downtown stores and banks. In the mid-1960s, a black ministerial association mounted a money exchange in area churches, where hundreds of parishioners exchanged parts of their paychecks for $2.00 bills. Suddenly in February—timed to coincide with Black History Month—hundreds of downtown merchants found customers paying for their purchases in $2.00 bills, a vivid reminder of the growing economic power of the black community.[34]

By the mid-1960s, much of the overt discrimination and segregation had vanished from Lima. This victory was partly a result of changing racial attitudes among whites and the power of the federal government, which finally ended the era of Jim Crow with the Civil Rights Act of 1964, but it was also a product of decades of local agitation by the local African American community. By the late 1960s, this community could also measure its progress through its small but growing political influence. Woodard made an unsuccessful bid in the Lima mayoral race of 1968, finishing a poor third. But in 1968 he was still a relative newcomer to Lima; more success came to those whom the public deemed had paid their dues. On May 1, 1968—as many of the nation's urban areas exploded, perhaps coincidentally, with the riots following Martin Luther King's assassination—William Davenport capped his two-decades-long rise through the ranks with his appointment as Lima's first black police chief. A year later, Furl Williams took another step in an even longer rise to local power when the voters of the sixth ward—Lima's south side—sent him to the Lima City Council, the first person of color ever to win elective office in the city's history.[35]

By this point, however, many in Lima's black community judged such measures of racial progress to be too little too late. They perceived local courts passing out more severe sentences to black teens than to white teens for the same crimes. They watched as their kids came home from college and were unable to secure summer jobs even in fast-food restaurants. They wrung their hands over the poor quality of teaching their children received at schools like South Junior High. They kept a mental list of which white cops would beat them up for the catchall crime of "resisting arrest"; not even the efforts of Chief Davenport, Woodard said, could change the subculture of the Lima Police Department.[36] As rows of outhouses festered and stank across the south side, its residents watched political forces routinely derail efforts to pass something as minimal to progress as a city housing code. Four times—in 1958, 1963, 1966, and 1971—the city council passed a housing code, but each time a powerful local coalition of realtors, landlords, and small businessmen—aided by editorial fulminations on behalf of personal freedom in the *Lima News*—arose to defeat the measure, three times by popular referendum. On the city council, in 1971, Williams pushed for more power for the largely toothless Lima Human Relations Commission, warning his fellow council members that if they refused to grant it, "You are saying to a segment of our community, 'you are down, we have our foot on your neck, and, by God, we are not going to let you back up.'" Undaunted, the council voted down Williams's measure.[37]

Elsewhere in the United States in the late 1960s, urban communities were ringing with cries of "Black Power." New voices arose, chanting in the strident cadences of black nationalism that the time had come to change such conditions whether white politicians liked it or not. Decades of pent-up frustration and rage gave way to spasms of rioting. With the country's black ghettos burning, much of black Lima likewise moved into a new era of militancy. Older solutions no longer sufficed. Take, for instance, the fate of a south side agency called the Mizpah Center. Since its establishment in the late 1930s, Mizpah had functioned, in the words of one activist, as "a quiet little center paternalistically aiding the poor." By the late 1960s, an energized new board—primarily an ecumenical Protestant agency called Churchwomen United—wanted the center to do more than its usual slate of cub scouts, after-school tutoring, and head start programs. In 1969, they hired a new director, a Presbyterian minister and experienced community organizer from Philadelphia named Dennis Loo. Soon Rev. Loo had Mizpah bustling with street academies and other activities, and the center quickly emerged as the staging ground for new African American confrontations with Lima's white power structure. A group called the Concerned Parents Association met there to plan a boycott of South Junior High. So did a new group of activists, whose members now felt they had enough momentum to take a name. Casting around in the national waters of radical black activism, they found the perfect one to convey their seriousness of purpose and overall agenda. They decided to call themselves the Black Panthers.[38]

In reality, the Lima Black Panthers were disorganized and consisted perhaps of two dozen young people. They existed for barely more than a year, during which time they devoted much of their energies to a breakfast program for local poor children. With the benefit of hindsight, even a local police officer admitted a grudging respect. The Panthers, local policeman Thomas Nelson saw, "drew the public's attention . . . to how things were out in the south end. You hate the violence but usually progress comes in that way." The single major accomplishment of the Lima Black Panthers seemed to be to steadily stoke the racial fears of white Lima. Following the assertive agenda of the national Black Panther movement, the Lima group regularly appeared in public carrying weapons. Periodically they engaged in open military drilling, and distributed around Lima the organization's national paper, *The Black Panther Speaks,* with its casual references to killing cops—"offing the pigs"—and other violent fantasies. When, in July 1969, Lima mayor Christian Morris appeared at a community meeting at Fourth Street Baptist Church on the south side, a dozen or so Panthers, clad in trademark brown berets and with bandoliers of ammunition draped across their bodies, broke into the meeting to deliver an ultimatum. The city had exactly one month, they told Morris, to "do something" for its African American residents, or face a "war." Many white residents returned the hostility in kind. Individual Panthers discovered that mere mention of their association with the group would eliminate any chance they had for local employment. Lima police kept their headquarters under close surveillance, as did the Toledo office of the FBI, which quickly infiltrated the group and sent regular reports on its activities to the Lima Police Department. The Panthers became a particularly convenient explanation for the racial trouble that had begun to roil the city's school system. School superintendent Earl McGovern publicly blamed them for the increased racial polarization in the schools; it was their circulation of "hate literature," their spreading of rumors and "psychological harassment" that kept "everyone on edge."[39]

Many African Americans would have pointed to other reasons for the city's racial tension, but by the late 1960s, it was clear to everyone that the Lima schools were in racial turmoil. In November 1969, fed up with what its members saw as abusive teachers and administrative indifference to racism at South Junior High, the Concerned Parents Association launched a student boycott. It lasted into the following February, when sixty students, parents, and Black Panthers picketed in front of the school, calling for the resignation of the principal, John Wolfe; another dozen occupied Wolfe's office before they were arrested. In fall

1969, school officials cancelled night football games, unable to control the racial violence that erupted among spectators in the parking lots and streets outside the grandstand. Racial fights among individual students and then larger groups broke out repeatedly at Lima Senior High. Police responded with arrests, along with ambulances to carry away wounded combatants, and administrators closed the school for days afterward. After a particularly violent mêlée in 1971, police arrested twenty-nine teens and eleven adults, among them Rev. Loo, who spent ten days in jail before accepting a new job out of state. For several years running, hostilities at Lima High peaked during the ceremonies of Black History Week in February, with a regularity and intensity that provoked a front-page newspaper story as far away as Cleveland. "It's like this," an African American teenager named Antelle Haithcock explained to a reporter. "The white kids all resent Black History Week, and the black kids all resent that they resent it."[40]

The principal representative of the white power structure against which such activists reacted was a Lima native and the city's mayor, a thirty-eight-year-old Republican named Christian Morris. The owner of a local sporting goods store who previously had been uninvolved in public affairs, Morris took office in 1965 as a self-described "political neophyte" pledging to govern in a nonpartisan manner. Circumstances later cast him as an embattled small-city mayor, and in some ways he fit the description. Believing that the public had entrusted him to maintain the rule of law and protect public safety, Morris, by the late 1960s, was carrying out those responsibilities with enough vigor to have received several death threats. As a result he began to carry a gun in a shoulder holster as part of his everyday attire. Yet in other ways Morris seemed an ironic choice for the role of tough racial adversary. He resolutely pushed for a housing code and looked for ways to crack down on slumlords even in the absence of a code. He took a lot of pride in his efforts to modernize Lima's police department and particularly in his appointment of Davenport as the department's new chief, even though placing an African American in such a position triggered several blistering phone calls to the mayor's office from angry whites. Undaunted, Morris brought in several outspoken local black ministers to meet with city administrators and conduct early efforts in racial sensitivity training. Speaking at community Lenten services in 1967, he called on area churches to shake off their "complacency" and get more involved in the struggle for racial justice.[41]

Morris's efforts were not enough to stem the tide of black anger, however, which soon began to spill over from the schools into Lima's streets. In January 1970, 150 Panthers and other demonstrators marched from the Mizpah Center to downtown to demand an official holiday for Martin Luther King. Most were peaceable; a few broke downtown windows, blocked traffic, and taunted local police, who responded with arrests. Tensions built steadily. Later that month a Lima policeman, Ted Lee, was hit by a sniper and critically wounded as he investigated a fistfight after a dance at the Mizpah Center. "When people get frustrated, they don't care," Rev. Woodard later explained. "They'll do anything."[42]

Over his two terms as mayor, Morris managed the city through twenty-one separate civil disturbances. The unrest peaked one evening in early August 1970, when two white officers, Glen Pierce and Ted Boop, apprehended a teenager they found stealing a bicycle on the near south side. As Pierce turned to put the youth in his cruiser, a group of bystanders attacked Boop, breaking his nose. Simultaneously, a forty-two-year-old black woman, Christine Ricks, came flying out of a nearby house, grabbed Pierce's pistol out of its holster from behind, and began shooting. Pierce fell with an ear shot off before Boop returned fire, killing Ricks. Rumors rapidly began circulating through the south side that the officers had opened fire on Ricks first and then pumped bullets into her body; militants spread the word, Morris remembered, that "the pigs have killed a sister." A crowd of two hundred angry residents, many of them armed, began to march up Main Street on the south side. Police forced them back with a skirmish line, but elsewhere across the district, firebombs exploded and police cruisers began to come under sniper fire. Gunshots burst from the Black Panther headquarters on Fourth Street, wounding one officer before police stormed the building. At 8:30 P.M., Morris declared a state of emergency and instituted martial law across the city, while Governor Rhodes sent in the National Guard. Troopers rolled into town in half-tracks and trucks, and for five days, five hundred guardsmen patrolled the streets of Lima.[43]

As the tide of black militancy crested and then ebbed elsewhere in the country, so too did local racial tensions slowly ease. By the mid-1970s, a rough racial truce had set in at Lima Senior High, the Black Panthers had disappeared, and even a mainstream group like the NAACP appeared largely moribund. Yet the impact of angry confrontations would continue to reverberate in subtle ways for years. The proper, middle-class residents of Lima—the great white "silent majority" successfully courted by people like Richard Nixon—were increasingly fed up. Lima crime rates had escalated steadily through the early 1970s, their children were unsafe at school, and now racial unrest so reverberated across the city that it apparently took the National Guard to maintain order in the streets. In this climate, imagine their reaction when in 1969 the *Lima News* inflamed their frustration by asserting that racial violence had so permeated Lima High that assaults on innocent students were frequent and "many female students have come to expect molestation attempts as an inevitable part of school life." If nothing else, Lima's angry era of racial confrontation further propelled a demographic shift that may have been unavoidable anyway.[44]

"Everybody's just leaving town"

Americans, historians tell us, have almost always been drawn toward suburbia. In its idealized form, suburbia held out a way for them to enjoy the jobs and dynamism of the city while retreating at night and on weekends to the pastoral setting of the countryside, at least in miniaturized form. To instigate the suburban push, all Americans needed were manageable ways to commute back and forth between city centers and their green lawns outside city limits. When capitalist entrepreneurs provided such means of access, the suburbs steadily advanced across the American landscape. In the later nineteenth century, vast waves of "streetcar suburbs" rippled out from the urban cores of expanding metropolitan giants like New York, Philadelphia, and Chicago. Yet even this substantial rate of suburban growth paled in comparison with the possibilities offered by the automobile in the twentieth century. Formerly sleepy villages located far from urban centers suddenly exploded in population, as people discovered they could both keep their downtown jobs and, when the workday ended, drive away from the congestion, crime, and environmental stress of the city. The tiny hamlet of Warren, Michigan, on Detroit's northern rim, for example, saw its population jump from 727 to 89,000 people in the 1950s alone; Parma, south of Cleveland, tripled in population in the same ten years.[45]

In the years after World War II, retailers began to follow their customers to their suburban homes. Americans reoriented their shopping patterns from downtown department stores to new shopping centers in the growing suburbs, which retailers had designed with ease of automobile access primarily in mind. When GM and other giant automakers, seeking to eliminate competition, bought and destroyed dozens of municipal streetcar lines after the war, few people objected, because they saw the car and the suburban home as the epitome of progress and the way of the future. Neither was there much of a public outcry earlier, in 1939, when, faced with declining numbers of streetcar riders, Lima's city leaders did away with its declining streetcar lines and replaced them with buses, which could easily run to the city limits and beyond.[46]

His sensitive political antennae ever attuned to the subtle desires of voters, Franklin Roosevelt threw the power of the federal government behind the rush to the suburbs with New Deal agencies such as the Home Owners Loan Corporation and especially the Federal Housing Authority (FHA). Indeed, in the words of suburban historian Kenneth T. Jackson, "No agency of the United States government has had a more pervasive and powerful impact on the American people over the past half-century" than the FHA. Combined with the famously affordable "VA mortgages" awarded to veterans with the GI Bill of 1944, the FHA reconstructed the face of housing across the country. By insuring the low-interest loans made for home construction and sale by private lenders, these agencies opened the doorway to homeownership to millions of Americans. Untold numbers of people discovered it was suddenly cheaper to buy than to rent, and new postwar mass housing developers like William Levitt stamped out thousands of standardized suburban homes to provide them the opportunity. Yet FHA insurance flowed more easily to residential developments on the edges of cities than to those in the urban core. Moreover, the agency funded home repair projects only reluctantly, rendering it easier to finance the construction of a new home than the rehabilitation of an older one. In this manner, FHA policies accelerated the decline of inner-city neighborhoods by easing the exodus of their middle-class residents.[47]

Fueled by such developments, Lima's new housing boom initially took place both outside and inside the city limits. In 1961 alone, six new developments were built within Lima's limits, while stick-frames rose in twenty-two developments beyond the city limits. In 1966, with newspapers referring to a "Limaland construction boom," the city added three thousand homes. Soon the growth of the townships began to outrace the city, however. When he was a young man before the war, Red Parker recalled, the countryside just west of Lima's city limits was "all farms"; he used to enjoy catching a city bus out to Eldora Farms on Cable Road for delicious home-churned ice cream. From 1956 to 1966, however, in surrounding townships like American, to the west of Lima, Shawnee to the south, and Bath in the east, residential growth rates rose by 20 percent, and the open farmland Parker recalled from his childhood filled with the concrete slabs and balloon frame construction of housing developments.[48]

In Lima as elsewhere, where middle-class homeowners went, retailers followed. In 1956, a Cleveland developer bought nineteen acres in rural American Township just west of Lima and built Westgate Shopping Center, the area's first. Shoppers rushed to the center's eighteen stores, where they could purchase everything from children's shoes to refrigerators in just one automobile trip. This was only the beginning. In 1960, a Youngstown developer obtained a larger parcel near the Northland area that the city had recently annexed, just north of where homes once filled with Irish and German immigrants clustered around St. Rose's parish. There he constructed a slightly bigger shopping center, which opened in 1965 and boasted twenty-one stores, a bowling alley, and parking for more than two thousand cars. Yet before this new Northland Plaza opened, two more developers (one of them the retail magnate Edward DeBartolo) revealed, in boffo announcements two days apart, even bigger plans for a veritable shoppers' paradise that would rise in American Township a little farther west than Westgate. Both would outdo previous shopping centers with an exciting new concept in retailing. Rather than the stores pointing outward, toward the acres of parking lots, the storefronts would open inward, toward each other, and all under an enclosed roof, offering shoppers comfortable shopping no matter what the weather. The new American Mall and its larger cousin the Lima Mall both opened their doors to customers in 1965 and drew in shoppers from three counties away. Chamber of Commerce officials recited thrilling annual totals for retail trade that seemed to rise steadily year after year.[49]

Who could doubt the declarations in the *Lima News* that the entire area was "a *growth* community which is bound to boom"? Depending on the particular yardstick used to measure it, the boom lingered at least through the early 1970s. Residential building in the Lima metropolitan area grew by 28 percent in 1971, and a work survey by the Ohio Bureau of Employment that year forecast that five thousand new jobs would open in the county in 1972. Local unemployment levels steadily fell from 1970 to 1972, and a regional newspaper spotlighted Lima's rise from its racial "doldrums."[50]

Even as the Chamber of Commerce boasted of a shoppers' paradise, however, Lima city officials carefully watched the trends and worried; they knew that the retail and construction bloom harbored hidden blights. The first shopping centers, Westgate and Northland, had presented no open threat to the viability of downtown, because their stores sought to supplement rather than replace the bigger establishments in Lima's city center. But when in 1964 Montgomery Ward announced that it would be the first major downtown Lima business to relocate to the American Mall, city officials did what they could to resist the tide. Mayor Homer Cooper briefly raised traffic barriers along West Market Street, the major traffic thoroughfare to the new American Township retail district. More effective at slowing suburban growth was the "no-annexation, no-service" policy that Lima officials tenaciously retained for several years in the early 1960s. If outlying districts refused to annex to the city, Lima officials would deny them water or sewage service. By 1967, however, Mayor Morris had abandoned this policy, which he came to believe had created undue animosity. Although Lima still demanded a 50 percent surcharge from suburban water and sewage users, the malls boosted local economic power, which helped the region as a whole. In any case, Morris recalled later, "the deterioration of the downtown community had already started." Within five years most of the other large downtown retailers, including Sears and J. C. Penney, had relocated to the malls west of town, and a brief *Time* magazine feature on Lima in 1974 reported that the city's "downtown district and the tax base were disappearing at approximately the same rate."[51]

By the early 1970s, perceptive observers were noting that people, not just businesses, were fleeing Lima. Once again the FHA had set the basic pattern. For decades the agency had allowed the personal prejudices of insurance underwriters to play a major part in determining which loans were granted, while even official agency policy had permitted restrictive covenants and favored racially homogenous neighborhoods. As Jackson has argued, the result was that the FHA's "policies supported the income and racial segregation of suburbia." The civil rights revolution of the 1960s, and particularly the Civil Rights Act of 1968, had tried to alter this, yet the laws left plenty of loopholes and paled at any rate against the power of millions of suburbanites determined to live and raise their children in secure environments and among others of the same race and economic bracket as themselves. In the ten years of the 1960s alone, for instance, the population of Lima's Garfield neighborhood changed from having a minority of blacks to a minority of whites. "It was a matter of 'they're coming, let's run,'" observed an African American resident. "It was an exodus of whites." Even as the city's total population dropped dramatically from 1960 to 1990, the proportion of its people of color increased from 10 percent to 23 percent, while its white population declined from 89 percent to 74 percent. Meanwhile, the nearby American and Shawnee townships remained overwhelmingly white; in 1980, fewer than five hundred residents out of the twelve thousand in each township were people of color.[52]

Almost imperceptibly, many Lima neighborhoods entered a downward economic spiral. One or two homeowners would depart for the suburbs, leaving vacant homes that slowly declined. This process encouraged other residents—at least, those with the economic means to do so—to leave in their turn. Neighborhood institutions, in many cases, followed the same trajectory of flight. Father Norbert Howe had served St. Johns Catholic Church on South Main Street in the south side loyally and well from 1967 to 1977; like several other activist clergy, he had thrown himself into the struggle for racial reconciliation. By the early 1970s, however, Howe could only watch as white enrollment at the church's parochial school dropped by about half, from five hundred children to two hundred. The school closed shortly thereafter. Local residents did not need government experts to tell them that Lima was losing population and businesses. It was left to the old south side entrepreneur Williamson to articulate something of what the trends were costing his city. "When they built the mall people started running," he declared. "We have a town full of vacant lots. That's what happened. This town was really a beautiful town then . . . it had life, really life. But putting in the malls and the theaters out there and everybody's just leaving town, everybody runs out of town."[53]

One way American cities have historically combated such trends was by annexing outlying areas. By the mid-twentieth century, the pattern had become clear. Cities fortunate enough to have parcels of undeveloped land within city limits flourished, while those surrounded by (increasingly hostile) suburban or township governments did not. Many early suburbs had initially welcomed annexation because of the superior services—particularly utilities—that bigger cities could supply. In the early 1960s, several nearby subdivisions readily accepted their absorption into Lima for just this reason. Yet as suburbia increasingly emerged across the country as a racial and class refuge, its leaders began to resist annexation, and state legislators responded with new laws strengthening their hand. The superior services that suburban governments had begun to offer their residents—principally schools—strengthened their resolve. The profile of the suburban resident most resistant to annexation, notes historian Jon Teaford, was that of the blue-collar homeowner who feared racial change and higher taxes.[54]

Morris was an astute administrator, but it didn't take a mayoral Einstein to see that Lima needed to push its city limits deeper out into the townships. However, the obvious direction was not toward the new malls in American Township, for retail jobs and businesses furnished nowhere near the high wages and tax revenue as did manufacturing jobs and industry, but to the south. In 1966, Lima officials had managed to annex a large but sparsely populated tract of Perry Township, on the city's southeast border, for industrial expansion. In the ensuing three years they had attracted a Westinghouse facility to locate there on land now within city limits. By the late 1960s, however, the top target for annexation was the industrial complex just south of town, home to the refinery, the steel foundry, and other plants whose taxes were enriching the coffers of Shawnee Township rather than Lima. Morris saw his chance in June 1969, when two residents of Shawnee Township petitioned to have their homes and a 1,700-acre tract located immediately south of Lima's city limits, annexed to the city. By the fall, the proposal had expanded to include six hundred other residents of Shawnee and, more importantly, such industries as the Sohio refinery and chemical plant, Ex-Cello, Westinghouse, the Ohio Steel Foundry, and the tank plant. If the county commissioners approved, the annexation would result in an annual loss of $138,000 in tax revenues for Shawnee Township, and a $47 million increase in the tax base of the City of Lima. A survey of the affected residents revealed a slight majority in favor, and the industries were open to the plan as well, although they advocated that the annexation should include not just their facilities but all of Shawnee. In their November meeting, arguing the annexation was just too large, the commissioners voted down the proposal. Morris blamed the industries, certain that their insistence on the annexation of all of Shawnee had killed the deal. "Someday we'll be more concerned," he told the press, "about the entire metropolitan area, rather than a township or a school district as such."[55]

In November 1973, Lima voters dumped these problems and a host of others into the lap of a new mayor, another downtown Republican businessman named Harry Moyer. But whatever Moyer's strategy, he could do little to stem the underlying demographic and economic forces that continued to eat away at the economic viability of his city. Lima's population continued to decline, those of the townships continued to rise, and only a fool could deny the relationship between the two. Even the genial Moyer gulped at the figures he received from the Census Bureau in 1980. After peaking at more than 57,000 in the mid-1960s, Lima's population had dropped to 45,000 residents by 1980. The totals were "unbelievable," Moyer fretted openly; at that rate of population loss, the city could well lose millions in federal revenue-sharing dollars. Meanwhile, in the previous ten years alone, the populations of American and Shawnee townships had jumped 27 and 24 percent, respectively. Having in previous decades benefited from a virtuous economic/demographic cycle pushing Lima upward, the city now faced instead a vicious cycle, leading down rather than up, a cycle likewise being experienced by urban areas across the country. As businesses and middle-class taxpayers left town, they took their jobs and benefit plans with them, along with an increasing percentage of the city's tax base. At the same time, the economic demands on the city increased, because its increasing proportion of lower-income residents, increasingly hard-pressed to find employment, required more health care and social welfare services. To meet this need, city officials upped income taxes, which spurred still more middle-class homeowners to flee, and the cycle spiraled further downward.[56]

Urban mayors across the country could take scant comfort from the fact that their cities shared the same set of economic ills. A host of economic doctors diagnosed the problem, and pointed to one additional factor that could either reverse or accelerate the cycle.[57] A city's prospects for recovery, they prescribed, depended in large part on the relative vigor of its manufacturing base, the reliable foundation for economic health for cities across the country. But by the late 1970s, economic cancers were eating away at this base, cancers that not even the most skilled ministrations of businessmen-mayors could heal. Hidden away in cost-benefit analyses, locked in corporate file drawers, these tumors had been quietly metastasizing for decades. Now their symptoms began to emerge, blotting the shiny chrome faces of industrial cities with ineradicable smears of rust and decay.

"Little Detroit"

In the twenty-five years after the end of World War II, with U.S. corporations dominating global markets, levels of economic inequality in America had gradually but unmistakably eased. In their postwar social contract with labor, corporations had shared some of their profits with their workforce, to the point where vast numbers of workers, while still blue collar in occupation, in economic status were joining the great expanding middle class.

Beginning in the early 1970s, however, the gap between rich and poor gradually widened again, a trend maintained through much of the rest of the century. Economists point to several reasons for this development, but a key one had to do with new initiatives by American corporate managers. Industry's deal with labor held as long as profits rolled in, but even by the late 1960s conditions were changing. A tight labor market in the late 1960s led to wage increases, squeezing corporate profits. By the mid-1970s, foreign competition was also reducing corporate profits. For years, U.S. corporate managers had maintained profits simply by raising prices; when GM, for example, raised the price of a new car model, Ford and Chrysler did as well. Left with no other options, consumers paid what the industries asked. By the 1970s, however, foreign companies had become too adept to allow American financial dominance to continue. When competitive imports appeared, the old strategy of "mark-up pricing" no longer maintained U.S. corporate profits. From 1969 to 1979, the value of American imports doubled, and in industry after industry, European and Asian corporations established significant beachheads in U.S. markets. And as corporate profits stagnated, the great postwar contract began to unravel. Frustrated managers began to focus instead on cutting costs instead of raising prices.[58]

U.S. corporations responded to the profit squeeze by taking two different courses, one domestic and one pertaining to foreign markets. Internally, the American economy witnessed a centralization of production, with control held by fewer and more powerful corporations. This had been a gradual, century-long trend that began in the days of Rockefeller and Carnegie. But now it accelerated, driven by tighter corporate profit margins, and individual businesses increasingly reshaped themselves into ever-more-hierarchical chains of command. Through the postwar years, economic power became increasingly centralized. These domestic developments both fed and in turn were fed by a set of external trends. In some ways these trends, too, were merely a rapid intensification of an earlier development that had begun with the rise of the modern industrial corporation. A century before, the steel titan Andrew Carnegie had perfected "vertical integration," that is, the assimilation of all aspects of the production process under one corporate roof. In this manner, Carnegie Steel had become not just a steel company but also a coke company, a railroad company, an iron-ore-mining firm, and an ore boat company.[59]

Now Carnegie's mid-twentieth-century descendents took this process a step further. Aided by technological breakthroughs like satellite technology and the computer revolution, corporate managers suddenly found it possible to engage in something like a "vertical *dis*integration." On the administrative level, they engaged in another wave of mergers, forming massive corporate conglomerates that would have made Carnegie proud. At the same time, however, they discovered they could "outsource" the production of their goods, or part of that process, to overseas subsidiaries that promised to build them cheaper. Corporate managers could reallocate their capital into different regions of the country, or into different countries altogether, letting it flow to wherever labor was cheapest and the hand of governmental regulation lightest. Total U.S. investment abroad jumped from $50 billion in 1965 to $124 billion in 1975 and $213 billion in 1980. Again, this was no brand-new development: Henry Ford had set up assembly lines in Europe as far back as 1911.[60] But the process inexorably accelerated in the 1970s, when corporate managers increasingly began to look abroad to recover declining domestic profits. It was facilitated by the trajectory of a growing "permissive technology" that increasingly allowed them a global focus and presence. Through such developments as the telephone, the jumbo jet, containerized shipping, then the laptop, the cell-phone, and, finally, massive computer systems, corporate heads sitting in New York or Tokyo could manage global corporate systems and track the productivity of every spindle or loom thousands of miles or oceans away. Over the past thirty years, U.S. corporations have globalized their production to such a degree that it no longer makes sense to call them American businesses at all. They have become multinational corporations transcending the boundaries of particular states. Increasingly they take on a national coloration only when they appeal for tax breaks or special favors from one national government or another.[61]

This process is a multifaceted development of Byzantine intricacy with far-reaching, even revolutionary implications, and the process resists easy condensation. Struggling to name it, social scientists finally came up with imprecise, catchall words, such as "deindustrialization." Whatever the term, the intricate set of processes signaled the destruction of the old social contract and the arrival of a new set of relationships between corporations, their labor forces, and the particular communities where they decided to locate. Simply put, globally oriented corporations quickly obtained the upper hand, and took their business to wherever the corporate bottom line—their major moral consideration—demanded they go. In the United States, the profit-driven dictates of corporate mobility often meant relocating plants from older industrialized areas, where organized labor had been strong and wages high, to formerly rural, nonunionized, "right-to-work" states in the South where fatter profit margins beckoned. Such relocations devastated many industrial areas in the Midwest in the 1970s and 1980s, as a long string of automakers decided to quit dealing with the UAW and head south. One after another, the big names in transportation technology and auto parts—Rockwell International, Eaton, Allis-Chalmers, Caterpillar, Borg

Warner—closed midwestern plants to move to new facilities in places like Texas or the Carolinas. Some shifted production even farther away. As early as 1966, RCA decided against expanding an older, unionized television plant in Cincinnati, and instead built a large factory, employing 4,000 workers, in Memphis. When the Memphis workers themselves unionized, RCA shut both plants and shifted its TV production to Taiwan. In the late 1960s, General Electric responded similarly to two strikes at its facility in Ashland, Massachusetts: it shut down the plant and moved the entire operation to Singapore.[62]

With untold millions of people in developing countries around the world desperate even for low-paying work, their governments watched these shifting strategies and assessed the possibilities. In 1965, the government of Mexico, taking advantage of various loopholes in the U.S. tariff code, encouraged foreign corporations to open plants in a special twelve-mile strip next to the U.S. border. There U.S. companies could produce goods using Mexican labor and ship them back to the United States nearly tariff and tax free. This offer of corporate-friendly locations abroad spawned a new term that would become familiar in the growing vocabulary of globalization: the *maquiladoras*. In the late 1960s, scores of U.S. companies—Litton, GE, Motorola, and Hughes Aircraft, for example—flooded into the Mexican zone and created these *maquiladora* assembly plants; by 1974, the Mexican government had issued licenses to 655 different U.S. manufacturers. U.S. automakers arrived relatively late, in the late 1970s, but by 1982, Mexican workers in seven GM and two Chrysler plants were cranking out auto parts in Ciudad Juarez, just across the border from Texas, for far less in wages than these companies would have paid to U.S. autoworkers. The new Mexican autoworkers referred to the area as "Little Detroit." Whatever such corporate mobility meant for U.S. workers, it brought smiles to the financiers of Wall Street. With profits rising from such savings in labor costs, corporate stock prices usually rose, pleasing investors immensely.[63]

Certainly, as corporate spokespeople insisted, at least some of the plants they closed simply had died of old age; with their machinery worn out and their facilities dated, they had gradually become unprofitable in an increasingly competitive global marketplace. One could not just pick up and move massive, multimillion-dollar operations like poker chips; market pressures, including the relatively high cost of U.S. labor, drove the unfortunate decisions to close plants. Yet from this small kernel of truth, skilled corporate public relations experts constructed a widespread and superbly functional myth: of greedy unions pulling down high wages running obsolete plants until their patient employers had no choice but to close down and move away. So reflexively and successfully did corporate managers, and their allies in the halls of government and conservative think tanks, disseminate this caricature that it soon wound its ways into public discourse.[64]

More perceptive observers, however, pointed out other realities that corporate spokespeople had passed over: that the responsibility for modernizing equipment lay with management, not unions, and that management often ignored that responsibility for years, especially in traditional industries like steel. Even as, in the late 1970s, plant shutdowns rippled down through the river valleys of the Monongahela and the Mahoning, the heartland of the American steel industry, many workers knew that, as political scientist R. Jeffrey Lustig pointed out, U.S. Steel had "not built a new integrated facility since 1953." Plants did not become obsolete overnight. A major cause of the huge job losses following closures lay not with union members, who usually scrambled for concessions when they saw their jobs were on the line, but rather with the cumulative financial decisions of management. Some of these decisions went back decades; others—like the increasing corporate trend toward nonproductive forms of investment—were of more recent origins. In both cases, such decisions had a devastating impact on their partner industrial communities. For example, it was a series of quiet corporate decisions to invest in new facilities elsewhere, rather than in the established plants of Akron, Ohio, that fueled the exodus of rubber companies from the nation's old rubber capital and the loss of ten thousand jobs. Rather than invest in new machinery, management often preferred a more ruthless strategy: acquire older plants, milk them for all the profit they could, close them down, and invest elsewhere. This is what apparently happened in the great old steel town of Youngstown, Ohio. Certainly the decline of the American steel industry dates at least to 1959, when cheaper Japanese and European steel began to undercut U.S. markets. But the refusal of U.S. steelmakers to modernize and the takeover of the Youngstown Mills by a new corporate owner, the Lykes Corporation, were the final blows to the industry in that city. Lykes quickly invested its profits in other industries and then, on "Black Monday," September 19, 1977, suddenly shut down its Youngstown plant, throwing 4,100 workers out of their jobs with three days' notice. In *Day of Reckoning*, a sobering 1989 analysis of the United States' exploding national debt levels, Harvard economist Benjamin Friedman noted that "the 1980s has been the worst period for business investment in physical assets like plant and equipment since World War II. Instead of borrowing to build new facilities or even to build liquidity, the corporate business sector as a whole has mostly used the proceeds of its extraordinary volume of borrowing since 1980 to pay down equity through mergers and acquisitions, leveraged buy-outs and stock repurchases." By 1982, oil companies had ploughed the immense financial rewards they had already reaped from Reagan-era deregulation efforts into $16.2 billion of acquisitions of other firms, many of them in noncore businesses.[65]

Indeed, by the early 1980s, corporate power had increased to the point that the fate not just of individual workers but of entire industrial communities could lie simply with how much fealty to the old social contract was recognized by individual corporate heads. Some CEOs seemed to go the extra mile, working tirelessly to soften the blow through such solutions as finding buyers for their plants or creating employee ownership arrangements. An International Business Machines (IBM) facility in Greencastle, Indiana, for example, was the town's largest employer and the foundation of the local economy. When in 1986 IBM officials elected to close the plant because of financial contraction, they arranged for the transfer of most employees to other plants and agreed to purchase their homes. The company created generous early-retirement schemes, found job-retraining programs for workers who elected to leave the company, gave the city $1.7 million to replace lost taxes, and continued its substantial United Way contribution for three years. Other corporations felt no such sense of responsibility. In 1977, for example, Envirodyne Industries purchased Wisconsin Steel, which had served as an economic cornerstone of South Chicago since 1902, and shut down the plant three years later, citing declining profits. There was no warning: Envirodyne announced to its workforce of 3,400 steelworkers that the mill would close the following day. Through various legal loopholes, Envirodyne officials then escaped paying their former employees all severance pay, vacation pay, and pension supplements, or for hospitalization care and early retirement plans, costing the unions altogether $29 million worth of benefits.[66]

Soon the cumulative impact of thousands of such decisions began to register job loss totals of staggering size. Between 1963 and 1982, according to one analyst, 100,000 manufacturing plants employing nineteen or more workers closed, a full fifth of them located in the industrial Midwest. During the 1970s alone, losses ran at about 900,000 manufacturing jobs per year, resulting in upwards of 22 million lost jobs by the early 1980s. Individual lives reflected the impact. By the mid-1980s, suicide rates were twice the national average in the Monongahela Valley south of Pittsburgh, an area that had lost 20,000 jobs because of the closure of the steel mills. In nearby Aliquippa, Pennsylvania, at the same time, only 700 steelworkers labored where 15,000 had worked a few years before, and the town's population dropped by 35 percent in a half-dozen years. After property taxes fell dramatically, city administrators laid off half the police force and firefighters.

Disturbing trends developed among laid-off workers and the communities where they lived. Social workers saw increases in the rates of domestic violence, alcohol and drug abuse, mental health problems, and other indices of social trauma. Economists noted other "ripple effects." The U.S. Chamber of Commerce estimated that a community lost an average of two service-sector jobs for every three jobs lost in manufacturing, an impact that often snowballed when other local manufacturers, discerning an unfavorable business climate, moved as well. As population rates and tax revenues fell, schools declined. At the same time the social needs of the unemployed—for food, health care, social welfare services, and the like—increased, putting additional economic pressure on local governmental structures for increased aid.[67]

Given the advantages that increased mobility gave international capital, Lustig argues, "Private corporations have acquired the power to issue birth certificates and death sentences to entire communities." Industrial communities came to bow and scrape at the doorsteps of local manufacturers, begging for corporate largesse. Multiplant firms with a single facility to close could dangle the threat over the home communities of several of its plants, and then watch the ensuing scramble among different sets of municipal officials to see which one could come up with the most lucrative package of financial incentives. In their wooing of new corporate partners, financially desperate cities in such a competitive jungle could be led to ever-more-amazing levels of economic inducement. When in 1980, GM approached Detroit with the possibility of replacing its aging Cadillac plant with a huge new facility requiring 6,500 workers, city officials outdid themselves: they offered GM a 50 percent tax abatement for ten years and sent in bulldozers to level four hundred acres of the historic old neighborhood of Poletown, including churches, 160 businesses, and the homes of 3,200 Detroiters. The city did get the new GM plant, but with, in the end, far fewer jobs than GM had originally promised. So vulnerable did cities become to the dire economic consequences threatened by the new corporate mobility that political scientists began to refer to the late-twentieth-century urban center in terms like "the Dependent City."[68]

Altogether, the collapse of the old social contract between management and labor, the new corporate upper hand, and the raft of plant closings began to wreak a grim transformation of the American economic and cultural landscape. Americans today may have become numbed to plant closings as a sad but inevitable aspect of globalization, but twenty years ago such closures were a new and shocking development. They particularly caught the public eye between 1980 and 1983, when the United States experienced one of the worst financial downturns since the Great Depression. The recession clearly started under President Jimmy Carter, but the inflation-fighting, tight monetary policies of the new president, Ronald Reagan, exacerbated it, and month by month the nation's unemployment rolls swelled. In February 1980, 6.3 million Americans were searching for work; by the following June, the number had jumped to 8.2

million. That August, the national unemployment rate stood at 6.7 percent but the rate was considerably worse in particular demographic pockets. Among blacks, it stood at 14.2 percent, among white teenagers, at 19 percent, and the economic misery only deepened with the relentless waves of plant closings, especially in the nation's former economic base, the once-mighty industrial Midwest. "Nowhere in the country was the misery of economic downturn more acute than in the factory towns of the nation's industrial heartland," *Time* told its readers in 1982. For half a century, the Midwest had tied its prosperity to the ever-upward boom of the automobile industry. Now, with Japanese imports like Hondas and Toyotas taking an ever-increasing share of American auto sales, that industry was in decline. New car sales hit a twenty-one-year low, and about 23 percent of the U.S. car industry's labor force of 1.1 million was unemployed. So pervasive was the economic gloom shrouding the Midwest that cultural commentators began searching for a phrase to encapsulate it. Before long some of the nation's best songwriters seized on especially hard-hit cities as epitomes of what had begun to happen, and set that pain to music: to Bruce Springsteen it was "Youngstown," to Billy Joel, "Allentown." To most Americans, however, the Great Depression of the 1930s remained the ultimate metaphor for financial collapse, with its images of weather-beaten residents of the plains states watching their livelihoods disappear in the dust bowl. From there it was an easy leap to the new images of hard-pressed midwesterners, staggering from the punches of another financial calamity, and, finally, *Time* magazine hit on the perfect term. In its summary on the economic distress brought by the single year of 1982, *Time* titled its story simply, "Booms, Busts, and Birth of a Rust Bowl."[69]

In the early 1980s in the heart of the rust bowl, along the I-75 automaking corridor leading south from Detroit, citizens of yet another midwestern manufacturing city waited to see what kind of fate these dark economic indicators had in store for them. For a century, the people of Lima had anchored their fortunes in the bedrock of hard labor in the industrial workplace. Given the portents of the economic storm that approached, it would be a thin reed upon which to base their hopes.

Chapter 4
Resistance

David Berger arrived in Lima in the summer of 1977 for what he thought would be a two-year break before resuming final studies for a career as a Catholic priest. He had come to town as executive director of the Rehab Project—a heady title for a twenty-two-year-old philosophy student whose professional training had consisted largely of nine years in seminary. Driving through the city's streets on a hot July day, Berger was not initially impressed by what he saw. But as he settled himself in his new lodgings and began to poke around the city's streets, he found that behind Lima's gray façade were currents of energy in its human resources that he hadn't expected. "I really found an energetic, caring group of people," he remembered later, "who were wanting to create positive change."[1]

When James Schaefer, commercial manager for British Petroleum's Midwest operations, was sent to Lima in 1991, he likewise encountered new realms of hidden, untapped potential. His corporate superiors at BP had assigned him a single major task: to carefully assess the huge old refinery south of town and see if he could halt what they characterized as its irreversible decline. The conditions Schaefer encountered surely must have confirmed the hopeless forecast: a demoralized workforce, a management wracked by constant turnover, and a physical plant suffering from environmental liabilities and a mounting list of long-deferred maintenance problems. But "what I was struck by," he remembered later, "was the enormous capability for improvement . . . there was opportunity for creativity." For years, well aware of the official skepticism toward refineries they detected in corporate executives, workers had been struggling to keep operations going at lower and lower levels of output. Schaefer began to suspect that the declining output and negative attitudes were working in tandem and that by reversing the direction of one, he could reverse the direction of the other. After two months of quiet observation, he signaled the change of direction at a conference of BP senior refinery staff. "You've been listening to pessimistic outlooks for years," he announced from the podium, but "it doesn't have to be this way." They were going to fix the problems, reengage the workforce, run the refinery at higher volume, and put it in the black once again. "These refineries are going to be restored to profitability," he declared, "and we're going to have a lot of fun doing it."[2]

As it turned out, there was a lot of creativity and energy available to Lima in those years, and both the city and the refinery would need all of them they could get. Immediately on his election as an untested young mayor, Berger would watch another round of plant closings stagger the city once again, as one by one industrial jobs left the county. Berger recognized that new retail positions could not really replace the steady exodus of bedrock manufacturing jobs, positions he characterized as "good paying jobs with benefits, the kinds of jobs where you make things."[3] He pushed the mayor's office to unprecedented levels of municipal activism to fight such trends, but to little avail; by the mid-1990s, the struggle had focused on saving the city's foundational industry, the old refinery spreading out south of town. For four years, Schaefer and his colleagues there waged a determined campaign amidst the complex mass of pipes, pumps, and valves, and in the end, they met with stunning success. But in the age of the new global economy, did this really matter? Even as the dedication and energy of Lima refinery workers transformed the plant into one of the most productive such refineries in the country, BP executives in London were pursuing a different logic toward closure.

Both the city and the refinery, in fact, were facing the same underlying reality: that many of the basic decisions determining their own viability were made

The last remaining buildings waiting to be leveled at the site of the old Lima Locomotive Works, about 2002–3. *Photo courtesy of the* Lima News.

not in Lima but in corporate boardrooms thousands of miles away. By the mid-1990s, two decades of decision making in such places had resulted in the rapid transformation of the American Midwest into the rust belt. The same dynamics seemed to be at work in Lima; despite the success of local efforts to revive production, BP executives elsewhere seem to have determined that it was now time for the refinery and the city to quietly take their places on the industrial scrap heap. In the face of such outside forces, both Lima and the refinery would have to wrestle with the same basic question: Was there any initiative they could take, any resources and creativity they could harness, to somehow escape that fate?

"Lima is now at the bottom"

David Berger took office between two waves of plant closings, both of which devastated his city. The first wave had begun in the early 1980s. At first, Mayor Moyer and others with their fingers on the pulse of Lima's economic prospects had reason to hope that their city might be spared the worst ravages of the recession then fastening its teeth in the national economy. The downturn was already hitting the auto industry hard, prompting layoffs out at the Ford engine plant, but the region around Lima had a diversified economy and many local firms seemed to be holding their own. The Sohio refinery had managed to retain its 600-person workforce, even though a secretary had posted a seemingly permanent shingle on the main lobby door reading, "We are not accepting applications at this time." The neighboring chemical plant, then called Vistron, likewise reported solid sales and a secure workforce. At the Procter and Gamble plant in Bath Township, corporate officials reported little impact from the recession, and their 200 workers seemed safe in their jobs. As for Ex-Cello, maker of jet engine parts, its executives had discovered that when the auto industry suffered, their industry usually boomed, and, given the current conditions, their company's prognosis seemed rosy. The firm had nearly 900 people on its payroll and even planned to hire a few more. The Chrysler tank plant seemed similarly "recession-proof," with tanks sales not only steady but boosted by regular government contracts. Even Warner & Swasey, a small machine-tool company, had workers putting in nine-hour shifts to meet demand, and had just recently finished an active expansion of its workforce. Yet other employers were struggling. At Lima Electric, a local manufacturer of generators for agriculture and industrial work, 80 employees were on indefinite layoff, and the 200 remaining workers had spent three weeks on furlough without pay. Westinghouse seemed in a downward spiral. In 1978, 300 people lost their jobs, and the 150 white-collar managers at division headquarters likewise had experienced furloughs.[4]

The most alarming signals of local economic distress emanated from Clark Equipment, the functioning remnant of the old Lima Locomotive Works. In 1971, Baldwin-Lima-Hamilton had sold its Lima facility to Clark, which had continued to build construction equipment at the cavernous old plant on South Main Street. Clark flourished for several years; in the early 1970s, employment had shot up to 1,600 workers, highs not witnessed since the heyday of the old locomotive works during World War II. In 1979, the Lima facility had introduced four new models for construction cranes, and as late as February 1980 planned yet a fifth. However, the high interest rates and inflation of the recession soon combined with a slump in construction and mining to severely undercut sales. Within a year, Clark had laid off nearly 300 of its 800-plus employees, while the remaining workers, their morale plummeting, operated on four-day, thirty-two-hour workweeks and waited for the other shoe to drop. In the late summer of 1980, corporate officials announced that they were actively searching for a new buyer for the plant, but, in a declining market during a deepening recession, nobody harbored great hopes that a buyer would readily step forward. On its front page, the *Lima News* quoted a Wall Street insider, who commented that "the Lima plant—I don't think it's any secret—has been a big loser." To turn a profit, the plant required extensive modernization; some of the factory shops still had dirt floors. In October 1980, officials announced plans to close their Lima operation, telling union officials that they would produce replacement parts until December, but "beyond that—nothing."[5]

The closing of Clark could not have been unexpected, but it still seemed to hit many workers like a hard punch in the stomach. Shifts had changed at the factory gates and work whistles had blown from roof gables at the plant in South Lima for nearly a century. Like their parents before them, many of Clark's workers had known no other place of employment and scarcely knew where to turn. For two years, they had been "living in a bubble," a welder said. While they at least now knew their economic fate, the news was hard for many to digest. "I don't know how to go out and get a job," one worker confided. "I've worked here all my life." Younger people still had opportunities to pick themselves up and start over, many recognized, but what about older workers who "have given half their lives to the company and are too old to get a job"? As far as they were concerned, Clark owed something to such men and women. But little was forthcoming from Clark. Soon commercial realtors began stalking the empty corridors that had once echoed with noise, assessing the raw market value of old buildings where patternmakers had once modeled parts for unique locomotives and skilled craftsmen had riveted together the engines that had dominated the nation's great era of railroading.[6]

While the cultural loss was beyond measure, it was left to the city to begin counting the economic impact. The most obvious cost was the loss of tax dollars from former Clark workers, which, at less than 3 percent of the city's total budget, Lima could absorb. Moyer put the best face possible on the outcome, cheerfully offering hope that the new buyer of the Clark site might develop it into an industrial park, which might provide more jobs than Clark had. But even the name of the new buyer, Kovalchick Salvage Company, suggested that its agenda for the property would not lend itself to prospects of economic development. Instead, city officials began to realize that the open cost of the plant closing came accompanied by other, even more destructive hidden ones. A local Chamber of Commerce official estimated one of these hidden costs at $2.5 million in lost retail sales that missing Clark paychecks would have brought to area businesses. Since those lost dollars turned over roughly three times as they worked their way through the local economy, officials calculated, the final cost to Lima of Clark's closure might exceed $7.5 million—and this figure didn't even take into account the kind of domino effects that a perceived unfavorable business climate could trigger in the community at large.[7]

As the national recession fastened its claws deeper into Lima, the local business climate began to take more hits. Clark was only the beginning: also in 1980, the corporate conglomerate of Sheller-Globe, which had begun building buses and funeral coaches in Lima in the 1930s as the old Superior Coach Company, announced the closing of its plant on East Kibby Street. By the end of 1981, more long-standing firms had issued pink slips to their employees; another plant, National Standards, had shut its doors entirely, while Westinghouse, once the county's largest employer, had eliminated 135 more jobs because of a further slump in the aerospace industry. By 1983, the once-rosy economic outlook of Ex-Cello had faded, prompting it to cut back its workforce; the auto-parts maker Dana Corporation did likewise.

The costs of these developments to the local community were high. A new county economic development director admitted that the loss of Clark and Sheller-Globe had cost Lima and its environs 3,000 jobs, but those numbers paled in comparison with the economic pain dealt out by the continuing malaise in the auto industry. Many local workers, including those at such companies as Ohio Steel, were represented by the UAW. The union repeatedly made concessions to local corporate officials, giving up things like paid personal holidays in order to save jobs, but to little avail. By 1983, UAW officials reported that local layoffs had cast 6,000 members out of work. Nearly half had suffered in the waves of cutbacks at the Ford engine plant in Bath Township, which in five years had shrunk its workforce from 4,500 workers to 1,600. "Ford's telling us we'll be lucky if we ever get back up to 2,500 again," a union official remarked. "We're telling our laid-off people that they can forget working here if they were hired later than 1973." With the entire Midwest saturated in bad economic tidings, prospects for relief seemed slim. “Ohio’s Jobless Rate Up to 14.5%,” headlined the *Cleveland Plain Dealer*, but in Lima, in the spring of 1982, the rate stood at 15 percent, a level that held steady for at least a year and was the highest recorded since the Ohio Bureau of Labor Statistics began keeping track of such numbers in the late 1960s.[8]

Jobless adults still had children to feed and mortgages to pay, and careful observers began to measure the rising levels of economic desperation with different yardsticks. The Lima police noted a marked drop in local crime rates, at least partly because high unemployment rates kept many more homes occupied during daylight hours when burglars would otherwise be active. When a pizza parlor advertised two jobs paying $4.00 an hour, including tips, its owner received a deluge of applications, many from former factory workers who had previously been pulling down three times that rate. Another Lima restaurateur noted that the number of applications he was receiveing each week jumped from ten to fifteen to upwards of forty, many from older people for whom, he suspected, unemployment benefits were running out. Nursing homes witnessed a regular stream of people stopping by to inquire about low-level, minimum wage positions, while a local department store advertising ninety new positions watched a huge crowd of five hundred applicants stand in line for hours in hopes of securing one. A local woman remembers glancing at the want ads in the *Lima News* during these years and being shocked at the paltry number of “help wanted” listings: “I mean, some days there were none.” By 1983, the number of Lima schoolchildren eligible for free or reduced-price school lunches had jumped markedly: two of every three children qualified. In the new, evolving economic standards of the community, commented Earl McGovern, the school superintendent, teachers and school staffers were “probably well-to-do.” Serving as priest at St. Rose in the mid-1980s, Father Howe frequently heard tough stories from his parishioners about their inability to pay their bills, and saw such economic woes reflected in decreasing personal contributions to the church’s offering plates at Mass. In December 1981, the county unemployment rate reached almost 18 percent. “Lima is now at the bottom,” summarized the president of the Teamsters local.[9]

Area social workers noted other costs of the city’s economic decline. The Lima director of United Way estimated that half of the area’s jobless refused to apply for services from social agencies because of the stigma they associated with accepting charity. Plans had circulated among such agencies to begin a soup kitchen at the Salvation Army, but administrators rejected the plan because they were not convinced that the new unemployed would consent to patronize it. These were proudly independent people who until now had usually achieved what they needed through their own willingness to work hard. As many locals discovered that such virtues were irrelevant in the new global marketplace, however, some released their frustrations in destructive ways. In 1981, the county health department saw a 100 percent increase in admissions to alcoholism outpatient programs, an increase that a departmental study clearly linked to systemic factors like high local unemployment levels and economic distress. Likewise, a shelter for battered women and children called Crossroads Crisis Center reported an intensified demand for its services, as the incidence of domestic violence escalated. The United Way funneled money to such groups and did what it could to help—although its own budget was declining. Clark and Sheller-Globe had been especially generous corporate contributors, and for several years in the early 1980s, the United Way's fund-raising—upon which twenty-three area social service agencies depended—remained essentially flat. Other groups also did what they could. Father Howe and local church-based activists founded a food bank that helped distribute free groceries to thousands.[10]

Yet the economic pain spreading across the city was not restricted to Lima's blue-collar stratum. Within a single year, the congregation of the Market Street Presbyterian Church, traditionally the church home of many of the city's upper crust, witnessed the departure of twenty families because of the layoff or transfer of family heads. Pricey summer classes at the Lima Art Association went unfilled, and in the 1983 Christmas season, for the first time in memory, the Lima Symphony had unsold tickets for its annual performance of *The Nutcracker*. Parents told teenaged children that they had begun to rethink the possibility of sending them to college. Within two years, from 1980 to 1982, three local car dealerships liquidated their inventories and closed their doors because hard-pressed area employees lacked the confidence or the capital to buy new cars, while others came to regret the big-ticket purchases they had made. Personal and business bankruptcies rose rapidly, and area bankers repossessed so many cars that "sometimes it appears like we're running a used-car lot," local banker A. D. "Sandy" MacDonel remarked. Delinquent home mortgages presented new challenges. One banker admitted that he had quietly begun to refuse to foreclose on delinquent mortgages unless the buyer abandoned the home, simply because there were no buyers for foreclosed properties. Local housing prices gradually declined, creating all sorts of budgetary problems for a city government still partially dependent on property taxes. In 1982, facing a $250,000 budgetary shortfall because hard-pressed Lima voters had vetoed a proposed tax increase, administrators furloughed fifty-six city workers, including fifteen members of the police department and thirteen firefighters. Mayor Moyer's longtime personal assistant opted for early retirement to save the city money.[11]

In the early 1980s, perhaps because Lima was a small city and its pain more easily grasped by the public imagination than the massive economic woes of a megalopolis like Detroit or Chicago, the city began to join other wounded industrial centers like Homestead and Youngstown as a poster child for the rust belt. The national newsmagazine *U.S. News & World Report* featured the city in 1983 as the epitome of industrial decay, with an accompanying photo of the deserted old "cathedral" hangar of the now abandoned locomotive works prominently displayed above the header. But it was another story, a year earlier in the *Wall Street Journal,* that really seemed to hurt local pride. The story contrasted declining Lima—"reeling from an unemployment rate of 15.4%, and people there despair of things getting any better"—with the expanding sun-belt town of San Angelo, Texas. In the hands of the *Journal* reporters, the latter city, with its booming local economy, its go-getter spirit and "favorable business climate" (a result, the reporters clearly implied, of its lack of unions), made Lima appear by comparison like a graying, industrial relic magically transported *in situ* from the Great Depression. The story stung civic activists in the Lima Arts Council into action. They sent out a letter that passed, through a series of lucky breaks, into the hands of a Texas concert promoter named Sam Lewis, who brought it to the attention of an old childhood friend, country singer Willie Nelson. When Nelson read the letter and the accompanying *Wall Street Journal* article describing the gloom permeating Lima, he told Lewis, "we need to take them some sunshine." On a scorching hot summer day in July 1982, Nelson, Lewis, and Nelson's band all came to Lima at their own expense, and gave a free concert to twelve thousand enthusiastic fans at the Allen County Fairgrounds.[12]

Nelson and his entourage were a smash hit; Lewis even brought along his pet armadillos and sent them pattering down Market Street on their little armored feet. The event "raised spirits at a time that was pretty depressing otherwise," remembered arts council leader Martha MacDonel, and attracted some favorable national publicity to Lima. But city leaders knew that recovery needed more than Willie Nelson and armadillos and plugged away at the task of economic development. The city's downtown—which the *Journal* had described as a "depression scene"—remained a particular concern. "I guarantee you we're not going to close," pledged Thomas Gregg, owner of the city's last downtown department store, in 1982; after eighty-five years downtown, he argued, the shuttering of Gregg's would be a "death blow" to Lima. Three years later, however, blaming the "negative" attitude of Lima's city council, Gregg cancelled plans for a $6.5 million minimall and closed the store for good. Lima's oldest remaining corporate partner, Standard Oil, brightened spirits a year later when, to commemorate a century of its presence in the city, it refurbished the handsome Victorian façade of its downtown headquarters. But an even bigger boost came in 1984, when the city brought in native son and daughter Hugh Downs and Phyllis Diller to lead the bill in a star-studded night of opening ceremonies for its sparkling new $8.5 million civic center fronting the downtown square. City officials had resolutely pushed through the new center over a long and difficult decade fraught with, in the words of local columnist Mike Lackey, "planning, scrambling for funds, legal entanglements and political wrangling." Tightfisted Lima voters had provided the crucial level of support in 1979 with their approval of a public referendum pledging $1 million of city taxpayer funds for the project. Now, in October 1984, officials celebrated with a gala opening, a series of concerts, and a parade that snaked its way through downtown streets. By the middle of the decade, enough positive indications had appeared to spark hope that the economy's long decline had bottomed out and maybe had begun to tick upward. Slowly, the unemployment rates fell, from 14.9 percent early in 1983 to 13.7 percent by the spring of 1984 and 10.7 percent the following December. The economic picture was further brightened in 1984 by massive infusions of federal dollars into the tank plant that accompanied President Reagan's huge defense buildup. Property values gradually rose once again through 1985, and the worst of the recession seemed over.[13]

By 1987, Lima had struggled through two tough decades. When the Diocese of Toledo placed Father Howe in Lima in 1967, he had found his new home a busy, prosperous place, where sprawling rail yards bustled with activity and working men and women thronged through the gates at massive industrial facilities like Clark Equipment and Ohio Steel. Their paychecks not only had fed their kids and paid their mortgages in a dozen solid blue-collar and white-collar neighborhoods, but they also had maintained churches and schools and kept ledgers in the black in a still-thriving downtown. For ten years, Howe had served the community in various ways, baptizing its babies and burying its dead, and also, perhaps most importantly, helping it with the sometimes traumatic but also long-delayed and vitally necessary task of admitting all of its citizens to the good life that Lima offered.

In 1977, the diocese sent Howe away to the city of Norwalk, Ohio, for seven years, before returning him to Lima, now assigned to St. Rose Parish, where he would serve out the rest of his career. When Howe came back to Lima in 1985, he was shocked to find it "a different town than when I had left." Many downtown stores were empty, many houses seemed run down and suffering from a general air of neglect. Things were "all closed up," he remembered; "a great decline" had occurred. The trials of one Lima couple encapsulated what had happened while Howe had been gone. Patricia Merriman's husband had lost his job on a shipping dock, found another job for lower pay after a year of looking, and lost it a few months later. In the interim, the couple's marriage had nearly disintegrated. By 1982, they were surviving on his unemployment checks and her part-time job driving a school bus, and she tried to put words to what the experience had done to her. "It's like," she said, "somebody pulled out a cork and let the air out of all of my dreams."[14]

Further, it was hard for Howe, Merriman, or anyone else who had watched the city's decline to identify a single culprit to blame for it. Like that of a tide-pool community left high on the beach by the underlying shifts of waves and sand, Lima's fate seemed determined by mammoth forces far beyond its control. Like so many other towns and cities that had tied their fate to industrial opportunities in an increasingly postindustrial age, Lima's fortunes had moved and shaken in correspondence with the grinding of economic plates deep beneath the surface. Like that of other rust belt cities, Lima's life seemed to have arced and entered what appeared an irreversible descent. The only major decision left for the city was whether or not to accept the limited future that the underlying currents of the global marketplace had laid out for it, or to find some way to turn back the tide.

"My work here was very engaging, she was very engaging"

From the late 1980s on, any economic resistance to the forces of deindustrialization mounted by the City of Lima was led by a new and much younger mayor. The resources David Berger brought to Lima were mostly internal, developed through a childhood and adolescence oriented around two fundamental lodestones: working-class labor and the Catholic Church. Born and raised in Mansfield, Ohio, Berger was the son of a union electrician father and a mother who labored for decades at a small manufacturing plant. Throughout his working life, Joseph Berger had remained an active and dues-paying member of the International Brotherhood of Electrical Workers, and he frequently cited to his family the good wages and decent working conditions that union membership had brought. The family later learned the lesson in an experiential way when Joseph Berger, in old age, lapsed into dementia that lingered for years before he died, and his family stayed afloat financially largely because of the pension and benefits that his hard work and union membership had earned.[15]

Beyond his family, David Berger's primary source of training and nurture in his youth was St. Peter's Catholic Parish of Mansfield, a huge church with a half-dozen priests, dozens of Franciscan nuns, parochial schools for the children, and a busy enough round of religious education classes, youth groups, and bake sales to keep ten thousand members thoroughly involved. Looking back years later, Berger concluded that, without question, "the focus of our lives outside the family was St. Peter's." He and his brother eagerly trained as altar boys, memorizing the Latin prayers and liturgies and serving at regular masses, weddings, funerals, and special services. At a junior high youth group retreat, the young devotee began to discern a sense of life calling, and after the eighth grade he transferred to the diocesan seminary, Holy Spirit Seminary, in Toledo, where he blossomed, serving

Lima mayor David Berger. *Photo courtesy of the Mayor's Office, City of Lima.*

in leadership positions and pulling down high grades. It was a trajectory clearly designed to place Berger in the priesthood and, throughout his adolescence, Berger could not imagine any life course more fulfilling or meaningful.

Upon graduation from Holy Spirit in 1972, Berger continued on a course toward priesthood to St. Meinrad College, a Benedictine school in the rolling hills of southern Indiana. There and later, at Catholic University, the two intellectual halves of Berger's world came together when new mentors introduced him to the teaching and practice of his church on matters of social justice. Classmates at Holy Spirit had warned him that St. Meinrad had too fully absorbed the dangerous new liberal currents coursing through the church in the wake of the Second Vatican Council. For Berger, the new liberal ideas seemed personified in Fr. David Kahle, a priest the Diocese of Indianapolis had assigned to the college staff. "Dave Kahle's academic specialty was physics," Berger remembered, "but his passion was social justice." Fr. Kahle's classroom lectures often left the world of science and focused on matters of poverty and justice, taking their bearings from the teachings of the French Jesuit Teilhard de Chardin. A theologian who was also a respected paleontologist, de Chardin had followed an interweaving of evolutionary theory with Christian theology to an understanding of a God intimately involved with the world and actively nurturing its development. As mediated to St. Meinrad students through the fervent teaching of Father Kahle, de Chardin offered an optimistic view of human action in the world. He saw the universe as still in creation and fundamentally dependent on the personal involvement and sacrificial service of dedicated Christians. Individuals could make a difference in the world, Kahle told his students; committed personal action could right systemic wrongs. Thirty years later, Berger had "never forgotten the power" of Kahle's words and had "never lost the sense of hope that de Chardin set exploding" in him.

Ever the dedicated Catholic seminarian, Berger lost himself in both his studies and their practical application. After two years at St. Meinrad, he discovered a passion for philosophy and won a special scholarship in philosophy to Catholic University in Washington, D.C. He took a room in a residence hall at the Theological College there, living with other seminarians, and threw himself at his books, completing not only a bachelor's degree but also a master's degree in philosophy in three hectic, crammed years. He found life in the nation's capital enthralling, as he took in the symphony, wandered the halls of Congress and the Smithsonian, and followed the drama of political intrigue, then at the apex of the Watergate trials. At the same time, he did not forget to practice what he had learned from Fr. Kahle and from another mentor, a homiletics professor at Catholic named Fr. Geno Walsh. Berger began spending his Saturdays at a soup kitchen for the homeless in downtown Washington run by the Community for Creative Nonviolence, and his Sundays clad in clerical garb taking communion to bedridden Catholics at the Washington Home for the Dying.

Berger's three years at Catholic University were rich but exhausting, and as his graduation approached in spring 1977, he felt he needed a break from the intensity. Instead of proceeding straight to Belgium for final theological studies before ordination, therefore, he wangled approval from the local bishop for a two-year leave and set his sights on a job interview that Walsh had lined up with the editor of *Time-Life* books in downtown D.C. At the interview, however, he froze up miserably and blew his chance for the job. With no other options, he headed back to his parents' home in Mansfield, flat broke and unsure of what to do next. When the Diocese of Toledo called Berger about a position directing a service agency that fixed up homes for the poor in the economically pressed city of Lima, two hours to the west, the idea just seemed to fit. By that fall, the seminarian had settled into the work with vigor, soliciting funds from churches, learning the intricacies of local real estate, and beginning to tackle the problem of how to find free labor in an old industrial city still dominated by unions.

Within two years of his arrival in Lima, Berger made a life decision that abruptly and finally closed the door on returning to seminary and ordination as a priest. In spring 1979, he met Linda Musto through the spouse of the director of Lima's housing authority, who gave him Linda's phone number and suggested he give her a call. Having been on track for the priesthood since the age of twelve, Berger was unsure of how to proceed; he had rarely dated. So he kept phoning Linda Musto, then working as a clerk in the county commissioners' office, "and she kept coming up with excuses about why she couldn't go to lunch" with him. Soon Musto would discover, on a more intimate level, the same maddening aspects of Berger's character that would become apparent to numerous corporate executives in the coming years: he was relentless, he wouldn't take no for an answer, and he wouldn't give up. Berger kept calling until Musto agreed to go to lunch. Soon, he commented, "one thing led to another, and ultimately I decided that my work here was very engaging, she was very engaging, and going to Belgium just didn't look like something I needed to be focused on right now." The two were married in January 1980.[16]

Berger directed the Rehab Project for a dozen years, from the summer of 1977 to August 1989, when he resigned to campaign full time for mayor, and by any standard the project seemed a success. In his first ten years as director, he and a former seminary colleague, Howard Elstro, working with inmates from Lima Correctional Institute, built or repaired more than three hundred homes. Almost inevitably, these efforts led them into politics. The Rehab Project faced, for example, the resolute opposition of Allen Dobnicker, the city's law director and a committed archconservative who was nearly as obstinately stubborn as Berger himself. Dobnicker ruled—arbitrarily, it seemed to Berger—that the federal dollars the city received could not be applied to city housing. When Dobnicker refused to reconsider his ruling, Berger and Elstro filed suit against the city, and when city attorneys managed to bottle up the case in the courts for several years running, Berger and Elstro finally turned to Lima's voters. They recruited a young Democratic lawyer, Richard Siferd, to run against Dobnicker the next time he came up for reelection. After a vigorous campaign, with Berger, Elstro, and a small but growing number of progressive activists knocking on doors through the streets of Lima, Siferd swept into office and, soon afterward, lifted the city's ban on applying federal money to housing repair. Exhilarated by this victory, the Rehab Project directors hungered for more. They found an African American school principal, Will Thomas, to try to unseat a conservative city council member from Lima's north end. Thomas was an old Ohio State University football player who had once blocked tacklers for Ohio State's legendary coach Woody Hayes, and during the campaign, he even brought Hayes to walk precincts with him on Lima's north side. Thomas lost the council race, but the effort indicated to Berger the direction they needed to go. Housing issues had never seemed high on the political agendas of Lima's recent mayors; by the late 1980s, after nearly thirty years of agitation, Lima still lacked a housing code. The Rehab Project had begun to receive attention from national news media and major foundations, and in 1988 the National Realtors Association flew Berger to San Francisco to crown him "Citizen of the Year." Meanwhile, back in Lima, he perceived "a larger deterioration going on." When two national housing organizations contacted him with interesting job offers out of state, he and Linda began to wonder whether the time had come for him either to take on a more direct political role or to move on.[17]

Thus, when in the early spring of 1989 several downtown Lima businessmen approached Berger about mounting a political race of his own, they found him inclined to listen. The general mayoral election of 1989 promised to be a blockbuster. No less than five candidates were already in the race, all of them known city politicians, the most prominent of whom were current mayor Gene Joseph, running for reelection, and former mayor Moyer, gearing up to try to win back his old job. By any calculus, a bid by Berger would be a long shot. As someone reared in a household echoing to union songs, he could never be anything else than a Democrat, and Lima voters had not put a Democrat in the mayor's office in thirty years. But he went home, talked it over with Linda, and threw his hat in the ring.[18]

The downtown businessmen were right about the voters' openness to a fresh political face, but it still took the precise falling of a unique set of political dominoes to land Berger in the Lima mayor's office. The multicandidate primary—in which the top two vote-getters in the May primary faced each other in the fall election—gave an outsider like Berger an opening, if he could turn out his base of support and hope that Lima's more established politicos split up the rest of the voters. He was also helped by widespread dissatisfaction with the incumbent and by a lingering perception among many residents that Moyer's day had come and gone. Graying and fit at age 71, with a distinguished air and an easy affability, Moyer was still the one to beat. He had a seasoned, tested campaign apparatus that had put out yard signs and mobilized voters through three elections. Moreover, he enjoyed a political alliance with Furl Williams that went back two decades, and could count on Williams to cross party lines and deliver much of the black vote to his column. Nevertheless, Berger's candidacy seemed attractive to other longtime members of Moyer's old political base, including many of the downtown, Rotary Club Republicans, such as influential banker A. D. "Sandy" MacDonel and the Republican state representative, Ben Rose. As Rehab Project director, Berger had enjoyed a close working relationship with much of Lima's business community, and now much of this "growth coalition" deserted Moyer for him, convinced he would more actively endorse their agenda of economic development and community revitalization. For his part, the pragmatic Berger quickly discerned that, in a city dominated by the Republicans for decades—and where downtown money had routinely bankrolled Republican political campaigns—

a nonpartisan approach was the way to go. He placed prominent Republicans like Rose in key campaign roles and engaged in a delicate dance with the county Democratic Party, whose political ground troops he needed but whose leadership he sometimes seemed to keep at arm's length.[19]

It was a difficult political act to pull off, and it infuriated the Democratic Party's county chair, Bill Angel, who began to consider joining the campaign of Gene Joseph, the Republican incumbent mayor. If there was a key moment in the election, at least for Angel, it occurred at a Candidates' Forum before the spring primary, sponsored by the local branch of the League of Women Voters, where all six mayoral candidates were asked to respond to a question about how to bring Lima's people of color into a more integral role in community life. Five of the candidates, as Angel remembered, quickly bypassed the question and "turned their answers into attacks on minority hiring." In shades of condescension, Moyer grandly offered to help teach minorities how to apply for city jobs, while Joseph dismissed the significance of the issue, declaring, "Things are fine as they are." The question struck a nerve with Berger, however. Temporarily deserting what Angel saw as his "dryly professorial" style and speaking with a power and emotion that the Democratic leader hadn't before seen, Berger denounced the inadequacy of the responses from Joseph and Moyer, shouting out, "This community has never faced up to the issue of race, and we've got to consider it." For Angel, it was enough. The Democratic political organization mobilized party voters, Republican money and endorsements spoke to the independent-minded, and, in the end, Berger

Local judge William Lauber administering the oath of office to Mayor-elect David Berger for his first term, December 4, 1989. Lima City Council president Furl Williams seated third from left. *Photo courtesy of WLIO-TV, Lima, Ohio.*

coasted to victory. In the spring primary, Berger led the pack with 32 percent of the vote, versus 28 percent for Moyer, and in the November runoff, outspending Moyer by two to one, he beat the older candidate handily by 1,800 votes.[20]

"How many years can a city exist when all it has is retail?"

It would have been nice had external conditions allowed Berger and others in city leadership the unhampered time and energy to solve pressing problems at a deliberate pace, but as matters stood, the new young mayor found himself, to a great degree, crisis driven. Berger had been in office barely a month when, in January 1990, Dick Cheney, then the U.S. secretary of defense, announced the Pentagon's plans to close the Lima Army Tank Plant, at that time the county's largest employer. Within days of that bombshell, Amtrak issued new timetables that signaled the suspension of service on its last lines through Lima. Both the Broadway Limited and the Capitol Limited would be rerouted, stated a regional Amtrak spokesperson, thereby severing the city's last remaining passenger connections with its 150-year-old heritage as a train town. Berger and other city officials scrambled to fight the move, pulling together a special task force on the issue, and sending a delegation on the train to Amtrak offices in Chicago to protest the planned reroutings. But Amtrak officials appeared undaunted when they heard of Lima's response. Why were they coming? one bureaucrat wondered, adding, "I wouldn't hold out a lot of hope."[21]

Once again, the lesson was clear: critically important decisions affecting the future of entire communities were being made not by elected local leaders but by corporate heads in distant cities who knew little and cared less about their local impacts. To make matters worse, Berger soon learned that more than trains would be leaving Lima. The city had hardly recovered from the economic dislocation of the 1980s when it was hit, early in the new decade, by a new and equally devastating second wave of plant closings.

This second wave of shutdowns reverberated through Lima with particularly cruel force, partly because the city could ill-afford to lose any more manufacturing jobs after the losses of the rust belt era, and partly because promising signs had begun to suggest that the local economic recovery might be accelerating. Not only were manufacturing firms holding steady, local economic development experts reported, but a golden new future beckoned through growth in the county service-sector, retail jobs. William Bassitt, president of Lima's Chamber of Commerce, admitted that the area had not been very successful in attracting new industries, partly because of the lack of suitable industrial sites, but asserted that the boom in the retail sector more than made up for the stagnant industrial base. “We are going to grow our economy,” Bassitt guaranteed as a new decade dawned. “The growth that we have seen in the late 1980s is going to be continuing and expanding.”

Local unemployment rates had declined to around 6%; housing starts and business investment were up; houses were selling; and local real estate prices were climbing. The city even had regained most of the seven thousand jobs lost in the 1980s, although Bassitt admitted that most of the new jobs were lower-wage retail positions. Indeed, the recovery had taken such firm root it clearly had permeated the lives of individual city residents. The *Lima News* made sure to report on the mending fortunes of Patricia and Kenneth Merriman, whom the *Wall Street Journal* had earlier singled out as emblematic of Lima's financial decline. Mrs. Merriman was still driving a bus, but her spouse had found steady work at a small manufacturing firm. Altogether the couple's finances had returned to their 1980 level, allowing them to enroll their son in college.[22]

By 1991, however, a few troubling indicators had appeared, tarnishing the optimistic forecasts. The clerk of courts noted that declining auto sales might herald an economic slowdown, while the Lima refinery manager asserted that unless the area attracted small to medium-sized industries, it would continue to lose economic ground. Retail sales alone, he warned, were inadequate to build sustained economic growth. But none of these warnings could have adequately prepared Lima for the kinds of job losses that loomed.[23]

Scholars of other old industrial cities have underscored the kinds of wrenching repercussions that follow when the “civic capitalism” of longtime local owners is replaced by an emerging set of new corporate owners lacking those local loyalties. In Lima, this process played out in 1990 in one of the city's last remaining foundational industries, a homegrown plant currently named Teledyne Ohio Steel but known to most residents for nearly a century only by the latter two words. From World War I through the Vietnam War, Ohio Steel had been run under the firm but paternalistic rule of John Galvin. Galvin had called Lima home for most of his adult life and made his mark on his adopted city in a wide variety of ways. Not only had he actively recruited the African American workers who ushered in such sweeping demographic changes, but he had dutifully played the role of local philanthropist, giving generously to local charities and churches, donating land for a city park and also providing the purchase price for the tract of land east of town where state officials would construct Ohio State University, Lima. Six years before his death in 1974, at age 96, Galvin had sold his company to Fifth-Stirling, a subsidiary of the Los Angeles–based conglomerate Teledyne, Inc. Galvin had sold Ohio Steel to Teledyne because of what he discerned as its outstanding management and potential for growth. “The steel foundry was his life,” Galvin's daughter said, and he clearly wanted to leave his company in good hands.[24]

Galvin had always been an astute corporate boss with an eye for talent, and he was right about Teledyne. Its management—and especially its founder and chief executive, Henry Singleton—exuded business acumen, and when Teledyne bought Ohio Steel from Galvin in 1968, Teledyne was growing like crazy. Singleton had begun the company eight years earlier as a small electronics firm but, in line with his immense ambitions, had expanded it rapidly. In the eight-year span from 1960 to 1968, Teledyne had acquired eighty other companies of all kinds, twenty in the single year of 1966, when it began to gobble up metal companies, and ten more in 1967. When Teledyne acquired Ohio Steel, the former's massive corporate structure meant that the latter's existing workforce would receive much less in the way of solicitous consideration by their new managers than under Galvin. To Teledyne's top executives, responsible for managing eighty different companies, it seems doubtful that Lima steelworkers were much more than items on a spreadsheet, while Henry Singleton may not even have been able to place Lima on a map. Worse, Lima's steelworkers would also discover another unpleasant reality of the new corporate economy: what the top boss had so easily acquired, he could just as conveniently cast aside. By 1990, Singleton had begun to ease into retirement at his handsome New Mexico ranch, and therefore had begun to sell off parts of his conglomerate to investors, who eagerly anticipated the dismantling of Teledyne's corporate core, the $1.5 billion military and electrical equipment business but were considerably less interested in the more marginal outposts of the Teledyne empire. The particular team of corporate managers going over the Lima account would have followed the numbers to an easy conclusion. As increased international competition lowered steel prices below the costs of U.S. labor, the Lima plant, like much of the rest of the U.S. steel industry, was losing money. It needed to go. Teledyne sold it to a Cleveland manufacturing concern called WHEMCO, which would keep a small portion of the foundry running with only a fraction of the old workforce. In November 1990, the Teledyne management told Lima's hourly workers not to report the next day, and 350 of them entered local unemployment lines.[25]

The same month that doors swung shut on the old Ohio Steel plant, R. G. Dun likewise closed up shop. R. G. Dun was the successor firm to another of the city's historic industries, the old Diesel-Wemmer Cigar Company. Its managers announced that, in the face of declining sales, they had sold the firm to a competitor that also planned to cease operations. The move ended not only the jobs of thirty remaining cigar workers but also 106 years of cigar making in Lima.

As when Clark had closed the door on many older locomotive workers, the shutdown of another long-established Lima industry, Ohio Steel, represented particular hardship to what had been a remarkably stable and faithful workforce.

At the time of the closing, most of Teledyne's Lima workers, whose average age was forty-six, had worked for decades in one job, and many had an especially difficult time finding decent-paying jobs elsewhere. Three months after Teledyne's closing, the Lima area manager of the state unemployment office issued broad assurances that plenty of service-sector jobs beckoned, such as nurses' aides and cashier positions, with starting pay ranging from minimum wage to upwards of nine dollars an hour. A reporter following up on the fate of the old steelworkers four years later, however, discovered that many had taken positions in area fast-food restaurants. In the winter of 1990–91, Lima unemployment rates ticked slowly upward again—and this was only the beginning.[26]

The next major Lima industry to indicate signs of distress was Airfoil Textron, a manufacturer of fan blades for military and commercial aircraft. As Ex-Cello, its previous corporate identity, it had moved into an arm of the old Ohio Steel foundry and began production in 1951, employing 850 people as late as 1980 before its decline and resale, in 1986, to Textron. By 1993–94, the plant began to repeat the same sad pattern, so familiar to local residents that local manufacturers might appear to be reading from a standard script. First, workers ending their shifts receive a company notice that profits are down, layoffs will occur, and total plant closure is possible. The *Lima News* leads with a headline story full of regretful comments from the appropriate corporate CEO. In this particular instance, the Textron chief, G. L. "Topper" Long, outlined severe profit losses in the previous business cycle and announced the company was transferring corporate headquarters from Lima to Thomasville, Georgia. Textron, he informed the Lima public, was in a "quest for survival." Next, the press records conflicting emotions among the stricken workforce: some, with confusion and anxiety, wondering about their own economic prospects, others, with anger, remembering grand corporate promises made in earlier years that their jobs were secure as long as they worked hard and delivered for the company. As if on cue, Textron workers in Lima initially displayed a mixture of defiance and determination; as one worker put it, "It's a darned shame, but we're not giving up."[27]

The next scene in the standard script opens with the local press revealing intransigent unions in an apparent suicidal posture, unwilling to give an inch to save the plant. As for the Textron plant, in June 1994, the Lima public read that the UAW local there was refusing to make any job concessions, while Textron's management assured the press that if labor would only bend a little, they could save the plant. Next came the managers' announcement that they would make a decision on the plant's future within two weeks, while the Shawnee school superintendent, William Lodermeier, detailed the decline in local property taxes that closure would bring. Finally, the basic playbook has the corporate

CEO issuing another statement, fluttering with regret, that external financial exigencies render it necessary to close the facility in question, and the press takes comments from dismayed and angry workers. In the final episode of this particular Lima narrative, on June 24, 1994, Long announced that over the next eighteen months, Textron managers would close the Lima facility and shift its production to other plants in the South. A reporter jotted down a response from Textron worker Randy Beck, who sputtered angrily, "We've done everything they want. We met their demands, we made top quality parts . . . We have made big money for this company and this is how we get treated . . . we got the shaft."[28]

That was the script, at least as it played out in the eyes of the local public, reading about the course of events in the newspaper or watching them play out on Lima's WLIO-TV. Behind the scenes, however, a different kind of narrative unfolded. Mayor Berger, newly reelected in November 1993, heard word of the possible closure of a major area employer and jumped into action to avert it. A Textron task force, consisting of Berger, several consultants he selected, labor representatives, the county's economic development director, and the Allen County commissioners, quickly began meeting with local Textron management at the county courthouse in downtown Lima to do what they could to induce the firm to stay. However, Berger soon noticed the emergence of an unmistakable pattern in the negotiations: whenever he or task force colleagues agreed to new Textron demands, company officials would raise the bar. City and county officials offered training grants and special water rates, union leaders put forth wage, benefit, and work-rule concessions, but all met with the same response. Textron management, Berger said, "would come back at the next meeting and say, things have changed some more, this is what else we're going to need, and ultimately we could not put anything together that could save that plant." The negotiations had him at times pounding his fist on the table in frustration, he later recalled. Although he remained sympathetic to Textron's financial difficulties, Berger knew that at the same time that Textron managers were blaming declining sales for forcing them to close the Lima plant, they were building a new one in the South. In the end, Berger concluded that declining profits in aircraft manufacture were not the real issue at all. "Fundamentally, it came down to the fact that the plant manager didn't like his winters here in Lima and he wanted to be in Georgia." And because of that hidden, bottom-line reason, four hundred more local people lost their jobs, further eroding the community's tax base.[29]

In 1994, the script revolved around Textron; a year later, the drama was replayed around another firm, Sundstrand. Just as Textron was a re-formation of Ex-Cello, Sundstrand was the latest corporate metamorphosis of another old Lima company, an arm of the Westinghouse division that once had been the county's largest manufacturer, employing three thousand people to produce generators for the heavy bombers of World War II. As late as 1991, the Lima Westinghouse plant remained an important aerospace firm where seven hundred employees made ignition systems for both jet aircraft and NASA's space shuttle. But in January 1992, after months of rumors, these workers learned that their primary competitor, Sundstrand, had just bought them out. After years of reading sad stories of plant closings in the newspapers, they feared the worst. "It's a sad situation after you put in all those years for the company to treat us like this," said a Westinghouse inspector. "Where is a 46-year-old going to get a job in Lima if they close us? McDonalds?" But Sundstrand's manager was reassuring: Sundstrand was a highly regarded Fortune 500 company that had enjoyed $1.5 billion in sales the previous year; its executives had no intention of closing their new Lima plant. By the following May, suspicions had eased and workers were apparently "celebrating" the takeover with cake and refreshments.[30]

In light of the national downturn in the defense industry in the early 1990s, however, it was too early to celebrate. Within months of the cake and refreshments, Sundstrand's managers, citing slumping sales in the aerospace industry, began a series of layoffs. They handed out pink slips to 87 employees in July 1992, 60 more the following November, and then 115 more, a full fifth of the remaining workforce, the next August. They reminded the public that business conditions unfortunately left them with no choice, and that the layoffs were no reflection on the quality of the work of Sundstrand employees. Local people had heard it all before, and knew how the movie ended. Nobody could have been terribly surprised in February 1995 when company officials announced the closing of the Lima plant and the termination of the last 400 local employees. All that remained was the bitter epilogue: the usual round of hand wringing by local officials and the grappling by the newly unemployed to somehow grasp the human terms of yet another economic blow. Berger called it a tremendous loss for the community, while Shawnee superintendent Lodermeier focused on the coming cost to the schools. "We're about to get whacked big," he admitted. Workers gathered at a pizzeria near Sundstrand and the refinery. Defiantly still calling themselves Westinghouse employees, they had their own diagnosis of what had happened at Sundstrand and of what it meant for their city. "The bottom line is: we were dedicated; we were loyal. They tell us we did better than they expected and they still close us down," one of them remarked. "A town can't make it if companies treat their workers like that."[31]

If the prevailing narrative of the Textron and Sundstrand episodes was a death watch, then in the face of similar gloomy portents at the tank plant, local people could only conclude they were watching the precursors to a replay of the same story. The facility had received a boost of energy in 1976, when the Pentagon had selected it as the main production site for the new M-1 tank, and within five years the plant, then run by General Dynamics, was rolling out the huge battle wagons at the rate of thirty per month. In another five years, as President Reagan intensified his military buildup against the Soviet Union, the rate approached 120 tanks per month, and the Lima plant hummed with the energies of more than four thousand skilled industrial workers. Not since World War II had the county seen such a large number of workers gathered at a single plant. They labored in a facility sized to the mammoth, sixty-three-ton military beasts they produced: 370 acres with 47 separate buildings, the largest of which was nearly 1 million square feet. At a time when much of the rest of the area's financial base was reeling to news of plant closings, the $17.00 per hour paychecks brought home by the army of workers at Lima Army Tank Plant served as a source of economic salvation through the 1980s.[32]

By early the next decade, however, the Berlin Wall had fallen, the Soviet Union had ceased to exist, and incoming waves of fat defense contracts seemed as distant in time as the days of Benjamin Faurot. By the time of Dick Cheney's sudden announcement in January 1990 of administration plans to terminate both the M-1 and the Lima plant in three years, the facility was down to 2,600 workers, but nobody in Allen County could doubt that they needed to fight the planned closing. The plant's $100 million annual payroll by itself accounted for a full tenth of the total wages earned in the entire county, and losing the tank plant by itself, warned Bassitt, president of the Chamber of Commerce, could easily push the local unemployment rate up three points to over 10 percent. Whatever he thought personally of his own church's peace teachings, ex-seminarian Berger understood the economics of the tank plant, and quoted scripture in the cause. "Beating swords into ploughshares," he told *Business Week*, "is not an option." So the mayor and other civic leaders formed a special "Save the Tank Task Force," worked their own contacts, and, in this instance at least, benefited from the attention of district congressman Michael Oxley. Late in his career, Oxley would become notorious for his endless round of junkets with lobbyists and devotion to the financial interests of his corporate patrons, but through the 1990s he and his staff pushed the Pentagon on behalf of Lima.[33]

As in other cases, however, the economic survival or decline of any particular locality rested not on local efforts but on outside forces: what saved Lima's tank plant were new foreign orders and the sacrifice of a competing town. Cheney's axe spared Lima, but when it fell hard on Warren, Michigan, eliminating an older tank production facility there, Lima remained the only tank assembly plant in the country. Even so, by 1992, President George H. W. Bush's military budget had proposed phasing out the M-1 for the third year in a row. The fate of the Lima plant rested on an annual struggle between the tank's supporters in Congress and its detractors, who argued that the weapon was an expensive and unnecessary relic of the cold war. General Dynamics saved its big weapon by turning away from its primary customer at the Pentagon and peddling it overseas. By 1992, the governments of Saudi Arabia, Egypt, and Kuwait had placed orders with the contractor for over 1,200 more tanks, and the corporation had wheedled enough money out of Washington for modifications of existing stock to keep the plant going into the new century.[34]

The tank plant was spared an ugly death rattle but its survival still did not mean a happy ending for Lima. The long period of uncertainty had left the plant a long way from its glory days. Four thousand workers had given way to fewer than five hundred, a number that combined with the shutdowns of local defense plants to total nearly eight thousand more jobs lost in this second wave of plant closures. The economic multiplier effect that those lost jobs registered on other businesses, in addition to the declining revenues garnered from a shrinking local tax base, amounted to a staggering loss of more than $250 million to the local economy. Local officials tried to put the best face possible on the developments. "Even though we've taken some pretty stiff hits, there's still a positive feeling in the community," said the county economic development director, Marcel Wagner. Surprisingly, in contrast to the human toll taken by the economic dislocations of the 1980s, this time local people seemed to have fared better. Unemployment rates did not skyrocket into double digits, local real estate kept its value, and in 1996 welfare caseloads were actually dropping. Still, when describing current economic development in the Lima area, the best local boosters could point to were solid retail sales at the Lima Mall, a big new home-improvement center, and the construction of a few new fast-food outlets near the refinery. The question asked by one of Sundstrand's laid-off employees in 1995 was all the more pressing and appropriate. "The city of Lima, I think, is done for," she concluded. "How many years can a city exist when all it has is retail?"[35]

"That's my role, to figure out ways to solve these kinds of problems"

By the late 1990s, a scholarly consensus held that the mobility of international capital in the new age of globalization had placed local municipalities, and the public officials who led them, in positions of inescapable dependency. The extant literature in the fields of urban sociology, labor studies, and industrial economics rings with a shared pessimism that, in the words of one scholar, "it is futile to fight the decisions of the corporate elite." In 1993, the consensus stood so solidly grounded that two experts in the field could refer in shorthand form to the "community dependency thesis." Charles Craypo and Bruce Nissen summarized this thesis as holding that "conventional norms and established political structures in industrial communities are such that economic, social and political institutions are limited in their ability to control or influence the direction of economic change."[36]

In such a world—where market mobility tips economic power so decidedly to the corporate side that, as one scholar argues, "market systems imprison policy"—the choices left to elected local officials will necessarily remain quite limited. The three extant municipal models available to public officials like mayors were identified in academic language as the "bystander," the "offset," and the "proactive player" roles. To someone in Berger's position, the first two would have seemed especially impotent models of municipal leadership. Witness, for instance, events in the early 1980s in South Bend, Indiana, at the local facility of the Torrington Company, a heavy bearings manufacturer. Confronted with a decline in profits because of increased overseas competition, Torrington faced a basic choice about how to respond: should it renovate its plants in the Midwest and Northeast or instead shift production to nonunionized facilities in the southern states? Torrington was already beginning to implement the second course of action as early as 1961, when it constructed a state-of-the-art plant in open-shop South Carolina while declining to invest further in its flagship plant in Connecticut. The Ingersoll-Rand Corporation had affirmed the policy when it acquired Torrington in 1968. Union officials at the Torrington plant in South Bend saw the trend developing and brought it to the attention of corporate CEO Thomas Bennett, who issued firm guarantees to local workers that as long as they continued to work hard their jobs were safe. He assured workers in July 1982, for example, that "you people have earned the right to keep this plant open, and we are going to keep it open." Two months later, however, Bennett sent internal memos directing that the company close the South Bend facility. Even as workers intercepted company documents revealing Bennett's duplicity and demonstrating to union leaders and the local public that the decision to relocate the plant had already been made, however, South Bend public officials declined to challenge Torrington management before or after closing, afraid that doing so would poison the local business climate and make it harder to attract new firms to the area.[37]

The human devastation wrought by plant closings was so great that in some cases public officials did abandon the cheerleading role of the bystander position, or the reactive, refereeing, offset stance, to carve out a third possible role for themselves when facing a possible plant closing in their communities. Such officials have entered the economic field themselves as proactive players in the struggle, often in overtly populist ways. Allying themselves with labor and community groups, they have used a variety of legal tools and political pressures to try to avert a plant closing or mitigate its effects. Moreover, such officials have begun to pioneer new political understandings legitimating such governmental intervention, arguing that communities have a stake in the movements of private enterprise and that the sacrosanct wall of private business sometimes may be breached to protect the public interest. These new analyses are important, for opposing arguments—holding that any actions by government or workers to hamper business activity constitute an unwarranted infringement on the right of property and a negative drag on the productivity of the free market—are deeply rooted in American society. Such widely spread notions constitute a significant barrier that more activist public officials must overcome, though doing so can be difficult. Since increased corporate mobility in the new global economy allows businesses to relocate their jobs to areas they discern as offering the "good business climate" they desire, actions by local officials perceived as damaging that climate may meet with substantial opposition within the threatened community itself, as the South Bend case illustrates.[38]

Because of the financial, legal, and political barriers that corporate adversaries tend to raise, the academic literature offers many instances of local officials working with labor activists in such populist player roles, but fewer cases where they have been successful in stemming corporate power, much less in stopping a plant closing. In the early 1980s, for example, activists in the Monongahela Valley south of Pittsburgh created an agency called the Steel Valley Authority as the spearhead of a widespread campaign to resist the devastating series of plant closings in the heart of the nation's steel belt. They mobilized churches and voters, created new mechanisms of political authority, enlisted scores of elected officials, and even sketched out a trenchant critique of capitalism—but none of these tactics managed to markedly slow the tide of job losses in the valley. In 1990–91, a similar coalition of activists, the Calumet Project, actually succeeded in persuading a Chicago-area industrial facility, LaSalle Steel, not to relocate some of its production to a nonunion plant elsewhere, but the victory amounted to a lone, isolated bright spot on an otherwise dismal horizon.[39]

The risks of resistance to corporate hegemony, moreover, could be substantial. In the late 1980s, for instance, as part of a $10 billion modernization effort, GM decided to close or relocate twenty-three separate plants. One of them had functioned for years as the economic lifeblood of Norwood, Ohio, a small city of 25,000 people with an excellent school system located in suburban Cincinnati. Losing the plant and its 4,300 employees would have cost the city about a quarter of its operating budget and dealt Norwood a crippling blow; indeed, the prospects were so dire that city officials briefly considered declaring bankruptcy. Norwood's mayor, Joseph Sanker, pulled out all the stops. He pleaded with GM to stay, reciting all the zoning changes and traffic adjustments the city had made at GM's request. He unsuccessfully tried to enlist state and national politicians to pressure the giant automaker. With all other means of recourse exhausted, Sanker resorted to the municipal equivalent of nuclear war. The City of Norwood filed a $318 million lawsuit against GM, charging breach of contract and violation of fiduciary duty. One local official went so far as to accuse the corporation of "economic terrorism." The huge automaker responded in the manner of a giant swatting a mosquito. First, GM hired the Miller-Valentine Group, a respected major developer of industrial space, to assess and develop its Norwood site, pleasing city officials tremendously. Then it announced that it would not continue paying Miller-Valentine as long as the city pursued its legal action. When Sanker's administration persisted with the suit, GM refused further cooperation with the developer, triggering its withdrawal from the project. Shortly afterward, a judge dismissed the city's lawsuit and GM proceeded with the demolition of its former plant in Norwood City. Instead of GM-funded development efforts, all Norwood won from its resistance was a fenced-off former industrial site and 4,300 lost jobs.[40]

By the mid-1990s, any number of academic experts could have told Lima's mayor that it was hopeless to try to change the fate that the new global economy had mapped out for his city, but Berger, a politically inexperienced former community activist, seemed to carry a basic naïveté with him into his new job. Nobody had told him that the only remaining role left to Lima was that of helpless victim. Immediately on taking office, he faced a series of decisions about how to respond to more bad economic news. "Every day," it seemed to Berger, "there was another negative announcement about plant closings," and in response, he decided "that's my role, to figure out ways to solve these kinds of problems." So when Amtrak announced, in Berger's first month in office, to terminate passenger service in Lima, the new mayor drove to Washington, found a high-powered attorney to push the city's case on a pro bono basis, and did what he could to bring Amtrak to the negotiating table. When the tank plant and Textron appeared to be spiraling downward, he created special task forces to try to reverse their courses.[41]

Certainly, like other public officials around the county, Berger discovered that decisions resulting in local economic dislocation were made far away, and recognized the difficulties this presented. Despite his best efforts, he witnessed the disappearance of eight thousand area jobs in his first two terms. But Berger persisted in his activism, weathered his own personal learning curve, and, in at least one instance, was able to slap a new and different ending on the established local script of economic decline. Through 1993 and 1994 he continued to work at what to do with the Sundstrand property. As the company prepared to leave the area, a Sundstrand official telephoned to tell Berger that the company planned to demolish its huge central building. When Berger asked why, the official confessed that the entire facility was saturated with ground contaminants; before the passage of laws prohibiting the practice, Westinghouse had routinely taken them outside and dumped them into the soil. To escape environmental liability, Sundstrand planned to level its 700,000-square-foot major building and cover the entire property with a huge asphalt cap, sealing the contamination but also rendering it useless for any future development. Berger talked a friend with a private plane into flying him to corporate headquarters in Rockford, Illinois, where he prevailed on senior Sundstrand management to give him time to find another solution. He and the task force then located an environmental engineering firm in Atlanta, and persuaded Sundstrand to sell it the property at a heavily discounted price, on condition that the new owner indemnify Sundstrand from future environmental liabilities. The Atlanta firm spent two years cleaning up the site, literally vacuuming the contaminants out of the soil, while the City of Lima found a grant to fund improvements to the property, such as additional water and sewer line extensions and a roadway on its southern and eastern sides. In this manner, instead of remaining a sealed-off site of environmental contamination, the property became attractive enough to lure in new occupants. A local developer bought the site and "condominiumized" it into separate units. Within a few years, thirteen new small manufacturing firms had located there, employing upwards of two hundred people.[42]

Nor was Berger finished with the property. Having worked so hard to rescue the site for further industrial development, he had no intention of allowing it to remain solely within the tax base of Shawnee Township. After a fair bit of digging, Berger and his administrators discovered a loophole in the intricacies of state annexation law. Within the creative space that existing law allowed, his administration proceeded to invent a new mechanism called "non-withdrawal annexation," in which a border area could technically remain part of the township while becoming attached to the city. Through this new method, the township would retain the right to tax property, but the city gained the power to tax wages employees earned in the annexed area. Of course, Berger admitted, "Shawnee fought us all the way," but in the end Lima won, as did other Ohio cities when the area's state senator amended state law to fully legitimate the new annexation method in the Ohio code. A quarter of a century before, Lima mayor Christian Morris had dreamed of somehow extending Lima city limits into the tax-rich industrial zone just south of town. Now the city had found a way.[43]

In January 1994, the reelected mayor turned his attention with renewed vigor to the city's deepening economic woes, and soon he would face the biggest challenge of them all. Over the preceding two decades, the acids of economic transformation had eaten away at the city's old industrial base. One by one, nearly all of the city's traditional industries had eroded or completely disappeared. The locomotive works, the steel foundry, the cigar works, the rail yards—all were gone; Ex-Cello and Westinghouse were gone; and as for the tank plant, it had lost seven-eighths of its workforce. By 1996, although the Ford engine plant east of Lima remained healthy and the Lima Correctional facility still employed hundreds, a key symbolic change had occurred in the old industrial town: Lima's biggest employer within city limits was now located not in manufacturing but in the service sector, St. Rita's Hospital.[44]

Financial decisions made far away had already eroded Lima's traditional industrial base; now they were threatening the city's bedrock industry, the one manufacturing concern above all others that had given birth to Lima as a modern industrial city. Gas flares still burned brightly from the tops of pipes at the massive complex south of town, a drawing of an oil derrick still bent and buckled when the wind hit the city flag, and in five years' time, James Schaefer and a skilled and creative workforce had accomplished mechanical and financial wonders at the Lima refinery. Increasingly, however, little of this seemed to matter to the hierarchy of corporate executives who technically held title of ownership to the refinery. They had reasons of their own for no longer needing or wanting the refinery in their financial picture, and they had the power to eliminate it. In this decision, however, they would be opposed by an uncommonly stubborn mayor, a determined workforce, and a solid phalanx of community leaders, all of whom would unite with their arms folded, point to the refinery, and say, no, not this last plant, not this time.

Chapter 5

Scorched Earth

In 1996, two parallel but fundamentally incompatible trajectories collided at the Lima refinery. One of them emanated from the agenda of its owners, the corporate executives of British Petroleum. As seen from BP headquarters in London, or through the eyes of American management executives in their beautiful, red granite skyscraper in downtown Cleveland, the logic of international finance and corporate priorities began to point unmistakably toward shutting Lima down. BP had never focused its major energies on refining anyway; instead, its particular corporate genius had always been in finding and producing oil. Now, as profit margins from refining shrank in the 1990s, the logical policy from the corporate perspective was to reduce BP's refining capacity in an increasingly tough market. As a minor star in the BP firmament, the Lima plant increasingly appeared a prime candidate for closure.

This agenda only made sense, however, to those overlooking or ignoring a parallel series of developments occurring at the Lima refinery itself. When their corporate superiors repeated the company consensus that BP's midwestern refineries were losers, Lima's managers and workers wondered if perhaps they had been lost in a time warp. Beneath the corporate radar, Lima refinery workers had accomplished a remarkable turnaround, transforming a neglected and declining refinery into a facility that even outside oil industry experts had begun to characterize as one of the most improved and productive in the country. If one trajectory spoke in the language of closure and decline, the other responded in the idiom of revitalization.

BP's corporate executives and the people on the ground at the Lima refinery were locked on a collision course, and their conflict would play out in front of a set of local people whose recent history had rendered them unable to look on such struggles dispassionately or abstractly. At stake in this conflict was yet another rendition of the same question the people of Lima had been wrestling with, in one form or another, for the past several decades: whether, in the new global economy, a local community and ordinary people could still imagine themselves as the masters of their own economic fate. Lima's mayor still thought they could and threw himself into this conflict with all the energy and resources he could muster. Whether these or any efforts could make a difference remained to be seen.

"The queen of the fleet"

Since 1886, when John D. Rockefeller had directed his brother Frank to purchase farmer Hover's old bean field south of Lima and begin building an industrial complex there, history had largely been kind to the old Standard refinery. By 1995, while other local firms and entire industries had come and gone, Lima's facility had been transforming raw crude into gasoline and other products for more than a hundred years. For most of that time, it had remained under the ownership of the functioning remnant of Rockefeller's core firm. In 1906, amidst the trust-busting fervor of the Progressive Era, President Theodore Roosevelt had instructed his attorney general to bring suit against Standard Oil. Even after the U.S. Supreme Court provided the final legal sanction for the breakup of Standard Oil five years later, the separated pieces of Rockefeller's original massive monopoly were still large enough to remain major players by themselves in the American oil industry through much of the twentieth century. Standard Oil of New Jersey, for example, metamorphosed into Esso and then Exxon, while Standard Oil of New York gradually emerged as Mobil. The original mother company, Standard Oil of Ohio, or Sohio, retained Rockefeller's legacy, headquartered itself in his old hometown of Cleveland, and continued to refine crude in Sohio's two remaining refineries, in Toledo and Lima. Because it lacked its own sources of crude, Sohio's potential for growth was limited, and it remained a regional refining and marketing company with operations largely confined to the state of Ohio. Even so, it evolved into an adept company with a firm tradition of managerial independence and a dominant position in the Midwest. By the 1960s, with nearly four thousand filling stations across the state, Sohio still controlled about a third of Ohio's gasoline market, then the fourth-largest market in the country, and the Lima refinery, as one of Sohio's major facilities, benefited from Sohio's active attention. In 1970–71, Standard invested $75 million in expanding and improving the refinery, transforming it into one of the largest and best-equipped such plants in the country.[1]

As Sohio revamped its refineries and contented itself with its regional market, however, developments under way elsewhere would inexorably pull it into the international nexus. In 1968, the larger oil world jumped to exciting reports that the Atlantic Richfield Company had discovered huge new fields of crude oil beneath Prudhoe Bay on Alaska's far North Slope. Nine months later, after nearly a decade of searching, British Petroleum announced similar finds. At the time, BP was already an established player in the world of international oil. Its roots stemmed back to 1901, when a wealthy Englishman, William D'Arcy, won permission from the shah of Iran to search for oil in his northern provinces. Within eight years, D'Arcy's firm, then called the Anglo-Persian Oil Company, had begun to export oil to a world newly mad with the automobile craze and ravenously thirsty for gasoline. The real growth of the company followed the collapse of the old Ottoman Empire and England's rapid extension of its own empire into the Middle East. In 1914, the British government became the majority shareholder in the Anglo-Persian firm, and it eagerly granted its chosen company long oil rights to huge swaths of some of the most oil-rich territories in the world. By the early 1950s, the mammoth oil company, by then renamed British Petroleum, owned almost a fourth of the world's oil reserves. When waves of nationalism rippled through the Middle East—and Iran briefly nationalized BP's assets there—the corporation began to look elsewhere for new and more stable sources of supply. It worked to develop reserves in Nigeria and Libya and pushed exploration into South America and the Caribbean, but its big breakthrough came in Alaska.[2]

Shortly after its big strike there, BP controlled more than half of the massive Alaskan oil reserves. The company's huge Alaskan reserves, signaling new opportunities for entry into the American market, would quickly lead it to reconfigure its global strategy away from the Middle East toward efforts to capitalize on those opportunities through a deal with Sohio and ultimately through the planting of thousands of green and yellow BP signs across the American Midwest. Two problems remained, however: first, how could BP transport its oil out of the frozen tundra around Prudhoe Bay? And second, how could BP locate and control established North American outlets for its new crude?

BP solved the first problem, in conjunction with other oil companies, by pushing for and helping to engineer construction of the Alaskan pipeline. As for the second problem, BP met this need by buying up smaller U.S. oil companies. In April 1969, it acquired the Sinclair Oil Company. In exchange for a payment of $400 million, BP gained ten thousand gas stations from Maine to Florida (double the number of its own stations in England) and became, in one fell swoop, the largest single all-British investor in the United States. Sinclair was not enough, however, and soon BP entered into negotiations for a partnership with

Sohio. In contrast to Sinclair, Sohio offered firm financial capacities of its own, little debt, its two excellent refineries in Lima and Toledo, and a much stronger market position concentrated in urban areas. For its part, Sohio, which had lacked its own source of supply for seventy-five years, saw in BP the prospect of an alliance with an international company awash in crude. Sohio employees were enthusiastic about the initial agreement, which began as an affiliation between equals; soon, however, BP's global presence and injections of Alaskan crude into Ohio soon overshadowed its smaller partner. By the early 1980s, BP had acquired 55 percent of Sohio stock, and then, in a "boardroom coup" in February 1986, it summoned Sohio executives to London to inform them that BP would fully subsume the lesser company. Within three years, BP's green and yellow signs had replaced the red and blue of Standard, and the last vestiges of Rockefeller's old company had disappeared.[3]

BP executives did their best to assure the old Sohio employees that aside from the new name, little really had changed: the Lima facility remained an integral part of BP's operations, it was still producing adequate profits, and the workers' future was in good hands. Indeed, so efficient was the Lima plant, workers often heard from their new bosses at BP, that it held first place as "the queen of the fleet" among BP's refineries. Because of this, BP executives declared, local people in and outside the plant should harbor no doubt about their security under the new management. "Our hope is to remain in Lima for many years in the future," pledged BP's new refinery manager, Gary Greve. "Lima will play a key role in our operations for the foreseeable future," soothed another official in 1987.[4]

The Lima refinery's workers did notice subtle changes occurring as they became smaller parts of a much bigger company. In contrast to the easy familiarity that had characterized management-employee relationships under Sohio, refinery worker Clarence Roller recalled, BP's managers tended to treat the Lima employees more impersonally; sometimes, under BP, he felt like a mere "tool." Roller and his fellow hourly employees also noticed a much higher turnover rate among local refinery managers under BP than under Sohio. Workers suspected the new refinery bosses saw Lima as merely a stepping stone; often they stayed for only a year or two before moving on to other postings in the BP empire. Moreover, the BP managers who did stay were sometimes bosses that workers wished would quickly move on. Greve's tenure in the mid-1980s was especially confrontational, both in terms of his hard-edged approach to the refinery's union, and in terms of his personal style. "He was very authoritarian," Gilbert remembered, "very brusque and abrupt about it." One union official summarized refinery labor relations as "tumultuous" throughout the entire decade of the 1980s. Equally troubling to many in the workforce was top-down neglect of the plant itself. Roller and other longtime refinery workers discerned top management devoting less care to issues like routine maintenance at the refinery, and investment in equipment and technology needed to keep the facility running at its most productive pace. Roller also noted a tendency to reduce the workforce. He watched the number of co-workers in the plant's pipe shop decline by a dozen guys in four years, while retiring maintenance workers likewise were not replaced. The refinery could get by like this for a while, they knew, but sooner or later the bill would come due.[5]

These issues remained largely invisible outside the refinery's gates, and at any rate the cumulative effect of such trends would not emerge until later. In the community of Lima, local people instead focused attention on the suitability of BP as neighbor.

"In bed with BP"

Oil refineries, by their very nature, are dirty, inescapably dangerous, and environmentally dicey enterprises. Without the jobs and other economic benefits they provide, few communities would invite them into their backyards. No matter how carefully they are run or how strictly their safety procedures are enforced, refineries are likely to subject their neighbors to spills and fires, and a few of their own workers to injuries. Whether run by Sohio or BP, the Lima refinery was no exception. Periodically it released toxic fumes, spilled damaging pools of oil, paid fines to the EPA for other environmental transgressions, and, on rare occasion, mourned the deaths of employees. In 1963, for example, an explosion and fire burned four workers, killing one, while in 1988, a furnace fire killed another refinery worker, Kevin Nichols. A more severe accident occurred in January 1969, when an oil spill came close to blowing up a fair portion of Lima. Cracks on a welding job done seven years earlier led to the rupture of a high-pressure crude pipeline deep beneath the ground, and two thousand barrels of highly flammable oil began seeping into an open field on the far south side of town. Declaring a state of emergency, Mayor Morris evacuated six thousand residents from a hundred blocks on the south side and managed to find most of them sheltered from the cold winter night before the oil reached the city's sewage treatment plant, where vapors ignited and blew up the plant.[6]

BP's neighboring chemical plant likewise struggled with how to adequately dispose of its waste and how to handle the inevitable accusations that it was failing to do so. For several years beginning in 1988, Ohio Citizen Action, a statewide environmental group, published reports depicting the chemical plant, with an annual level of toxic emissions of 57.7 million pounds, as the worst polluter in the state and the eleventh-worst polluting plant in the entire country. The group claimed that the kinds of chemicals routinely released by BP could clearly be linked to birth defects. BP's spokespeople vigorously disagreed, pointing out that BP had injected most of those 57 million pounds deep into the earth, but even neutral observers recognized the staggering levels of pollutants that the plant emitted and something of the risks they posed to human health. By 1991, according to the *Cleveland Plain Dealer,* the refinery and the chemical plant were together releasing a daily total of more than ten pounds of toxic chemicals into Allen County's water or air, and of the twenty-two toxic chemicals making up this daily total, six were known to cause cancer. In their defense, the two companies reiterated that they injected most of their chemical waste into "deep wells"—2,800 feet into the earth. At such depths, BP officials claimed, the chemicals would remain immobilized from human contact for ten thousand years. However, newspaper reporters could do the math, and continued to draw uncomfortable inferences. With the companies injecting an average of 540,000 gallons of waste every day for twenty-three years, they reported, the reservoir of toxic waste a mile below Lima had grown to more than 4 billion gallons—a poison pool large enough to fill the Cleveland Browns' football stadium fourteen times over. Moreover, the *Cleveland Plain Dealer* noted that two such deep wells elsewhere in the state had already leaked, and went on to list several other ways that the buried wastes might find their way into local drinking water.[7]

Long before such specific controversies over deep well injection, Allen County had begun to witness local manifestations of a more general concern over the environmental impacts of industry that was erupting into conflict with increasing frequency elsewhere in the country. Locally, rumors of the possible negative effects of BP's activities on public health had given birth to environmental activism. By 1985, a group of area activists had formed the Allen County Citizens for the Environment, or ACCE, to hold BP accountable on such issues. The ACCE was never very big, but its core group of twenty people included several savvy activists and lawyers who quickly learned how to make things tough for BP. One of these was local attorney David Little. By the time Little began his work with the ACCE in the mid-1980s, he had served for years as the director of the county's legal aid office, railed against racism, advocated for the poor, and generally functioned as a thorn in the side of the local power structure for about two decades. Now he and his fellow environmentalists harnessed their skills to focus the public's attention on BP's perceived environmental liabilities.[8]

According to Bruce French, an ACCE activist and local law professor, the ACCE had been quietly agitating for several years, but its first public protest came in 1988, when its members marched to the gates of the chemical plant to protest its proposal to burn its hazardous waste in an incinerator. Although BP wanted the incinerator, it abhorred the negative publicity and quietly worked out a compromise with the ACCE: it would withdraw its application for a permit for the incinerator if the activists with ACCE would in turn refrain from opposing its applications for more deep wells. The ACCE agreed to the deal but later regretted it as a mistake, recognizing, French claimed, that BP's guarantees that its wastes would be safe for ten thousand years was at best a guess, particularly when the New Madrid earthquake fault lay only a few miles away. Despite such second thoughts, the episode set the pattern for later confrontations and deals. While BP quickly learned that the legal expertise of Little and French could enable the ACCE to bottle up matters like permit applications for a long time, the ACCE, for its part, learned that BP would usually win in the end. To avoid lengthy court fights with the ACCE, BP found it easier in the long run to compromise and modify its waste disposal proposals. In the short run, though, the two sides publicly squared off in a series of acrimonious permit hearings.[9]

For a dozen years, the ACCE and other activists launched a variety of assaults on BP's environmental record, and BP's capable staff consistently beat them back. In 1991, BP successfully resisted an ACCE lawsuit against the refinery for improperly releasing several pollutants into the Ottawa River, and three years later, it fought off a $1 billion, class-action lawsuit brought by three Lima citizens charging that the deep well injections underneath their residences amounted to trespass and an assault on their property values. The refinery refused to provide the ACCE with any information unless forced to do so by the state and petitioned the federal Environmental Protection Agency (EPA) for rule changes that would allow it to report lower emissions levels. French, acting for the ACCE, charged in turn that the only reason BP insisted on reporting emissions from the chemical plant and the refinery separately was to make each level appear lower. On other occasions, the corporation argued, quite accurately, that its emissions standards fully complied with state and federal EPA guidelines; the ACCE did not deny this assertion, but French noted that this only proved the "worthless" nature of the Ohio EPA.[10]

Meanwhile, prodded by law, public pressure, and also perhaps its own sense of corporate conscience, BP worked to lessen its emissions levels at both the chemical plant and the refinery. In 1991, BP Oil announced plans to spend another $120 million at the refinery alone to bring it into compliance with the new federal Clean Air Act. The ACCE continually called such claims into question, although French, after getting past the public relations staffers at the front desks and actually talking to some of BP's technical people, conceded some years later that BP probably had been trying harder to reduce emissions than the environmentalists had realized at the time. In case people missed the message, James Ross, head of BP America, journeyed to Lima in 1989 to outline the company's efforts in a speech to the Rotary Club. Over the previous decade, he told the Rotarians, the company had spent $168 million on environmental improvements at the two plants, $20 million of it in 1988 alone in an attempt to cut the chemical plant's emissions by half. "We are proud of our environmental efforts in Lima," Ross declared, "and we believe we're a good citizen and neighbor."[11]

Ross had not come to Lima to make such statements on a whim. Apparently, BP executives felt threatened enough by the growing environmentalist critique that they embarked on a well-funded public relations offensive to communicate the corporation's views to the residents of Lima. At least in part, the fact that BP had a local public relations staff at all was because of ACCE environmental activism. This staff was led by Judy Gilbert, formerly a local schoolteacher who had left the classroom in 1984 to take a job in human resources at the refinery. Sparked by environmentalist "attacks" on the plant, she began urging her superiors to respond in some way. In 1988, they acted on her suggestion by creating a local public relations department—the first such office BP established in any of its plants around the world—and putting Gilbert in charge of it. Her staff busied themselves with efforts to "focus more on outreach, to be proactive, and to tell the story from our perspective. Because if you don't tell the story, somebody else tells the story, and it isn't always right." They distributed a newsletter to 4,700 local residents who lived near the plants, assuaging their environmental concerns. In 1991, they mounted a special exhibit in the city, "Exploring the World Beneath Your Feet," designed to ease local concerns about the deep well injections. Visitors walked

Judy Gilbert, public relations specialist for the BP Lima refinery, March 2006. *Photo courtesy of WLIO-TV, Lima, Ohio.*

past geologic depth-charts comparing the 375-foot depth of local drinking-water wells to the abyssal depths of the Mount Simon layer, 2,800 feet down, where BP was storing its toxic wastes. That geologic stratum, BP informed visitors, acted liked a "giant sponge," absorbing hazardous wastes and rendering them unable to ever permeate the relatively shallow zone containing Lima's drinking water. In a single month, more than five thousand people—better than a tenth of Lima's population—took in the exhibit. Perhaps even more indicative of the work of BP's adept public relations staff was an expensive, attractive pamphlet, apparently distributed widely in the community, called "What Is BP Doing to Protect My Family, My Neighborhood, and the Environment?" Amid glossy photographs of wildflowers and waterfalls, the breezy text supplied answers to any troubling questions that might crop up in local minds. For example, a person might wonder, "Have BP pipelines ever leaked?" The answer: "Yes, but, fortunately, leaks are rare." The brochure outlined the many different safety procedures that BP staff and workers had mastered and cited scientific studies underscoring the lack of connections researchers had found between local cancer rates and BP industrial air releases. Company publicists were also reassuring about the release of contaminants into the water, announcing that BP was working closely with the Ottawa River Coalition, another local environmental group, "to study the watershed and develop ways to achieve full attainment of EPA standards." As matters stood, BP claimed, "the Ottawa River has virtually been reborn."[12]

Really? In 1992, environmentalists pounced on a study released by the Ohio EPA documenting horrible rates of fish disfigurement in the Ottawa. At a test site near the refinery industrial complex and the Lima sewage treatment plant, the EPA found half the fish it checked to be deformed or disfigured from disease, rates far higher even than those of Ohio's most notorious polluted river, the Cuyahoga Ship Channel, near Cleveland. The local manager for health, safety, and environmental quality for BP Chemicals called the EPA data "very inconclusive." Baloney, retorted ACCE's Little. "That's the standard BP line: they say the link cannot be made," he said, "but we say they cannot disprove the link either."

Back and forth the volleys shot. In 1990, Allen County obtained state funds to hire an outside consultant, the well-respected Battelle Memorial Institute, to investigate any possible connections between BP air emissions and area cancer rates. After two years of study, Battelle concluded the risk was slight; local residents had a cancer risk of one in 10,000. The ACCE said Battelle's monitors had been poorly placed and called for more testing. Meanwhile, BP claimed victory. "It confirms what we've believed and said all along," a company spokesperson crowed. "This is not modeling. This is not guessing. This is proof."[13]

In the all-important arena of public opinion, BP seemed to be winning hands down. Signs of this victory included the size of the turnout and the sentiments expressed by the crowds showing up when the state EPA conducted local hearings on new waste discharge permits. At one such hearing in early 1991, more than 350 people gathered to cheer a steady stream of speakers denouncing proposed EPA regulations intended to further restrict wastewater emissions from the refinery. Of the 70 individuals lined up for a chance at the microphones, all but 3 objected to the new regulations. A similar-sized crowd showed up nearly two years later to support BP's request to increase the pressure rates it used in its deep well injections. The matter of pressure rates was important, since the EPA had valid concerns—which the ACCE did its best to amplify—that increased pressure would fracture the rock formations deep in the earth and facilitate the flow of waste upward toward drinking water levels. However, when BP spokespeople testified that the company had spent $4.5 million on a test well to confirm that no migration of wastewater was occurring, only 3 of the 31 locals voicing an opinion that evening—all 3 members of the ACCE—challenged BP's assurances that the injection pressures were safe. "I believe what we have heard tonight is a conspiracy, a lobbying effort," Little told the press.[14]

Little also knew, however, that the crowds of people at the hearings had not just wandered in out of the blue. They had come because they worried that their jobs were at stake. Of the hundreds who came to the 1991 hearing, most were current or former employees of the refinery who had been urged to demonstrate support for the company by the BP Retention Task Force, a coalition of business leaders. If BP workers harbored any doubts about the real costs of the proposed EPA restrictions, their bosses quickly reminded them. "BP Official Says Lima Jobs Hinge on Petition Approval," the *Lima News* headlined, and James Walpole, the chemical plant manager, frequently repeated the company's position. Refusal by the EPA to allow increased pressure on BP's deep well injection, Walpole stated, would put BP at a competitive disadvantage, forcing the company to eliminate two hundred jobs, nearly half of the plant's workforce. Such a prospect was unthinkable, both to local workers and to the area's elected officials, who were already watching a steady hemorrhage of manufacturing jobs and were desperate to staunch the flow. Among those pleading with the EPA to see things BP's way on the issue of the well injections pressure were an Allen County commissioner, the Chamber of Commerce president, and Lima's Mayor Berger, who worried openly that an EPA ruling stipulating lower pressures "will threaten our local economy." In their confrontation with the ACCE, Gilbert and other BP managers clearly saw Berger as an ally. Lima city officials from the mayor on down presumably wanted clean air and water as much as anybody else, but they also understood the economic dynamics in play. To a community undergoing the loss of eight thousand jobs, maybe stricter environmental safeguards were luxuries it could not afford.[15]

The activists with the ACCE also grasped perfectly well the obstacles that economic desperation presented to their environmental advocacy and grappled with how to find their way around them. They tried several times to convince church groups on Lima's south side of the connection between environmental degradation and racism but met with limited success. It was hard, they found, to reach across the ingrained suspicions that blue-collar workers and people of color had for a group consisting mostly of white-collar professionals, and even harder to overcome the underlying approval of BP that many people had formed, as a company providing both jobs and economic protection. Many ACCE activists, French admitted, were not surprised when they saw much of the local business community lining up as "cheerleaders" for BP, chanting incessantly that all development, all industry, is desirable. They had expected better from Mayor Berger, however. They thought he "should know better because he was a smart man." As an old community activist and, by some measures, a progressive Democrat, Berger might have been a natural ACCE ally. Instead the environmentalists watched him line up with the business crowd to urge the EPA to lay off the corporation. Many in the ACCE, French said, found it disheartening to see Berger so "in bed with BP."[16]

No, it would not be environmental pressures that would threaten the five hundred jobs at the Lima refinery. Instead, like so many other economic changes that had hit the area, the real locus for change was located thousands of miles away, where people far removed from local matters made the important calls. The fate of the Lima refinery—and to some degree, the fate of Lima—did not lie in the hands of its mayor or other public officials but instead was measured out in spreadsheets at the BP headquarters in London, in decisions in BP corporate boardrooms, and in the very culture of BP itself.

"The corporate equivalent of perestroika"

BP's ultimate decision on the future of the Lima refinery would emerge out of financial calculations, certainly, but also, in a strange way, as the logical outgrowth of a gradual transformation occurring within the corporation's culture. For BP's first sixty years, its managers had reflected the company's imperial heritage as a quasi-official arm of the British Empire. Wherever in the Middle East that corporate strategy had assigned them, BP executives regarded themselves as semiofficial ambassadors of the crown. Royal directives issued from the BP headquarters in London, where the managing clique reigned as a tight-knit group. All six BP executive directors of the early 1950s shared the same Cambridge University background and had spent years rising to the top of a steep, centralized, pyramidal hierarchy. The company remained a tightly run, somewhat closed entity, driven by a huge and unwieldy bureaucracy.[17]

In the late 1960s, BP attempted to seriously alter such dynamics. To some degree, this cultural change followed the company's strategic change, as it switched its focus away from its roots in the Middle East to enter the American market with its big bonanza in Prudhoe Bay, and develop a huge new oil field in the North Sea. However, the cultural shift also emanated from key changes in personnel. This started in the 1960s, when, as its wealth and prestige attracted the top young talent in management, BP began an active graduate recruitment effort. BP took an emerging coterie of bright young men—for example, future corporate chairs like Peter Walters, David Simon, and Robert Horton—put them in responsible positions, and groomed them for the top. In 1964, BP enlisted a bright young Briton named Russell Seal; after stints in Asia and New York, he was brought back to London, where he took up duties in the supply department, the real training ground for future BP elite.[18]

Another of these rising stars was John Browne, a Cambridge-educated physicist who would, in the end, take BP to a level of glory and financial success that few of his predecessors could have imagined. With his Cambridge degree and later an M.S. in business from Stanford, Browne signed on with BP in 1966 as a university apprentice and then willingly followed company orders to wherever he was directed, including postings in such places as Anchorage, New York, London, and San Francisco. Superiors recognized his talent and initiative and rewarded him with steady promotion. In 1984, Browne advanced to group treasurer and chief executive of BP Finance International, and two years later, in the wake of BP's complete absorption of Sohio, he became executive vice president and chief financial officer of the new BP subsidiary of Standard Oil. Schaefer saw him as an "incredibly brilliant" and innovative manager who was absolutely devoted to BP. Never marrying, he lived with his mother for much of his adult life and worked constantly, regularly putting in fourteen- to sixteen-hour days through entire shifts of secretaries. Once Browne set his sights on a goal for his company, Schaefer said, he would not deviate an inch from his path toward it. In this determination, Browne reminded Schaefer of another chief executive he came to know, Lima's mayor, David Berger. Both men, Schaefer realized, were capable of an intense, bulldog-driven single-mindedness in pursuit of an objective, and neither would rest until he had won. If ever their spheres touched, he knew, they would generate some heat.[19]

But that would come later. By the late 1980s, the young recruits of the 1960s were staffing the upper echelon of BP management, and they were determined to launch an assault on the company's stodgy, heavily bureaucratic corporate culture. Two key appointments manifested the change. First, in 1989, BP's board of directors placed Browne in charge of BP's exploration division, and within months, he signaled the transition to a tough new management style and to a leaner, more efficient BP: Browne cut a tenth of the staff, sold off a wide range of secondary assets, and outsourced smaller operations such as finance in a relentless effort to cut costs. Browne also refocused exploration down from thirty countries to ten, but invested more resources in new areas, searching for another big bonanza. Second, in March 1990, Robert Horton took over from Peter Walters as BP's overall chief executive. He arrived in office determined to bring the same kind of changes to the corporation as a whole by remodeling BP into a hard-driving reflection of himself. Like his chief lieutenant, Browne, Horton had spent years in the United States, running BP Chemicals and then Sohio, where he had fully absorbed the adroit and even sometimes ruthless American style. Now he applied it to BP, sending shock waves reverberating to the company's core. By 1985, BP had already switched its internal financial management parameters to American dollars from British pounds. Soon after that, Horton created Project 1990—"the corporate equivalent," he said, "of perestroika and glasnost"—which axed entire layers of bureaucracy, wiped out dozens of committees, and merged the company's sixteen separate divisions. Horton eliminated nearly a thousand jobs at BP's corporate headquarters in downtown London and moved the entire operation from a skyscraper back to BP's smaller but elegant older headquarters. Like other corporations that moved rapidly to "decentralize" operations in these years, Horton wanted to shake the company into new and more efficient modes of operation; he wanted, for example, lower-level managers both to have the power to make decisions and to take responsibility for them.[20]

Horton and Browne were able to move their company in such a dramatically different direction partly because the new financial realities that BP faced allowed them—perhaps even forced them—to do so. The global oil market had changed drastically over the course of their professional careers. When they had started with BP in the late 1960s, the global demand for oil had pushed oil prices onto a high plateau, while the succeeding developments of the 1970s—the formation of OPEC, the penetration of the automobile market to the farthest corners of the developing world, and the soaring levels of global oil consumption—promised to keep them there permanently. Instead, by the middle 1980s, confounding all the experts predicting the emptying of the world's oil reserves and the end of the auto age, the world had entered an oil glut, and oil prices inexorably began to fall. When he took over as head of BP Exploration, Browne soon realized that dreams of oil prices rising above $30 or $40 a barrel were unrealistic; his company's costs were rising while prices were heading in the other direction. By the mid-1990s, oil prices had dropped two-thirds from their peak fifteen years earlier. Moreover, BP found itself financially pressed in other ways. In the stock market instability of the late 1980s, a group of Kuwaitis had acquired a minority of BP stock, forcing the corporation in 1989 to spend $4.2 billion to buy them out. In many ways, the new efficiencies Browne forced on his division were a matter of financial necessity.[21]

Those who missed the lesson paid the price, and among them was Robert Horton. He continued to believe as a matter of faith that oil prices would once again rise above $25 a barrel—and he spent accordingly; regal living for CEOs was another American business tradition he brought to BP. Horton designed his own office in appropriate style, bought his own corporate jet, accelerated acquisitions of what the trade press called "noncore business," and alienated many of his subordinates. Even Horton's cost-cutting could not keep pace with his level of spending, and corporate debt expanded tremendously. In 1992, when oil prices had not risen as Horton predicted they would, BP's board abruptly shelved him and brought in the No. 2 executive, David Simon, to run things. Simon had watched Horton and Browne carefully and fully grasped the new program. He spoke quietly, stressed the virtues of teamwork, sold the jet, and attacked the entire BP structure with a meat-ax. Within six months, he had peddled off a billion pounds' worth of BP's more peripheral assets—such as Kennecott Copper and Purina pet foods—and directed the elimination of more than twenty thousand jobs from different BP operations around the world. "We were selling all kinds of things trying to reduce debt," a BP executive remembered. By the mid-1990s, the company appeared to be back from its own doldrums. Financial analysts loved the new, slimmed-down company. "In the past two years," wrote the *Investors Chronicle* in 1995, "British Petroleum has been one of the stock market's best recovery stories." Its corporate profit levels were climbing once again, it was pumping more energies and resources into exploration, and the word went out on Wall Street, in Tokyo, and in London: buy BP.[22]

For all Simon's success, however, BP's Board of Directors apparently had intended his tenure to be transitional; in June 1995, they appointed the heir apparent, John Browne, as group managing director, BP's functioning CEO. Browne took the helm of a hugely successful corporation that had undergone extensive cultural and financial remodeling but still retained some continuities with its past. The two characteristics, in fact, existed at some tension with each other. On the one hand, perhaps reflecting a slight residue of colonial-era paternalism that the company had exhibited in its days as an arm of the British Empire, BP retained a firm corporate commitment to the health of the communities where it operated. As new BP top boss, Browne firmly accepted such responsibilities, demanding that the company actively promote the social and economic good of its partner cities and towns around the world. He was a hard-nosed businessman, not a sentimentalist; he reasoned that the company could flourish only if its home communities did so as well. "These efforts have nothing to do with charity," he insisted, "and everything to do with our bottom line." Whatever the rationale, BP's efforts along these lines were impressive. In Zambia, for example, the company donated two hundred solar-powered refrigerators to local health clinics so doctors could properly store antimalarial vaccines. In Peru, it ploughed $3 million into connecting remote areas of the country with a solar telecommunications system, while in Brazil, it spent $10 million on the creation of a photovoltaic power system for 1,800 schools. In Columbia, BP spent its resources on transforming certain of its waste materials into bricks that local people could use in home construction. BP funds facilitated the replanting of a forest around the Black Sea in Turkey and furnished computer-based technology for flood-control efforts in Vietnam.[23]

On the other hand, Browne epitomized the development of a new BP corporate style, a kind of take-no-prisoners efficiency that he helped create and that paralleled his own rise to the top. Perhaps the new global economy required such a stance toward the world, though in this respect, nothing was new about the oil business since the days of John D. Rockefeller. To the degree that the capitalist marketplace remained a competitive Darwinian jungle where only the strong survived, BP by the mid-1990s had fought its way, by tooth and claw, close to the top of the heap. As recently as 1992, it had stood eleventh in profitability among thirteen major oil refiners and marketers. Three years later, it ranked sixth, right behind Exxon and ahead of its historic rival, Shell Oil. The new corporate culture had permeated BP outposts around the world, and reigned supreme at the old Sohio headquarters in downtown Cleveland, now the nerve center for BP operations in the American Midwest. There the president of BP Oil in the United States, a competent, forty-nine-year old American named Steven Percy, enthusiastically preached the gospel of cost-cutting and corporate efficiency. When he had started in his position in 1992, BP was earning one cent for every dollar of capital it had invested in the oil business. Now it earned ten cents for every dollar, and Percy searched for ways to push it to fifteen.[24]

In some ways, as the company neared its centennial birthday, it found itself in a fundamental tension between what one might see as its heart and its mind. BP certainly remained committed to the good of the communities where it operated, but the priority given that agenda when it conflicted with the company's pursuit of its own financial bottom line remained unclear. John Browne remained confident that his corporation could pursue its own financial good and that of its partner communities at the same time—but what would happen in a situation where it decided it could not?

The "programme to reposition BP's international refinery network"

It would be BP's refineries that pushed this question. Through the later 1980s and into the 1990s, all around the world, the refineries of most oil giants had been losing money. As the global oil glut settled in and prices dropped, a nagging overcapacity had emerged in the international refining industry. Analysts noted that in 1995, refining margins in the United States hit twenty-year lows, and the industry had responded accordingly. Within the previous fifteen years, the United States alone had seen its number of refineries drop from 300 to 165, and the oil and gas industry in general had suffered the loss of half a million jobs in a single decade. The astute managers at BP, carefully tracking these trends, certainly would not have found it difficult to follow them to their conclusion. BP, Schaefer said, had never been particularly good at refining oil anyway. Like many of the major oil companies, it had gained fame and fortune from exploration, from big strikes, and from pioneering new fields and sending tankers of black crude back to Europe or America for someone else to deal with. For its own operations, Schaefer observed, it had preferred "the least sophisticated refineries possible to convert crude oil into products." It was the drama of the hunt for next big bonanza that quickened the hearts of the big oil executives.[25]

By the early 1990s, several BP executives mindful of the bottom line had begun to conclude that it would be better not to have many refineries at all. The chief champions of this view were some of the sharp new hires of the 1960s, notably Russell Seal and Rolf Stomberg, who had, like their colleague Browne, risen far up the company ladder in thirty years. In 1995, Stomberg had taken over from Seal as head of BP's refining, and in July he was appointed a managing director of BP, joining Seal, who remained a senior executive. Their high-level corporate positions ensured that both men operated in an immediate financial climate consumed with divesting BP of marginal operations and otherwise reducing BP's debt load. "They were under pressure to generate cash," Percy recalled, and the numbers on their spreadsheets highlighted particular ways to do it. At one point, Seal's office issued an internal corporate study—written by his special assistant, Gary Greve, once the manager of the Lima refinery—advocating that BP collapse its refining capacity around the world. When he headed BP's European refining operations, Seal had advocated the closure of a number of refineries on the continent, a stance admired as courageous by many in the industry. In fact, according to Schaefer, his promotion to the top echelon of BP executives came partly as a reward for such actions. This bias against refining was certainly shared by the top boss. Browne had headed BP's exploration division for six years and, like BP itself, had made his reputation in the "upstream" side of the oil business: the discovery of oil and the development of new fields. Refining, in contrast, was a dirty, complex, problem-laden activity, often a public relations headache now yielding diminishing profits. It was time, BP's developing consensus held, to reduce the company's refining capacity.[26]

The "initial step" in what Stomberg called the "programme to reposition BP's international refinery network" came in November 1995, with the sale of BP's refinery in Marcus Hook, Pennsylvania, for $235 million. Located not far from where the Delaware River emptied its waters into the Chesapeake Bay south of Philadelphia, the seventy-year-old plant had come to BP as part of its purchase of the holdings of the old Sinclair Oil Company. It was far from BP's other midwestern facilities and it was losing money; selling it presumably was not a hard decision for the company to make. The ensuing developments at Marcus Hook, however, would send chills up the spines of hourly workers at BP's other refineries and probably of oil workers everywhere. At the time of the sale, BP lacked a contract with the existing local of the Oil, Chemical, and Atomic Workers Union (OCAW), and the new purchaser, the Tosco Corporation, requested BP to shut down the plant before turning it over to Tosco. Almost immediately, Tosco announced that in order to make a profit it planned to reduce production at the plant by a fifth, eliminating 130 of its 530 jobs. Contract negotiations with OCAW soon collapsed, the workers walked out, and the refinery remained staffed by a skeleton crew until the following August. Then, with benefits and strike pay long having run out, the union caved in to Tosco. In the end, Tosco reemployed only 360 people, of whom only 215 were members of OCAW, a net loss of about a hundred union jobs. "They were holding all the big cards," the local OCAW president admitted ruefully. Whether or not the larger public cared much about union jobs, the episode at Marcus Hook also raised questions about hidden corporate motivations in refinery shutdowns. Marcus Hook was a big refinery that had processed 190,000 barrels of crude every day. Throughout the months it was closed, gasoline prices steadily climbed in the Northeast, and the laws of supply and demand certainly hinted at a connection. Soon, union activists and area congressional representatives began to ask some hard and public questions.[27]

The sale of Marcus Hook alone reduced BP's worldwide refining capacity by 10 percent, but Stomberg had clearly indicated that it was only a first step, and rumors soon began to swirl about its old Sohio refineries in Ohio. Of the two, in Toledo and Lima, the latter plant appeared the more endangered. Viewed only in a snapshot moment of 1990, it had fallen far from its glory days as "queen of the fleet." Clarence Roller, who had begun at the old Sohio refinery in 1969, recognized that the deterioration had begun in the last years under Standard's oversight, but many people thought it had accelerated under BP. Maintenance had been too long deferred, upgrades had not been made, and equipment had been neglected. Some workers blamed Greve in particular, viewing him as a "slash and burn" executive who readily opted for the cheap fix rather than the more costly investments that the refinery really required. Under Greve, the plant's number of plant inspectors fell, leaving the maintenance staff to patch things up as best they could as they watched hidden problems slowly accumulate. By 1995, the press had routinely begun to refer to BP's two Ohio plants as its "money-losing refinery operations," but the outlook seemed grimmer for Lima. Standard and then BP had long operated the two plants as "sister" refineries, designed to complement each other. But many of the key processes required for refining—industrial aspects like alkylation and desulphurization—remained at Toledo, which received processed crude from Lima via a complex of underground pipes.[28]

BP had quite clearly embarked on a program of disinvesting in refining and, viewed from the outside, the Lima plant seemed the logical choice for the next refinery to go. It was only when examined from inside the plant that things appeared differently. The "queen of the fleet" had been in a state of sad decline in 1990, but in the ensuing five years, marvelously interesting developments had occurred.

"Don't just fix it; improve it"

Schaefer later recalled that he realized the magnitude of the task ahead on his very first day on the job. Just appointed as commercial manager for BP's Midwest and Southwest operations, Schaefer met with his immediate boss, senior vice president Michael Press, to learn of his new duties. "Well, Jim," Press began, "I brought you into this job because if there's anyone who could do something about this, it's you. But I don't know if this situation can be salvaged." He handed Schaefer a portfolio containing numerous studies of BP's two Ohio refineries by BP's corporate management in Cleveland and London. All of the reports pointed toward a single conclusion: profitability at both plants was spiraling downward. "All of the options are bad," Press summarized. "Further decline is inevitable, and eventually we're going to have to close one or both of the refineries unless you come up with a different plan." He didn't know if Schaefer could do it, Press admitted, but he pledged, "I'll give you all the support that you need."[29]

Press was right on several counts: the situation was grim and he also seemed to have picked the right person to try to reverse it. By the time of his appointment to manage BP's refineries in Ohio, Schaefer had already accumulated a broad range of experience in managing industrial facilities and developed an uncanny instinct for diagnosing corporate problems. On the face of it, he appeared a sharp corporate whiz kid on the fast track to the top. The son of a Cleveland-area engineer, he had absorbed college-level chemistry in high school, graduated at the top of his class, and won a scholarship to study chemical engineering at Catholic University in Washington, D.C., where he filled his spare hours as captain of the tennis team and student body president. After four positions in three years at an Exxon refinery in New Jersey, he completed a Harvard M.B.A. and then steadily scaled the corporate ladder at several firms. With an iron ore company called Hanna, he correctly forecast the collapse of the mining industry and addressed the firm's senior management and its board of directors on the need to begin planning for such a possibility. Drawn back into oil, Schaefer left Hanna and joined Sohio in operations planning for the company's crude oil training and marine fleet activities. He found a way to save millions of dollars, so impressing his bosses that they appointed him special assistant to the company president, where he found himself sitting in on corporate strategy sessions. At the same time, however, Schaefer had come to a more nuanced view of the business world than his resume perhaps indicated. During summer breaks from study in high school and college, he had worked in factories and at manual labor jobs like bricklaying and plumbing, where he had learned the language of unionism and developed a special respect for people who labored with their hands.[30]

Now, in 1991, he sat in his office at BP's Cleveland headquarters preparing to tackle the thorny problem that his boss had laid in his lap. First, he decided to work out an answer on-site. Renting an apartment in Perrysburg, Ohio, a convenient twenty minutes south of the Toledo Refinery and an hour north of Lima, he spent so many hours over the next three years commuting between the two facilities that he burned through three hundred books on tape. The solution had leapt out at him after his first sixty days, however. BP's two old refineries, he realized, were truly mammoth facilities, designed to process crude at much greater rates than they currently were. Greater levels of production would be more efficient, so, at a Refining Department conference for BP's managers, he laid out a plan to increase output levels by a fifth in three years. "They'd been studying how to run this refinery with less and less throughput," he recalled later, "and I said, 'No, your challenge is to figure out how to operate this refinery at higher outputs than at any time in its history, and here's how we're going to do that.'" After he walked the audience through his plan, Schaefer could sense a growing enthusiasm. "It was just so much more fun to think about growing rather than declining."

Douglas Farris, BP's Ohio refineries manager, expanded the session, calling in BP staffers from a variety of groupings—refining, marketing, pipelines, and retail—to a conference at Maumee Bay State Park, on the shores of Lake Erie east of Toledo. For the first two days, Farris and Schaefer listened as managers vented an accumulated backlog of complaints. Then they called a halt. Massive problems obviously existed, they admitted, but what are we going to do about them? London executives had asked for a miracle, the managers told the audience soberly. BP had given up hope of the two refineries running in the black but had also given them three years to increase their joint earnings by $7 million. How can we do that, Schaefer asked the audience? Hours of brainstorming produced a variety of suggestions before a key moment came. If we implement all the suggestions, Schaefer wondered aloud, perhaps we could increase earnings by seven million in the first year alone, and double them the year after that. It was an old technique in personnel management—challenging workers with a lofty goal—but then people in the audience began upping the number, thinking beyond the limits of what they had previously thought realistic. By the end of the conference, the participants had settled on what were probably impossible goals: to increase earnings not by the $7 million over three years that London had requested but by $20 million each year over the three-year period, for a total of $60 million in improvements. It was an audacious idea, this "$20–40–60 million plan," and Farris decided it needed a more dignified name. To manage the program, he announced, they would meet at the same state park every three months, where they would together take the pulse of what he termed the Maumee Mission.[31]

The harder part, they knew, would be selling the plan to the workers. BP top executives had already poisoned whatever well of good feeling had remained among the Ohio refinery workers by enthusiastically embracing the exciting new gospel of "reengineering" that had swept through top corporate management in the 1990s. The movement had begun with an article in the *Harvard Business Review* in 1990 and had then been reinforced by a 1993 book by management specialists Michael Hammer and James Champy. Quickly translated into fifteen languages and selling nearly 2 million copies, *Reengineering the Corporation* soon became the best-selling management book of the decade. The authors intensified their influence delivering high-priced seminars to eager corporate heads around the world and by a series of successor books. Asserting that all previous models of corporate management were now hopelessly outdated in the new world of a global business environment, they had come, they boldly announced, to replace "yesterday's paradigm" with a new one. "If American companies want to become winners again," Hammer and Champy declared, "they will have to look at how they got their work done. It is as simple and formidable as that." In breezy, confident tones, they laid out the required program of corporate reshaping, expressed in neat little bullet points—"checks and controls are reduced"; "Several jobs are combined into one"—that belied both the fear tactics underlying the analysis and the thorny problems that, they freely admitted, most corporations would encounter in achieving their desired results. In spite of this, corporate heads across the United States and Europe eagerly took Hammer and Champy's gospel to heart. Within two years, the term "reengineering" had permeated the management literature. Major consulting firms and dozens of smaller ones had reoriented their practices along these lines, and by 1994, upwards of 70 percent of more than eight hundred firms surveyed in the United States and Europe had "engaged in 'significant' re-engineering efforts."[32]

By the time the Maumee Mission was launched, BP had become one of these newly reengineered corporations. Some of the bullet points that Hammer and Champy proscribed (for example, "peoples' [*sic*] roles change—from controlled to empowered") were later ones that lay at the heart of the refinery's transformation—an ironic development, since, in the main, what reengineering brought to the Lima refinery was headache and heartache. As BP's local public relations manager, Judy Gilbert, later recalled, in the early 1990s, BP hired business consultants from Anderson to reengineer the Lima and Toledo plants "and they tore the structure on paper apart. I mean, everything was up for grabs, you could change everything." The consultants refigured job descriptions, combined and separated positions, issued new titles by the score, and "totally reworked" the management organization chart. So confusing were the results that "it took us months to figure out what the new terminology was" for a simple maintenance worker. As for the reception of this program among the rank and file at the refinery, Gilbert summarized, "It was an understatement to say that it was unpopular. It was chaotic. When I say that people hated it, that just doesn't describe it. People were furious." It was, moreover, a direct and personal anger, because reengineering also meant, both at BP and elsewhere, the elimination of a lot of jobs. As summarized by one business technology magazine, "reengineering ultimately became a dirty word in business, most known for its predominant side effect of downsizing." In Lima, about the time that Schaefer and Farris began the program of plant revitalization, Clarence Roller had just witnessed the termination of his boss as part of the reengineering efforts. When Schafer first met him, Roller said, he was "beyond angry" and profoundly demoralized.[33]

As a result, the Maumee Mission got off to a rocky start. At an early meeting with refinery workers in Toledo, Schaefer entered a room to encounter "a really, really tense atmosphere," with union members lining the walls, arms folded across their chests, and staring at him, many of them sporting the various buttons and insignias they had worn during different strikes. By nature an earnest and cultivated man, Schaefer soon learned that he sometimes had to confront his most vocal critics to make progress with the rest. At one of his first Toledo meetings, he laid out the plan to a group of about eighty people, and one old worker growled out loudly, "We've heard all this old shit before." "And I looked at him," Schaefer remembered, "and said, 'No, you haven't. This is *new* shit . . . . This is different. This is going to change this refinery and you guys are going to be part of it.'" Later he learned that the worker in question was a reliable grouser, and once he had faced him down, "the rest of the audience just erupted in questions."[34]

The big breakthrough with the hourly employees came in the context of such individual meetings, where Schaefer began to practice a kind of a "grassroots-based management style." In his years in corporate management, he knew some executives who seemed almost "afraid" to actually venture out into the plant. But this was not the case with Schaefer. From his own days as a factory worker, he enjoyed working with hourly employees and union people and knew they could furnish a wealth of valuable ideas if management took time to listen. So he began to cultivate such suggestions with the help of what emerged as his secret weapon: pizza. Early on in his work at the Lima refinery, he called the local OCAW president, Hugh Winterstellar, told him he wanted to begin having lunch with the workers, and invited him to attend all of the meetings, assuring him, "I want you to be comfortable that I'm not trying anything subversive or anything." Winterstellar attended the first such meeting and found the new manager to be doing exactly what he said he would do, sincerely cultivating ideas. Winterstellar said he didn't need to come to subsequent meetings and sent out the word along the union grapevine that "it's okay to go to lunch with Jim." Schaefer began meeting with groups of six to eight people at a time, always bringing along pizza or hoagie sandwiches for the group, and in three years he had lunched with the nearly thousand employees at both refineries.[35]

Slowly, like one of the engines at the old locomotive works, the project began to pick up steam. It took a while at first; managers had solicited ideas before and then done nothing with them. Schaefer recalled a key early meeting. A group of workers told him that any time pumps in the distant tank fields had a problem, they had to call maintenance, which had to send out a truck. Hours later, they'd have the pumps up and going again. But all of these men, he knew, had been working with tools at home all of their adult lives. If they had the tools, they could diagnose the pumps themselves and dramatically speed the repairs, they told Schaefer. In fact, one of the men knew a hardware store in town that had the kind of toolboxes they needed on sale right then. Fine, Schaefer told them. He'd have the requisition for them within an hour—and he did. By the end of the day, he recalled, everyone in the refinery had heard of the event and was anticipating lunches with him "because they all had ideas they wanted heard and acted upon."[36]

Soon the suggestions came pouring in, so many that Schaefer sometimes found it difficult to keep track of them all. Out on the far reaches of the refinery, for instance, were certain mechanisms called propane and propylene cavern pumps. They were expensive and time-consuming to repair and failed regularly. One worker, noticing that they failed most frequently during electrical storms, reasoned that since these pumps extended metal deep into the earth, they might be so well grounded as to actually attract lightning. Why not put up some lightning rods? Once they did so, the pumps' rate of failure declined precipitously. Workers identified another pump that broke down repeatedly because of heavy vibrations, and then solved the problem by leveling its foundation with a laser. In fact, pump reliability became an area of particular success. This was an important variable, because refineries need a lot of pumps; the Lima refinery by itself had more than a thousand of them. Across the industry, the mean time between failure (MTBF) of the pumps averaged thirteen months (that is, each pump averaged thirteen months between repairs). When workers at the Lima refinery launched what their managers began to call their "continuous improvement plan," their MTBF was at twelve months. Exxon, they learned, had a rate of more than double that, and they took it as a personal challenge to beat their competitor. By the time he left BP in 1996, Schaefer saw the MTBF at Lima reach forty-four months, and recently he learned that workers there had it up to eighty-four months.[37]

Another example of a problem solved by the workers concerned a particular piece of refinery apparatus called the fluid catalytic cracker unit, or, in oil worker parlance, the "cat cracker." The refinery paid several bored employees to sit next to it and watch a dial all day long to make sure it maintained its rate of a certain number of daily barrels. Schaefer encouraged the workers to see if they could figure out how to nudge the cat cracker up a notch. They began discussing ways they could do it, and the next shift took up the challenge to see if it could get the rate still higher. Before long, they were pushing an extra 3,000 barrels through the cat cracker every day. With oil running at $3.49 a barrel, this produced an extra $10,000 a day, or $3 million a year. The ingenuity and dedication of Lima's newly reenergized workforce amazed Schaefer. One particularly telling instance of this concerned the lit flares shooting out of the refinery. Locals might regard these flames as emblematic of industrial production, but the refinery workers knew that they really consisted of the release through burning of valuable gasses, symbolizing lost resources and revenue. Almost 1.5 percent of the oil entering the Lima refinery went up the flare as waste, and in a refinery processing 150,000 barrels of crude every day, that 1.5 percent equaled the loss of nearly 2,500 barrels daily, at the cost of $20 each. During periodic shutdowns, workers placed sonic devices on the huge pipes that traversed the refinery and listened for sounds of a flow. If they heard the right noise, they traced it back to where two pipes joined, and then to smaller pipes and eventually back to leaky valves. "It's like they were detectives," Schaefer realized, "going through the entire refinery tracing these leaks"; he likened the process to "following tree roots down to the very tip of the source." In three years' time they were so successful in reducing the flaring that the refinery achieved one of the best such rates in the BP world, second only to a refinery in Germany that released its gasses into underground caverns and had no flaring at all. In fact, the refinery received at least one call from a cranky neighbor, who demanded to know what problem they were concealing. He had been living nearby for many years, he said, and could always tell when the refinery had shut down by watching the flare. Now the flare was gone, and he kept insisting they tell him the whole truth about why it had disappeared.[38]

As the hourly workers were enjoying seeing their good ideas implemented at last, refinery personnel specialists like Paul Monus and Jim Griffith worked to extend the same spirit of "continuous improvement" to midlevel management. Convinced that within the workforce were "ten years of good ideas waiting to be released," Schaefer began meeting regularly with a grizzled old section foreman named Steve Watters. Other section heads, Schaefer knew, carefully watched Watters as a model, and if he could break through to him, the others would follow. So Schafer began pressing Watters for more than the usual reports that "nothing was wrong"; instead he begged for just two or three suggestions for improvements. It took a while, but within three years, foremen like Watters were regularly handing Schaefer upwards of thirty sheets of paper detailing specific improvements that their sections had made. Meanwhile, Monus and Griffith made headway with a board game called the Manufacturing Game. Created by the management guru Winston Ledet, the game required both salaried and hourly workers to role play, to break down and solve hypothetical problems together, and to exchange ideas. Since they provided people with opportunities to air long-held grievances with each other, the sessions sometimes became emotional, and union leaders resisted the process at first. In spring 1995, they held organized protests at the meetings, folding their arms and refusing to join in the discussions. At one point, Griffith and the plant manager, Donovan Kuenzli, discussed privately whether or not they had the means to force the unions to participate, but slowly union resistance broke down. In three years, upwards of 95 percent of the refinery employees had played the game, and while some attitudes never changed—Roller dismissed the project as a "damned board game" that "would drive you crazy"—others saw potential for conflict resolution and, through it, progress. Union boss Winterstellar watched carefully for a while and remarked to Monus that it was "good to see that you company people are finally listening to the union people about the problems around here." Kuenzli attended many sessions and bore the heat patiently, partly because of a personal commitment he had made. In contrast to many of his predecessors, who had moved on to other positions, Kuenzli had decided he wanted to retire at the Lima refinery. So he attended many sessions, role-playing problems from a union perspective, and seemed responsive to the critiques he received.[39]

What swept through both the Lima and the Toledo refineries as a result of such efforts was a whole culture of improvement. Schaefer remembered hearing an anecdote that a number of people passed around; whether apocryphal or not, it epitomized what had occurred. Two refinery mechanics, the story went, were having a conversation about a problem they had just tackled on a particular piece of equipment. "I just fixed it," one of them had reported. "What do you mean, you 'just fixed it'?" demanded the other. "Don't just fix it; improve it." That kind of culture and commitment achieved some amazing results. In 1995, at the Lima refinery alone, the collective improvements achieved by the workforce saved more than $12 million. In the end, the effort to reduce flaring saved $10 million in formerly wasted product all by itself.

As Schaefer and other senior staff began to total up the cumulative impact of such changes, they realized they would have a different kind of narrative to report back to London. BP's top management in London, having lost confidence that the refineries could ever run in the black again, directed them in 1991 to try to improve their performance by $7 million. Instead, in a burst of crazy but probably misplaced enthusiasm, their senior staff in Ohio had launched the impossible $20–40–60 million goals of the Maumee Mission. Three years later, as Schaefer and others examined their numbers, they were immensely pleased at what they found. They had achieved their successive goals of $20 million, then $40 million, and then $60 million in those years, improvements dramatic enough not only to pull the two refineries out of the red but to achieve profits of between $10 million and $20 million annually. When an expert from the Saloman Brothers, a firm of respected industry analysts, visited the Lima plant, he told Schaefer that it was the fastest-improving refinery in the country, if not the world.[40]

Equally exciting to the senior American executives was how the changes had happened. In the end, Schaefer knew, all he really had done was to permit an "enormous explosion of creativity" to occur. The workforces at the two Ohio refineries had not knocked themselves out only for the abstract and disconnected goal of increasing BP's profits. From the beginning, the planners of the Maumee Mission had hooked the workforces' own financial interests into the plan. All gains made by the refineries, they announced, would be "gainshared" with all employees and all at the same percentage rate, from local refinery management down to the janitors who swept their floors. Every six months accountants at both refineries wrote out checks to a thousand employees that shared the plants' productivity gains with its workforce. Schaefer suspected that local car dealers in Lima and Toledo benefited from the policy, because in three years, the refinery management paid out $8 million in gainshare bonuses to the combined workforce.[41]

However, even the prospect of personal financial gain would not by itself have been enough to sustain the excitement that had accompanied the new culture of improvement. From the beginning, Schaefer had seen the potential in the Lima workforce, and as he became acquainted with the hourly employees, he noted how many held second jobs like removing tree stumps and saw the "mechanical inventiveness" many had inherited from farm childhoods. "Lima people work hard," he realized, "and there's a lot of innate intelligence in the Lima workforce." If he could combine the intense local work ethic with the bright mental capacities of the workers, then "amazing things can happen." He also saw that, in contrast with Toledo, where the loyalty of many of the hourly employees lay with the union, in Lima the primary focus of allegiance was not the union, and certainly not BP, but the refinery itself. Lima refinery workers understood what Schaefer and other management officials were doing, and responded with a kind of driven enthusiasm. For years, they had been doing the actual labor of refining oil, but few of their bosses had ever bothered to ask them how they could do it better. Now they saw management not only soliciting but also implementing their suggestions, and Schaefer was right: amazing things had happened as a result. All they could do now was watch, wait, and see if it all mattered to the senior executives in BP's corporate headquarters in London.[42]

"I could see how upset he was in the improvements"

BP executives responded to the amazing success stories coming out of their two refineries in Ohio in different ways. To the BP senior management at the old Sohio headquarters in downtown Cleveland, the numbers they received from Lima and Toledo initially seemed hard to believe. They had been aware of the $20–40–60 million plan from the beginning and first regarded it with a skeptical eye. Steven Percy, president of BP Oil in the Midwest, journeyed to the meetings of the Maumee Mission enthusiasts, participated in the discussions, and responded to the newfound energies as would any responsible manager in his position: he gave the plan his blessing and then quietly watched the numbers. Percy may have had more hope for improvements in Cleveland; he knew the long record of decline at the refineries. But the numbers he kept receiving from northwest Ohio were undeniable, and slowly his sense of possibility grew.[43]

Likewise, BP senior executives in London had a hard time initially grasping what was occurring in Ohio (though, as chemicals plant manager Walpole knew, they certainly were aware of the upward trend of Ohio profits). One day, when he was visiting the Cleveland headquarters, Schaefer ran into one of London's top people, an American in charge of planning for BP worldwide, who told him, "You know, Jim, we really appreciate your enthusiasm and your effort. The strategy that you proposed for these refineries is really insightful. But it's completely unrealistic." After all, the London man continued, "You're talking about eventually running these refineries at 300,000 barrels per day, and you can't possibly run that much through the refineries. It's physically impossible." Moreover, "even if you could run that much through the refineries, you can't sell it, there's no market for it. That's why we think you're doing the best that you can, but it's inevitable that this is going to fail. You can't run 300,000 barrels a day; you can't sell 300,000 barrels a day."[44]

"You haven't been back for about six months, and I haven't really publicized this," Schaefer replied, "but do you know how much throughput we're up to now?"

No, the official confessed. "How much are you running?"

"Today we're running 317,000 barrels a day," Schaefer informed him, "and we're selling every bit of it." Schaefer found the executive's reaction almost bizarre; rather than becoming excited or pleased, he appeared surprisingly "crestfallen." Schaefer encountered similarly peculiar attitudes elsewhere. Equally unsettling was a report he heard from his immediate superior, Michael Press, who relayed Russell Seal's comments to him during Press's recent visit from London. "Russell was really upset over the Lima turnaround," Press told Schaefer, "because of all the improvements you're making." Seal told him, Press revealed, that "'we should not have spent any money on improvements at the refinery.'"

"What do you mean?" Schaefer wanted to know. All the improvements they had made "have quick paybacks; some of these things are going to pay back in eight months, fifteen months, whatever, we're going to make a lot more money on that." Press agreed with Schaefer, but admitted, "This gives me a bad feeling, but I could see how upset he was in the improvements. I don't know if I should read anything more into that or not."[45]

Schaefer, Percy, and other senior Ohio management did what they could to reverse London's attitudes. In 1995, BP's board of directors flew to Cleveland to look over the Ohio numbers. The Maumee Mission was already under way, and Percy ticked off all the good things they were doing. The directors, Percy remembered, saw that costs were going down, but also saw, from Percy's own charts, that refining margins continued to fall as well. On other occasions, Schaefer would recite the accumulating arguments for closure—that refining had become a "miserable business," that closing one refinery would reduce supply and perhaps raise demand and prices for BP's remaining products—and then argue in rebuttal that it was "the less sophisticated, higher-cost refineries [that] should close, not a BP refinery." Lima and Toledo, he went on to say, had become so inextricably integrated that the closure of one by itself would be extremely problematic, and governmental environmental regulations accentuated the cost and difficulty. Moreover, since the two refineries together were producing about half of the total oil product consumed in the state, closing one facility would suddenly award BP's competitors access to a quarter of the Ohio market—in a competitive business environment where firms normally scrabbled hard for an additional 1 percent.

BP's refining was struggling in part, Schaefer and others knew, because its marketing was closing stations so rapidly and losing market share. Schaefer remembered attending a conference of regional managers in 1994–95 when he publicly pressed the company's head of retail in the Midwest for BP's current market share and she finally admitted that she didn't know what it was. Later he discovered that BP's regional market share had fallen from around 35 percent in earlier years to less than 25 percent by 1995, partly as a result of deliberate corporate policy. In pursuit of higher rates of return on investment and greater volume per station, BP closed more than half of its six thousand gas stations in Ohio from 1992 to 1996. In the face of such declining demand, BP retail executives were supporting the closure of one of the two Ohio refineries, and Schaefer later admitted that the sag in BP's market share meant that BP in reality did not need the full production of two large refineries; at best, it needed about one and a half. (The remaining production was sold to third parties to allow high utilization rates at the refineries.)[46]

To expect BP's high command to rethink its decision to close refineries was probably an unrealistic hope, given the hierarchical nature of corporate governance. The decision, after all, had been building for years. Percy, having been stationed in Britain in the late 1980s, recognized that BP's strategy to exit from refining was fully under way. While most Western corporations exist and operate within the framework of popular democracies amenable—at least in theory—to the popular will, employees quickly learn to leave most democratic pretensions behind them when they report for work in the morning. Historically, corporations have been run by strict hierarchies that do not allow much questioning of established policy directives, particularly after the consensus has solidified under senior management. This trend may have intensified in the 1990s, a decade which one business historian has called the age of the "imperial CEO." Once a corporate chief decides on a course, he or she relies on subordinates to carry it out. Such subordinates are by nature reluctant to revisit a CEO's decision even if they disagree with it. Overturning an agreed-on course of action can cause tremendous upset within a corporation. Doing so upsets the clear sense of direction established by the high command, poses a grievous loss of face for the reigning CEO, and seriously jars the established chain of command.[47]

Although BP may well have permitted its senior management more autonomy and greater latitude to question established decisions than other corporations, the growing corporate momentum to close the Lima refinery left senior American managers deeply disturbed. They knew what the workers had accomplished, the incredible rate of improvement in both refineries, and their ongoing and triumphant ascent out of the red. In light of these achievements, these senior American managers pushed their superiors to justify their case for closure in hard numbers, and London obliged. Late in 1994, BP London directed Schaefer to get the best analyst he could find and conduct an in-depth study on the relative value of keeping open two Ohio refineries or only one. Schaefer was happy to explore the question; at the very least it would give him the chance to describe in detail all the improvements they were making. So he hired the best person he could, a "top-notch refining expert," who went at the question, reviewing reports, analyzing the numbers, and scrutinizing both refineries carefully. Then Schaefer and the expert flew to London and presented their conclusion: that in all circumstances, in every case, for BP, the two Ohio refineries were more profitable and efficient than running one by itself. London's reaction, Schaefer remembered, was "cool": the study contradicted Browne's larger strategy directives and Seal's decade-long program of shutting refineries. Schaefer must have become too close to his work, the London office reasoned, in a manner that clouded his ability to examine the numbers objectively. So London directed senior American executive Paul Fowler to redo the study with a different analyst. In early 1995, Fowler brought in a renowned oil refinery expert from Australia for the job, and together he and Schaefer sifted through the records from Lima and Toledo again. It took them months, Schaefer recalled; there could not have been an angle on the relative profitability of the refineries that they could have missed. Fowler and Percy once again took the results and presented them to London, demonstrating conclusively that in every case, the system of two combined refineries was better than one.[48]

In retrospect, it seems clear that it was not the American managers who were working from preconceived ideas, but London's. London had laid out a good deal of money for expert opinion, yet when the hard data they had paid for came in, they rejected it because it did not fit with the strategy they had previously agreed on. In the end, the two studies made no difference. Word came back from London: close the Lima refinery. Later on, Percy better understood BP's rationale. Certainly, the refinery was now making money, they admitted, but at an investment of $16 million a year. How much more profit could the company make, London wondered, if it invested that sum somewhere else? At the time, however, Percy and Fowler were deeply unhappy at the directive, according to Schaefer, and "took real risks" in conveying their unhappiness to London. Fowler chose to leave the company shortly thereafter, perhaps partly as a result of its decision. As for Schaefer himself, he recalled, he was stunned. Hearing the news in a phone call, "I absolutely couldn't believe that they couldn't accept" the results of the two studies. In his four years as manager of BP's two Ohio refineries, he had been haunted by what would happen to the workers if the Maumee Mission failed. Throughout that period, he regularly had trouble sleeping at night. Always, at the back of his mind, hovered the knowledge that "if there were any slips it could cost hundreds of jobs and hundreds of families would really be harmed by this. I had that pressure, the kind of thing that I couldn't talk to anybody about." Now to hear that, despite their dedicated labor and the many improvements they had successfully implemented, the workers at the Lima refinery were soon to enter unemployment lines—to understand that it was the success, not the failure, of the Maumee Mission that had sealed the refinery's fate—simply floored Schaefer. When he heard the news, he remembered later, "it took the air out of my lungs."[49]

To quell objections from BP's American executives, London compromised, telling them that instead of closing the refinery immediately, they could try to sell it. In January 1996, newspapers both in Ohio and around the world blared out the news. "BP Selling Rockefeller Legacy: Lima Refinery," headlined the *Cleveland Plain Dealer.* "BP Oil Co. put a piece of its John. D. Rockefeller legacy on the auction block yesterday," the story led. "The Company put its Lima refinery up for sale."[50]

"Deep Well"

For most people in Lima, apart from its mayor, the headlines of January 1996 were the first inkling any of them had received that the refinery might be in trouble. The portfolio that Press had privately handed to Schaefer in 1991 laid out the decline of the refineries in Lima and Toledo, but about the same time, local refinery manager Farris assured the public that the Lima plant had just come off the most profitable and productive year in its history, and expected another. In fact, through at least the mid-1990s, local worry with regard to BP centered on the possible economic costs of environmental legislation, such as the federal Clean Air Act of 1990, and muttered threats from the chemical plant about possible job losses if its managers did not get their way in the matter of deep well injection pressures. By 1995, the *Lima News* had begun to trace the financial malaise hitting the nation's refining industry, but it also reported the gigantic profits reaped in that year by BP International.[51]

Moreover, many local people were aware of the exciting series of developments reverberating through the refinery itself, for senior BP executives in both Lima and Cleveland had loudly trumpeted the transformation wrought by the Maumee Mission. Noting that productivity at the Lima plant had risen some 30 percent, BP executives at a national conference called such results "spectacular" and directed other refineries to adopt similar innovations. In the February 1996 edition of the refinery's newsletter, plant manager Donovan Kuenzli announced that in the previous year, employees there had set thirty new records for operation efficiency or improvements reinforcing the plant's total value, and Schaefer outlined the $30 million in income enhancements that the refinery had recently completed, most of them requiring no major capital investment. "BP's Lima refinery has improved so markedly that it generates profit even at low refining margins," Schaefer stated. In the April 1996 newsletter, BP's vice president, David Atton, called the Lima plant a sophisticated refinery, affirming that the facility was "in the top quartile in product yields and costs." With such a profitable, technologically advanced, and improved refinery, and given BP's rapidly accelerating profits worldwide, who could blame local people for continuing to view the plant as an enduring and stable economic anchor of the community?[52]

Privately, however, Berger was worried. By the spring of 1995, as senior American BP executives in Cleveland were scrambling to head off London's growing consensus in favor of closing the Lima refinery, the city's mayor was beginning to pick up danger signals of his own. For years, Berger, along with the county commissioners, had met periodically, often monthly, with local refinery managers in downtown Lima to talk over common concerns. Through these meetings, Berger and Schaefer had developed a mutual respect and even a kind of friendship within the professional limitations imposed by their positions. Berger found Schaefer to be a model of professional rectitude; he always, Berger recalled, "walked the line between what he could share with me versus what he could not." Through these meetings with senior refinery staff, Berger learned of their ambition to put Lima in the top tier of the world's refineries, and of the amazing climate of improvement developing in the plant that was bringing them closer to that goal. However, while he was naturally pleased at all the improvements at the refinery, which seemed likely to enhance its value to its corporate ownership, the mayor also began to piece together something of the larger set of financial considerations in London that might induce BP's top executives there to dispense with the plant anyway.[53]

Berger had also received more direct signals of trouble. In August 1995, for example, he had been disquieted by two incidents at a small but elegant banquet in a downtown Cleveland hotel. BP's board of directors had flown in for a series of meetings with Cleveland's political and business community, and the city's elite had gathered to inaugurate the conversations in fine style. Perhaps big-city mayors routinely operate in such high-powered environments, but for Berger, from little Lima, the evening was especially memorable. The dinner was held in a richly paneled dining room overlooking the Cleveland skyline, and Berger could look around the room and identify the luminaries assembled there: former Ohio governor Richard Celeste, several high-profile bankers and businesspeople, the publisher of the *Cleveland Plain Dealer*, and, of course, BP's top command. Berger had been invited because he was the mayor of one of BP's stakeholder communities in Ohio, and the maître d' led him to a table that included the mayor of Oregon, Ohio—the suburb where the Toledo refinery was located—and seated him between two BP executives. On his left, Berger met the president of BP chemicals worldwide, and on his right, he found himself talking with Russell Seal—actually, Sir Russell Seal, because he had been knighted by the queen.

Halfway through the festivities, about an hour into the dinner, he recalled, Cleveland's mayor, Michael White, suddenly appeared. White had just returned from Columbus, where he had met with Ohio's governor, George Voinovich, and inked a deal to provide state support for the proposed new football stadium for the Cleveland Browns. White, Berger recalled, was "higher than a kite," just "thrilled. And he gave this incredible stem-winding speech about all the things that were going on in Cleveland," about how the city had made its way back from its dark days when it had suffered as the butt of national jokes, and "why it was such a terrific thing to be part of Cleveland at this time." At his climax, White suddenly turned to John Browne and David Simon of BP and asked them, pointedly, if BP was going to be a permanent part of the wonderful future unfolding in his city. Both of them stood up and issued clear and unqualified assurances that, of course, BP would. "There was absolutely no hedging to the commitments made by BP," Berger remembered, "to the fact that they would always be part of the Cleveland community." The crowd greeted the news with enthusiastic and sustained applause.

The second incident that stuck with Berger from that evening was his conversation with Seal. As the dinner proceeded, and between speeches, Berger listened as Seal laid out his argument for how BP "could grow the business by collapsing its refining capacity. And I really came away pretty shaken by the idea that here was somebody in this very large company who had lost faith in refining as a fundamental way to make money."[54]

The more Berger looked into the kinds of considerations underlying Seal's comments, the greater his disquiet grew. He realized that the five hundred jobs at the Lima refinery were in deep trouble. As he dug into the matter privately, he was helped greatly by a few sources he had developed inside BP itself. A few individuals in BP's ranks, Berger discovered, had also grown discomfited by the corporation's apparent decision to discard its refinery in Lima. As time went on, these individuals began, in various quiet and private ways, to share their information with the city's mayor. On one significant occasion, a source deep inside BP's American headquarters in Cleveland passed Berger an internal company memo that clearly laid out the company's plans for an alternative source of gasoline supply to replace the refinery's output, long before it publicly announced final plans to shut the facility down. In fact, throughout Berger's escalating confrontation with BP, he came to rely heavily on the wisdom and advice of another executive placed fairly high in BP's own hierarchy. This source suggested certain lines of analysis for the mayor to explore and, especially, additional questions to ask, lines of inquiry so astute that Berger often knew far more about the corporation's internal decisions than its executives were publicly telling him. Though BP apparently remained unaware of Berger's conduit of private information, members of the local press corps spent so much time fruitlessly guessing at the person's identity that they finally decided to give the individual a name. Watergate had its "Deep Throat," *Lima News* editor Ray Sullivan remembered, and since Berger apparently had developed his own parallel source in the realm of oil refining, Sullivan suggested they call the figure "Deep Well."[55]

Berger's increasing worries stimulated him to a new level of activism, aided now by his new private contacts. He called the regional public radio station to challenge its routine use of the phrase "money-losing Lima refinery" and moved to develop allies among other Ohio public officials. Deep Well agreed with Berger that he should contact Governor Voinovich, both to discern what the state knew about BP's plans and to urge state government involvement in forestalling a closure or facilitating a sale. Voinovich, Berger learned, had a personal relationship with John Browne at least a decade old, begun when Voinovich had served as mayor of Cleveland and Browne had been stationed there as BP's head of the old Sohio. Perhaps the governor would have some special access to BP decision making—if Berger could prevail on him to use it. Deep Well also called the mayor's attention to an article appearing in London's *Financial Times* in November 1995. The piece laid out BP's movement toward divestment of its refineries, Browne's disdain for facilities he saw as second tier, and the difficulty that BP would encounter in closing its European refineries because of the stricter regulations imposed by European governments. The article so alarmed Berger that he sent off a careful letter to Browne, citing the *Financial Times* piece as reinforcing rumors "running rampant in the community" about BP's intentions toward Lima's refinery, and stating that he was eager to talk with Browne personally about the matter, even if it meant a trip to London. Berger admitted that he was "tremendously concerned" about the five hundred jobs at the refinery, and he urged Browne to do what he could to restore trust. In case Browne had somehow missed the gravity of the issue to Lima, Berger bared his teeth a little. Over the years, he reminded BP's chief executive, many in the community had stood "shoulder to shoulder" with BP against "some minority environmentalist views which were vociferously voiced," particularly on the issue of deep well injections for BP's chemical plant. It had taken much courage for people in the business community and in public leadership to take such positions—the kind of courage and commitment, Berger noted, that BP would need again soon, when it applied for more deep well permits. It was important, Berger told Browne, for BP to act in ways that maintained this kind of "trusting relationship."[56]

Although Browne did not invite Berger to London, the mayor had clearly spoken in a language he could understand, and he responded by dispatching Percy and others to Lima in late November 1995. Berger liked the BP executives who came to the municipal building for an extensive meeting and saw them as positive figures he could work with. However, he also realized that he needed to defend the interests of his city as tenaciously as they defended those of their corporation, and he pushed Percy hard. He recited the impressive track record of the Lima refinery, a record that had been pushed to ever-ascending levels of efficiency and profitability by the recent initiative and energy of its workforce. In the face of this record, Berger wanted to know, why had BP apparently placed the plant on a fast track toward sale, particularly in light of the three to six years they had allotted to sell Marcus Hook? Who was making the decision to sell the refinery, he asked, and when can I meet with them? Had BP adequately considered the environmental risks and costs involved in a sale? If BP really wanted to maintain local trust, he argued, its managers should immediately take the closure option off the table. Even the hint of closure, he reiterated in a follow-up letter to Percy, "would become a self-fulfilling prophecy": it would damage morale irreparably both in the plant and the community and create a "fire-sale mentality among potential purchasers."[57]

Finally, at the meeting with Percy, Berger raised another even more alarming possibility reverberating through the local rumor mill. He could understand the economics of oil refining and grasp why BP wanted to reduce its exposure to the uncertain profits that the industry offered. Yet the Lima refinery had improved so dramatically that its profitability no longer appeared in question. Given BP's apparent momentum toward selling such a valuable asset, Berger articulated another possibility he feared BP might be considering, a worst-case scenario for Lima. Perhaps BP really had no intention of selling the refinery. What if the plant had become an asset too valuable to allow a competitor to acquire? If BP's leaders followed that line of thinking, they might move to permanently close, rather than sell, the refinery. Casting around for a name for such a policy, his mind ran back to old Western civilization classes at Holy Spirit Seminary, and what he remembered of Rome's campaign against Carthage. Instead of sale, Berger wondered aloud, was BP really pursuing a policy of "scorched earth"?[58]

"I will not tolerate any sort of a surprise closing of the Lima Refinery"

Steven Percy would have quickly scotched talk of "scorched earth" as unreasonable paranoia. Although he later admitted that he and fellow BP executives in Cleveland had initially feared that London might do something "irrational," such as the immediate closure of the Lima plant, the reluctant recognition by

London executives of Lima's greatly enhanced value meant they would have been "crazy" not to try to sell it first. Percy thought highly enough of Lima's mayor to courteously phone Berger with a few days' advance warning before BP's official announcement, in early January 1996, that the refinery was for sale. Under the heading "BP Announces Outcome of International Refining Study," the company's official release left it to Schaefer to deliver the bad news. "After much discussion and analysis," the release quoted Schaefer as saying, "BP has made the difficult decision to sell our Lima refinery to reduce BP's exposure to volatile refining margins." Schaefer acknowledged that the refinery "has made excellent improvements in recent years," but then noted that "much of its production is surplus to BP's direct marketing needs." Nor was the Lima refinery alone. While BP would be investing $200 million in its Toledo plant to enable it to adequately process sour crude, the release read, the corporation would also be selling refineries in the Netherlands and in southern France.[59]

Knowing little or nothing of the dramatic improvements at the Lima plant, national media sources accepted BP's explanation without critical comment. BP's refineries were losing money, they reported, and, along with its competitors, BP was suffering from a "three-year overcapacity crisis in the oil refining industry." The combined sale of BP's three plants would shrink its total number of refineries to eleven and its daily total volume of refined products from 2 million barrels to 1.4 million barrels per day. Six of BP's refineries, Browne told the

BP refinery executive James Schaefer announcing that the corporation would be putting its Lima refinery up for sale, January 12, 1996. *Photo courtesy of WLIO-TV, Lima, Ohio.*

Financial Times, met BP's newly established criteria that they should remain within "the top 25 per cent in efficiency and profitability" in their respective regions, and it would be investing millions in the other five—including Toledo's—to bring them up to the same standard. Capable and efficient refiners, he added, could still make money at the refineries BP had put on the sale block, although he admitted that closure of the plants "was an option" if no adequate buyers emerged. Once again, investors loved the move. BP's jettisoning of its refineries, burbled the *Investors Chronicle,* "shows BP is the industry leader in tackling non-performing assets." BP's stock began rising as soon as the company released the news, and within a year had climbed nearly 40 percent.[60]

Berger greeted news of the refinery sale with a huge sigh of relief. From what he could tell, refinery workers and the larger community interpreted news of the sale in a similarly positive light. They had to have understood that their own excellent work had given the refinery a new lease on life, and if BP didn't want to pocket the profits the plant was now producing, surely some other oil company would be glad to have them. However, the mayor didn't talk with everyone. When Clarence Roller heard of the sale, he read it as a masked shutdown. The sale attempt, Roller said, was another quixotic struggle by the Ohio refineries' boss; it was "a Schaefer thing," he said, that's all. The fact that BP had left Schaefer—someone many hourly workers had come to regard as close to heroic—off the sales committee indicated to Roller that the company did not really want to sell it at all.

For his part, Schaefer knew that London did not expect to find a buyer. The top London executives had put up for sale only the refinery itself, not the pipelines going in and out of the plant, nor such key aspects of refining as alkylation and desulphurization. These processes had been carried out in Toledo and had enabled the two companion refineries to work effectively together. Now Toledo would retain them, leaving the Lima plant denuded and so structured as to render a sale difficult. Since Lima was not worth nearly as much as a stand-alone refinery and since the market for both refineries and for refining was poor, London confidently assumed that no buyer would emerge.[61]

Berger was not ready to give up, however. Even though London had devalued the refinery, he reasoned, "that didn't mean it had no value." In fact, any complete evaluation would reveal that the Lima facility offered potential buyers quite a deal. Schaefer had penned a special guest editorial in the *Lima News* to pump up community optimism, listing all the attributes the plant offered. It was an excellent, greatly improved, and sophisticated refinery, strategically located in a market with sufficient demand for the products it furnished. The plant was up for sale only because "BP has changed its business strategy and desires to reduce its refining capacity below its marketing capacity." The refining market was sagging, Schaefer admitted, but the community should not worry: "This will not be your typical refinery sale." The trade press listed an additional factor working in Lima's favor, namely, the common knowledge in the industry that BP was a poor performer in refining and marketing, and that a potential buyer might reason it could coax more profits out of the plant than BP.[62]

BP certainly began acting like a corporation seriously interested in selling one of its assets. It placed the job in the capable hands of senior executives like Fowler and Percy and assigned an old BP hand, David Atton, to lead the sales team. Atton had been with the company since 1967 and had served it well in various roles. He had spent years in Cleveland managing its Sohio affiliate and just recently had overseen the sale of Marcus Hook. He was very good, executives like Walpole knew, at selling structures like industrial plants. Among those assisting Atton would be a midlevel manager named Robert Paisley, an American who had worked for BP in London for years, where he had overseen several other similar processes of corporate divestment.[63]

In a media update that September, Atton and Schaefer announced that "the interest has been better expected in terms of the depth and breadth, confirming that we are selling a good asset with good people in a good community." That by itself appeared an understatement in light of the obvious attractions of the Lima refinery. In a poor refining climate, in which all other refineries sold in the United States over the preceding five years had attracted all of one bidder, BP had seen five solid buyers come forward with legitimate and reasonable bids for the Lima plant. Atton announced that BP would select one of them to begin negotiating with, and expected to close a deal by the year's end. Through Deep Well, Berger guessed that two of the potential bidders were the respected regional oil companies Ashland and Marathon. On his own, he had stumbled across the identity of a third. One afternoon that summer as he was sitting in his office, his secretary buzzed to say that a Mr. Robert Paisley was here to see him. Paisley came in and got right to the point. He had taken a leave of absence from BP, Paisley said, because along with several others he had become actively involved in a management buyout attempt; he and several others wanted to buy the refinery and run it themselves. "I came down here, as you know, with every intention of being part of the sales team with BP," Paisley told Berger, "and what I discovered was incredible. This is a terrific opportunity."[64]

The vision that Paisley laid out for the refinery must have made Berger's heart skip a beat. When he had started poring over the numbers on the refinery in preparation for a sale, Paisley explained, he had learned a lot. The improvements that Kuenzli and the refinery workforce had achieved had astounded him. Once refinery workers were "further unshackled by corporate issues," he was convinced, "they could find more innovative ways to cut costs, increase productivity," and bring the refinery to still greater levels of efficiency and profits. In fact, Paisley elaborated, he could see room for the refinery's workforce achieving even greater potential because he wanted to create a company that cut each of them a share in the profits and, to some degree, even in ownership of it. In doing so, they'd help him avoid the kind of labor-management disputes that could be fatal to a small company. The company that he envisioned would be to some degree community-owned and would be an integral part of the community of Lima. To emphasize this, he and his partners (Kuenzli and a Texas oilman named Steven Dove) had already copyrighted Rockefeller's old name for the refinery. If BP accepted their bid, it would once again be known as the Solar Refinery. Later they hoped to invest in gas stations up and down I-75, north and south of Lima, selling their own products in the same type of vertical integration pioneered by Rockefeller himself. "I think we could take a page out of history," Paisley urged his partners; "too bad we don't have a crude oil field." This was their intent, he told the mayor, and "also it was a way of getting more of a local identity." Even later, he envisioned the refinery's annexation into Lima. Paisley really believed that BP was open to this bid, he told Berger, and he had come by city hall to see if Berger could help him find other sources of short-term financing for the deal.[65]

Of course, Berger replied that he'd be happy to. Within a short time he had put Paisley's group together with two friends, Louis Nobile and David Drum, regional executives for Banc One in Lima. The two bankers spent several weeks looking over Paisley's management buyout plan and grew increasingly excited. Soon, Nobile came back to Berger to tell him, "Dave, we're not just interested in doing the short-term financing; we want to do the whole deal." Their bank had the capacity and active interest in financing the whole project, Nobile said, but before they went further, their superiors just wanted them to confirm that BP would see the management buyout as a viable option. The two Lima bankers drove to Cleveland and, as Berger remembered, "received absolute assurances from David Atton that the sale was for real" and "was sanctioned by the company. It was A-okay and, frankly, being encouraged."[66]

At the same time, however, Berger continued to hear insider accounts, primarily from Deep Well, suggesting that BP's real agenda in London was closure rather than sale. In March, for example, Percy had traveled to London for a meeting of the corporation's executive committee for what he thought would be a briefing on the sales process. Glancing at the agenda before the meeting started, Percy noticed the planners had scheduled him to speak not about a sale of the refinery but rather on the bulleted item "Timetable for Lima Closure." Percy protested, saying he had come to discuss the sales process. Quite right, came the reply. He could do that too, if he insisted, but the sales process might not work and the London team really wanted to hear his plan for closure. Percy was able to update his superiors on the possible sale of the refinery only because he demanded the process be given a hearing.[67]

Berger did not learn of this episode until some months later, but Deep Well did apprise him of comments that Stomberg had made on Wall Street, also in March. Characterizing the refinery as unprofitable, the head of BP refining had reiterated to financiers that London continued to hold out closure as an option. "In my opinion, comments from senior BP officials along these lines," Berger wrote in a tougher letter to Browne, "can only result in a 'fire-sale' mentality . . . The fact that these sorts of comments are being made causes me to question whether there is not a 'scorched earth' posture being assumed" by BP. Further, Berger wanted to know, did BP really want to dispose of the refinery in order to maintain "a short-term market position in the U.S. Mid-West?" Browne responded with a brief letter that included an actual transcript of Stomberg's remarks but failed to soothe the mayor. BP's refusal to take the possibility of closure off the table undermined prospects for a good sale. As Berger had noted in his comments to Percy, "If you're selling something, you dress it, you promote it. Here they are talking closure, that demotes it and devalues it," he argued. "The fact that they were on Wall Street continuing to trash-talk the Lima refinery to me was an indication that they were trying to undercut the sales process." Meanwhile, Deep Well began hinting that the sales process was not proceeding as swimmingly as it might appear. When the mayor queried Nobile and Drum, they reported that negotiations with BP on the management buyout effort were going fine, but Deep Well contradicted this. No, that's not the case, Deep Well insisted privately to Berger.[68]

The mayor's key moment of illumination came in early September 1996. A source deep inside BP's Cleveland headquarters explained to Berger the disjuncture between what appeared to be a legitimate sales process occurring in Ohio and London's apparent disinterest in a sale. While BP's Ohio team was trying to sell the refinery, this source revealed, London executives were trying to replace it with a pipeline. It was true, Deep Well confirmed. BP had entered into negotiations with a pipeline company to build a pipeline from its huge refinery on the Gulf Coast that, when completed, would supposedly award the corporation a huge competitive edge in the regional marketplace. Moreover, it would render the Lima plant not only unnecessary but, in the hands of another company, a real competitive threat to BP's new economic advantage in the Midwest.[69]

Until that point, Berger remembered, despite misgivings planted by the actions of BP executives in London, he had believed "in the genuineness of the sales process," but now, he suddenly realized, the game really was up. In fact, the true situation was exactly the worst-case scenario he had suspected and feared all along: BP had embraced a policy of "scorched earth" with regard to Lima. If it succeeded in building a pipeline, BP certainly would close its refinery in Lima—and might even close its Toledo refinery too—leaving Berger's city suffering under a staggering economic blow. It was a bitter, revealing moment, and to Berger, it changed everything. He would work with the company when he could. Yet if he was going to keep faith with his city and his responsibilities as mayor, he would have to shift his role from that of BP's partner to its adversary. He fired off a quick little note to Percy to express his "serious misgivings" at BP's refusal to take closure off the table and warned that unless BP did so, "I will consider other actions available to me and to the community." Then he laid out those possible actions in a long and blistering letter to the governor of Ohio.[70]

He had learned, Berger wrote Voinovich, that "there are corporate advocates for a 'scorched earth' anti-competitive strategy" pressing their case high in BP's ranks, and that the surprisingly competitive bidding interest in the Lima refinery—revealing to everyone in the company the value of the asset and the threat it would pose to BP's profits in the hands of another company—had strengthened their hand. "BP's short-term financial interests can be overwhelming in its decision-making," Berger summarized, and because of this, Lima would have to prepare itself for the announcement of the closure of the refinery in late October or early November. "I will not tolerate any sort of a surprise closing of the Lima Refinery," the mayor declared, "and I ask you to join me in this." In fact, he informed the governor that he was now preparing a multifaceted plan to create public pressure on BP to cut a deal with one of its bidders or to facilitate an employee buyout. First, he would urge area congressional representatives "to conduct a congressional investigation into the 'scorched earth' business practices of BP." Second, he would contact the presidential campaigns then under way and ask candidates Bob Dole and Bill Clinton to stop in Lima to "address the concerns of preserving American jobs in relation to foreign owners who pursue anti-competitive tactics." Third, his office was preparing a well-crafted public relations offensive to highlight BP's misdeeds. Fourth, he planned to contact local and national unions with this information because "their involvement will be critical in conducting local and regional boycotts of BP facilities and products." Fifth, Berger informed the governor, BP was now going to encounter a very different local mayoral administration with regard to environmental issues. They could now expect much greater difficulty in obtaining more deep well injection permits, and he also intended to "demand immediate and full restoration to residential standards of all BP property in Allen County not essential for its ongoing operations." Finally, he told the governor, he would push advocates of "ethical investing" he knew on Wall Street to discourage the purchase of BP stock. In sum, Berger's whole attitude had clearly undergone a sea change. He continued to view the management and workforce of the Lima refinery with respect and admiration, he concluded his letter; they had accomplished wonders. Yet "to understand now that the very strength of our community would be used against us by the 'scorched earth advocates,'" he wrote in bold type, "is to see an incredibly cynical and amoral set of decision-makers."[71]

In other words, Berger signaled to the highest public official in the state that he was inaugurating his city's own private offensive against BP. In retrospect, one can only marvel at the audacious nature of the enterprise. Perhaps its fundamental nature is best revealed by a quick comparison of the two major figures that would soon clash in this particular arena. John Browne and David Berger shared certain qualities that would accentuate the volatility of their encounter. Both were driven and talented workaholics on behalf of their respective organizations, and both possessed a dogged determination never to give up until they had won. Beyond this, however, they were very different men. Browne had studied physics at Cambridge, business at Stanford, and could converse insightfully about oil-price shares on the international market. Berger had spent nine years in Catholic seminary and could articulate a decent summary of the theology of Teilhard de Chardin. Browne was an opera buff who collected pre-Columbian art. Berger enjoyed nights at the Lima symphony and picnics at Faurot Park. Browne's employer compensated him at the rate of nearly a million pounds a year. Berger worked for the people of Lima for an annual salary of about $47,000. Browne cruised through the boulevards of Paris or Amsterdam in the back of expensive corporate limousines and could catch the Concorde to Moscow or a private helicopter onto BP oil platforms in the North Sea. Berger drove himself through the crumbling asphalt streets of Lima in an old Ford Taurus he took from the city's car pool. John Browne could reach for the telephone at any time of the day or night and get a highly placed official at No. 10 Downing Street. David Berger could pick up the phone at any time of the day or night and get the correct time.[72]

A sketch of the organizations that the two men headed likewise demonstrates the imbalance of the forces arrayed in this conflict. On the one side was the daunting global presence of British Petroleum. In 1996, it stood as the fifth-biggest oil company in the international arena, the largest single corporation in Great Britain, and the most profitable oil company in the world. It had steadily expanded its reach into the far corners of the globe. In 1997, it began launching hundreds of retail sites in Eastern Europe and was opening up new markets in China and Vietnam. Its total roster of staff and employees around the world easily rivaled the population of a good, midsized city. In the United States alone, by the turn of the century, it would employ more than 45,000 people. A vast majority of those employees were very good at their jobs, for in 1996, the company's profits exceeded $4.1 billion dollars. Collectively, BP had power.[73]

On the other side was the city of Lima, Ohio. It was home to a total population of about 42,000 people, spread over a dozen square miles of city blocks. This population was served by a total city workforce of roughly 450 people, who in 1996 managed to collect and budget a total tax revenue of $46 million dollars. For the past three decades, the city had undergone a steady and nearly unrelenting battering by negative economic forces. It had lost upwards of 12,000 solid manufacturing jobs, the kinds of jobs that local people had relied on for generations to feed their families and that had served as the lifeblood of the community. Now local residents stood with their backs to the wall and decided that they were going to stop the exodus. Collectively, Lima had determination.[74]

It would not be a fair fight.

Chapter 6

"It Was Like a Death—to the Town"

In the nineteen years from 1963 to 1982, America saw the closing of a hundred thousand manufacturing plants, resulting in about twenty-two million lost jobs. Like newspaper accounts of mass famines or war refugees, such statistics are so overwhelming as to be numbing. Lost, too, in the cumulative statistics is something of what such plant closings represented in individual communities. Of course, each closing was unique, and each occurred as the culmination of a thousand different decisions and calculations by a great many people. Individual workers had to repeatedly ask and answer for themselves a whole series of questions. Is my job safe or not? Will I survive the next round of cuts? At what point do I begin looking for another job? How rooted am I here? How rooted is my family? And how far away are we prepared to move to land another position? Midlevel managers had to sift through a variety of interrelated questions concerning what and when to tell their employees about the uncertain future of their jobs.[1]

Even senior corporate executives, from their more removed levels, found themselves gingerly entering a new field of corporate management for which few of their elite MBA programs had adequately prepared them. Certainly these executives were shielded by several layers of intermediaries from experiencing the full financial and emotional impact of the economic body blows that their corporations were delivering to individual cities. Yet the reverberations from such decisions still quivered far up the corporate hierarchies. All across the country, business executives were receiving informal, postgraduate crash courses in managing industrial decline. The experience had become so common that innovative new midwestern MBA programs would have been well advised to expand their course offerings; clearly, budding corporate executives needed to learn how to deftly manage relations with partner communities they were abandoning. As for BP, whatever else its decision did or did not accomplish, its experience in Lima at least prepared the company to offer special insights into such emerging subfields of business administration. By the time BP's divestiture of the Lima refinery was accomplished, such BP executives as Atton, Percy, and even John Browne must also have been singularly equipped to share with other corporate heads pointers on specific elements of the process, for example: Here's how you replace the lost product. Here's how you massage local public opinion. This is how much it will cost you to regain public favor. And here's how you handle troublesome mayors. In fact, as they recalibrated their corporate machinery to close Lima down, BP executives were being well trained to lecture at length on how to deal with a recalcitrant community that was doing its best to throw sand into the gears of the entire operation.

"Black Tuesday"

The minute that Atton and Paisley assumed management of the Lima refinery sale they must have noted the challenges of their new assignment. They knew the plant had problems. For one thing, BP had long designed Lima to run in concert with its sister refinery in Toledo. As a stand-alone plant, stripped of the subsidiary processes performed in Toledo, like desulphurization and alkylation, Lima was less valuable. Moreover, it ran on expensive feedstock. Both Lima and Toledo had been processors of "sweet" crude. While sweet crude had some advantages—it had less sulfur than "sour" crude and thus could produce a higher proportion of more valuable products like gasoline and jet fuel—its relative scarcity globally meant that it had a higher cost per barrel. When BP's executives decided to sell Lima, they also invested $235 million in the Toledo plant to enable it to refine the dirtier but more abundant—and therefore cheaper—sour crude. By itself, Lima had some structural problems that the new sales team could not get past no matter how they spun the story.[2]

On the other hand, hype or not, the Maumee Mission still left Atton with a number of impressive sales points that he did not hesitate to tick off to potential buyers. In a company newsletter that April, for example, he labeled the Lima plant a sophisticated refinery, proclaiming that it was "in the top quartile in products yields and costs." By the end of the summer, not only were significant regional oil companies like Ashland and Marathon showing signs of real interest but a bid suddenly emerged from within BP: Robert Paisley requested a leave of absence to develop a management buyout plan with his partners, Donovan Kuenzli and Steven Dove. Atton quickly won permission from London to let

Paisley take his shot and apparently encouraged Paisley in his bid through that summer and early fall. At one point, remembered Paisley's banker, Louis Nobile, Atton even offered some suggestions on how to lower the price of their bid.[3]

BP's senior refinery salesman remained optimistic about the prospects for a sale until late September 1996, when the actual bids came in. Bids for industrial facilities are complex matters, so much so that Atton and his team routinely gave themselves a week to evaluate them. The fundamental document, the "basic agreement to buy," consisted of two bound volumes, each four inches thick. But once BP officials had absorbed the details of the sets of documents from the various bidders, they could see that none of them would work, an insight ratified by their superiors at a meeting in London on October 15. Bound by the confidentiality agreements BP had signed, Atton and Percy repeatedly refused to publicly discuss the specifics of each bid, but their general outlines gradually leaked out in the press. Over eight days that September, BP said, all five bids fell apart. Two of the bidders withdrew, and BP rejected two others because they lacked the requisite financial resources to fully separate BP from any remaining legal responsibility in Lima. As for the fifth bidder—later identified by the press as Ashland—BP rejected its bid because the new owner would have charged BP too much for the refinery's products, requiring BP, on its own, to find an alternate source of supply to replace the products that the refinery had churned out.[4]

At this point, BP's executives, gathered in London, quickly reached a new conclusion on the fate of the Lima refinery. It was not a hard call: Browne had told them years before to reduce BP's exposure to refining. Shortly after Atton returned from London, he summoned Lima refinery manager Don Kuenzli to Cleveland. There he told Kuenzli the news: in two years' time, they were going to shutter the plant for good. Given what Atton told him of the bids, Kuenzli recalled later, he recognized the plan as a "legitimate decision." Still, "distraught and frustrated"—for this was the first word he had received that his and Paisley's management buyout bid had been rejected—Kuenzli returned to Lima under strict instructions to keep mum about the decision for a few weeks, until the company could prepare a formal announcement.[5]

From within BP's high command, that was how the decision to close the Lima refinery had unfolded. Except for Kuenzli, people in the plant itself had received only faint glimpses into this process, some of them unsettling. Refinery public relations officer Judy Gilbert did not know what had happened at the critical meeting across the Atlantic, but "when Atton came back from London, he was very quiet." No doubt this would have been tough for him, administering to another city what he had seen done to so many others. All Gilbert knew was that her boss seemed "defeated . . . energy seemed to go out of Atton a little bit when he came back from London."[6]

Even less news of BP's high-level deliberations had filtered out to the larger community. Nevertheless, Lima's mayor had been busy. His contained but angry letter to Governor Voinovich had sparked all sorts of responses. The governor quickly wrote to Percy to reiterate his willingness to do what he could to save the five hundred jobs at the Lima refinery. But Berger's tough letter had found its way to even higher authorities. On October 15—the same day that BP's high command gathered in London to make their final decision to close the refinery—Berger received a fax from John Browne. "Let me assure you," Browne soothed, "that BP is giving very deliberate thought to the future of our assets in Lima, and that no decisions have or will be made without careful consideration of a variety of factors." Among those factors, Browne insisted, were "the well-being of our employees; and the well-being of the citizens of Lima." On the same day, Percy tried to contact Berger, and, failing to reach him directly, left him a voice mail that revealed more than had Browne's declarations of good faith. While assuring Berger that BP planned nothing "precipitous," he acknowledged that "there are probably some misconceptions about the robustness of the bids that have been submitted." Berger read Percy's signals clearly, and, like a desperate football quarterback flinging wild passes in the last seconds of a game, tried a number of disconnected plays. He shot off a quick letter to Browne, asking for a meeting with him and representatives of the state government to facilitate a sale of the refinery to its employees for a dollar. He wrote to Voinovich, urging him to bring in the respected former chief of Sohio, Frank Mosier, as part of a team of people who would meet with BP on behalf of the state of Ohio. The governor instead delegated the state development director, Donald Jakeway, to work with the mayor. Although Berger met with Jakeway and found him competent, he did not believe the governor's choice represented the kind of intervention Lima needed at that critical moment. If BP had indicated they were about to shut down their massive operation in Voinovich's hometown of Cleveland, Berger suspected, Voinovich wouldn't have left the matter to Jakeway; he would have been all over the situation himself. Instead, it seemed to Berger that his city was "being relegated to a non-priority status" by the governor.[7]

Then, late in October, Berger learned from Deep Well and another well-placed source in BP what had happened at the critical London meeting a few weeks earlier. As Berger heard the story, Atton's job was to sell the plant, and he had gone to London not as a neutral evaluator of the bids but as an advocate for BP's acceptance of the bid from Paisley's group. Moreover, Atton had expected BP to accept this advice. However, Berger learned, "things happened at that meeting." At the London meeting on October 15—a date later labeled by the *Lima News* as "Black Tuesday"—representatives of BP's marketing group pointed to the Toledo fire as evidence that the whole deal was too risky. What if a major fire broke out at the Lima plant? Would Paisley's group of investors possess sufficient reserves of capital to survive it and still provide BP with product? BP's safest course, they argued, was to shut down the refinery entirely and replace it with a pipeline. Atton may have gone to London prepared to recommend the Paisley option, Berger learned, but he returned home with marching orders to close the plant. Since then, the *Lima News* informed the community several months later, he and Percy "have been playing the part of the good soldier, carrying out orders over which they have little control."[8]

Altogether, this series of developments left the mayor in a kind of a cold, possessed fury. By that October, rumors and innuendo about the refinery's fate were sweeping through the Lima community, Gilbert remembered, but "with the mayor, it was more than innuendo." Gilbert would run into him at various community meetings, and increasingly he hinted at knowledge that had clearly embittered him immeasurably. Once, as she filled in for BP management at a social function at the Shawnee Country Club, Berger angrily approached her, declared flatly that BP was planning to close the refinery, and directed her to tell her bosses that "closure is not an option!" Berger was seething and confrontational. "This company is taking you down the yellow brick road," he warned, "and there's no Emerald City out there. They're not what they say they are."[9]

Paisley's experience that October followed a similar path from optimism to despair. At first, as he awaited news from BP executives on his bid, his hopes soared. Like Atton, he knew the Lima plant's liabilities, but he did not find them daunting. Sure, Lima was a sweet crude refiner, but plenty of sweet crude was available; with sweet requiring less sophisticated equipment to process and producing a more valuable product slate, most U.S. refineries likewise processed sweet crude. Since environmental issues rendered it nearly impossible to build a new refinery in the United States, Paisley assured his bankers, "the market takes care of that variance" between sweet and sour crude, adding, "We will always pay for that premium in the U.S." Certainly, "you pay more" for sweet, Paisley reasoned, "but you get a lot better market out of it, and it's the margin that matters." The key to his confidence rested on his reading of the historic performance of crude oil margins, which experienced oilmen like he and Dove had plotted carefully. Defining "margin" as "the difference you pay for your crude stock, no matter what it is, and what you sell your products for, no matter what they are," Paisley and Dove graphed the sweet crude margins going back decades. They saw—as BP executives certainly would have seen—that sweet crude refining was in a forty-year cycle. Even though sweet crude was in its lowest spot in that year, 1996, the Lima refinery was still pulling in a $20 million annual profit. What would happen to its profits when the sweet crude margin again curved upward, as it was bound to do—particularly with Lima's highly motivated workforce, which had rendered the plant one of the fastest improving refineries in the world?[10]

The potential of the Lima refinery sparkled so brightly that Paisley was dumbfounded that BP even wanted to sell it. But if they did, he certainly wanted to buy. He and Dove prepared what they thought was a very attractive bid, structuring in the margin share profits that BP would have known were coming. Because they saw their major competition for the refinery as other oil companies—the prospect of closure barely occurred to them—Paisley and his partners offered BP a total of $365 million for the refinery: $50 million for the asset, $145 million for the crude oil presently sitting in the pipes and tanks, and $170 million in a market participation scheme. They further integrated into the bid three different options for BP to consider, based on the principle that the more of the margin BP wanted, the less Paisley and his team would pay for the asset. And if they wanted no market participation at all, Paisley offered a straight cash bid of $195 million. Paisley knew that here were aspects of their bid that he could not control: how strong BP would regard their financing, for example, or the fact that, in a world of giant oil corporations, a newly reborn Solar Refinery run by Paisley and his partners was pretty small potatoes. Even so, Paisley and his partners remained very optimistic that they could beat any other bid if BP considered their $365 million offer in full. Having presented BP with this offer on September 25, with the common legal proviso that it was valid for a month, they then sat back and waited anxiously for BP to make up its mind.[11]

As the days passed into a week with still no response from BP, the financing issue in particular began to eat at Paisley. Since their initial set of Boston-area bankers had pulled out, Berger had helped them line up new ones. Paisley liked Lou Nobile and David Drum of Lima's Banc One; they were "very good to work with and willing to be taught." However, they didn't fully understand the oil industry, and Paislely wondered if this was hurting their bid. In any deal to buy a refinery, the cost of crude already in the pipes was a major line item expenditure. With its oil being pumped in from stations along the Gulf Coast, on any given day Lima had a thirty-day supply of crude continually on its way from the gulf. A thirty-day supply times 170,000 barrels of crude a day equaled a lot of crude sitting in the pipeline. Of their $365 million bid for the refinery, $145 million was just for the inventory in the pipe, he assured his bankers. Even if the refinery goes down for some reason, you still haven't lost this crude; you could sell it to anyone else along the pipe. But Ohio bankers had difficulty grasping this fully. On their own they asked a number of questions from BP, most notably, If the refinery collapsed, would you guarantee that you'd still buy this crude from us? These questions may have intensified BP's fears that Paisley and his team did not quite know what they were doing. A Texas bank, Dove told him, wouldn't even have asked such questions; they would have known their collateral was in the pipe. The other thing that ate at Paisley was BP's possible reaction to Berger's aggressive tactics in pressing Lima's case. In his years at BP, Paisley had noted that the corporation did not like the intervention of outside parties. Paisley had seen copies of Berger's letters to Browne and others, and he "kept advising Berger, don't do that. Or wait until after October 25 to do that." He appreciated Berger's "shuttle diplomacy," but he told the mayor that it would be best to wait for guidance from BP.[12]

While October slowly passed, still without word from BP on his bid, Paisley's fear and disappointment intensified. He knew that companies usually accepted bids within a week or two. No news was indeed bad news. Moreover, he found that BP executives now would not return his phone calls, and his efforts to mollify them seemed fruitless. In mid-October, about the time of the important London meeting, he wrote Atton to ask what more the BP executives wanted. Can I clarify insurance? he asked. Can I clarify Banc One? Nobile and Drum offered to write a letter saying they were 100 percent behind the management buyout bid and didn't need guarantees , but Paisley still received no official word from BP, only the leaked word through the grapevine that their bid "wasn't sufficient." "They never started negotiations, at least not with us," Dove reported later. Paisley had been on the other side of the process enough to recognize that something was amiss. He began to wonder if the entire process was as fair as it was supposed to be. "What the hell is going on here?" he asked himself. Drum and Nobile of Banc One had been making periodic trips to Cleveland to talk with Atton, and suddenly BP's vice president told them, "These terms are not acceptable." At this point the conversation usually lead to questions such as, "OK, what terms would be acceptable?" and negotiations would begin. This time, though, Drum recalled, Atton made no counterarguments; he gave them nothing. On the drive back to Lima, Drum and Nobile looked at each other and agreed: it's over. When he got back to town, Drum called Berger to say, "Dave, it's not going to work. The negotiations are over."[13]

Sometime late that fall, Berger's secretary buzzed him to say that Mr. Robert Paisley had come to see him. The mayor welcomed a Paisley quite different from the well-groomed and tailored executive he had met previously. This time, Paisley appeared unshaven, in a golf shirt with an open collar, and began pacing Berger's office, venting at BP. He had just met with Atton, who remarked that the company was dissatisfied with the direction the bids were taking. He had been naïve and foolish for having believed BP, Paisley told the mayor. He felt, recalled Berger, "entirely used and abused by the process." In hopes of bringing Lima's old Solar Refinery to life once again, he had taken a ten-month leave from the company and paid for lawyers, environmental scientists, and insurance company officials out of his own pocket, incurring a bill that ran into six figures. Now he had come up with nothing.[14]

In early November, Berger called Percy as a follow-up to a last desperate letter Paisley had sent Atton, offering to join BP executives in a meeting with Paisley to try to assist Paisley's bid. Percy delicately voiced BP's distaste for "multilateral negotiations" and informed Berger that Atton would be communicating with Paisley himself. Percy added that since it had been so long since refinery employees had heard any official news, BP would be giving them an interim status report very soon, informing them that all the bids they had received were "unacceptable" (in previous conversations, Berger noted, Percy had used the word "unsubstantial"). Nevertheless, Percy continued, BP was committed to working with the bidders to render their bids acceptable, even though this process might become so "protracted" as to take years. If they failed to negotiate acceptable bids, Percy said, BP would "paint a picture of what would happen," but in any case the company would not do anything "precipitous."[15]

Within twenty-four hours of that conversation, Judy Gilbert was told by her superiors to prepare press materials and call a mass meeting of the refinery employees for 8:00 in the morning the next day, when BP would publicly announce the closing of the refinery.[16]

"I don't ever remember a time so bad for this town"

A day or two before the sudden mass meeting called by BP to announce the results of the sales process, James Schaefer emptied out his office at the refinery, removing pictures from the walls, emptying file drawers, and filling boxes. Superiors in Cleveland had passed word as to what the big meeting was going to reveal and suggested it would not do for him to be there. Schaefer readily agreed to make himself scarce and spent that day in Toledo. He knew he was a "symbol" to the employees "for the hopes and confidence in the refinery," and that his presence at a meeting announcing the plant's closure would be inappropriate for BP and severely disappointing for all its employees, including himself. He did not return to the refinery complex for upwards of five years.[17]

Except for the few people who might have noticed Schaefer carrying boxes of papers and books out to his car the day before, nobody at the plant seems to have had any clue of what was coming. Most expected that the company would reveal at the meeting who their next employer would be. All that fall, remembered refinery engineer Daniel Groman, various rumors had swept the plant about their next corporate owner. Bound by legal agreements, BP executives remained tight-lipped about the content of the bids or the names of the bidders, but the identities were impossible to keep secret at the plant. Workers routinely saw delegations from other oil companies touring the refinery, asking questions, and commenting on what they saw (usually, Groman said, about how clean it all was and how friendly people were). So the rumor mill hummed: Marathon had bought them; then, Groman heard, it was Citgo. One Kentucky newspaper headlined a lead story that the buyer would be Ashland. The latest buzz among the refinery rank and file, the day before the big announcement, focused on Ashland. Early on that Friday morning in late fall, refinery employees filed into various meeting rooms to hear the big word. Heading into the maintenance department lunch room, Groman recalled thinking it "weird" that secretaries were dutifully recording who was there and who was not, but at any rate closure "was the last thing on my mind." Clarence Roller reported as requested with a large group to the cafeteria, "and that's when they told ya, we're going to shut this place down."[18]

Of course, BP tried to soften the blow with all the reasonable financial cushions it could produce. In Percy's announcement to employees, he even avoided using the word "closure," instead assuring them that they would continue to refine crude in Lima for an approximate two-year transition period. BP, affirmed Percy, would do all it could to assisting employees with their personal plans. The soft soap didn't fool those listening, however.

The first emotional reaction inside the plant seems to have been stunned silence. "People didn't say much of anything at that point," Groman said. Most sought first to call their spouses, and then reaction set in, with responses running the normal range. Some responded in shocked disbelief that BP would close them after all the improvements they had made. For others, the moment just brought tears. Kuenzli admitted he lost his composure when delivering the news, and he was not alone. "I have not seen that many grown men cry in a plant, ever," one worker remembered. Judy Gilbert insisted that relations among employees at the plant had been close-knit going back to Sohio days. Generations of local people had worked there and tended to see themselves all as "family." Even hard-bitten union leaders like Roller used the same term. The entire climate of improvement that the workers had created at the refinery could only have rested in the tight collegial bonds they had shared. Now those bonds allowed workers to grieve as a family would. Following the closure announcement, many workers gathered for what one recalled as "a very emotional session" where individuals shared their "very intense, private feelings about the whole process. I was part of that and it was a staggering emotional experience." In the same manner that a family experiencing a death undergoes predictable cycles of grief, so too at the refinery the first initial shock gave way to immense sadness.[19]

Anyone reading the company's rationales laid out in the *Lima News* the next day would conclude that BP had no other choice. Refining margins were down

Workers leaving the refinery in shock and distress following BP's announcement that they planned to close the facility, November 8, 1996. *Photo courtesy of the* Lima News.

around the world, Atton pointed out. The paper quoted an industry expert that selling refineries in such a climate was "like trying to sell a farm with the price of grain going south." Moreover, who could blame the company, given the marginal offers it had received? "The bids were offering hardly any money at all for the refinery," Atton told the *Lima News.* "In fact, the bids can be characterized as being close to zero." But even if the prices had been better, he emphasized, BP still saw them as inadequate. None of the bidders had the requisite financial reserves to protect BP from future legal and environmental liability at the site. If a major environmental catastrophe occurred at the refinery in the future and its current owner went under, then the plaintiff in any lawsuit, under the U.S. Superfund law, could reach back and sue previous owners for damages. That was why the bids were unacceptable, Atton repeated over and over. BP just wanted a "clean break" from any link to refining in Lima.[20]

Local passions built quite quickly. Once again, the area media rang with quotes from devastated workers and politicians worrying about the impact of this latest and ugliest of Lima's plant closings on the city's people, families, and fabric of community life. "I feel sorry for these young people who can't even raise their families anymore," offered a retiree from the old locomotive works. "They can't find a job in this town, and if they do, it's some more of this retail. Everyone knows retail don't pay worth a dang." The blow was "pretty sudden and it leaves these families devastated," agreed Jack Rex, a former union head at the Ford engine plant and a Democrat who, in somewhat of a local political miracle, had gotten himself elected the week before as Allen County commissioner. Closure wasn't "fair for BP to do. It's like they don't care and don't worry much about these families."[21]

BP quickly indicated its willingness to pay dearly to counter such perceptions. A company that kept the health of its partner communities near the heart of its own identity—and carefully burnished a public image reflecting that commitment—knew that the way to ease a community's pain was by publicly opening its pocketbook. This effort began as soon as the stories of the refinery closing hit the press. First of all, the company highlighted its planned two-year delay in closing the plant, which gave the community ample time to adjust and also demonstrated BP's magnanimity, given that by law, under the federal Warren Act, it was required to give only sixty days' advance notice. "We're trying to make this fair," Atton pointed out, and a local union official agreed that they were "lucky to be given this kind of notice." BP managers also assured Lima that the company would continue to take good care of its workforce, announcing what Atton assured workers would be "generous" severance packages for salaried employees and preparing to grant like arrangements for hourly workers in its negotiations with the OCAW local. Moreover, BP signaled its intention to deal in a similarly munificent manner with the community. The company had historically been the largest single corporate contributor to the Lima United Way, a Cleveland PR chief quickly reminded people the day after the closure announcement; since 1980, the refinery and the chemical plant together had given $3 million to area charity agencies. Now BP announced its intention to maintain such contributions for "at least" the next two years and also to pay its real estate and personal property taxes through the same period (and of course, BP reminded everyone, the chemical plant would continue its presence in the community). Three months later, BP underscored this generosity with another press announcement highlighting plans to maintain tax payments to nine area agencies for two more years beyond the refinery's closing—no small contribution for a company that had paid nearly $2.8 million in local taxes in 1996. "We are bending over backwards to soften the blow for the community," Atton told the British press, just in case they had missed the point. "And we are doing it, believe it or not, out of the goodness of our hearts." Despite the self-serving nature of such comments, BP's actions in Lima, in an era when many corporations fled their partner communities with scant demonstration of any obligation for the financial distress they left behind, placed it at the far generous end of the corporate scale.[22]

Still, there was no disguising the financial hit that closure would impose on the entire Lima metropolitan area. The refinery's payroll annually topped $31 million. No matter how thick BP's severance packages, that payroll would be gone within two years, casting nearly five hundred workers into an area job market already saturated by all the earlier rounds of layoffs and plant closings. No one could imagine what the community would look like without the refinery's jobs—and the work it had granted a variety of local contractors and subcontractors—or how it would replace them. The refinery's three hundred or so hourly workers brought in an average base wage of twenty dollars an hour. The community's recent history provided the only clue about what kinds of jobs would probably appear in their stead, and the prospect cheered nobody. "We're replacing $20.00-an-hour jobs with benefits with $5-an-hour jobs without benefits," remarked local political activist Rochelle Twining—and that was only for those workers lucky enough to find work at all. BP's two-year financial cushion might have softened the blow initially, but the cushion would last only just that long. After the refinery was gone, what would replace the 62 percent of the budget of the Shawnee school system currently derived directly or indirectly from BP?[23]

The ripple effects of a loss of this magnitude sent shivers down the spines of all those who even half-glimpsed the numbers. By itself, the refinery was a major regional consumer of a variety of utilities, annually gobbling up $10 million worth of natural gas, $15.2 million in electricity, and massive quantities of Lima's water, providing $1.2 million yearly to the revenue-starved city. Once it closed, similar layoffs would certainly reverberate through all those industries as well. Lima's utility department, for example, did an annual business to the refinery that brought in almost $1 million; when the refinery closed, that department alone estimated it would have to lay off eleven employees. Similar layoffs could be expected by dozens and dozens of employers across the county. Buckeye Pipeline, which, along with the refinery, had been an economic presence in the community since the days of John D. Rockefeller, speculated publicly about having to close. Altogether, one journalist estimated, the cumulative financial cost of the refinery's closing would be in the neighborhood of $100 million. Whether or not they worked at BP, Lima-area residents soon would be able to count the cost of the plant closure in the declining value of their homes, the shrinking tax base of their schools, the for-sale signs dotting residential neighborhoods, and the growing fleet of rental trucks leaving Lima by way of Interstate 75 east of town with no plans to come back. These were scenes that Lima residents had witnessed several times before, but there seemed no escaping this last replay—the biggest blow of all.[24]

The damage went beyond the financial numbers, however. The closing of the refinery would inflict a deeper blow to more intangible aspects of life in Lima, aspects such as the community's self-respect and identity. At the very least, it represented the final emphatic punctuation mark to a vanishing era. For a short moment in time, perhaps six decades, Lima had epitomized the great working-class dream: a place where hard manual labor brought a secure job, a home of one's own in a decent community, and a means of passing on the same economic and emotional anchorage to one's kids. There was a time, recalled one lifelong resident, when "you could walk into any of those old-time plants—Clark Equipment, Westinghouse, and any of those—and get yourself a living in nothing flat." Now that day was done, and "I don't ever remember a time so bad for this town." To be sure, a declining number of blue-collar jobs still existed in Lima and other midwestern cities; working people still bent over engines along the assembly line at the Ford plant in Bath Township, though at a fourth of their former numbers. For Lima, however, the refinery was the big industry that had built the city and symbolized its prosperity. The city's flag did not display a fast-food franchise or an outlet mall; it bore an oil derrick. To have the refinery go down meant more than the loss of yet another industry. The metaphors that people reached for came from the human life cycle, and if that worked, then there seemed little doubt about what stage the city was in now. Judy Gilbert was a BP public relations official and publicly she said what her bosses told her to say. But she had lived in Lima all her adult life and she was sick at heart at what she witnessed now. Carefully watching the community's response, she was reminded of the work of psychologist Elisabeth Kübler-Ross on the end of a human life. She saw denial, then anger, and then maybe acceptance. But to her the one metaphor was inescapable. The end of the refinery, she said, "was like a death—to the town."[25]

"Get resigned to it and get on with it"

"BP owes Lima some answers," asserted the title of a *Lima News* editorial a few days after the shutdown announcement. "It owes Lima more than BP executives simply waltzing into town on Friday and saying, oh, well, the bids were lousy and we're just going to pull the plug." The corporation needs to provide some hard data about who the bidders were and why their bids were so unacceptable, the paper demanded. Otherwise, Lima was left with such questions as, "Did BP ever really intend to sell the refinery to a new operator? Was the bidding exercise simply a ruse?" To the editors, there seemed little doubt of the fundamental lesson. Lima was "caught up in a competitive global economy and financial or even geopolitical decisions made far away can affect us. Through no fault of our own we get hammered." If they were going to save their community from such distant, impersonal market forces, the editors declared, Lima needed "a crisis team to work with BP and the bidders to save the refinery." But in throwing down such angry lines, the editors of the *Lima News* were implicating themselves in a desperate quest, the full implications of which they could scarcely yet imagine.

Strategizing ways to resist: community leaders gather at the Lima Chamber of Commerce in the wake of the closure announcement, November 1996. Mayor Berger is to the immediate left of the flag; county commissioners Alberta Lee and Robert Barr are to the flag's immediate right; chamber president Jon Rockhold is standing; county commissioner Jack Rex is three to the right of Rockhold; Banc One executive David Drum is holding up a sheet of paper. *Photo courtesy of the* Lima News.

The task at hand seemed to demand that they and others like them in the community take on strange and probably uncomfortable roles. In the end, saving the refinery might require the metamorphosis of faithful devotees of Ronald Reagan into a loathsome species of political being from which, in saner times, they had recoiled in profound distaste. To save their town, they had to embark on a quest that demanded the temporary transformation of free-market conservatives into aggressive, left-wing political activists.[26]

Five days after BP announced the refinery's shutdown, forty local governmental officials and business executives came together at the Chamber of Commerce offices in downtown Lima to form a task force to alter or reverse the corporation's decision. "The message they sent was clear," reported the *Lima News,* "the people of Allen County are not ready to accept the refinery closing without a fight." Except for the mayor and a few labor leaders, it did not seem to be a group accustomed to confrontational political agitation. As finally configured, along with Berger and three union officials, the task force mostly consisted of people like Superintendent Lodermeier of Shawnee Township and prominent Republicans like county commissioner Alberta Lee and Congressman Oxley's aide, Kelly Kirk. Lima's City Council president, Keith Cunningham, rapidly emerging as Berger's major political antagonist, participated regularly. In its

Ken Belcher, leader of the Refinery Task Force, being interviewed by a local television reporter, December 17, 1996. *Photo courtesy of WLIO-TV, Lima, Ohio.*

very composition, the group thus had the potential for much conflict; at the time, Lima's mayor and the Shawnee trustees were also deep into a political tangle over Berger's attempt at "nonwithdrawal annexation" of small parts of Shawnee Township. The task force also included Jonathan Rockhold, president of the Chamber of Commerce, and Marcel Wagner, the county economic development officer. Two local leaders were appointed co-chairs, retired banker MacDonel and power company official Kenneth Belcher. The latter was, perhaps, a surprise choice. A Navy veteran who had spent much of his adult career as district manager for American Electric Power, Belcher attributed his selection as chair to the group's need to have someone from the private sector, rather than a local politician, out front. His employer encouraged his involvement—particularly since BP was one of their biggest customers in a ten-state region—but the position required Belcher to proceed carefully, because the task force had to be, he admitted, "adversarial at times" with BP.[27]

At the beginning, at least, the new task force came out swinging, listing three initial goals. They would push BP to openly state its minimum acceptable criteria for a sale. They would ask it to agree to a six-month delay in separating the refinery from the neighboring chemical plant. And more immediately, they would contact the three rejected bidders and learn from them all they could about what exactly BP wanted. The nature of these goals seemed to require some dedicated wooing of BP, or at least a more compliant local posture, but task force representatives had few soft words for the corporation. He left the first meeting, Cunningham told the press, "confident that BP fully expects to close the refinery and has manipulated circumstances to achieve that goal." BP had intended the move, he concluded, long before they had even put it up for sale. A representative from the OCAW Union international was just as damning. "BP has a plan and will use you to their advantage," he warned. "Most of you would have to pay a healthy cover charge to see the kind of dancing BP is doing."[28]

In their initial gathering, the newly forming task force met with Atton and James Walpole, manager of the chemical plant, both of whom asserted that BP remained willing to sell the refinery to an appropriate buyer, although they now doubted that such a buyer could be found. The task force charged into that slight opening. Over the next few weeks, members threw themselves into a variety of interrelated efforts. They surveyed area businesses to get some hard numbers on what the refinery closing would cost them, both financially and in terms of planned employee layoffs. They alerted the Ohio EPA and other related environmental agencies to make sure they kept monitoring BP with special intensity. They likewise contacted other state and federal officials to see what levers they could apply from those sectors. And they called the three bidders to learn what they could of their offers and the bidding process. Dove came to Lima to relay what he could of the bid process. While stating his conviction that BP had carried through a real sales process, rather than just going through the motions, he confirmed that BP had firmly rejected the management buyout plan. He also admitted that he had no idea what BP would accept as an adequate offer, either in terms of a specific amount of money or in terms of types of preconditions for a sale. Finally, Dove cautioned the group against much hope, noting that since several bids had failed to produce a successful buyer for the refinery, the

"We are bending over backwards to soften the blow": BP senior executive David Atton in Lima, explaining why the corporation had no choice but to close the refinery, December 1996. *Photo courtesy of the* Lima News.

odds seemed long for finding one now. Berger disagreed. The task force would "keep plugging," he assured the press. "We've got to."[29]

The task force devoted its main efforts to pushing Atton hard. They pumped him for all the additional specific information they could get and also tried hard to slow the closure process. In accordance with the group's wishes, Atton drove down to Lima again in mid-December to reiterate orally what he had already communicated on paper. Both in correspondence and in person, Belcher recalled, Atton was always polite and thoroughly professional, but he did not deviate from the corporate line. He readily gave permission for the refinery's local managers and local OCAW officials to involve themselves with the task force, but on nearly all the larger issues pertaining to the plant's sale or closure, his answer was a firm and unequivocal no. In fact, Atton said no with such predictable regularity that he might have saved himself considerable effort by simply posting the word in gigantic letters on a hot-air balloon circulating over Lima. No, BP would not accept any financial risk in any bid. No, BP would not agree to a six-month delay in locating an alternative source of supply for the refinery's products. No, BP would not pay a higher price for the refinery's products under any new owner than it would pay for "the cost of equivalent supply from other sources." Task force members got the message loud and clear, to their immense frustration and despair. "In BP's responses to our questions about a sale," one task force member exclaimed, "I seem to be hearing an unspoken message. That message is 'No, no, no. How many times do we have to say no?'" Percy was quick to suggest what BP thought a more helpful local attitude. Two years, he pointed out, "is a long time to make other plans . . . if people would kind of get resigned to it and get on with it, that's a lot of time there."[30]

From the very beginning of their work on the task force, Belcher and others had known that the odds of saving the plant were low, but they still had no intention of taking Percy's advice. Belcher had negotiated with BP in his role as a power company administrator, and he knew for a fact that its executives could be effective and demanding negotiators; perhaps these were just signals from a tough corporation that it expected concessions. So Lima scrambled for extra inducements. The OCAW local readily agreed to permit BP to reclassify whatever refinery workers it thought it needed, even if that meant replacing some workers with contractors. Area contractors—especially the city's water department, vendor of such massive quantities of fluid to the refinery—promised a reduction in rates.[31]

BP remained unmoved. Again, it blamed the hard facts of the refining business. Whatever profits the refinery had made were largely, Percy told the *Lima News,* because BP had pumped so much money into improvements; in effect, the plant had been a "break-even proposition." Only half-hidden behind such rationales was an implication that cut local people to the quick. BP had clearly decided, Percy said, to retain only "world class refineries," namely, those that could be structured to produce a $4–$6-per-barrel profit margin. With a $235 million investment, Toledo could be brought to this level, but Lima never could. Percy and Atton were diplomatic with their terminology in the papers, but the people in the refinery heard other words like "mediocre" whispered down through the grapevine from higher-ups. Such implications rubbed salt into wounds that were already open and sore. It was "very hard for people to hear," Gilbert admitted, "that this plant that they prided themselves on so highly" was "mediocre, and not worthy of upgrade." BP had been so impressed with the improvements the Lima facility had made that it had directed its other refineries around the world to copy them, yet now it asserted that this wasn't a "world class" plant? People at the refinery "couldn't understand it," Gilbert said. The fact that BP could extol the refinery's profitability when trying to sell it and then claim it made no profit when rationalizing its closure struck many in the community, the mayor especially, as the company simply shifting numbers around. The refinery's workers, one and all, remained convinced that they had built a first-class facility.[32]

All that late fall and early winter, BP on the one hand and the task force (and especially the mayor) on the other traded charges of such wide variance that most observers might have concluded that the two sides were operating in differing planes of reality. "BP is sending private signals that they in fact do not want to sell," Berger told the press, a charge the task force later repeated to state development director Jakeway. Rubbish, BP countered; the company would be foolish not to entertain any reasonable bid. The company, claimed the mayor, was using confidentiality agreements to control the process. Wrong, BP replied; these were legal documents and confidentiality agreements were standard operating procedure in such sales. They couldn't get around them if they wanted to. Atton and Percy repeatedly returned to a central reason why BP judged some of the bids inadequate: BP's need for a company with deep enough pockets "to assure," as Atton put it in a special editorial in the *Lima News*, "BP's separation from the day-to-day operation of the refinery." This had been the primary flaw in Paisley's bid; Banc One had asked BP to guarantee that the money Paisley borrowed would be paid back, creating an ongoing financial liability in Lima for the corporation.[33]

The only flaw in BP's argument concerned the matter of timing. A decade later, Paisley's disappointment had long since vanished, leaving him with only praise for his former employer. When his leave of absence finished, he returned to work at BP and nobody seemed to hold his absence against him; he remained on good terms with BP executives. When Berger and others charged that BP had never intended to sell, Paisley adamantly disagreed. "I trust BP explicitly that they dealt fairly," he declared. Certainly he was disappointed that BP had rejected his bid, but it had done so for understandable business reasons—all except for one. "I don't know what changed it," he admitted quietly, but "I felt the goal line moved on me at the end without me knowing why." His pitch for the refinery was a business gamble, and business gambles sometimes fail; he could accept that and put it behind him. But what got to Paisley in that hard autumn of 1996 seems to have been the sense that the game had somehow changed. Atton and Percy's contention that Paisley and his team of investors lacked pockets deep enough to ride out a disaster were true; they were legitimate reasons to reject his bid. However, BP had been aware of all those objections early on in the process when it encouraged him to submit a bid. "Well, you knew that when I started," he wanted to tell them. Yet despite that knowledge, BP had continued to encourage Paisley all through that summer and early fall. Why did the corporation's misgivings suddenly rise in importance in October? "If BP knew at the beginning that they weren't going to value an independent bid I could've saved a lot of money not trying to do this," Paisley admitted. "The bar moved up on me at the very end and I don't know why."[34]

It was exactly this point that the task force stressed in a long letter to Jakeway in mid-December. "Ohio and Allen County are caught in a global repositioning strategy by British Petroleum," they informed him. "We believe that the company decision to close the refinery was made in London, not by BP in Ohio," a decision "based on corporate market and financial strategies, not on poor operating results or inferior prospects for the refinery itself." Given this logic, the task force would do the opposite of the course Percy had recommended. Instead of resigning themselves to BP's decision, they would mobilize their community to resist it to the end. As the major next step in this agenda, they planned a big public rally. Belcher, who helped plan the event, recalled the agenda. "We wanted to make sure the community knew what was going on," he remembered, "keep them in the loop and get them stirred up a little bit." In meeting all three goals, the rally succeeded brilliantly.[35]

The rally to save the refinery, December 17, 1996. *Photo courtesy of WLIO-TV, Lima, Ohio.*

At first glance, the prospects for a large crowd seemed poor; the most paranoid of activists might have concluded that BP controlled even the weather. Lima is located right on top of the imperceptible Ohio continental divide, where rivers begin to flow north toward Lake Erie rather than south toward the Gulf of Mexico. Positioned just south of lake-effect snowstorms but north of the comparative warmth of the Ohio Valley, Allen County typically suffers winters that are long, grey, and ugly. The precipitation received in Toledo as snow and in Dayton as rain sometimes pours down on Lima as a mixture of both, or worse, as slushy snow that accumulates in slick piles in the streets and makes not just driving but even walking a tricky affair. On the day of the rally in mid-December, such a storm drove into northwest Ohio, and all day strong winds blew piles of ice-snow down on Lima. When evening fell, it was such a "nasty night," Gilbert recalled, that she was sure most people would stay at home. They didn't, however. Vast numbers filed into the downtown Civic Center despite the dreary weather. As Berger looked out at the packed auditorium, he could not quite believe the size of the crowd. The *Lima News* estimated it as upwards of eight hundred people, a gathering larger than any Berger had seen in his terms as mayor. Among them, Belcher identified union people, community leaders, and, he thought, "every employee of BP." It was the last group that the mayor specifically addressed. "We are your friends and your neighbors and the people you work with," Berger told them. "We want you to understand that we value you. You are an important asset to this community."[36]

Chamber of Commerce leader Rockhold led off the evening with the task force's own chronology of the closing of the refinery. Then Wagner summarized its survey results on the impact of the refinery's closure and their dark conclusions regarding the scale of the coming financial hit. This disaster, the mayor continued, emanated from a sharp conflict occurring among BP's upper managers, a conflict occurring entirely "in London, not in Cleveland. I believe the process has been ongoing," Berger told the crowd, "and it is a process we ought to question." Every visitor to the refinery from London had drawn the same conclusion, he said: that the plant "is a valuable asset, one that should be invested or sold. But London made the decision to do something else." If the event's planners were hoping to stoke community outrage, they realized they had succeeded before the event began. The crowd clearly arrived in an angry mood and the events of the evening merely intensified that anger. The signs people waved spoke to the night's theme. "Save our jobs," read one; "BP = Broken Promises," proclaimed another. Gilbert, who had been assigned by her bosses to attend and take notes, assessed the crowd as "emotional but under control." Still, few of the night's events could have assured the higher-ups that Lima was beginning to accept the closure decision. One member of the audience

The unveiling of the billboard at the rally to save the refinery, December 17, 1996. *Photo courtesy of WLIO-TV, Lima, Ohio.*

asked the task force what assurance workers might have that BP would honor the pledges it had made to treat the refinery employees fairly. Groans rippled among the crowd and several people shouted out, "None!" Altogether, Berger remembered, the "dismay and distrust of BP" people expressed that night were "enormous . . . . I think this was universally seen as a crisis for the community and that BP was precipitating it. This wasn't just an act of God and this wasn't just an act of the economy, you know, like rust belt economics. This was seen as a deliberate violation of the community."[37]

The task force ended the evening with what they called "the unveiling." They dropped a sheet from a large sign which the next day they affixed to a billboard on south Metcalf Street, right across from the major entrance to the refinery. The billboard's message proclaimed that Lima supported the refinery and affirmed to the employees that "the community is with you." It would remain there for most of the next eighteen months, reminding the employees, every morning when they came into work, that they were not alone in their hopes of retaining their jobs. For much of this period, and especially as that winter darkened and its cold settled in, the billboard would be about the only source of encouragement they would get.[38]

"Project blue"

When BP executives spoke of their company's future in Lima, all through that fall and winter, they repeatedly used a special phrase. To replace the gas and jet fuel that the refinery had produced, Atton and Percy affirmed, BP needed to find "an alternative source of supply." Internally they had their own secret corporate lingo for the same item. The special project in question, Gilbert's superiors instructed her to say, would be known as "project blue." This secrecy was ludicrous, however. Everyone in Lima knew what BP's managers were talking about no matter what euphemism they used. At the refinery, workers no doubt called "project blue" by all sorts of uglier names because they saw it as the direct threat to their jobs that it was. The night of the rally, Berger bluntly told Lima's public that "resupply" was just BP's way of saying that they were working to replace the refinery with a pipeline.[39]

By that winter of 1996, BP had already been working on various pipeline options for nearly a year. The initiative, not surprisingly, had come from a pipeline company called Teppco, which had approached BP executives in Cleveland the previous January, soon after BP had announced the refinery's sale. Teppco already had in place a system of underutilized pipes extending up from the Gulf Coast through the Midwest into the northeastern United States. Instead of selling the refinery, Teppco executives urged BP, close it down and use our pipelines to move finished product up from your Gulf Coast refineries. The proposition certainly would have made sense to BP. Since the Lima refinery by itself supplied the corporation with about a quarter of all the gasoline it sold in Ohio, its closure required BP to directly address the question of an alternative supply. A pipeline, or a combination of pipelines and barges, could be the answer to that problem. Once the refinery sales process failed, BP renewed talks with Teppco with more intensity. However, Percy firmly maintained that the refinery closure decision drove the pipeline plan, *not* vice-versa.[40]

The refinery task force and especially Berger read the situation the other way, as the pipeline driving closure. Berger knew much more on this point than BP realized because, late that fall, a source deep inside the corporate headquarters in downtown Cleveland had passed the mayor a copy of a memo from BP to Teppco that appeared to lay out their whole relationship. The basic idea, they agreed, was to convert a Teppco natural gas pipe into a siphon to bring up oil from the gulf. Lima was uniquely situated, both geographically and in terms of pipeline connections, to facilitate such an arrangement, but the refinery had to close for the economics to work. The project, the memo's author summarized, would take two years to complete, but it would bring the equivalent of 300,000 barrels per day into the Ohio market, an amount roughly equal to that produced by the Lima and Toledo refineries together. In September 1996, BP had apparently informed Teppco that if they could reach an agreement, London would endorse the pipeline over any sale of the refinery because BP executives in London thought their company would receive "preferred tariffs" on the pipe. According to the memo, this would grant BP a "unique competitive edge" over other Midwest oil companies, which would be allowed to use the pipeline but only at "a significantly higher tariff." The next month, the two partners agreed to work through two New York banks as middlemen to avoid direct meetings. They also agreed to delay public announcement of the deal until mid- to late 1997, when the smoke had cleared over the refinery sale. In any case, BP assured

Teppco in November, there would be no backlash to the plan because the public reaction to the sale had "gone well" and BP didn't expect any "major fallout." Given the breaking waves of public anger in Lima over the refinery's closure, the latter seemed an especially astounding claim, but this is what BP apparently told its potential partner. (See, Berger explained later, corporations "lie to each other too. They don't just lie to communities.")[41]

If the memo could be believed, its implications were potentially severe and far-reaching. It would prove that some of BP's key claims that fall—for example, that it had rejected certain offers primarily because the bidders lacked the financial wherewithal to fully separate the company from its former refinery—were completely bogus. That the mayor and the task force trusted the memo explicitly is clear from many of their subsequent analyses and actions. That December, Belcher and MacDonel summarized them for Jakeway. The closure of "a major league asset" like the Lima refinery, they stated, would "cause great harm not just to the Lima region, but also the entire state of Ohio." As refining capacity in the country continued to decline, motorists would feel the pinch in their wallets. Moreover, the task force urged Jakeway to think hard about the implications of BP bringing in oil in such massive quantities. The Lima and Toledo refineries together produced 300,000 barrels of product per day; how long would it be before BP decided it no longer needed the Toledo plant? If BP succeeded in securing retail product from outside the state and pumping it into Ohio through a pipeline, they warned, "Ohio consumer dollars will be making the reverse trip, figuratively through that same pipeline, right out of the Ohio economy." The next month, one trade industry publication cited a Wall Street source saying that BP was now undecided about the future of the Toledo plant. From any perspective other than the narrow financial interests of BP, the task force contended, "project blue," if allowed to go through, would be a complete and unmitigated disaster.[42]

Soon thereafter, BP announced that James Schaefer would be leaving the company. Since Schafer's job had been to manage BP's two Ohio refineries as an integrated "Ohio Refinery System," Percy explained to the press, and since the closure of the Lima refinery, leaving only the Toledo plant, would eliminate the need for such a system, "in a sense, Jim's job has been eliminated." Schaefer knew another reason for the move: even in Toledo, his corporate superiors saw that he embodied workers' sense of prerogative and was not shy in challenging corporate decisions that ignored the improved economics of the refineries. Stomberg had passed word down to "get Schaefer out of there." Kuenzli implied the reason was that Schaefer had been too aggressive in his defense of Lima. Workers at the refinery—whom a reporter the following spring found championing Schaefer as a lost hero—would not have been much surprised. Schaefer was "too honest," Roller claimed, to rise very far within BP. Moreover, there was no doubt he was unhappy. At a large meeting at the refinery not long after BP's announcement that it would face sale or closure, Roller recalled, Schaefer stood in front of a crowd of workers in the plant gymnasium. "I'll take questions now," the manager had said, "but I'll answer the first one. You're going to say, just how stupid is this board of directors and I'm here to tell you they're very stupid." Now BP abridged Schaefer's contract and sent him on his way with a healthy severance package. As the holiday season approached, Schaefer said goodbye to his staff in Toledo and packed up his office. A short time later, he landed an executive position with a Cleveland chemical manufacturing company, where he was soon bringing pizza lunches to the rank and file and asking them for advice on how to run the plant more efficiently.[43]

For many back in Lima, that Christmas was anything but cheery. Not long before the holiday, discussions by the task force had begun to shift from stopping the refinery's closure to dealing with its immense effects. Belcher knew that once BP had the pipeline in place, "the game was over." Lima seemed to have only a short remaining window of opportunity before the final blow fell. In a mid-December meeting between Atton and the task force, the BP vice president had estimated that the company would have its "alternate supply" locked in within five weeks. At best, then, the mayor and the task force maybe had a month, until early February at the latest, to save the refinery.[44]

Chapter 7

"Whether We're for BP or against BP, We All Sound Conspiratorial"

Throughout their long struggle to save the Lima refinery, Mayor Berger and his comrades on the task force never seemed to raise their heads above the immediate crisis and take an honest look at the odds they faced. If they had done so, they might have realized, as any number of specialists would have assured them, that their cause was hopeless. As they battled on over the course of the following year, Lima community leaders ran up against that hard truth time and time again, but they persisted in their resistance until the end. As their employers could testify, local residents had long cultivated a reputation for stubbornness, and they were led by a mayor who was fond of quoting Winston Churchill in the depths of World War II, enjoining his fellow citizens to never, never, never give up. It soon became clear that at least a small collection of local people would keep after BP with unshakable determination until the company finally decided either to save its refinery or destroy it.

"No matter what BP may or may not be telling you"

After a subdued celebration of New Year's Day, 1997, Lima leaders could not have been much heartened at the refinery's prospects. They had maybe a month left in BP's timetable and an uncertain portfolio of social capital to work with. Social scientists like Carmen Sirianni and Lewis Friedland define social capital as "those stocks of social trust, norms and networks that people can draw on to solve common problems." As the city of Lima geared up for its final rounds of engagement with BP, it became increasingly clear that its social capital differed somewhat from that of other industrial communities in similar circumstances.

The greatest difference was a fundamentally different dynamic of community politics operating in Lima. In many other industrial cities, opposition to a devastating plant closing generally coalesced from the ground up, forming a coalition of labor and community groups that sought every angle of leverage to motivate municipal officials toward greater activism in the struggle to reverse the damaging financial decisions of the corporation in question. In Lima, however, the calculus worked somewhat the other way around. There it was the small set of local citizens on the refinery task force, led by an activist mayor, who would try to prod an unwieldy coalition of Chamber of Commerce and labor officials into an intensified engagement with BP. Nor could these activists count on support from a largely unified community. Although the flame of public anger did blaze white-hot against BP in a few specific moments of crisis, Berger would have an increasingly difficult time stoking that flame into the kind of sustained, long-term opposition that the crisis required. As many union activists withdrew in bitterness and despair and growth officials—aghast at the possible creation of a "negative business climate"—became eager to accept whatever BP would give them, in the end the mayor and a few allies would carry on largely alone.[1]

Still, Mayor Berger and others in the Lima community who were determined to fight to the end to save the refinery were able to draw on a few of the elements of social capital that had facilitated some level of successful resistance to corporate decisions in other communities. At times, they could rely on the critical factor of an "aroused local community," and also at least the possibility of a critical and engaged local press. BP was a powerful global corporation, but it was not yet conclusively apparent that an adept marshalling of local political, economic, and cultural forces could not alter its decisions in some way. As labor studies scholar Bruce Nissen argues, a successful confrontation requires the existence of certain cultural/political dynamics that render corporate decisions amenable to public pressure. In Allen County, real possibilities appeared along that line. According to Belcher, the task force realized that BP was very "sensitive to public opinion." The community was already outraged. Nobody on the task force could see the harm in further stoking that anger and then watching where the public reaction led.[2]

To mobilize public opinion, Berger knew, the most immediate need was to recruit the assistance of a venerable local institution that had historically viewed activism of any sort as an anathema. He needed the *Lima News*. Despite the paper's conservative history, Berger believed there was at least a faint possibility of obtaining its support, for the paper had come a long way since the 1960s, when it had functioned as the reliable voice of arch-libertarian conservatism. On the one hand, the *Lima News* remained firmly anchored, editorially at least, at the Republican far right. Its publisher, Thomas Mullen, insisted that one did not need to be a libertarian to work for Freedom Newspapers and even contended that the newspaper chain would grant limited space to liberal columnists. However, Mullen did admit that the Hoiles, the family controlling the chain, maintained "a very clear sense of its political or philosophical viewpoint and it . . . traditionally wanted that viewpoint expressed on the editorial pages of its member newspapers." In Lima in the 1990s, that viewpoint often took shape as a shrill and venomous conservatism, especially as expressed toward the national Democrats in the White House. Lead editorialist Thomas Lucente specialized in such bile, portraying Bill Clinton as a "lying crook who should be in prison" and who had turned the presidency into a "cesspool," and branding Vice President Gore a "slimeball politician" and "pathological liar." The paper could not even bring itself to print the president's name without labeling him "our national embarrassment"; by the time Clinton left office, Lucente reported proudly, they had found occasion to attach the phrase to Clinton more than two hundred times.[3]

On the other hand, on local issues the paper had evolved into a good community newspaper, loyally serving its city and the surrounding county. It no longer instinctively opposed library bond issues or other commitments to the public good. It assigned one reporter, Kim Kincaid, to offer a weekly story on interesting highlights into area history, and employed two others, Michael Lackey and Bart Mills, to pen regular, humorous, and insightful commentary on local affairs. The Freedom chain brought in the upper echelon of management to its member newspapers, transferring in publishers and editors from elsewhere in its empire, but the ones assigned to Lima, Mullen said, tended to develop strong ties to the community and stay longer than they did at other posts. During the 1990s, an able editor named Raymond Sullivan was particularly important in this regard—but over that decade the paper took many of its major cues from its publisher. For, in contrast to the rest of the paper's management, Mullen was a local product. Born in town and graduating from Lima Senior High in 1957, he had started with the paper the next year as a rookie reporter and found promotions coming quickly. Within six years of his hiring, at age twenty-four and yet lacking a college degree, he found himself elevated to the position of general editor, a post he would hold until 1981, when the Freedom Newspapers chain sent him west to edit their paper in Colorado Springs. A decade later, they directed him back to his hometown to take on the new job of publisher. Certainly the new post would have fit him as comfortably as an old shoe; Mullen had grown up in Lima and chimed along with the main tone of its politics. "I'm a conservative Republican," he affirmed, "pretty much an economic conservative," a "free-market guy," a "limited government guy."[4]

When Mullen returned to town in 1991, however, he realized that he was entering a community in profound economic transition. He immediately decided he would take a particular interest in issues of economic development. This meant paying close attention to and working with the local political structures, even with Lima's mayor. Mullen developed a genuine respect for Berger. His paper had never endorsed Berger in his races for office, but then, it almost always refrained from endorsing any politician, as a general policy. Berger, said Mullen, was "rare among local politicians in that he has a high level of talent and intellect and focus." By and large, Mullen admitted, Berger had "a very difficult job as mayor of Lima and has done that job well." As in any relationship between a city newspaper and the local politicians it remained independent of and to some degree critical of, the *Lima News* had experienced occasional "friction" with the mayor. This tension was magnified by the distance between their positions on the political spectrum, especially with regard to the proper usage of the tools of government. Whereas, according to Berger, the *Lima News* generally contended "the less government the better," Berger's own "general approach is an activist kind of approach to improve, stimulate positive change in the community. They would generally have the opinion that if it's not coming from the private sector it has no merit, and if it's coming from the public sector it ought to be criticized and suspect." Given Berger's actions as Lima's mayor, the paper had had a lot about which to be critical. Regardless of their position on mayoral activism, however, Mullen and the rest of the *Lima News*'s management cared deeply about Lima, were committed to the economic health of their city, and were dismayed and outraged over BP's plans to pull out one of the last remaining major props of the local economy.[5]

Thus, when Berger approached the staff of the *Lima News* hoping to possibly enlist it as an ally in saving the refinery, the potential existed both for collaboration and disaster. He had first made his pitch to them the previous August, deeply disturbed by the warnings he had received from Deep Well that the BP's sale of the refinery was going awry. One evening in late summer, he and Banc One executive Nobile drove down to the home of *Lima News* editor Sullivan in suburban Shawnee Township to meet with the paper's editor and publisher. The four men seated themselves around Sullivan's dining room table and Berger laid out his idea. He was going to be engaging BP a lot in the coming months, he explained, and would have a great deal of information to share. But he wanted to make sure that he would have the ability to "control that case" against BP in the city newspaper. He was not asking for editorial control, he assured the journalists, nor requesting permission to vet the paper's stories. But he needed, he clarified, to be able "to look on the *Lima News* as a strategic weapon in the effort to deal with the company." If they really wanted to save the refinery, his office "needed to control the story and the pace of the story and make sure the story had legs and would sustain itself over a long period of time." Over my dead body, responded editor Sullivan; you're stepping over the line between politicians and a free press. Under no circumstances, he informed the mayor with some heat, would he agree to work with any politician in such a manner. Okay, responded Berger, and got up to leave. But then the two other men—most notably Mullen, Sullivan's boss—intervened, calling Berger back and asking both to return to the table and try to work something out. So Berger sat back down and the discussion continued. The more the mayor talked, Mullen remembered, the more they realized that "he could be very valuable to us because he was ahead of everybody else in the community at that point in understanding what was going on inside BP and that he had sources we didn't, and that it would be in everybody's interest to work together." By the end of the evening, Berger and the *Lima News* had reached an unwritten understanding. The paper would devote considerable resources to a full and sustained investigation of BP's actions in Lima. In that investigation, the mayor would function as a privileged source of information and allowed, not a veto but, some measure of guidance over the story's flow.[6]

Fundamentally, Berger concluded, the agreement with the paper gave him what he wanted. From then on, for at least a year, the conservative *Lima News* of the far-right Freedom Newspapers chain began to function in the best tradition of progressive, muckraking American journalism. Within days of the closure announcement, the paper went after BP with a blistering editorial penned by Mullen himself, and, especially in the first months of the city's confrontation with the company, the paper often offered two, three, or more penetrating stories on the matter every week. Some of the stories revealed particularly interesting insights into the higher workings of BP from unnamed "anonymous sources." Whenever the paper made such references, Berger admitted later, "that was me." In this manner what the mayor learned about BP's high-level deliberations from his own sources like Deep Well regularly found its way into the mainstream press. Before long the oil trade press began to consult the *Lima News* on a regular basis and so did highly placed staffers in the Ohio governor's office. The paper's management would have been delighted with the arrangement. On one occasion, when the chief executive of Lima's WLIO-TV complained to Berger that the *Lima News* had "scooped" his TV reporters on a particular BP story, Sullivan and Mullen reminded the mayor to remain coy about their arrangement. "They want to protect their 'source,'" Berger wryly noted in his diary. Mullen in particular began working closely with the mayor on other BP matters as well. In January, sparked by a suggestion from Berger, he wrote to the CEO of the Teppco Corporation, then busily negotiating with BP about its pipeline, offering to share "some of our coverage" of the story from the perspective of Lima. It "seems highly unlikely," Mullen informed Teppco executives, that the pipeline would benefit people in his part of the state. Further, Mullen did his best to remove whatever blinders BP had placed over the eyes of Teppco's executives about how the closure decision was being received locally. "In any case," he continued, "you need to know that this project, as it is presently understood, is not being greeted with any warmth or enthusiasm in Ohio, no matter what BP may or may not be telling you."[7]

In his letter to Teppco, Mullen also put his finger on one other powerful resource his community might be able to utilize against BP, a resource partly mobilized by the publicity his paper was generating. "Frankly," he told Teppco, "BP's credibility is in doubt not only in the Lima area, but also in the state capital of Columbus." If Lima's advocates stood any faint chance of saving the refinery, then they would need to enlist more powerful players to their side. "Our whole goal" on the task force, Belcher said, "was to keep this in front of the public." State politicians such as the governor might or might not want to intercede with BP, but they would act, Berger knew, if the glare of the public spotlight grew hot enough. By early in 1997, all the publicity was beginning to achieve the desired effects; some of Ohio's big politicians began to stir.[8]

"British Petroleum will have him for lunch"

From the beginning, Berger and the task force fully understood that some measure of state intervention would be critical to their hopes. There were all sorts of things the state of Ohio could conceivably do to help. It could pressure BP to drop the pipeline arrangement, as lawyer and local environmental activist David Little suggested, or it could "discomfort" BP by intensifying environmental oversight at the refinery and the chemical plant. Apparently, the governor and the state development director generally disliked tax abatement deals, yet the chemical plant had recently secured one, and similar overtures to possible refinery buyers might spark more interest. However, from all Berger could see four months into the effort to save the refinery, the state's crucial importance had been reinforced only in a negative way. By mid-January, the task force had made contact with two new potential buyers, but one had quickly dropped out when it deemed the state's support insufficient and the other, Berger told the press, was voicing reluctance to put more effort into constructing a bid unless it received indications of active interest from statewide politicians.[9]

Governor Voinovich had already made it clear that Lima would be dealing primarily with Jakeway, and what the task force had seen of him so far did not inspire confidence. He made a convincing initial impression, striking Berger as "a salesperson, very affable, optimistic." Moreover, "he had come to Ohio well regarded," as someone with "significant Midwest economic development credentials" who had done a credible job for the state under Voinovich. But the task force had steadily pushed him all that late fall of 1996 without noticeable effect. In addition, when the *Lima News* shot off a tough editorial criticizing the state for its lack of involvement in December 1996, Jakeway's rebuttal seemed curiously nonspecific. "I've probably spent more time on this issue than any other single project I've worked on for the governor," he assured local people. "I would hope that people don't fall into the old trap of believing that silence means we are not doing anything."[10]

Nor did personal contact with Jakeway ease local doubts. Right before Christmas, Belcher and Berger drove down to Columbus to meet with Jakeway, his staff, and several other area politicians. At the meeting, the state development director tried to calm local fears by announcing that BP had given him the green light to serve as an intermediary between the corporation and potential buyers. Yet he astonished the task force representatives by naïvely insisting on separating the pipeline from the possible sale of the refinery, claiming that the two were unrelated issues. Even more worrisome was his reminder that "BP is the largest investor in the state of Ohio." The conclusion seemed clear to Belcher. "It is pretty obvious," he told the *Lima News*, "that the development office doesn't want to do anything to upset BP." Plainly stung by the remark, Jakeway sent off a quick letter to the editor of the *Lima News*, reiterating his willingness to do whatever he could to facilitate a sale, but two weeks later, he was still seething over Belcher's remarks in a phone call to Berger. The central lesson in the little episode seemed plain to longtime observers of BP back in Lima: Jakeway "had better take a more aggressive posture," refinery worker Roller observed in a letter to the *Lima News*, "or British Petroleum will have him for lunch."[11]

Altogether these incidents signaled to the task force that they needed higher-level intervention—specifically, the assistance of the governor. But that kind of help remained elusive. British Petroleum, Berger knew, had a large, very effective lobbying effort active in Columbus and he also was aware of what BP was saying there. Their chief lobbyist was a tall, suave, and very articulate old gentleman who knew everyone important in the state capital. Berger had heard through the grapevine what he was saying: "Lima, Ohio? That refinery is a century old, governor. It's just not the place where we can make the investment that's required, and there's a better option for us." Lima was one of the fifteen largest cities in the state, and in his years as mayor Berger had previously met with Voinovich several times to discuss local concerns. Now, suddenly, when he showed up in Columbus for an appointment with Voinovich, the governor's staff made excuses for the big boss and the mayor found himself instead shunted off to a meeting with Jakeway. Berger had no doubt that it was BP's influence that had "shut that access off."[12]

It was possible that Voinovich's sudden refusal to meet with the mayor was because, as he geared up for a campaign for election to the U.S. Senate, his staff had become extra protective. However, it might instead have been because, throughout his political career, the governor had enjoyed a warm and profitable relationship with BP. After all, Voinovich had been born and raised in Rockefeller's old hometown of Cleveland, graduating from high school and practicing law there, representing an East Cleveland district in the state House of Representatives and then serving for five years as Cuyahoga County auditor. In 1979, after a year as lieutenant governor, Voinovich had returned home to Cleveland to run for and win the office of mayor, a post he held for a decade before being elected governor. As an emerging and powerful area politician, it was inevitable that he had forged collegial ties with Cleveland's large financial interests, a list that certainly included BP. He and Percy, a senior executive said, had developed a good working relationship and "talked on a lot of issues." Their relationship may well have drifted over into a personal friendship; Voinovich's letters to the vice president of BP America began, "Dear Steve." Moreover, it was nearly inevitable that BP had sought to lubricate its relationship with the emerging local political star with plenty of campaign cash. In 1990, as Voinovich geared up his run for governor, BP funneled $25,000 to his campaign. A decade later, the company was still a faithful campaign contributor to Senator Voinovich; its donation in 2000 of $32,500 ensured that BP remained one of the largest single contributors to Voinovich's campaign chest.[13]

Voinovich's ambitions cut both ways, however. With his eye on a U.S. Senate seat in 1996–97, he needed voter support as well as cash, and the largely rural counties of northwest Ohio had long functioned as a happy hunting ground for lots of Republican votes. The governor clearly needed to do something tangible to address Lima's concerns. In early January, he wrote another letter to Percy that went beyond the usual broad platitudes to include specific actions. He had heard rumors, Voinovich admitted to Percy, "that, for economic reasons, BP has no intention of selling" the Lima refinery. The Lima newspaper, the governor had learned, had recently run a story on some kind of a pipeline from the Gulf of Mexico that could affect refinery sale possibilities, and his office was experiencing "difficulty" in learning "what adverse effects a pipeline could have, not only on the Lima refinery, but on similar facilities in Ohio." BP had not been forthcoming with many details on the operation, and he was hoping that Percy would "share whatever information you have on this subject." He and Jakeway, the governor said, were eager to meet with him to facilitate that process. Moreover, the governor revealed that he had "recently heard from an interested investor" and stood ready to "do whatever I can" to help ensure that all interested parties emerge as winners in the "limited window of opportunity" left. Belcher told the *Lima News* that the governor's letter signaled "very significant progress," but privately Berger could only hope that Voinovich was serious. In his few first days of dealing with this new investor, he had already learned that he would need as many soothing ministrations as a politically distracted governor could provide, and maybe more.[14]

"Vulture investor"

Right after the New Year, Berger had received a call from a businessman from a corporation he had never heard of, Stanley Phelps and Company. Phelps wanted to explore the possibility of purchasing the Lima refinery, specifically to add to the holdings of a subsidiary he owned called the Commonwealth Oil Refining Corporation (the Phelps Company, Berger learned, included a variety of such energy-related affiliates). The Phelps Company initially seemed to Mullen to be a "bottom-feeder" among oil companies, but Berger phoned a few of his contacts in the oil industry and concluded that Phelps was a "legitimate prospect." (Among Berger's phone contacts was Schaefer, who vouched for a Phelps chief executive named Joseph Sheperd, whom he had known from their mutual days with Sohio.) Admittedly, Berger figured that BP's constrained timetable now rendered any bid a long shot, and he also had a few other misgivings. Phelps initially struck him as "the type of New York/Connecticut businessman who comes across as very aggressive [and] ruthless." The mayor knew, moreover, that Phelps's company was not the kind of major industry player that BP was looking for. Yet at that point Berger was mostly interested in wedding the refinery to a new owner before BP's timetable expired and was not very picky about potential suitors. Berger encouraged Phelps to proceed quickly with the bidding process. Then he alerted the task force and the *Lima News* of a possible buyer, without revealing his name.[15]

In his first conversation with Phelps, the mayor also encouraged the businessman to contact the governor. Phelps jumped on the idea. Apparently going right to the top was just his style. A few days later Berger again reached Phelps by phone and found him in a rage. He had called the governor's office, he told the mayor, left his name with the secretary along with a pointed reminder of the immense monetary contributions he had made to the Republican Party, and confidently awaited a return call from Voinovich. Instead, Jakeway had called. Phelps had spoken to him for only five minutes before handing him off to an aide. He wasn't going to play, Phelps told Berger, "those kinds of games." The deal was off, he stormed; he would find another place to spend his money. "I gave that governor of yours and Bush $50,000, I am prepared to spend $50 million in the state of

Ohio, and that governor of yours won't even give me five minutes." Berger tried to calm him and pledged that he would call the governor and encourage him to return Phelps's call. Later that day, however, he endured another angry phone call, this one from Jakeway, who was upset at being left out of the loop. Jakeway wondered if Phelps was a legitimate player, since he was not making himself available to the development director's office. "Is he a phantom?" Jakeway wanted to know. Berger managed to reach Voinovich by phone the next afternoon and found him indignant. "You know, mayor, we have a policy around here that I don't return calls like this," Voinovich complained. "The staff returns the calls and does the necessary follow-up work." He was particularly offended by the idea that a campaign contribution would nudge him into action. "I don't do business like that," Voinovich declared. "Good government does not depend on money for access." Making no excuses for Phelps's behavior, Berger hastened to agree with Voinovich, but pleaded with the governor to go the extra mile. Jakeway's comments had alienated potential buyers, Berger explained, and now, with less than a 1 percent chance of saving the refinery, Phelps would not proceed without an opportunity to talk with the governor. Finally Voinovich relented—"Mayor, the only reason I am making this call is because you asked me to"—and then things started to move.[16]

Within a few days, Berger had decided on a promising but very delicate strategy. He would push the story into the public arena, hoping that the heat of public attention might pressure both the state and BP into working together on a deal with Phelps. He would do this with an unstated wink of approval from Phelps, but without his explicit knowledge or concurrence, so that the businessman could truthfully adhere to a confidential relationship with BP. And he would have to make as much of the story as possible as public as he could as quickly as he could, before BP could envelop Phelps in a confidentiality agreement and pull the affair out of the public eye. It would be a tricky thing to pull off, but these were desperate times for his city and the mayor was a desperate man.[17]

So, in the ensuing weeks, with the ready cooperation of Mullen and his newspaper, Berger played the press like a clarinet. With the governor's political needs in mind, the mayor encouraged Mullen to run an editorial praising Voinovich's involvement, and the *Lima News* promptly did so. Meanwhile, in an effort to throw as many state hurdles as possible in front of the pipeline effort, Berger urged a Voinovich staffer to look into state regulations on pipelines, refinery closures, and possible violations of antitrust laws. The mayor maintained a steady phone relationship with a key Phelps aide, methodically building the case for Phelps to emerge publicly. He had a "nightmare," Berger told the aide, that BP would break the story first in such a manner as to discredit Phelps, just as, in his view, they had done with the previous bidders. Instead, he urged, "the first headline about you guys should be ours, since it will be good news." Phelps signaled his openness to the idea but informed the mayor that Atton had just forwarded him confidentiality agreements for his review. Berger immediately fed details on Phelps to a *Lima News* reporter, releasing biographical data on all the main Phelps players, so that, as the paper quoted him, "the entire community has the ability to understand that we have people of substantial means and experience who are interested in the refinery." He was concerned, the mayor told the Lima public, that "BP is using confidentiality agreements to keep everyone from knowing there were substantial bidders and substantial bids before." This time around, Berger promised, "before BP and the bidder talk too much, all concerned should know we have a credible buyer and credible bid." The paper also relayed the news that Atton had delayed any announcement about alternate supply arrangements, presumably to give BP time to consider Phelps's offer.[18]

Altogether the story delighted the mayor—"it was great!" he noted in his diary—and for a few short moments it appeared that the Phelps deal might be inching its way forward. The OCAW local at the refinery reached an effective bargaining agreement with BP that gave the company an out if they sold the facility—in effect promising the company a $10 million bonus for completing a sale. Berger worried over comments from a Phelps aide that, after receiving yet a second phone call from the governor, Phelps had begun to insist that the state keep out of the negotiations. No, no, Berger urged. "We had spent weeks turning the state around" on the matter, he told Phelps, and to exclude it now would cost serious momentum. Besides, he urged Phelps, you can say it's not you insisting that the state be present, it's the task force that's insisting on the state's intervention. Meanwhile, a source Berger trusted at the refinery quietly passed word to the mayor that, contrary to what the newspaper had reported, back behind the curtain at BP, Teppco and Atton appeared to be close to cobbling together a deal on the pipeline. If the Phelps deal disintegrated, BP's alternate supply seemed ready to click into place.[19]

Then, in the space of a few days, the mayor watched his work systematically unravel, and with it the last apparent hope of saving the Lima refinery. *Platt's Oilgram News,* a staple organ of the trade press, suddenly broke the story that Phelps was a "vulture investor" who was currently operating a terribly polluted oil tank farm and terminal called Corco—a site the EPA had demanded that Phelps clean up as one of the worst such sites in the nation. Moreover, the story continued, Phelps's company included in its executive ranks Schaefer's old friend Sheperd, a former official of a company called Arochem. At Arochem, the other chief executive, Sheperd's partner, had gone to prison to serve a fifteen-year sentence for money laundering and bank fraud. Berger quickly contacted Schaefer, who told him that the data on Sheperd's partner was true but meant nothing. Sheperd was innocent of any wrongdoing and only the victim of guilt by association. In fact, Sheperd was a hero who had blown the whistle on his partner the moment he had heard of wrongdoing and cooperated with the FBI in prosecution of his former partner. The mayor jumped on the phone to Phelps and demanded answers. The *Oilgram* story was mistaken, Phelps insisted. He had bought Corco committed to cleaning up the pollution that the previous owner had left, and had hired Sheperd because he was honest and competent. But the mayor could see that the "vulture investor" charges had upset Phelps, further undermining his ardor for a possible deal with BP.[20]

Even more disturbing to Berger was how all that potentially damaging information on Phelps had come to the eyes of the press at such a critical time. Suspicion began to harden in the back of his mind. A *Lima News* reporter he had been working closely with, Mike Mender, had described to the mayor a curious e-mail he had recently received out of the blue from someone he didn't know but who had carefully recited, with perfect "insider jargon," much of the content of the *Oilgram* "vulture investor" story. Berger asked a BP friend to check the sender's name against BP's corporate employee roster. Sure enough, Berger's source produced the name of a BP security chief, a former CIA officer with the same surname as Mender's correspondent, whose e-mail handle began, revealingly, "intlguy." Pressing Phelps for what he knew, Berger quickly learned that after the story had appeared, Phelps's staff had contacted the *Oilgram* reporter, James Norman, who had broken the "vulture investor" story. Norman had admitted that a contact at BP had fed him the negative data on Phelps.[21]

For the mayor, all the pieces fit into place, and he did not hesitate to make them public. The same day the *Lima News* led with a big story on Phelps's bid, the paper included a second feature article on the "vulture investor" charges. Both stories had Berger's fingerprints all over them. Phelps had offered $50 million in cash for BP's refinery, the paper reported, an option that Phelps underscored as far preferable to any pipeline arrangement. After nudging from Berger, Phelps had consented to an interview with the *Lima News* reporter Mender, and his point by point defenses of his company and of Sheperd rang with sincerity. The story included a quote from Paisley's old associate, the Texas oilman Dove, testifying to Sheperd's integrity. But the real bombshell in the story came from Berger, who charged that BP had planted the "spin that seems to have been put on some of the background information about Phelps."[22]

Phelps, for one, seemed pleased with Berger's work. In talking with the *Lima News,* he could defend himself against the *Oilgram* charges without seeming to violate the confidentiality agreements he had now signed with BP. "You told me to trust that reporter, Mike Mender, and you were right," he assured Berger. All other players in the story seemed less certain. For the mayor of Lima to have informed the press that BP had planted negative stories to try to kill a potential bid—and with it, Lima's refinery—escalated tensions to a new level. BP hotly denied Berger's charge. In a letter Atton sent to the mayor and released to the press the next day, he denounced the mayor's claim as "totally untrue" and added that BP was "deeply offended" at the accusation.[23]

Now it was Berger's turn to sit back and watch a master player work the press. A Phelps executive called him with a confidential heads-up: BP would soon be announcing that Phelps was withdrawing his bid. Don't worry, Phelps's associate executive soothed. BP would be handling the media, but Phelps would explain that his company was withdrawing only because he had become convinced that BP did not want to sell. At any rate, the executive hinted, "the day is not over." Phelps was not done playing his hand, he said, and more activity would be occurring behind the scenes. However, all the public saw was the curtain coming down hard on the Phelps deal, with the finger of blame pointing squarely back at the mayor and the publicity tempest he had stirred up. To make matters worse, BP released a memo to all the refinery employees and also to the press, stating that Phelps's withdrawal had resulted from all the negative publicity he had received. It was true, Phelps admitted to Berger, but not really. Percy had read him the release over the phone and he had approved it so as not to alienate BP. He had done this because he still hoped to cut a deal with the company when personally visiting London. The major *Lima News* story on the matter seemed incapable of entirely making sense of what had happened. It printed a statement from BP, on its letterhead, reporting that Phelps had withdrawn the offer because of the recent negative publicity, but a few lines down, it also quoted Phelps himself, who contradicted BP's press release, expressing hope that a deal would still go through, though declining to elaborate. Further on in the story, a BP public relations official in Cleveland professed confusion as to why Phelps would blame the negative publicity. Instead, she insisted, BP was still waiting for more specific details from Phelps so it could evaluate his company's offer against the "other supply possibilities" it was considering. In all, the episode seemed best summarized by environmental lawyer Little, who had been contacted by a reporter from the *Oil Price Information Service* for comment. "Whether we're for BP or against BP, we all sound conspiratorial," Little had explained. "That's the way things are down here."[24]

At least one local media outlet readily accepted BP's portrayal of Phelps's withdrawal, and so did at least one state official. Dennis Shreefer, a local radio talk-show host, read BP's memo to refinery employees over the air, Berger noted in his diary, "and immediately began to blame me and the *Lima News* for losing the Phelps deal." Even more aggravating to Berger was the fact that Jakeway likewise immediately accepted BP's line. The state development director released a public letter blaming the area media for undermining the Phelps bid. For its part, the *Lima News* blasted BP with another angry editorial. “Cheapshot artists and second-guessers are encouraged by BP’s murky statement,” the paper thundered. “It is difficult not to think BP intended such speculation.” These strong words accomplished little, however, and the deal really did now seem dead. In periodic phone calls to the mayor over the ensuing two months, Phelps kept reiterating his confidence at closing a deal on the refinery, at one point upping his offer to BP to $100 million. Through his BP contacts, however, Berger never discerned any real movement by BP toward serious consideration of any of Phelps’s offers. In late March, after relaying to Phelps the advice of one oil executive that he offer $300 million, Berger observed that the businessman’s interest in any deal seemed to be waning.[25]

From BP’s perspective, the whole thing had worked out satisfactorily. “We were trying to settle things down in Lima,” a senior executive admitted later, and Phelps’s withdrawal of his bid came as a big relief. Now it was too late to consider any more bids, BP’s public relations officer in Cleveland told the press, and the company could get on with the business of closing the Lima refinery.[26]

“Fresh coffee, doughnuts, and company jackets”

For the mayor and other interested people in Lima, the Phelps episode had at least been an educational experience. They had learned a lot. For Berger it became a means of testing the sincerity of BP’s claims that they really would sell the refinery to an interested bidder, “and I think they failed that test.” As the affair terminated, he also heard the company loudly slamming the door on any future bids. “That had always been their private resolve,” he stated; now, with the end of the Phelps deal, it became BP’s public position as well.[27]

The intense few weeks dealing with Phelps’s bid had also taught Berger and others in Lima something of the level of support they could expect from the state of Ohio. They reluctantly recognized that BP, with its deep ties to big Ohio politicians, had a lot more pull with state officials than did the needs of little Lima. At best, the mayor said, the state had given him “lip-service” on the issue; when push came to shove, state officials took BP at its word. Berger told Jakeway, and tried to tell the governor, that BP was closing down the refinery for its own narrow commercial reasons, in an attempt to secure a product flow at a lower price, corner the Midwest market, and ratchet up area gas prices. In the end, however, as far as Berger could tell, the state rejected such reasoning. “They didn’t want to hear about a premier international company and the way it was doing business in Ohio.” To them, his warnings would have “just seemed like the ravings of a desperate local politician." Even as someone as loyal to BP as Judy Gilbert characterized Voinovich's role as "minor." He and his administration, Gilbert said, "didn't care about Lima and they were looking at the bigger picture." Local people had even fewer kind words for the state development director. Not long after the Phelps deal fell through, Jakeway came to Lima to strategize with the task force and Berger refused even to attend the meeting, so angry and disgusted he was with Jakeway for his public letter blaming the local media for killing the Phelps offer. In his mind, Jakeway was simply "fronting for BP." Mullen was equally damning in his assessment. "I'll tell you when I blew up," he later explained to a reporter for the leftist national newsmagazine *The Nation*. "I was at a dinner with the Ohio Department of Development, when we were told that the state would not involve itself without the approval of BP! You understand? Our efforts have to be approved by BP? The state has simply taken the view that it is powerless, that all this is inevitable."[28]

Now, with the Phelps bid finished and BP's announcement about a pipeline deal expected at any time, the task force quickly began to ease back from the edge of confrontation. They had decided, Belcher told the press, to rework and rethink their efforts. Privately that meant, he admitted later, that the task force then "started falling apart" because of a prevailing sense of despair. At a meeting of the group in mid-February, Berger ticked off a couple of small points he felt the group should raise with the company, and met with immediate objection from several people, who argued that the group "had to stop alienating BP" and instead get what it could from the company. With the exception of a union representative, he noted, he was the only person at the meeting with anything other than a "hat-in-hand" attitude toward BP. This left him, he recorded in his diary, "thoroughly disgusted and depressed." Early the next month, with Atton now declining to return its phone calls, the task force scaled back their meetings to once a month. Meanwhile, in preparation for the refinery's closure, BP began trying to induce the Lima plant's workers to accept jobs at the Toledo plant.[29]

The mayor quickly discovered the futility of nearly every other possible angle of activism against BP. After consulting with key staffers who told him of lukewarm community support for the idea, he decided against a unilateral city boycott of BP diesel fuel for Lima city vehicles. Since the memo he had received on the pipeline suggested an attempt by BP to corner the Midwest gasoline market, he phoned a few Washington attorneys and asked about a possible legal basis to sue BP for antitrust violations. Forget it, the lawyers advised; it was a hopeless case. He drove up to Toledo for an hour-long meeting with Democratic representative Marcy Kaptur, the only sympathetic representative in the congressional delegation from northwestern Ohio. Kaptur relayed the interesting news that when Percy had visited her nearly a year before, as the company announced plans to sell the Lima refinery, he had confidently assured her that they would have no problem finding a buyer. Then, as she read of BP's recent decision to close the plant because of overcapacity in the refining industry, the congresswoman had been skeptical. "I mean," she asked Berger, "does overcapacity in an industry happen overnight, or does it exist for some time?" The mayor pushed Kaptur to explore possible antitrust aspects of BP's actions and any means by which she could link BP into upcoming congressional hearings, headed by Representative Joseph Kennedy, concerning a heating oil shortage. In the end, nothing came of Berger's advice. Nor, he learned, could he expect much help from Lima's own congressman. Oxley, Lima's local representative, showed up in February at a local Chamber of Commerce event and Berger asked him publicly if he thought the refinery closure had any national security implications. Oxley replied that he didn't think so, since more than 150 other refineries had closed; moreover, Oxley continued, BP officials had assured him that since gasoline remained in abundant supply in the Midwest, Lima's closure would not be a big problem. The congressman followed with some "stupid remarks," Berger thought privately, about how, adjusted for inflation, current gas prices were equivalent to those of the 1950s.[30]

Neither, the mayor discovered, could he expect organized labor to mount much strong action against BP. This was partly because of reasons peculiar to local union history. The last major strike at the Lima refinery had occurred in 1980 under Sohio management. Then, midway through that decade, facing a routine contract renewal, the local union had apparently committed a major blunder that lessened the effectiveness of further militancy. Facing Greve as local refinery manager—a sharp and aggressive businessman who would readily press his advantage—the union had neglected to request in writing a contract renewal six months in advance of the deadline, as their contract had specified. Claiming the union had broken the contract, Greve had adamantly refused to negotiate, and it had taken the warring parties a year to sort it all out. As a result, when the OCAW local finally did renegotiate its contract, it had become off-cycle from the rest of the OCAW. When the national union struck, the local union was contractually unable to, and vice-versa.[31]

Moreover, the OCAW local seemed temperamentally disinclined to confrontation. Years of corporate magnanimity had apparently lulled it into a deep slumber. Greve's toughness had fed a deep bitterness among the Lima rank and file, but, beyond his short tenure, the general relationship between the union and the company had soothed much of the local OCAW membership into complacency and inaction. Workers at the refinery had tended to see each other as family, an attitude reinforced by the fact that so many members of individual families had worked there over succeeding generations. Apparently, Browne's emphasis on

Local OCAW leader Hugh Winterstellar. *Photo courtesy of the* Lima News.

the "special relationship" that BP enjoyed with its "partner communities" had sunk deeply enough into the plant's culture that even union members tended to include management within that sense of an extended workplace family. When he hired on with Sohio's Lima refinery in 1969, Hugh Winterstellar, president of the OCAW local, decided after just two weeks that he wanted to retire there. "It was great," he remembered. "Lima was like no other place—hourly and salaried people lived next to each other, worked together, even went on vacations together." Now, in the spring of 1997, looking back on what BP had done to the refinery, his misgivings spoke volumes. "We probably would have been better off in a more adversarial situation," he realized. "As it is, they put us to sleep with fresh coffee, doughnuts, and company jackets."[32]

The greatest crisis in its history thus found the OCAW local unprepared and its members strangely apathetic. They would raise a stink with BP about comparatively small issues, like the company ignoring the accustomed way of filling new positions. Yet when Winterstellar called a key meeting to vote on the pact called "effects bargaining," the legal terms of the refinery shutdown he had negotiated, only roughly half of the 286 members bothered to show up. When one leader, the OCAW's recording secretary, Karen Lombardo, tried to rouse her fellow union members to greater militancy, they told her that "the time isn't right," and some "resented" her efforts to stir things up. It was only in late spring 1997, with its members facing the loss of all of their jobs, that the OCAW local finally began to rouse itself into action, proposing to send delegations to Columbus and Washington to press state and federal officials for intervention. That June, in a effort it dubbed the Save Our Jobs Campaign, it officially launched a boycott of all BP products, but such action seemed too little too late. Both the union vice president, Mike Edelbrock, and Mayor Berger admitted they had little hope that anything the union did at that point could cause BP to change its mind. Berger, Edelbrock, and others still inclined to confrontation found themselves increasingly alone for another reason too: BP still had a large chemical plant in Allen County, and some workers feared that if they pushed things too hard with BP, the company might retaliate against the chemical plant employees. To one angry member of the task force, the reasoning seemed clear. "It's like BP was holding the Lima refinery as a hostage," this individual said, "and then after it shot that hostage, people said we better do nothing because it has other hostages."[33]

All that remained for anyone in Lima to do, it seemed, was wait for the final irrevocable blow they expected from BP: its official announcement that its pipeline deal was complete. For inexplicable reasons, local people kept waiting. Throughout that spring of 1997, Berger's sources kept his ear attuned to BP's rumor mill, and when he had solid confirmation he released the rumors to the *Lima News* and the public: BP's alternate supply arrangements were once again delayed. Atton's signatures on the final documents, Berger heard, had been postponed from mid-February to early March, and then to late March. By early May, BP had released no word, and late in the month the *Lima News* revealed that BP had broken off negotiations with Teppco and begun to explore other pipeline options. Refinery workers must have felt like condemned prisoners whose execution date was being repeatedly set back. Why had the final axe not yet dropped?[34]

The delay may have been caused by simple snafus in corporate bureaucracy. The soil underneath the American Midwest is interlaced with lines of all sorts: electricity and telecommunications cables, utility lines, sewer siphons, and pipes for moving all kinds of material—even oil. Many of those lines promised to lend themselves to BP's purposes. Knowing that it had to replace the considerable volume of liquid produced by the Lima refinery, BP had entered into careful negotiations with a variety of companies. Then, considering that Teppco's demands had become too expensive, BP dropped that pipeline firm and started talks with another one, Mid-Valley. Nor was BP limited to a single solution. Ohio was a big state and presented BP with several possibilities. A combination of pipelines and Ohio River barges might work. BP executives were talking intensively with Shell about using some of its pipelines. In the southeastern part of the state, BP had engaged in discussions with Ashland about resupply possibilities from its Kentucky refinery, while for northwestern Ohio, the corporation was talking to the Sun Oil Company. Still other possibilities may have included tapping into sources as far away as southern Illinois and Ontario, Canada. Carefully considering all possible options, BP was not in a particular hurry to commit to a single course of action. After all, they knew they had two years to complete a deal. Lima's mayor could agitate for information all he wanted, but BP would outline the pipeline deal when it was ready to go public, and not a moment before.[35]

But Berger thought he knew of another reason why the pipeline deal hadn't yet gone through, and would not go through no matter how many pipeline partners BP considered. He had received another clue from Deep Well. Check with the Interstate Commerce Commission, his source had urged, and especially U.S. "common carrier" law. If the secret memo Berger had received late in 1996 about the pipeline was as solid as he thought it was, then the BP executive whose pet project this was had apparently managed to sell the company on an idea based on a fundamentally erroneous assumption. Apparently, BP thought it would receive preferred tariffs on any pipeline—a preferential insider arrangement that would award it a slight but immensely profitable edge on the midwestern gasoline market. However, Deep Well told the mayor, BP's London executives did not fully understand American interstate commerce regulations, particularly those pertaining to "common carriers." They failed to grasp that these regulations prohibited any one company from receiving a preferred rate on a shared pipe. Berger quickly phoned an ICC lawyer and confirmed these details. All at once, it seemed to him that BP had put itself in a very tight spot from which, it would soon discover, it had only two equally distasteful ways out. The corporation still needed to supply its hundreds of midwestern gas stations with fuel. To secure its needed product, it would either have to venture onto the spot retail market—where it would get hammered by its competitors—or it would have to reopen the Lima refinery. Kuenzli was certain that under no circumstances would BP reopen the plant, but what better option did it have? According to sources Berger trusted, by June 1997, with the ending of the Teppco talks, BP must have been growing desperate to find a solution. To use a Lima metaphor from its older days, from what the mayor could tell, BP America was barreling straight down the track toward its own private little train wreck. Maybe all he had to do was just sit back and wait for the company to figure it out.[36]

"Paying your social rent"

In the meantime, the only card left for the mayor to play was one that seemed to have backfired on him earlier. He would do all he could to publicize BP's actions in Lima more widely. As it would turn out, such efforts would have a greater impact than he or anyone else around him realized at the time.

Back in late January, as Berger tried to shake off the emotional toll of the failed Phelps bid, he had suggested to Mullen that Lima's citizens would benefit from seeing something of the BP correspondence accumulating in his office. The two men decided it would be best if the newspaper obtained it through an official Freedom of Information Act request; as Berger recalled, "it needed to be seen as something that was driven by the *Lima News* as opposed to driven by me." Mullen's staff promptly filed the necessary paperwork, and Berger happily handed over a burgeoning file of letters to a *Lima News* reporter, assuring him that he now had the material for "several days of stories." The ensuing exposé carefully led readers through the entire chain of events leading to BP's decision to close the refinery, though most readers probably did not realize that the story reflected entirely the perspective of the mayor. This was only a beginning, however: Berger was eager to do what he could to push the story in front of a wider readership.[37]

At his initial meeting with Berger in late summer 1996, Mullen had agreed to do what he could to interest the national media in the story. All that fall he had tried to catch the interest of publications like the *New York Times,* but to little avail; who wanted to read another story about another plant closing in the industrial Midwest? Early in the new year, Mullen told the mayor that he had finally caught the eye of someone in the Pittsburgh office of the *Wall Street Journal.* Jumping into his car, Berger drove the five hours to Pittsburgh, where he placed a thick binder full of supporting material in the hands of an editor. Late in January, he eagerly welcomed a *Journal* reporter, Paulette Thomas, to Lima and spent the morning ushering her around town. Berger even drove her into the refinery just as a plant "town meeting" was breaking up, and while Kuenzli begged off an interview himself, he readily gave Thomas permission to talk with several employees. Thomas got her interviews, and her ensuing story could have brought no joy to BP. Certainly the reporter couched it in the usual respectful tones toward business that characterized the *Wall Street Journal,* but she still adroitly shaped the story in ways that did not enhance BP's image. She described the massive improvements of the Maumee Mission, BP's decision to sell, and the initial optimism over finding a buyer, followed by the local devastation at BP's decision to close. Thomas allowed BP a voice, principally in a quote by Atton that "BP's first responsibility is to our shareholders." However, Atton's words did not juxtapose well in the story with the advice that followed from respected former Sohio chief Frank Mosier, who spoke of the obligations companies had to their communities. "It's called paying your social rent," Mosier explained. When a corporation faced a close call with regard to a possible plant closure, "I think you ought to give great weight to how it affects the community."[38]

The *Wall Street Journal*'s national story, Berger and Mullen discovered to their satisfaction, soon paved the way for others. Within weeks, other reporters were contacting the mayor. Berger soon enjoyed a lengthy interview with the major newspaper in BP's American home city of Cleveland, and left the interview confident of the ensuing story's tone, given the "suitably cynical" comments the reporter had made about BP's official statements. Certainly the *Cleveland Plain Dealer* was careful to let BP get in its side, carefully relaying a variety of company rationales for the closure decision, notably the poor economic climate for refining and the supposed low profitability of the Lima plant. However, the story also portrayed Lima's perspective in depth, including a quote from a Phelps lawyer picked up by several other papers, implying that BP did not want the Phelps deal to succeed.[39]

Even more discomfiting to BP was the fact that the British press was likewise beginning to focus on Lima. The same day the *Wall Street Journal* piece appeared, Berger received a phone call from the *Guardian* of London, which a week later flew a reporter and a photographer across the Atlantic to do a major story. At a lunchtime meeting, the reporter, Richard Thomas, informed the mayor that his paper had a readership of about 3 million. He also noted that BP seemed intensely interested in its image in Great Britain, endlessly repeating the message that it cared about its employees and the communities where they worked. The mayor and Nobile did their best to educate the British reporter about their increasing unwillingness to believe BP's claims about anything. When Thomas later stopped by Berger's office on his way home, the reporter told the mayor he could expect the story to be published within days, and then added, "I don't think you will be receiving any Christmas cards from BP for a while." Certainly, parts of the *Guardian* story would have cheered the company. Thomas had been careful to include a number of BP's rationales for its Lima decisions, along with plenty of quotes speaking to what he implied was widespread local anti-British sentiment, a matter not likely to win Lima the sympathies of many British readers. The *Guardian* reporter had also laid out the multitude of ways in which the company was trying to ease the financial blow for the community, quoting Atton's assertion that BP was doing so "out of the goodness of our hearts." However, the story also included Berger's snarl in response—"I don't like being patronized"—along with descriptions of the efficiencies of the Lima refinery that BP had persistently ignored. Making profits, the story contended, was no longer the main issue. In the new global economy, corporate managers continually have to ask themselves if they could make even more money by making their capital "sweat" elsewhere. As a result, and more damning to BP, would have been the story's major image: that of a stricken city seemingly helpless against the cold decisions of a corporate giant located four thousand miles away.[40]

In early May, Berger sat down for another long interview with another national political reporter, this one from *The Nation*, a newsmagazine at the opposite end of the political spectrum from the *Wall Street Journal.* An immensely influential publication with a mass readership, *The Nation* was the oldest opinion magazine in the United States and had long ago emerged as the great lion of the American left. The reporter, Marc Cooper, readily indicated his sympathies with Lima's plight, and Berger found the interview moving quite easily between on- and off-the-record conversation. When he first saw the draft of Cooper's story, however, Berger worried briefly that the reporter had gone too far. The first sentence began with a reference to Lima's city flag and explained that whenever Berger saw it, "he swears that the oil derrick in the center of the banner looms ever more as a taunting, erect middle finger." Berger laughed out loud when he read the opening lines, but he was a sensitive politician and knew that he had not sworn or said any such thing. Over the phone Cooper hastened to agree, saying that he had used the raised middle finger image only as a symbol of the mayor's general feelings, and explaining that it had been his editors who had removed his qualifiers.[41]

At any rate, the story ran with that lead, and it set the tone for Cooper's piece. In midsummer, the mayor found a photo of himself, set against the backdrop of the refinery, gracing the cover of *The Nation,* with, beneath, a banner headline reading "A Town Betrayed: Oil and Greed in Lima, Ohio." Inside the magazine, readers encountered a devastating portrait of corporate arrogance running amok in the rural Midwest. Cooper admitted that, unfortunately, the tale of a plant shutdown and a community's destruction was not a new story in rust bowl America. But he added that what made the Lima story "tragically unique" was that Lima's refinery wasn't an outmoded, rusting dinosaur but a superbly impressive facility with a highly motivated workforce whose increased efficiencies in 1996 had garnered a $46-million profit for its corporate owners. Cooper developed the same line that had appeared in the *Guardian* piece: that BP had decided to shut Lima down mainly because its accountants had told the company that it could make even more money by investing elsewhere. The reporter also included local suspicions that another reason behind BP's decision was not because the refinery was a poor plant but because it was a good one—too good to let fall into the hands of a competitor. "It's the Napoleonic tactic of scuttling your own ships," he quoted a "very bitter Mayor Berger" as saying. In the end, the story left readers with the same fundamental image conveyed by the *Guardian* piece: that of the sway of global capital and the relative helplessness of the individual cities and towns where it operated. "When you come down to it," Belcher said, "it really hurts to see how powerless we are as a community." Cooper left the last and best lines of the piece to Mullen. "We feel our community is nothing but a red pin on a wall map somewhere in London," the *Lima News* publisher had smoldered. "It matters not that our refinery is 'spectacular' and viable. A financial decision is made and our pin is just pulled out and thrown away."[42]

A BP senior executive later denied that the spate of international publicity that Berger had stirred up had bothered BP's higher executives in the least. They had expected the bad PR, the individual said, and they were used to it. Actually, it could have been worse. Cooper had mentioned that he knew people working for the popular investigatory television program *60 Minutes* who might be interested in the story, and Berger pushed him hard on it before Cooper's contacts lost interest. Even without a *60 Minutes* story, the negative publicity was bad enough for BP. Despite the denials of the senior executive mentioned earlier, other BP employees testified to the emotional impact of the bad press on the company. Senior executive Greve, whom BP had recently directed back to Cleveland, admitted to Berger several times that June that the articles, especially the *Guardian* piece, had upset the higher-ups in London. Gilbert, who also was in a position to observe such things, agreed. From what she could tell, the national news stories "made BP crazy" and her bosses "extremely angry" and more determined than ever to just "get out of this town." At that point, BP executives might have preferred drinking rat poison to further encounters with Lima's mayor. Senior BP executives outside Lima, Gilbert reported, read Berger only as "very confrontational." Altogether, "they were furious with him."[43]

Of course, for Lima's mayor to so energetically stick his thumb in the eye of one of the world's largest corporations was a risky move, and periodically he received small hints of the further price he and his city yet might have to pay. Scholars have described the possible economic cost to cities for creating what corporations perceived as a "negative business climate." Greve informed Berger that this was exactly what was happening in Lima. He personally knew executives in other companies who were looking for new sites to establish businesses, Greve said, and when he suggested they consider Lima, they looked at him as if he were crazy. Local friends would have told the mayor not to worry about it. Belcher thought that the immense lengths to which the city was going to save the refinery would attract other businesses rather than repel them, while Mullen dismissed Greve's charges as a "red herring." He had heard such accusations many times over the years and read them only as manipulative ways of pressuring the media. Usually, Mullen observed, the person making such charges did so in a self-interested attempt to control a situation and not in the best interests of the community. However, Greve's concerns were echoed by others in the Lima area. The county commissioners signaled their discomfort to Berger about his moves in a private sphere, where governmental action seemed to them inappropriate, and the county economic development officer worried about the economic impact of further confrontations with BP. Berger also had to consider the personal political risks of his aggressiveness; he was up for reelection again that fall and knew that the coming campaign would soon place all of his actions under the local political microscope.[44]

Yet the more feedback the mayor received, the more he realized that his aggressiveness toward BP was not hurting him politically at all. If anything, people seemed to like it, for nearly the entire Lima community seemed deeply, pervasively, resoundingly angry at BP. All that local people saw was an excellent local plant—and with it, to some degree, their city—being thoughtlessly thrown onto the industrial scrap heap by a company they had once regarded as a benevolent partner. For years, BP had taken a prominent public role as a good, helpful corporate citizen. Now it had revealed a darker, uglier side. The men and women who labored at the refinery and whose jobs now faced elimination were the neighbors, fellow PTA members, soccer moms, and Little League coaches to uncounted thousands of local people, and the pain of the refinery workers became shared across the community. That spring, the *Lima News* rang with their stories. It told of Edelbrock's five sons, whose college plans now seemed on the rocks. It described Roller's daughter and the cloud now darkening her imminent graduation from high school. It discussed Steve Moening, a forty-five-year-old refinery worker whose father had worked at the Sohio plant for thirty-six years and who had once assumed that he, too, would be there until he retired. Now Moening struggled instead with how he would pay for medical insurance for his wife and three kids once his union benefits ran out nine months after the refinery's closure. Looking into the cost of maintaining it on his own, Moening had been stunned at the $520 monthly fee one insurance company quoted him—an unreachable mountain of money, since Moening figured he would shortly be unemployed. And then there was refinery engineer Dan Groman, who was methodically updating his resume and preparing to spread it widely around the local area. He had assured his family that they wouldn't move—he had married a local woman and was deeply rooted in the county—but warned that they would probably have to adjust to a big pay cut. Anybody in Allen County listening to the undercurrents of community distress that spring could readily hear these stories and five hundred others like them.[45]

BP senior executives, of course, lived elsewhere and functioned at a fair remove from local community feelings. But people like Gilbert did not, and she readily discerned that around Lima, "people were hating BP . . . it was terrible. You can't imagine; it was really ugly." The company employed a whole professional staff of PR people like Gilbert, whose jobs were to measure such reactions, and that staff produced data that would have alarmed the higher-ups in London had they looked at it carefully. Lima PR staffers even charted the community polls they had done in neat bar graphs, polls that people like Greve and Walpole carried around to various community gatherings. Greve once pulled out the charts in a private meeting with Berger in the mayor's office, telling him curtly that he'd probably take pride in what they showed. The mayor quickly saw that one figure on a bar graph, quantifying responses to a query as to whether local people agreed with the statement that BP was "a company I trust," had dropped from nearly 60 percent agreement in 1996 to around 20 percent one year later. "Gary," Berger said, "I am actually surprised these results are as high as they are." But he took no pride in such numbers, he stressed. For years, he told Greve, BP and Sohio had "stood head and shoulders" above other area companies in the immense contributions they had made to the community: in their generosity to the United Way, for example, or in the many volunteers they had fielded for a range of local needs, from teaching science classes in local schools to appearing with brooms and dustpans in the city's streets, picking up litter after community celebrations. For years, BP had put itself on a local "pedestal"; now it had chosen to knock itself right down by its decision to close the refinery. He had been laboring hard, Berger said, to show the company the "irremediable damage that they would do to themselves if they proceeded" with such plans. Now BP was seeing the results.[46]

Meanwhile, one of Berger's contacts with insight into BP's Cleveland headquarters told him that morale that summer was very low among the staffers there, who saw Lima as a symbol of how London would handle all its American employees. Moreover, many at BP remembered—and if they did not, the environmental activists of ACCE were quick to remind them—that the nature of BP's remaining chemical plant in Lima required particular sensitivity to matters like good public relations. Among the other nasty commercial chemicals conjured up by BP on the south edge of town were fair quantities of cyanide. Local activists do not know if "BP is causing health problems," warned one from ACCE about the same time, but they do know that not enough research has been done to explain why the Lima area had a breast cancer rate eighteen times higher than the rest of the state, substantially elevated rates of other cancers, and a much higher level of obstructive pulmonary disease. Environmental worries gnawed at Lima leaders in other ways too. Federal and state law placed the responsibility for environmental cleanup on the last owner of an industrial facility. Since Sohio or BP had been refining oil south of Lima for a century, Paisley noted, who knew what nauseous brew of poisons had seeped into the ground out there? But if BP could keep even a small portion of the defunct refinery open for use in some minor way, Berger and other city officials learned, extant laws allowed it to defer environmental cleanup responsibilities indefinitely. Already, the mayor told Greve bluntly, he and other city leaders suspected that "BP has figured out a way to keep portions open in order to avoid the expensive costs of environmental remediation on the entire site." Certainly such worries would have percolated widely across the Lima community.[47]

By the summer of 1997, such anger, doubt, and suspicion were the reactions confronting British Petroleum in Lima. As a wealthy corporation that had prided itself on the mutually beneficial relationships it enjoyed with its partner communities around the world from its earliest days as a semiofficial arm of the British Empire, BP's position in Lima by this point must have seemed a sad and intolerable state of affairs. Such a situation could not be allowed to stand. Soon the company sent in a new executive with all the abundant resources he needed to set things right again.

"That is what we owe the community"

Late in the winter of 1997, BP transferred Percy to New York City to better look after its interests on Wall Street. To replace him in Cleveland, the company sent back Gary Greve. Given his hard-charging, take-no-prisoners operating style of a decade earlier (one local activist remembered him as a "barracuda in business"), Greve seemed an inauspicious pick for the job of easing BP back into the community's good graces. Immediately upon his arrival, however, he indicated that he had changed. Kuenzli saw that he had "had lost some of that brusqueness" of his former days; Gilbert quickly perceived that Greve had "mellowed." He openly stated to her that this time around he would be "much more conscious of how his actions affected people," and he gave every indication of honoring that pledge. Not long after he arrived, he showed up in Berger's office for what became a series of long, frank, but seemingly relaxed conversations. Greve was "taller than I remember[ed] him," Berger noted privately, "dressed very well, hair perfect (not unlike though not as overdone as Bill Clinton's); has a very ready smile." BP's new executive-in-charge listened to Berger patiently, interacted cordially, and did not take offense at the mayor's sometimes irate descriptions of BP's recent track record in town. To Berger's more blistering charges, he merely promised to "do more research" and report back.[48]

Now installed in Cleveland as head of BP Chemicals (and thus, Berger learned, the highest-ranking American with operating responsibilities in all of BP), Greve threw himself into the major task at hand. He quickly tore off the blinders that had obscured the vision of the Cleveland executives already in place. The Cleveland people, Gilbert claimed, had never seemed to take the needs of Lima seriously. For nearly a year she, Kuenzli, and chemicals plant manager Walpole had continually tried to focus their attention on the deepening crisis in Lima. It had several dimensions. First of all, the refinery produced several of the materials, such as propylene, that the chemicals plant still needed. Was anyone planning for what the plant would do when the refinery was gone? Second, any industrial facility needed harmonious community relations if it was to run at peak efficiency, but BP's local reputation had plummeted. Did Greve have any idea, Gilbert pleaded, of how poorly regarded BP is around here? Cleveland executives had continued to overlook this deepening crisis except in one instance, Gilbert said; "you can bet your sweet life that when it landed in the *Wall Street Journal* they noticed it and got very upset."[49]

Within weeks after his arrival, Greve had fully grasped the sad state of affairs, although he was apparently convinced he was the only one who did. Late that spring, Gilbert remembered later, she and Walpole were attending a BP company conference in France. The phone rang in her hotel room and when she picked it up, she heard Greve's voice: full, booming, and agitated. What was she doing there in France? he wanted to know. Did she realize how upset people were with BP in Lima? How could she leave in such a crisis? Catch the next available flight back to Cleveland, he ordered, be in my office at 9:00 Monday morning, and bring enough toothpaste and clean underwear to last a week. Gilbert and Walpole did what they were told. That entire ensuing week, they followed Greve wherever he went in northern Ohio, trailing luggage, staying in three or four different hotels, diligently noting Greve's suggestions, and working sixteen to twenty hours a day. But at the end of the ordeal, Gilbert said, they had together produced a big, new, exciting future for BP in Lima that her boss grandly called the Lima Integrated Complex (LIC).[50]

Berger returned from a week of vacation in mid-July 1997 to a community buzzing with rumors about something momentous coming from BP. Walpole had apparently advised one of Berger's old comrades on the task force to "think positive and think big." Speculation filtered down corridors about what it all meant—maybe even that the company had decided to keep the refinery open. Greve showed up in the mayor's office the next afternoon to give him a confidential heads-up. The governing philosophy of BP America with regards to Lima, he informed Berger, was, "Go hard on the asset, soft on the employees," meaning that if they had to make hard decisions about facilities, they'd be generous with people. BP had been the third-largest employer in the area, Greve said, and they intended on staying that way. If they discounted the number of refinery employees who had already transferred to Toledo or taken other jobs and took into the account the forty or so chemical plant employees opting for early retirement, Greve and his aides had figured out a way to integrate enough aspects of the refinery into the current chemicals operation so that few or maybe even none of the remaining refinery workers would end up losing their jobs. Granted, most of those employees would have to learn new and different kinds of work, requiring the full cooperation of the union, but Greve estimated to the mayor that the new complex could make adequate use of three-quarters of the old refinery facilities, leaving the last quarter to careful demolition. This would allow BP to employ as many as one hundred former refinery workers

BP senior executive Gary Greve explaining the decreasing number of local jobs at risk because of the Lima Integrated Complex, July 1997. *Photo courtesy of the* Lima News.

for a full decade in doing little else but pulling apart the rest of their old plant. However, the point was they would have jobs, thanks to BP (and also thanks, in no small part, to Greve himself, who apparently had agitated hard for the program within upper-level circles of BP management).[51]

Greve rolled out the new program for the Lima public in a series of high-profile announcements, meetings, and press briefings at the refinery over the next few days. Proclaiming that "this site has a future," he outlined the merger of most of the old refinery into a giant new petrochemical facility, to be managed by Walpole. He carefully walked reporters through the math, demonstrating that under the new plan, the greatest number of refinery employees in danger of losing their jobs hovered at 90, whereas a few weeks before it had stood at 401. The planners were not even sure yet what all the jobs would entail, he explained excitedly; maybe they would rely on the creativity of the workforce to define them. As of that day, Greve declared, he had issued Walpole a "hunting license" to find any pieces of the old refinery that he could usefully integrate into the new plant. Plans for the LIC only had one restriction, symbolized by the new motto "ABC—Anything But Crude." By this, Greve explained, he meant that Walpole's workers could incorporate any pieces they could use of the old refinery into the new complex as long as they could run it through the new units and make money at it, and as long as it didn't involve crude oil. The *Lima News* highlighted its coverage of the new proposal with a huge photo of workers from the two facilities, having just

The birth of the Lima Integrated Complex, July 17, 1997: refinery chief Donovan Kuenzli, left, and chemical plant head James Walpole, right, cutting the fence between the two facilities. *Photo courtesy of the* Lima News.

removed the fence that had formerly stood between the two plants, rushing eagerly forward to shake hands in a happy symbol of new togetherness.[52]

Community reaction, initially guarded, soon turned to gushing. The news hit hard those refinery workers who had recently quit the plant for new jobs (including the unfortunate Moening, who had resigned only one week earlier, surrendering fifteen years of seniority). Others resisted Greve's overtures, at least emotionally. One worker wanted to see the deal in writing, explaining that "when you deal with a rattlesnake and get bit enough times, you're careful when you grab the thing." Berger likewise cautioned that actions speak louder than words, telling the press, "We are going to measure this thing over time." But most people inside and out of the refinery seemed eager to once again rush into BP's embrace. "I think it's very positive," Winterstellar admitted, while a workmate declared "there's not much to complain about anymore." Outside the plant, the reaction glowed even brighter. "I think it's great news for the community," said the local United Way head. Lodermeier, Shawnee's school superintendent, likewise said he was "ecstatic," and with good reason: BP's new plan restored to his district $1.7 million of the $2.8 million in lost taxes that he had been trying to plan for.[53]

Greve followed his big announcement by pushing his local good news publicity campaign into even higher gear, demonstrating previously unnoticed new abilities to charm and schmooze. At a lunch at the refinery for community leaders, he pulled out a big photo of boilermakers at the old Solar Refinery in 1908,

Refinery workers at left greet BP chemical plant employees at right in a BP media event celebrating the creation of the Lima Integrated Complex, July 17, 1997. *Photo courtesy of the* Lima News.

some of whose hands rested on each others' shoulders. It was his favorite photo, Greve informed the crowd, because it showed how much the workers cared for each other. At that meeting and elsewhere to the press, he also hammered away intensively with BP's rationales for closing the refinery, as if to erase any lingering doubts about the fundamental rightness of all BP decisions. Indeed, that week the *Lima News* published the most full-blown explanations for the closure decision than it had in the previous eight months—only this time, the reasoning was all from BP's side. Berger wasn't about to let that go unchallenged. After the lunch broke up, he quietly told Greve that if he wanted to talk publicly about where the community was going "from this point forward," then the City of Lima would be a "willing participant." But if he was instead going to use public occasions to defend BP's decision to close the refinery, then he would find the mayor "publicly debating" him. Greve agreed, commenting that he would need to do a little more research to convince Berger. Berger retorted that he didn't need any more research, asserting that, having been around the previous eighteen months, he knew more about things than Greve gave him credit for. Nevertheless, it did suddenly seem as if the days of confronting BP really were over. Later that month, the six remaining members of the old refinery task force met and announced they were changing their name to the LIC task force. Belcher told the *Lima News* that the sale process was clearly over. Now the task force could devote itself to its new mission: supporting the Lima Integrated Complex.[54]

Nor was Greve finished yet. In late August, he made another grand announcement at a meeting of the Lima Rotary Club, to which he had invited the press, an event he designated as "C-Day" for "Community Day." There he took some time to elaborate on the larger question, "prompted by the Lima closure controversy," of "What does a company owe a community?" As such, "C-Day" became a significant occasion, underscored by BP printing up Greve's analysis in a little pamphlet and distributing it widely around town. Greve forthrightly addressed the local crisis of morale that his company had found itself in. He could personally see the sense of hurt and missing pride in the eyes of refinery employees, he admitted, and it was clear from talking with people in the community that the prevailing sense was that "BP had let them down." This troubled him, but it was partly because, he claimed, that BP had chosen to conduct the entire process of deciding what to do with the refinery "in a remarkably open manner. We chose not to conduct this exercise in private, in secret, like some companies do." He had no doubt that this openness had been the right approach for BP, but it had come with a price. "Unfortunately," Greve explained, "by being open with our plans, some people outside BP thought that they would be involved in the decision. That was a mistake on our part. We weren't clear enough with people that in the end this would be a BP decision. A BP business decision. Not," he added in a clear slap at Berger, "a referendum. Not a political decision . . . I am not comfortable when the community feels it should make our business decisions for us." Of course he had not expected the community to be pleased at the decision to close the refinery. But "I do expect the community to accept that this is our decision to make and then judge us on the way we execute that decision. That is fair! On that basis I believe that BP would come out well—in fact, very well. That is what we owe the community."[55]

Having delivered the salt of his message, Greve quickly followed with the sugar. He reminded the Rotarians of the big announcement of "E-Day" a month before, when BP committed publicly to finding a job for every refinery employee who wanted one. "How many other companies," Greve wanted to know, "who have downsized in Lima or elsewhere have made a similar commitment?" In the future, he pledged, when BP makes a momentous decision that affects the community, the company would do its best to be "more clear about why we have taken that decision." However, he begged the community to please be patient, since BP managers were human beings who sometimes make mistakes. When they do, "and it certainly appears to have happened in this case, we hope you can find it in your hearts to give us a second chance." Greve then went on to describe what BP planned on doing with its second chance, a matter Greve hoped would help "officially begin the process of healing our relationship with the community." BP would dole out a lot more local money. Greve officially announced the establishment of a local, community-controlled, BP-bankrolled redevelopment account, to be called the D'Arcy Fund, after a site in Wales where the company had done the same thing. The company would make available $1.5 million in unsecured loans at rates below market value in order to attract new businesses interested in relocating on the rest of the old refinery site. This would be, Greve declared, concrete evidence "that BP cares about Lima." The decision to close the refinery wasn't one made against BP's employees nor against Lima; "it was a decision against refining oil—period!" Now, "hopeful that we can put all dissension and controversy behind us," he concluded, BP was eager to march into a bright local future, hand in hand in ready partnership with the Lima community.[56]

From Berger's perspective, Greve had "delivered a masterful speech designed to put the community on the defensive." The response from the audience seemed to have been stunned silence; one individual, Berger noted, began to clap but then quickly stopped. Mullen heard the speech as little more than BP's attempt to silence an outraged community. Local Presbyterian minister Richard Sheffield told Berger afterward that he was "enraged" by Greve's address, but felt they could do nothing about it. "Lima is a company town," Sheffield said, and they had all "just been taken to the woodshed by those who owned the town." The mayor and others on the task force at least consoled themselves with the conclusion, probably correct, that without their months of confrontations with BP and all the negative publicity they had brought, none of this would be happening. However, all such negative responses now seemed discordant in the new harmonious climate, for BP soon delivered on Greve's bright promises. Within weeks, the company began soliciting representatives from the community to serve on the board of the D'Arcy Fund. By November, Greve had reduced the number of refinery employees still at risk of losing their jobs to thirty-one, and a company spokesman voiced confidence at whittling down that figure even further.[57]

That fall, in fact, BP seemed to reign as triumphantly in Lima as it did elsewhere in the world. The intensified summer demand for gasoline had ratcheted gas prices—and oil company profits—skyward. In 1997, BP Oil international saw total profits reach $4 billion and enjoyed its status as the most profitable oil company in the world. "Everything is sunny in BP's garden," observed the *Investors Chronicle*. Locally, few people seemed ready to dispute the conclusion offered by Lima City Council president Cunningham, who had come a long way from his cynicism toward BP of eight months before. "Despite our natural inclination to criticize large corporations for not caring," he instructed local people effusively, "BP's willingness to recognize its long-enjoyed relationship with the Lima community serves as a spoonful of sugar in the bitter taste of business decision-making." Such tones did not augur well for the mayor, who began to worry that Cunningham planned to make BP an issue in his upcoming mayoral campaign. Perhaps, in the happy new climate Greve had created, Berger's aggressiveness against the corporation would come back to haunt him after all.[58]

Outside the mayor's office, the only place yet left in the world where Greve's charm and money had not entirely won the day was with the workforce remaining at the Lima refinery. There, almost unnoticed, they continued with the most remarkable development of all. Down among the curving pipes and flaring gasses, refinery workers still labored hard in the climate of improvement they had created, though now without any shred of hope that their efforts mattered to anyone except to themselves alone.

The Turm Oil Company

The news of the Lima Integrated Complex, and Greve's assurances that few if any of them would lose their jobs, had engulfed many refinery workers in waves of relief. Kuenzli recalled Greve's big "C-Day" a "great day." The news of few job losses accomplished wonders, he said, in restoring morale in the refinery. Not only was it a smart public relations move for BP, he said, but it also was efficient in a business sense, since it kept people focusing on their jobs rather than on worrying about an uncertain future. Others remembered Greve's program differently. People felt relief, sure, but a tempered relief. Groman obediently lined up with other refinery workers in the chemical plant's recreation room. BP had set up little cubicles there, and one by one, Groman and his workmates filed into the cubicles to interview for new jobs with the chemical plant. None of them felt that thrilled about it, Monus said; they were refinery people, oil people, not chemical workers. Gilbert, who had worked extensively in both facilities, knew the chemical plant had never been characterized by the same tight bonds, the same camaraderie, and the sense of extended family that had permeated the refinery. At best, Monus knew, many refinery workers regarded chemical plant employment as just better than nothing. Nor did Greve ease tensions by his apparently tight negotiations with the OCAW about various workplace matters in the new LIC. He knew he had the upper hand, said Roller, who had taken the lead in the talks; it was like negotiating, he recalled, with a knife at your throat.[59]

Yet the basic, foundational response inside the refinery that year was set on the very first day that BP announced its closure. Amidst all the emotion after Atton had made an initial speech revealing the bad news, Kuenzli remembered, a tough old refinery foreman named Steve Watters stood up to speak. He just had one question, Watters said to the crowd, and it hit Kuenzli later what a "class act" it was that his major question did not concern the issues running through a hundred other heads at that moment, like "How am I going to feed my family now?" No; instead Watters wanted to know, "How in the hell are we going to keep people's attention and focus on operating this refinery safely for two years and not kill somebody?" They all knew, Roller said, that in some ways an oil refinery "is just a bomb that's never gone off." It wasn't designed to explode, but it could, particularly if people became distracted or units became understaffed, as key people departed for new jobs elsewhere.[60]

Watters hit the major issue right on the head, Kuenzli recalled, and all that evening and much of the following day, the refinery's manager went around to the different units and visited each shift to repeat the same message. "We're in a real tough spot now," Kuenzli admitted, "but we've got to continue to run this plant safely and well, and the best way to do that is to not miss a beat with the continuous improvement program."

Perhaps the most amazing part of the whole story is that they did. Even as the Phelps bid came and went, as Berger generated negative publicity, and as Greve and Walpole hatched the LIC, even as their numbers declined by that September to the bare skeletal force essential to keep the plant running safely, refinery workers not only maintained the facility in top running shape, they managed to continue to improve it. One refinery maintenance staffer, for example, evaluated forty pieces of equipment in their unit and identified half a dozen in bad condition requiring high maintenance costs. He recommended repairing the bad ones first and budgeting in the next in the coming years. The supervisor insisted on replacing them all right away. One unit with high temperatures received permission to replace air conditioners, and quickly found that instead of having to replace eighteen control boards in one year (at a cost of $4,000 each), the next year they needed to replace four. Workers in another unit discovered liquid hydrocarbon leaking into the plant sewers at fairly high rates. They plugged the leaks and sold the hydrocarbon to a supplier instead, resulting in yet more productivity gains for the refinery at large. When flames engulfed the fluid catalytic cracker unit (the "cat cracker") in August 1996, executives in London would have seen it as further confirmation of their decision to lessen BP's exposure to refining. Back in Lima, workers read it instead as evidence of the continuous improvement subculture, noting how quickly they and the Shawnee Fire Department contained the fire, repaired the unit, and got it back up and running within weeks. Across the plant, the rate of mean time between failure (MTBF) of pumps, the standard yardstick by which refinery effectiveness is measured, continued to skyrocket. By June 1997, refinery workers had responded to the certain destruction of their jobs by winning four company safety awards. Even as the plant lost a hundred workers to transfer or new jobs, the improvements continued apace, and so did the profits BP received from the facility. Berger ran into an acquaintance from the refinery who informed him that BP had just announced inside the plant that it had made $38 million in the first six months of 1997 alone. All of this, one outside observer realized, was a result of the degree to which individuals in the plant had internalized the continuous improvement subculture. The "Don't Just Fix It; Improve It" slogan peeked out from buttons attached to a hundred shirts, and workers affixed a huge banner with the same message inside the plant gates, so that every truck driver or other visitor understood what was happening.[61]

Once again it is important to acknowledge, since Kuenzli and his local management team continued to gainshare such productivity gains with their workforce, the degree of worker self-interest in such improvements. Every dollar in profits that their initiative gained for their employer was shared proportionally with the workforce as well. But, given the extent of the improvements and also the intense bitterness toward BP circulating around the plant, such gains certainly also reflected more than mere self-interest devotion to BP's fortune. In fact, workers' anger at the company may have partly fueled worker commitment to the continuous improvement program. As hope for saving the refinery died among the workers, one senior manager discerned a new mind-set of bitter pride. It was as if the workers were saying, "We'll show those bastards that this is a good place." Gilbert noted a similar reaction, workers' realization that "the cavalry isn't coming and we will determine our own fate." Across the refinery, she noticed a prevailing attitude among workers that "we will continue to run this in the best possible manner we can. We will not have environmental issues; we will not have safety issues; we will show them that they are wrong" in their decision to close the plant. Monus likewise discerned a complex welter of feelings permeating the refinery's atmosphere. Part of it was simply workers' pride, he said, a "we'll show them" attitude, but part of it reflected a fierce determination among many to continue to function as masters of their own fates, an "it's not over 'till I say it's over" mind-set. However, Monus also contended that another reaction was involved, a "spiritual" element mixed with a residual loyalty to BP and a "quiet support" for senior leaders, even those in London. It was as if the workers were saying, "I may not like what you're doing, but you're the boss and I'll serve you in the best way I can, even if that means running the place as efficiently as possible and making the most money for you while you shut it down." With many workers reverberating to the evangelical subculture of rural America, part of the success of the continuous improvement program may have emanated from the commitment many of them felt to biblical notions of good stewardship of the resources God had given. Even as senior management accelerated plans to close the refinery, groups of forty or so refinery people would often meet at lunchtimes, Monus remembered, to pray for executives like John Browne.[62]

If BP senior management ever became aware of such attitudes, it would have been a mistake for them to have misread them. In effect the refinery's workforce had begun to do—to BP's benefit—what Greve and others in BP had found so objectionable in the mayor: they had begun to blur the difference between what was public and what was private. The continuous improvement subculture devolved at bottom from a sense of personal ownership that employees began to assert over a private asset. Entire shifts of workers were no longer regarding the valves and pipes in their particular domain as solely the concern of a foreign owner. They felt a growing sense of personal responsibility for the pieces of equipment they worked with, a sense of responsibility that fueled their shared determination across the plant to improve it to the amazing degree that they had. BP had not objected to that sense of responsibility; in fact, given all the financial rewards it delivered, the company had done its very best to foster it. In encouraging workers to take responsibility for the refinery, however, even in matters as minute as seeing if they could coax a bit more production out of this or that piece of equipment, Schaefer, Kuenzli, and other managers had, to some degree, let the genie out of the bottle. "The property which every man has in his own labor," Adam Smith had theorized in the eighteenth century, "is the original foundation of all other property." The refinery workforce was merely updating Smith for an industrial era. BP certainly held legal title to the physical asset of the refinery. However, the workers felt that they held title, not legally but perhaps morally, to what it had become. It was this sense of ownership that had rendered BP's decision to close the refinery such an emotionally devastating blow to its workforce. When Greve insisted publicly that BP was the sole arbiter of what it would do with its property—that BP's decisions with regard to the refinery were a private matter about which only senior BP managers could offer valid opinions—he was technically and legally in the right but in another sense, he was wrong. The only reason, the workers knew, that this property had any value at all was because of their own sweat, effort, and ingenuity and that of the five generations of workers preceding them, those who had refined oil here and given value to this asset long before BP had ever come to America. By their care, their steady work, and their ingenuity, the workers were letting it be known: "You just can't come in here now and act as if our work doesn't matter and that history had never happened. You just can't come in here like this and throw us away."[63]

Outside the refinery, it was this same fundamental conflict about public vs. private ownership that had propelled the mayor's year of confrontation with BP. Inside the refinery, the conflict was best exemplified in little symbolic ways over matters like colors and insignia and the company flag. In lunchroom discussions, refinery workers apparently batted around these questions a great deal. After BP announced they were going to close the refinery, Monus remembered, workers there entered a kind of two-year hiatus in which one of the key players in their world was suddenly missing. They continued to function as they had before, delivering product to their customers and maintaining the plant's relationship with the community. "We could identify who the customers were," Monus said. "We could identify who the suppliers were. We knew who the employees were . . . But we didn't know who the owner was." "BP clearly didn't want us," people reasoned, "and are going to close us. But until they close us," the analysis went, "we own this place." Workers demonstrated their ownership in a variety of ways. One was by taking down the company flag. They formed a small committee of their own, led by Doug Parrish, one of Kuenzli's managers, who designed a new flag. It was blue, with a drawing of a flare on it, and simply read "Lima Refinery." One day in late April they all gathered together in a little ceremony, lowered the green and yellow banner of British Petroleum, and raised their own Lima Refinery flag.[64]

To the refinery workforce, Monus recalled, that April moment amounted to their own personal "Declaration of Independence Day." And they quickly produced other insignia of their own defiance. Like any company, BP had readily distributed small items with its own insignia through the plant: BP pens, coffee cups, and the like. After the closure announcement, workers refused to use them anymore. They likewise pulled off and threw away nearly all other easily removable markers of BP's presence. "We didn't want green and yellow," Groman remembered. "Green and yellow wasn't looked upon too favorably." Years before, most people had sported a blue and red Sohio sticker on their hard hats. When BP consolidated its control, it had sent a memo around the plant directing workers to replace the Sohio signs with BP stickers. Now the Sohio brand reappeared on many hats and shirts, while other workers created their own signage, more expressive of their feelings. Many produced hard hats with the new blue Lima Refinery color and flare they had designed. Others were more creative. Groman decorated his hard hat with an oil company name of his own creation: "TURM OIL." The widespread rejection of green and yellow, Monus knew, also spoke to a deep and underlying attitude of bitterness and hostility toward BP that thoroughly penetrated the refinery. The sentiments of one maintenance worker were certainly emblematic of the feelings of many others. "What we accomplished wasn't done," he said, to merely make BP look good. "We were going to show them, 'We will run this place and we will run it better than ever.' Then we could turn out the lights and go home and say 'Kiss my butt.'"[65]

The conflicted relationship between the refinery workforce and BP was best exemplified, perhaps, in a project that the company began at the refinery early in 1995. Monus—who, as best as one outsider could tell, was employed around the plant primarily as an "idea factory"—had been following the work of scholars like Peter Senge, Arthur Kleiner, and also George Roth of the Center for Organizational Learning at the Massachusetts Institute of Technology. Independently of this, Walpole and Gilbert had been serving in various roles with a local historical consulting agency and, in that context, had come know the organization's main staffer, a capable writer and researcher with a Ph.D. in anthropology named Hans Houshower. In the early 1990s, they brought him in as a consultant to do team training for their leadership team in Cleveland, a process which involved Houshower transporting a cardboard mock-up of an old Lima locomotive to the Cleveland headquarters and leading senior BP managers through the process of rebuilding it. In the mid-1990s, with the work of the MIT management gurus in mind, Monus apparently coaxed a small sum of money out of Kuenzli to employ Houshower to conduct a small "learning history" of the successful effort by refinery employees to reduce the flaring. Houshower diligently interviewed the seven major workers involved in the "Butane Action Team" and wrote up the results. BP was pleased enough with what he produced to disseminate the account widely across its empire and direct other plants to copy the Lima process. Houshower knew for a fact that workers at a BP refinery in the North Sea studied the Lima model carefully. Early in 1995, Kuenzli produced a larger pot of funds—small by BP standards but a small fortune to money-starved academics like Houshower—to produce a similar but more extensive "learning history" on the entire continuous improvement program at the Lima refinery.[66]

Thus it was that for the following three years, while publicly BP downplayed its "mediocre" Lima refinery and prepared to scrap it, privately it employed a consultant to help it learn all it could from a workforce whose creativity and ingenuity had rendered the refinery one of the most rapidly improving of such plants in the world. Through upwards of forty separate interviews, sandwiched between trips to MIT and visits from people like Roth and Senge back to Lima, Houshower and Gilbert documented, for the good of BP, something of the subculture of improvement that had emerged in Lima. In doing so, they also gained valuable insights into what senior management really understood about what Lima's workers had done and how those workers accounted for their accomplishment themselves. The fact that the London headquarters valued Houshower's work was demonstrated by the generous time that a number of very busy senior BP executives gave him in extensive transatlantic phone interviews. While always quick to rationalize their decision to close the refinery in the context of the larger financial needs of BP International, Houshower remembered, they were also acutely aware of, and regretful about, the first-rate "asset" they were "shedding" and the incredible human capital they were tossing away with it. The ordinary refinery workers were also eager to cooperate with the interviews. While many of them were bitter toward BP, Houshower recalled, all of them regarded the refinery with immense pride. They understood their jobs as "contributing to something bigger than themselves" and likewise saw his project as a means by which some further good might come out of their work, good that could outlive their employer's termination of it. To anthropologist Houshower, who had spent much of the previous decade documenting Lima's history, the inheritances seemed clear. In his mind, the continuous improvement program was just a modern extension of the same local working-class subculture that had permeated Lima for a century, created by the women and men who had rolled cigars by the crate load, riveted entire locomotives together, and uncoupled rolling boxcars on frozen nights. "It's an argument," he concluded, "for the importance of community in America." Refinery worker Clarence Roller said the same thing in a gendered but also less academic sense. His father had always worked hard for a living, and "We're our fathers' sons. That's the kind of work you get out of us," he said; "that's what made the refinery."[67]

Now, apparently, it was finished.

"We want to make it very clear, the refinery is closing"

In November 1997, the two major adversaries that had dominated local affairs for the past year, Lima's mayor and British Petroleum, independently celebrated victories that would set the stage for one last enduring period of intensive interaction.

Early that month, contrary to his initial expectations, Berger enjoyed a surprisingly easy win over Keith Cunningham in the fall mayoral elections. Early on, it had looked to be a tough campaign. Some of Berger's early polling had indicated that Lima citizens saw both men as equally capable of doing the job, a finding that shocked Berger. Throughout his time as city council president, Cunningham had been a noisy and persistent critic of the mayor's proposals but had never, it seemed to the mayor, advanced a single proposal of his own. Now polls indicating that the public saw the two mayoral candidates as equivalent indicated to Berger that "I had a problem." The public also seemed tired of political negativity and wanted a more constructive engagement with local issues. So the mayor and his campaign staff constructed a series of campaign ads stressing Berger as "a positive choice," a theme that their opponent's caustic negativity seemed to play into. Moreover, Cunningham's attempts to parlay Berger's aggressiveness against BP into a potent campaign issue never took root. What could he point to, the mayor realized, except that BP seemed to have broken trust with the community? If anything, despite the recently mended fences, much of the public would have agreed with that charge. Instead, the mayor's clever extolling of himself as a positive choice seemed to resonate with the Lima public, and Cunningham's campaign, he recalled, fell apart pretty rapidly. On Election Day, Berger won reelection to a third term with 64 percent of the vote.[68]

The mayor had barely savored his victory before his bigger antagonist came back to consolidate its own. Two weeks after Election Day, Greve once again hit the local headlines with another exciting announcement. That day, Greve heralded, would be known as "Z-Day," because an exciting new development at the LIC now meant that zero of the refinery's old jobs were now at risk. BP, Greve revealed, had just decided to invest $100 million in the Lima Integrated Complex to enable it to produce a chemical complex called 1,4 butanediol, or BDO, a widely used chemical commonly employed in producing other products, such as a key compound in the construction of car bumpers, and another chemical called THF, used in various solvents and fibers. Altogether, the company soon hoped to be able to produce 1.6 billion pounds of BDO a year and thus become a major player in a BDO global market that was growing at 10 percent annually. Locally, the development meant all sorts of good news. "The new plant is further evidence that BP's Lima site has a bright future," Greve said, and no

Installing the BDO Unit at the Lima Integrated Complex, winter 1997–98. *Photo courtesy of the* Lima News.

one could doubt him. Not only would the BDO addition mean 50 new permanent jobs—at which old refinery workers would be given the first crack—but constructing it would require the temporary labor of 800 people. Moreover, in a few years, Walpole estimated, the BDO unit alone might be generating between 850 and 1,000 new permanent positions, spurring new levels of economic growth and perhaps also luring more businesses into the Lima area. The community reacted with joy. "We herald this as outstanding news," stated Lima Chamber of Commerce president Rockhold, praising the plan as "a promise kept to the community." Even the *Lima News,* which had greeted Greve's initial LIC overtures with a guarded, wait-and-see attitude, finally seemed ready to let down its guard. There's no more need for skepticism, the paper confessed. "BP deserves our support and encouragement as the company builds a promising future in the chemicals business at its Lima facility." Regardless of his private bitterness toward BP, Lima's mayor welcomed the BDO announcement because it promised new jobs, and actively promoted it throughout the community, even though the expansion of the chemical plant, as before, provoked the ire of local environmentalists. After Berger had defended the BDO decision at a hearing on the matter hosted by the Ohio EPA at Shawnee High School, for instance, one such activist told the crowd that the mayor was simply "BP's toady."[69]

Finally, Greve took the opportunity to remind the public once again of BP's wisdom in closing the refinery. That decision, and BP's ability to integrate part of the old facility into the new LIC, he claimed, had helped tip the balance toward BP's decision to locate the BDO unit in Lima. The refinery site offered the company a number of expensive capital items, such as large storage tanks, which would save it the millions of dollars it would have had to spend to construct them someplace else. Greve seemed unable to resist the public opportunity to reaffirm the company's prevailing and unerring wisdom on all business matters. "If the refinery had not closed, we could not do this with the same efficiency," he emphasized again. "We want to make it very clear, the refinery is closing."[70]

Two months later, with the refinery workforce down to a skeletal number barely large enough to keep it functioning, Berger received a phone call from his old BP acquaintance Schaefer, who told him of the contact he had recently had with Robert Payne, a broker at the respected Wall Street investment firm Wasserstein Perella. Somehow, Payne knew all about the workers' accomplishments at the refinery, Schaefer relayed, and was quite impressed with them. He suggested that Berger call Payne, since Payne knew some big players in the industry and was trying yet again to cobble together a deal to save the Lima refinery.[71]

Chapter 8
Victory

While traveling for BP in Japan in January 1998, Gary Greve placed repeated phone calls one day to Dave Berger's office back in Lima. The mayor's secretary passed on the message: Greve needed to reach Berger urgently. When Berger finally caught up with the BP executive late that afternoon, he was slightly stunned at what he heard him offer. Greve wanted Berger to fly down on a corporate jet to private game lands BP owned in Georgia to spend several days quail hunting with Greve and several other business executives. They could just relax, enjoy several days of leisure and business conversation, and also perhaps build up, Greve ventured to Berger, a "more trusting relationship." The mayor quickly begged off, citing various family commitments, and although Greve "seemed slightly offended," as Berger noted that day in his diary, he "kept from getting angry" and brought the conversation to a quick end. For his part, the more Berger thought about it, the more it seemed to him a "thoroughly petty perk" and an ill-concealed attempt to get him back on board BP's team in Lima.[1]

Yet in January 1998, there was perhaps a deeper reason why the mayor rejected BP's quail-hunting offer. As the winter of 1998 deepened and gave way to spring, Berger was involved in a much bigger project. He had once again begun to work intensively, in one last and probably quixotic effort, to rescue the refinery.

"Finding the Holy Grail"

It did not take the mayor long to put a call through to Payne, the broker Schaefer had mentioned, although Berger had not thought much about the refinery for a while. Events there seemed to have taken on their own momentum and appeared far outside his ability to influence anymore; at any rate, he had been consumed with his reelection campaign. But Schaefer had said Payne seemed genuinely interested. "So after a long drought of effort, I decided to make that call," Berger remembered, "and see where it would go, one last time."[2]

As it turned out, the mayor discovered, Payne knew a lot about the refining industry, a fair bit about the Lima refinery, and also appeared to know how to put deals together. He had worked for Sohio for some years in the 1980s, helping it buy, sell, and manage refineries. It was through this job that Payne had come to know Schaefer well, and he had even come to Lima "extremely frequently," sometimes as often as once a month during his Sohio days. Though he had left Sohio not long after BP's boardroom coup, Payne retained an impression of the Lima plant as "a viable refinery that ought to stay alive." Since the early 1990s, he had been assigned to manage refinery mergers and acquisitions for the rich and respected Wall Street investment firm Wasserstein Perella. It was his job to look for promising deals, and what he had recently learned from Schaefer had whetted his interest in the Lima refinery. Assessing the battle over the Lima refinery from his vantage point on Wall Street, Payne told the mayor that he believed BP's sales process had been essentially a "sham," designed primarily to assure the community that the company had tried to find a buyer. After all, Wasserstein had placed Payne on Wall Street with instructions to identify possible refineries for sale, yet BP's efforts to advertise the Lima plant's availability had been so weak that Payne had heard nothing of it. The only reason he knew of the refinery's predicament at all was because of a chance phone call to Schaefer. The more Schaefer had told him of the Lima plant, the more interested he had grown. Far from being shut down, he told Berger, the Lima refinery ought to have a bright and profitable future.[3]

At that point, the mayor must have responded to Payne with all the passion of a weary traveler far from home who had finally encountered someone speaking his native language. Best of all, Berger discovered, the broker seemed to have a real lead as to a possible deal. He had already been meeting with a major financial mover, David Stockman, who was eager to get into refining in a big way. Stockman was a name immediately recognizable to Berger and nearly any other politician in America. Payne went on to say that he had another meeting with Stockman coming up shortly and would be glad to raise the issue of Lima with him. Even more promising, he added, the Wasserstein group already had a meeting set up in London with John Browne for the very next week. Berger tried to contain his enthusiasm. First of all, he warned Payne that Greve had declared repeatedly that the planned BDO unit at the chemical plant would preclude a separate life for the refinery. Payne thought Greve mistaken, arguing that the two shouldn't be mutually exclusive facilities, but Berger promised to check. Second and even more important, Berger cautioned Payne never to use his name or allude in any way to his involvement in his conversations with Browne. After he sketched out something of the public confrontation with BP that he had spearheaded, Berger convinced Payne that he was "a liability in terms of trying to get John Browne to change his mind."[4]

Unfortunately, as Payne told the mayor a week later, even with no mention of Berger, the meeting with BP's chief executive did not go well. Browne's mind still seemed set. The only future he could imagine for the Lima plant, he had told the Wasserstein partners, was a shutdown. In fact, he seemed to think that the demolition of the plant had already started. Berger replied that Browne was either being disingenuous or was misinformed. The refinery had lost key people by that point, but it was humming along as productively as ever. Yet the door seemed locked as well as slammed shut when Payne told Berger that Stockman seemed no more open to a purchase of the Lima refinery than Browne. To Stockman, the Lima refinery on its own was too small to bother with; he wanted to purchase all of BP North America, an ambition both men knew he had no chance of fulfilling. Their only hope was to somehow stimulate Stockman's interest in the Lima refinery, either by itself or as a part of some other conjunction of refining interests large enough to tempt him. That February, Berger met with Mullen and a few other select members of the old Refinery Task Force to apprise them, in strictest secrecy, of the new possibility. The group agreed that, given the lateness of the hour, any chance of saving the refinery was "a very long shot," yet they urged Berger to maintain his contacts and see what happened. Payne still thought an opening existed. "Finding the Holy Grail is one thing," he knew, "but finding someone else who'll really see it as a holy grail is another." Yet Payne had been around the oil business long enough to learn not to give up on a deal until the wrecking ball actually appears. He and Berger together set out to lead both Browne and Stockman to a deal that neither knew they wanted. Their most immediate objective, Payne told his partner, had to be Stockman.[5]

In tackling David Stockman, Berger and Payne were unknowingly approaching a potentially sympathetic character. At that point in his life, Stockman was in the middle of a profound personal transition. A decade and a half earlier, as a twenty-nine-year-old Michigan congressman, he had burst into public fame when President Reagan tapped him for the post of budget director. From this position, Stockman had quickly emerged as a leading architect of Reagan's vaunted supply-side economic revolution, even while publicly admitting to journalist William Greider the bogus nature of the enterprise. Stockman had withstood the ensuing political firestorm but within a half-dozen years had washed out of politics, heading instead to Wall Street to parlay his fame and financial acumen into a fortune. By the mid-1990s, he was serving as senior managing investor for the Blackstone Group, a private equity firm, where, according to Greider, he had begun to pioneer "'labor-friendly' corporate takeovers" that worked carefully with unions and that won Stockman guarded admiration from his old enemies on the left.[6]

During several meetings between Wasserstein brokers and Blackstone executives that winter of 1997–98, Payne found Stockman "a very stimulating guy: brilliant, a quick mind, easy to talk to," and also someone with "a strong point of view about things." He didn't want a single refinery, Stockman made clear to Payne; instead he wanted to try to capture all of BP's holdings in the United States. Payne and Berger somehow had to lead Stockman to a smaller vision focused on Lima, but for the present, neither of them had figured out how to do that. Berger worked at the task from his end with every angle he could. He consulted with his private BP sources regularly and kept in regular phone contact with Payne, sharing everything he knew and asking for updates. Every week or so he'd call the broker to check in, asking for news and sharing any information he had gleaned from his end. Months later, Payne confessed to Berger that it was these repeated phone calls that kept him hard after Stockman, especially after the latter's initial statement of disinterest. He had to decide whether it was easier to stay after Stockman or shake off Lima's mayor, and the former task seemed easier.[7]

Meanwhile, in the dicey weeks of early spring 1998, both Berger and Payne kept a worried eye on BP for an answer to the most crucial question of all: had BP yet managed to lock in its alternate supply arrangements so it could start the final destruction of the Lima refinery? In March, Berger and the county commissioners journeyed to the plant for a meeting with its senior management. Walpole, the chemical plant manager, informed them that the alternate supply deal was about completed, adding that BP had been "playing one option off against another" but had scheduled a final meeting shortly to complete the arrangements. The demolition of the refinery would begin next month and accelerate that summer. Berger privately refused to believe Walpole, but the conversation still unsettled him. Hurriedly, he checked in with his private sources. Don't worry, the word came back: Walpole was misinformed. BP remained "indecisive" and soon would find itself forced to turn to Marathon/Ashland for its major market products. They would cherish the chance to dictate the supply and price of gasoline to their major competitor. Even so, the clock counting down to the refinery's final doom seemed to be ticking slightly louder.[8]

Then out of the blue, early on a Monday afternoon in mid-April, the entire equation precipitously changed. Berger returned a phone call from Payne, who told him, incredibly, that Stockman had called, suddenly "hot to trot" to buy the Lima refinery. What had changed his mind? Payne explained: the Blackstone Group had just accumulated its 65 percent controlling interest in Clark Oil, a small, St. Louis–based oil company. Stockman appeared to be the prime mover behind the deal because he had become convinced in the future of oil refining. The market, he and others at Blackstone reasoned, had reached its nadir and was now on the upswing. Enough refineries had closed across the country that profit margins were slowly beginning to rise. In grabbing Clark, Stockman and the Blackstone Group hoped to ride that new wave, transforming Clark into a major midwestern refining power. However, given what Payne thought was the "marginal" nature of Clark's two current refineries, they needed an additional major facility to cap off their new presence in the Midwest. Lima seemed exactly what they were looking for.[9]

All of a sudden, the mayor realized, he and Payne had a truly golden opportunity and they began working intensively. Explaining that Stockman had said he wanted all the hard data he could get on the refinery within weeks because he hoped to meet with Browne in May and complete the purchase shortly afterward, Payne asked Berger how much of that material he could obtain. "Plenty," the mayor said, and, together with his secretary Marlene, spent much of the two following days at the Xerox machine, copying vast reams of his private files. These he shipped overnight to Payne, who immediately passed them on to Stockman. Within a week, late on a Friday afternoon, Stockman himself called the mayor, wanting to know if he would be willing to serve as a "resource" for him as he put a bid together. Berger agreed immediately and added that he knew of someone else who could be very helpful, Schaefer. Quickly coordinating their schedules, Berger and Stockman, together with Schaefer, agreed to meet secretly, three days later, at the Cleveland airport.[10]

When Berger called and asked him to meet Stockman, Schaefer said he would be glad to help, but privately didn't harbor much hope. The odds were low that anything could break for the refinery at that late date, and besides, he remembered the Phelps deal. Still, he knew that the Blackstone Group was a much bigger enterprise than Phelps's company, and might have enough clout to shake something loose with somebody like John Browne. It was worth a try. Since Berger's schedule was impossibly full on the appointed day, he arranged to join the group by conference call. Following precise instructions, at 7:00 in the evening on April 27, Schaefer walked into the lobby of the Sheraton Hotel at the Cleveland airport and was met by Stockman's aide, who escorted him to a quiet meeting room upstairs and off the main floor. Stockman was informed once Schaefer was in the room. He came into the room alone five minutes later to make sure no one would see him meeting Schaefer in the hallway. Schaefer understood the need for secrecy—neither BP nor Blackstone would have wanted anyone to know of a possible deal at that point—but was still struck by it, and also by Stockman himself. He looked, Schaefer thought, a good deal grayer and a bit heavier than the photos of the young whiz-kid congressman of the old Reagan days, but he was "very businesslike" and they quickly got down to work.[11]

Stockman, Schaefer discovered, had read the data Berger had sent him very carefully. Now he first wanted to know how BP could have concluded the Lima refinery was that bad when everyone else was telling him it was that good. Schaefer carefully outlined a story he had lived for the past decade: the refinery's decline in profitability over the previous quarter-century, its slow physical deterioration, its amazing turnaround under the $20–40–60 million plan and the creation of the continuous improvement climate, and, finally, BP's decision to close the plant despite that turnaround. Stockman listened intently. "But then what's the upside for a new owner?" he asked. "If you've made all those improvements to the plant, haven't you already optimized it?" "Not necessarily," Schaefer replied, and explained that the $20–40–60 million plan had been accomplished through a culture of innovation that was ongoing. When he left, Schaefer pointed out, the refinery workforce was on track to further raise the profit level from $60 million to $90 million. About this point, Berger joined the conversation by speaker phone. Stockman spoke, he noted later in his diary, in a kind of driven rush of "run-on paragraphs." Yet through their exchange, the three men identified a whole series of reasons why a bid from Blackstone might succeed with Browne when so many others had failed. First, Blackstone enjoyed the cash reserves to offer a bigger bid than any BP had seen before. Second, it also had deep enough pockets to absorb the environmental liabilities—the major sticking point that had sunk Paisley's bid. Third, the Wasserstein firm had enough clout and money to gain direct access to Browne himself, a tactic that would allow them to avoid having to persuade a junior-level BP executive to summon the courage to approach the head executive about a matter he thought he had long ago dismissed. Fourth and best of all, Berger and Schaefer stressed, from all they could tell, BP's unresolved alternate supply question and its demolition schedule still afforded Blackstone time to work a deal if Stockman moved fast.[12]

In subsequent phone calls from Payne and Stockman, Berger learned that the arguments he and Schaefer had marshaled had impressed Stockman and Blackstone. Even as he had followed the story of the refinery shutdown as it unfolded in the press, Stockman admitted, he had questioned BP's actions. Now he was even more amazed at its decision over Lima. Payne learned that at some point during those months, Stockman had sent his people into the plant and may even have visited it himself. When you walk through a refinery, Payne said, you can tell a lot about it in terms of how it has been maintained and how the workforce has been treating it. In Stockman's own private assessment of the refinery, he had recognized not only the many capital improvements that characterized the place, but also, Payne said, the "pride of ownership there" that gave "a very important signal to Stockman that this thing has viability."[13]

Early that May, Berger looked up an old refinery acquaintance he hadn't seen in a while, the plant manager, Kuenzli. Since Berger wanted a private conversation that would have been impossible down at the plant, Kuenzli instead drove up Main Street and met the mayor in front of the municipal building one morning at 7:00 A.M. It was a bright spring morning, so the two decided to walk around the square and talk, there where the town's Union Army regiments had drilled and where the people of Lima had once received the news of the death of Abraham Lincoln. Berger swore Kuenzli to confidence and then told him of unfolding events—of Payne, Stockman, and the bid that would soon be coming to BP. Explaining that Stockman wanted more information, Berger asked Kuenzli if he would be willing to talk with them. Kuenzli thought about it and declined. He hoped to continue his career with BP and dealing with a potential buyer on the sly was just too risky for him personally. He wished Berger the best but saw the bid, and the refinery, as doomed. BP's retreat from refining began with Browne, Kuenzli insisted, and there was no way to reverse that decision.[14]

In mid-May, Stockman informed Berger that "we are trucking right along" in their preparation of a bid to BP. It all depended on Browne's receptiveness to an offer. Even if they somehow had access to BP board members, they would never be able to move the board against the chief executive. If he looked sourly on a deal, Payne told the mayor flatly, it was over. With Stockman now on board, somehow they had to win over the most unmovable obstacle of all: the chair of BP.[15]

"I am not interested in games"

In the third week of May 1998 Payne managed to put a phone call through to Browne. Schaefer had been right: the name Wasserstein had enough clout to get through the layers of intermediaries and go right to the top. "I am not interested in games," Browne informed him bluntly. "Just tell me the number." Payne said he had an offer of $150 million for the Lima refinery. Browne declined to give an immediate response, but told Payne he would have Chase follow up. Rodney Chase, Browne's immediate No. 2, reached Payne the next day with lots of questions, the "right questions," Payne summarized for Berger, "good quality questions . . . We have definitely rung a few bells." They could only speculate about what had changed. Perhaps names like Wasserstein and Stockman, and the kind of money they were talking about, were big enough to get Browne's attention. Browne certainly would have noted Blackstone's aggressive move into refining, seen in its acquisition of Clark. Browne hadn't wanted to be bothered by the Lima matter again, Schaefer thought, but for the kind of money Stockman was talking, he might reconsider. A week later, Payne reported, Stockman and a Wasserstein partner had flown to London to meet with Chase and Ian Conn of BP. They began negotiating a price, laying out a reasonable series of steps they would follow to a conclusion. Payne's tone was cheerful; he was confident that Stockman would quickly nail down the deal. But major dangers still loomed, he cautioned Berger, not least of which was Chase's insistence on the absolute need to envelop the whole process in total secrecy. If one word of the possible deal leaked out anywhere, it was dead. In particular, Chase had warned, if BP heard of any involvement by the mayor of Lima, they would terminate the discussions immediately.[16]

The veil of secrecy largely worked, and the negotiations proceeded at a "furious pace," the *Lima News* reported later, although back in Lima, the mayor mostly found himself in the dark. In mid-June, Payne called to say that Wasserstein had just received a copy of a six-page acceptance letter from BP to Blackstone/Clark. Among other tidbits of data, BP had apparently stressed to Clark that "secrecy and speed are essential." But the whole thing made him so excited, Payne told Berger, that he had to fight off the temptation to go outside and shout from the rooftop into the canyons of Wall Street. Nine days later, Payne called again to report that the two sides had agreed on a price of about $175 million. Berger's sources told him that rumors of something big afoot were swirling through the refinery, but Payne assured him that they had to be coincidental; nobody there was in the loop. He was right; in reality, nobody, not even the PR officer, Gilbert, had a clue that a deal might be in the offing. Freshly returned from a three-week sailing trip in the Caribbean—he had negotiated matters from his yacht—Stockman called Berger to provide other various details and again caution him to keep quiet until the paperwork had actually been signed. The mayor remained silent; not Mullen, not Belcher, nor anyone else on the old refinery task force had an inkling anything was up. Berger was particularly determined this time not to utter even a whisper of the possible sale to anyone with the State of Ohio. They "hadn't demonstrated they were a trustworthy partner," he reasoned, and had always, instinctively, taken the side of BP. Why jeopardize the deal with a heads-up to Jakeway or the governor? Instead he kept his worries to himself and sweated the delicate days through.[17]

"Ultimately, the dollar speaks"

At 8:00 A.M. on July 1, Berger arrived at his office and checked his voice mail to find a message Gilbert had left an hour and a half before inviting him to a meeting at the chemical plant at 7:45. That meant two things, he calculated: first, that they were about to announce the sale, and second, that he was late for the announcement. He drove through the streets of Lima like a madman but found no cars in the plant parking lot and nobody in the administration building lobby except himself. Within ten minutes, Walpole's secretary came out and escorted him to her bosses' office, where the chemical plant chief officer told Berger of the refinery sale and carefully walked Berger through the steps of the sales process—except, Berger thought to himself, he's starting in the middle of the story because he doesn't know how it really started. The mayor smiled, nodded, and let Walpole continue. Ten minutes later, Kuenzli walked in, told Walpole, "Well, Jim, it's signed," and then extended his hand to Berger with a hearty "Congratulations!" The three walked out of Walpole's office to encounter BP's Ian Conn and Clark's chief executive, William Rusnack, coming out of an adjoining room, where they had just inked the deal. Moments before, Clark/Blackstone had purchased the refinery from BP for $215 million. "I want to thank you for all you have done in this matter," Conn told Berger in an aside, "including the fact that you kept all this confidential."[18]

Back at the refinery, loudspeakers called the remaining 350 or so employees to a mass meeting in the plant's gymnasium, where they seated themselves on folding chairs. Kuenzli took the podium and addressed the crowd, his voice echoing out into the silence. "You've probably heard some rumors," the plant manager said. "Like most rumors there's an element of truth." After a pause, he stated, in a matter-of-fact manner but with an immense grin, that the refinery had just been purchased by Clark USA. Kuenzli's words came off like a bombshell, Roller recalled, "straight out of the blue." Like the rest of his comrades at

BP senior executive Ian Conn announcing the sale of the Lima refinery to Clark Oil, July 1, 1998. *Photo courtesy of WLIO-TV, Lima, Ohio.*

the refinery, he quickly began to envision a different professional future. "My future was going to be demolishing the place and tearing it apart," he told a reporter. "Now I'll keep it running." Groman remembered his jaw dropping as applause and cheers echoed around him and then turning to a workmate to begin strategizing about what further improvements they could make to the plant. By the time the meeting ended, they had sketched out a full page of new projects to work on before rushing back to their cubicles to search the Internet for information on Clark USA.[19]

The applause and cheers set the dominant tone of the day. Clark and BP invited Berger and other civic leaders to a lunch that day at the refinery gym, where Walpole, Conn, Rusnack, and Kuenzli spoke and handshaking and congratulations reverberated all around. Conn told the crowd that BP had always been looking for "a buyer that was committed to long-term future here," and that Clark's bid was the first they had received "that was a market bid." Kuenzli kept his remarks harmonious. "This is a great day for us," he told the crowd, "and, we believe, an especially great day for the company and the entire community." During the question-and-answer period, Berger rose to welcome Clark on behalf of the city and to thank all the major players. "How is it," Kuenzli remarked loudly, "that all of us have a sneaking suspicion that the mayor had something to do with all this?" Determined to be discreet to the end, Berger just laughed and said nothing, but he had his own rich moments. Grabbing Conn's hand as the luncheon broke up, the mayor asked him, "Please tell John Browne how much we appreciate this event." Admitting his emotion of the moment, Berger could only say, "This has been such a roller coaster." Conn confessed his emotion as well, adding, "I have some insight into your feelings. You see, I was John Browne's assistant when you started writing your letters. You represented your community exactly the way you should have."[20]

The *Lima News* greeted the announcement with a huge banner headline, "Oil Refinery Rescued," and devoted most of the day's paper to a half-dozen major stories on the sale; the story likewise dominated twelve of the twenty minutes of WLIO's television coverage that evening. Further away from Lima, the news stories stressed larger financial factors as the primary cause of Lima's good fortune. The trade press, for example, explored the move mostly from the perspective of larger corporate strategies, concentrating in particular on the sale as an indication of Clark's expansion into the upper Midwest. Such large-scale economic factors certainly remained critical in the saving of the refinery; as Payne commented, he'd always had a hunch that the deal would go through in the end because "ultimately, the dollar speaks."[21]

Yet to portray the salvaging of the Lima refinery as the result only of corporate strategy or self-interest is to airbrush out the equally critical factor of community

David Berger at the "Welcome Clark" celebration in Lima's Faurot Park, August 1998. *Photo courtesy of the Mayor's Office, City of Lima.*

and human agency in socioeconomic change. As the celebrations continued in the Lima area on and off, in various forms, for the rest of the summer, corporate saviors were noticeably absent in the community's list of people they wanted to thank. Berger came in for a lion's share of the credit. "It was great, it was wonderful, it was elating to see that Mayor Berger had accomplished his primary mission," Gilbert summarized. "Everyone was just thrilled with it." A local minister invited Berger to a lunch meeting of the Lima Rotary Club, where the assembled Rotarians gave him a standing ovation—"a humbling experience," he noted in his diary. The Freedom newspaper chain gave a private award to the *Lima News* for its service to the community in its coverage of the story. In late October, the city hosted another special "Welcome Clark" day of festivities in Faurot Park. Schaefer remembered it as "right out of a movie": a gorgeous fall day, green grass extending to the top of the hill, a high school marching band playing loudly and snaking its way through the crowd, people hugging each other. Clarence Roller, Berger later noted, "shook my hand at least two times." At the podium the mayor wound up his remarks by calling out something to the effect of, "If there's one person out there who is more responsible than anyone else for having this happen, Jim would you please come forward," and Schaefer enjoyed his own moment in the sun.[22]

Berger knew the crowd well; many people at the refinery credited Schaefer in particular for the plant's continued existence. But in identifying a key force in the refinery's survival, they would have been more accurate in pointing back at themselves. When Clark's executives began examining the refinery for a possible purchase, they later stressed to the community, they had expected to find a demoralized, unmotivated workforce and a plant in poor condition. Instead, to their immense surprise, they found the opposite: a "proud, talented, committed workforce" that hadn't lost a workday to accidents in nearly three years, maintaining a plant in superb condition. They would not have pursued the sale, they said, had matters been otherwise. Conn made similar comments on the day of the sale, and BP rewarded the workers' contributions with handsome bonuses. Once again, however, it was clear that such financial rewards were an effect, rather than a cause, of a commitment refinery workers had made long ago, as had generations of local people before them, to old values like hard work as the basis of identity and self-respect.[23]

"You must be a gorilla"

One morning in mid-August, Berger stopped by the Lima Memorial Hospital for a press conference they were holding on a local health care development. A local bank executive Berger knew asked him if he had heard the news. What news? Berger wanted to know. BP had just purchased Amoco, the executive replied. "You're kidding!" Berger said in disbelief, but the media confirmed the news. Technically it was a stock-swap merger of about $49 billion; in reality, BP had devoured Amoco. The oil giants had made "an aggressive move," Browne said at a press conference, but it was good for them both because "we can do more together than either of us can do separately." Moreover, it would save the combined companies more than $2 billion in operating costs through increased efficiencies. Translated, this meant massive job losses: about six thousand in BP offices around the world, including more than thirteen hundred jobs in Cleveland alone, since, as part of the deal, BP would be vacating its Cleveland headquarters—where Rockefeller had established Standard Oil a century before—for Amoco's corporate offices in Chicago. Wall Street loved the merger; stock prices for both BP and Amoco soared immediately after the announcement. "It's a marriage made in heaven," commented one financial analyst. Yet once he heard the news, Berger's mind shot back to that August evening in a posh Cleveland ballroom almost three years to the day before, when Cleveland's Mayor White had so pointedly asked Browne and Simon if he could count on them to stay in his city, and the two BP executives had answered with a resounding yes, assuring him that the company would remain there for another generation.[24]

At a community event at the Lima refinery the next day, Greve insisted to the mayor and others that BP's sale of the plant to Clark was totally separate from its Amoco deal, except that BP had delayed the Amoco announcement by one day so as not to overshadow the local "Welcome Clark" event. Certainly, on one level, Greve was right. Moves on such a gigantic scale transpired with scant regard for the day-to-day preoccupations of little communities. In this case, especially seen in retrospect, BP's absorption of Amoco devolved from macro-level trends in the global oil industry that had been brewing for years. For a century, the search for the next big strike had dominated the attention of the big oil companies and quickened the heartbeats of their chief executives. From the mid-1970s on, however, such efforts had produced only one great new field: the strike at Kashagan in 1999, in the waters off Kazakhstan in the Caspian Sea. Meanwhile, as pressure by stockholders for increased profits continued unabated, the dominant oil fields owned by the big players in the oil industry—Alaska's North Slope and the North Sea—entered into quiet decline. As a result, the big companies increasingly turned to a strategy of replacing their slowly ebbing oil reserves by devouring each other. By 2004, summarized one industry expert, the oil world had witnessed nearly a decade of "a relentless shuffling of oil fields and other assets," with the great oil corporations increasingly acting as "investment banks." And in the great oil company merger mania of the late 1990s, as in so many other key industry developments, BP led the way. Already by 1996, Browne had quietly begun merger negotiations with Mobil. When those talks disintegrated—partly because neither side could agree on which corporate chief would head the colossal new company that would result—he initiated discussions with Amoco. The big BP-Amoco deal of summer 1998 set off a huge scramble of ensuing mega-mergers by other oil giants: Exxon with Mobil, Conoco with Phillips, and Texaco with Chevron. Two years after acquiring Amoco, BP swallowed Arco.[25]

Of course, like dinosaurs thrashing in the swamp, such moves were carried out with little attention paid to the smaller entities—individual employees and communities—that got in the way; that was what Browne meant by the savings accrued by increased operating efficiencies. When Robert Horton ruled BP, he had already begun to initiate large cutbacks in the immense layers of bureaucracy enveloping the company, partly through increased communications technology; according to Schaefer, subsequent CEOs like Simon and Browne then "supercharged" this process, moving BP's London headquarters, for example, from a thirty-two-story skyscraper to a four-story building. The chiefs found similar cost savings elsewhere, thus eliminating thousands of superfluous employees. A perennial leader in communications technology, BP under Browne put in teleconferencing in the late 1980s. Right before he left BP in 1996, Schaefer could hold face-to-face meetings, from his computer in his office, with the 150 other top BP people scattered throughout the world. This was why the company could eliminate its Cleveland headquarters: BP did not need it anymore. Following BP's absorption of Amoco, Schaefer claimed, Browne accomplished the same increased operating efficiencies with that company in eight months that it had taken him eight years to do with Sohio. When BP ingested Arco, the process moved even faster. Browne eliminated the Arco headquarters in Los Angeles nearly as quickly, cutting thousands more jobs and saving the corporation additional hundreds of millions of dollars. No wonder BP stock prices skyrocketed and investors showered praises on Browne.[26]

Situated as he was in the far-flung periphery of BP's empire, the mayor of Lima began to put it all together. In these global calculations, of course, he and his small city counted for little. Still, Berger could not escape noticing the clear linkages between BP's relatively small deal with Clark and the big merger with Amoco. The Amoco acquisition, he realized, explained a lot about BP's actions with regard to Lima. This was why BP executives had never really worried much about lining up alternate supply arrangements and never would have reopened the Lima refinery if they had failed. They knew a merger with Amoco would give them all the gasoline they wanted. The Amoco prospect also explained the corporation's obsession about the speed and especially the secrecy of both deals. Indeed, the Amoco possibility had been such a tightly held corporate secret that it had flown under the radar screen of Deep Well and all of Berger's other private sources of inside information. Many of BP's upper-echelon managers had been unaware of the planned merger; even as highly ranked a BP executive as Percy had received word of the merger only two weeks before BP let the story break. Most immediately, Berger grasped, as BP had intended, the secrecy of both deals had certainly worked to substantially raise the price that Clark/Blackstone had paid for the Lima refinery. In the third week of May, Stockman had tendered Browne an initial offer of $150 million. Five weeks later, his company had bought the plant for $215 million. Blackstone/Clark executives would have figured, Berger realized, that once they acquired the refinery that had provided such a substantial portion of product for BP gas stations in Ohio, BP would remain their primary customer. They had assumed that they would recoup the increased amount they had paid for the Lima refinery from BP on the other end of the arrangement. Since Blackstone/Clark would pay the higher price for the Lima refinery only on that basis, it was essential to BP that Blackstone/Clark remain ignorant of any other possible sources of supply—like Amoco—that BP had in the works. Thus from BP's perspective, it was imperative that the Amoco deal remain super-secret until after it had closed its sale of the Lima refinery. The chain of events, coming so close together and with all the repercussions they had for both Lima and Cleveland, struck the mayor with particular force. "On the day Lima is resurrected," he summarized years later, "within twenty-four hours, the bell tolls for Cleveland . . . the irony is just incredible."[27]

The blow of losing BP hit Cleveland hard. There was the matter of 1,300 lost jobs, the effect of which would multiply as the incomes from those lost jobs disappeared from the local economy. There was also the $227 million in local taxes, now gone, that BP had paid. In addition, the company had been a major contributor to local charities and civic organizations, including the public schools, the Cleveland Food Bank, and the United Way. The previous year it had given $6 million to the Cleveland Red Cross alone. Now all of these organizations, and more, would have to adjust to substantially tighter budgets. Given the company's historic, hundred-year presence in the city, the loss registered a hit in other ways as well, and local leaders responded in immense pain and bitterness. As White, Cleveland's angry mayor, told the press, BP had "promised that they would stay and be part of our community for generations to come . . . They gave us assurances and they've broken their word. I join with many other community leaders in feeling betrayed." As it had in Lima, BP issued statements oozing with regret and grandly opened its wallet to soften the blow, promising to continue its current charitable contributions for at least two years after its departure. In addition, BP sent an additional $1 million check to the Cleveland public schools.[28]

Stung by a major blow to their hometown, Governor Voinovich and Mayor White both immediately swung into action, pledging a vigorous (and, as it quickly turned out, unsuccessful) public campaign to reverse the flight of BP jobs from Cleveland. Back in Lima, local people were especially quick to contrast the swiftness and intensity of Voinovich's response with his comparative lethargy the previous year, when their own city was in crisis. Their tone was mostly indignant, but the comparable circumstances might have drawn from them a little more sympathy. For the central lesson of BP's departure from both communities seemed the same: the needs and agendas of any partner communities, small or large, carried little or no weight in corporate boardrooms when big decisions were made. White's development director phrased it best. "Our ability to control those decisions is limited," he admitted. "We will not be passively accepting. We will always try to be a player in those decisions. But in some cases they are driven by forces we cannot control." Certainly the scale of these decisions—transpiring now on a global as opposed to a municipal or interstate level—made this a different era from the Gilded Age a century before. In many other ways, though, the Darwinian nature of business transactions seemed essentially the same. If Berger somehow missed that point, he would be reminded of it most directly a year later, when he journeyed to New York City for his second—and last—personal encounter with John Browne.[29]

In September 1999, Berger and his friend Parker MacDonel jumped on a plane to New York City primarily on the outside chance that such a meeting could occur. MacDonel, a Yale alumnus, had shown the mayor a brochure telling of a special seminar hosted by the Yale School of Management at the Yale Club of New York City, a swank high-rise across the street from Grand Central Station. There Browne would deliver, the brochure highlighted, a keynote address on the relationship between government and business. Berger was eager to hear what he had to say. Late that afternoon, half an hour before Browne's address, he found himself waiting in the lobby with other seminar participants when a vaguely familiar voice called out, "Well, mayor, how are you doing?" To his surprise, Berger met an old acquaintance he hadn't seen in years, a business executive who had grown up not far from Lima and who now worked, Berger learned, as the director of BP's External Affairs Office in New York. The executive was intrigued as to why Berger had come. The mayor simply explained that it was primarily to hear Browne's address. "Would you like to meet Browne personally?" the BP officer asked, and with Berger's okay led him to a private reception in a salon downstairs, where the seminar speakers and other VIPs milled around. The BP official excused himself and returned a few minutes later with a knot of full-suited BP executives, in the middle of whom was Browne.[30]

The BP officials surrounding Browne, Berger thought, appeared extraordinarily watchful and protective of their chief executive, almost as if "they thought I was going to take a swing at him." Browne himself seemed nervous and ill at ease, at a loss for how to start the conversation. So Berger dove in, reminding him of their one previous meeting at that banquet in Cleveland in the summer of 1995 and saying he was eager to hear Browne's remarks on the relationship of business and government. Big companies and industrial communities could benefit from a mutual "clarity of purpose," Browne admitted. Yet "if you shake the tree hard enough, an apple will fall." Berger struggled with how to respond, but continued with what he recalled as "fairly breezy, positive set of comments" on the refinery's importance, expressing his appreciation to Browne for his work in consummating the sale. The BP chief executive had only one other major thing to say. "You must learn," he instructed the mayor, "that if you're going to play with gorillas, you must be a gorilla." With that, the conversation seemed to be at an end. Berger again thanked Browne for the chance to talk with him and invited him to Lima sometime. Browne folded himself back into his entourage and walked away.

"Straight moral issues never make it"

For a decade, the city of Lima in general, and its mayor in particular, had found themselves up against huge global entities with power on a scale far beyond their control—yet had found a way to triumph anyway. Hence, Berger's final major encounter with the refinery was all the more galling because it did not emanate from the fundamental imbalance of power or scale between global corporations and their partner communities. Even as he celebrated the sale of the refinery, Berger remained haunted by one last bit of unfinished business. He had not gone through such strenuous efforts and risked his political career primarily to benefit wealthier Shawnee Township. Having done so much to save the Lima refinery, the mayor moved directly to annex it into the city.

Certainly the thought of annexation had percolated at the back of Berger's mind throughout his long struggle with BP. As the pieces began to come together for the refinery's successful sale, he acted on the idea immediately, gently broaching the subject with Stockman in their first conversation and then following up that summer. The day after the sale, Berger threw himself into the preparation of a lengthy power-point presentation on the economic benefits of annexation, which he delivered the following Monday to a visiting delegation of Clark and Blackstone executives, including Rusnack and Stockman. Both seemed open to letting the city limits encompass their new refinery, Berger thought, although they asked Berger to include BP in the discussions so that the refinery and the chemical plant might make the move together. The next day, the mayor met with Walpole at his office in Lima, who initially seemed agreeable to the move, as long as they could do it in concert with Clark. Nine days later, swallowing hard, Berger drove to BP's Cleveland headquarters for a morning-long conversation with Atton and Conn. As Berger methodically laid out the benefits to BP, both men, Berger thought, quickly warmed to the annexation idea. Matters remained slightly strained with Walpole and later with Greve. The mayor gently explored the moral dimension of annexation, unapologetically laying out the need for Lima to enlarge its tax base. His city functioned as a regional employer for a ten-county radius, he explained, where thousands of nonresidents "earned their livelihoods." These many employees, he claimed, "owed something back to the community in which their jobs and livelihoods were sustained." He put it to Walpole as a straight matter of morality, namely "the need for the city of Lima to be able to survive." Walpole remembered exactly how the conversation unfolded. "Dave, I'm in business," he replied. "BP Chemicals is in business. There are all kinds of moral issues. This is a capitalistic society. Give us a financial reason to do these things and we'll do it. But straight moral issues never make it."[31]

So the mayor stuck to the numbers, which he had structured in a way that even tough business executives would be able to understand. First of all, Lima had been officially designated by the state as an area in "situational distress," meaning that if the refinery and the chemical plant joined the city, both could expect sweeping tax breaks (worth $1.2 million and $600,000, respectively). Second, the refinery regularly consumed voracious amounts of city water, and the mayor had instructed his utilities department to declare the old water contract null and void upon the sale. Berger made it clear that if they stayed outside the city, they could expect to pay upwards of $2 million annually for city water. If they joined it, however, they would receive water at greatly reduced rates. Third and most important, the "nonwithdrawal annexation" scheme that Berger had pioneered would not cost Shawnee Township a dime. Technically, the facilities would remain in Shawnee and the township could continue to collect their property taxes, its major source of income. Ohio state code prohibited all townships from levying income taxes. The economically distressed City of Lima, however, had long been dependent on income taxes instead of property taxes. In 2006, for example, of its total income of about $16 million, $15 million had come from income tax payments. All that "nonwithdrawal annexation" meant was that the city would be able to impose a 1.5% income tax on the salaries of refinery and chemical plant employees, bringing in millions of additional revenue to its needy coffers.[32]

For more than a month, it appeared the deal might go through. The No. 2 official at the chemical plant told the mayor that they would come into the city if the refinery led the way, and Clark's Rusnack indicated his company's openness to the idea. Its major concerns were only how to tell its employees about the decision and also how to manage the unhappiness of Shawnee Township trustees, who would be sure to oppose the deal on general principle. "Light your votive candles," Berger suggested to his staff.

Then the hope died, just as quickly and easily as it had risen. In a conference call between the mayor and the plants' senior managers in mid-September, Kuenzli told Berger that they had jointly decided not to pursue annexation. It would have too great an impact on their employees and on Shawnee, he explained, for only marginal economic gain to themselves.[33]

The mayor had one final card to play, with the union members whose jobs his activism had saved. He had previously been bound from this because of a commitment to confidentiality that Rusnack had demanded on the annexation proposal. But when, in spring 1999, the Clark CEO had himself begun speaking publicly in defense of Clark's decision, Berger felt the matter was now fair game for public discussion. In a meeting with the OCAW's executive committee in early April, he laid out his case for annexation and asked the union to push it with Clark's management. "You know, Dave," Winterstellar, the OCAW president, told him, "if you had just come to us when the whole thing was going on and asked us then for support of annexation, we in all likelihood in order to protect our jobs would have voted for it." Explaining that he hadn't been able to do it then because of the promise of confidentiality he had given Rusnack, Berger then went on to ask, "If it was the right thing to do then, why isn't it the right thing to do now?" The union officers conceded Berger's point and agreed to take the mayor's recommendation to their membership for a vote. Soon Winterstellar reported back: the OCAW membership had voted unanimously against supporting the annexation of the refinery into the City of Lima. The refinery workers, Gilbert said, were just "furious" at the possibility of paying city taxes. Dealing with management had taught them, one refinery worker rationalized later, "that loyalty means nothing." As he explained, "You figure right off that you're going to pay city income taxes and what's in it for me?"[34]

"An ethical order must be imposed on business behavior"

In an era when giant corporations move across the global landscape like leviathans, what do the stories matter of the individual communities left in their wake?

The significance of this question fairly shouts aloud in Lima's case for, no matter how much local people congratulated themselves for saving the refinery, in retrospect it is clear that the plant's continued existence lay partly in just plain dumb luck. Payne ticked off the many lucky breaks that had had to line up like dominoes merely for him to bring off his own part in the process: that when Berger first called him, he had had a meeting scheduled with Stockman; that Stockman had just happened to be at Blackstone, where he had recently persuaded his partners to invest in the refining sector; that Blackstone had just acquired a majority interest in Clark; that Clark was looking to acquire a large refinery in the upper Midwest; and that BP, surprisingly, had agreed to reconsider the sale of its refinery. It just so happened that the two oil companies were able to work their way to a deal, past many of the obstacles—particularly BP's demand for speed and secrecy—which might have torpedoed it at any time. Perhaps luckiest of all for Lima, before this last series of fortunate events, was BP's long delay in lining up a pipeline or other alternate supply arrangement to replace the refinery. This left the mayor and others with enough time to search for a possible new buyer, a large and critical "window of opportunity," Schaefer said, "that should have been closed." If any of these decisive factors had not appeared or had fallen another way, events at the refinery almost certainly would have transpired as Walpole had outlined them to Berger in March 1998: the demolition of the storage tanks begun in April 1998, the dismantling of the coke apparatus and cat cracker a year later, and finally, the destruction of the vacuum and crude units and other integral elements of the dismantled refinery. Thanks to the mayor's aggressiveness, BP had agreed that creation of the LIC would entail no net job losses. Even so, Lima would have mourned the passing of the last remaining part of its old manufacturing heritage, and yet another traditional enterprise would have disappeared from the once-mighty industrial Midwest.[35]

Even with this element of luck, the stories of individual communities in an era of deindustrialization are critically important for many reasons. For one thing, they illustrate the zero-sum-game nature of the new global economy, in which the success of one community is linked, often inextricably, with the downfall of another. Knowing this, workers at manufacturing plants, along with the larger communities where they live, sometimes direct a fair part of their emotional energy not at the corporate managers weighing their jobs but at other plants and communities they must compete against for continued existence. At Lima's refinery, people like Monus and Gilbert admitted, part of the emotional bitterness with which local people greeted BP's decision to close them down stemmed from a sense of rivalry they felt with their sister plant in Toledo. To Lima-area residents, and particulary the refinery workers themselves, the Toledo plant had never enjoyed the same level of pride and efficiency characterizing Lima's, and, in fact, had accumulated a much higher record than Lima's of environmental and safety crises, fires, and the like. Why, the people of Lima wanted to know, does a plant like that get to survive—to say nothing of clearly less effective refineries like Ashland's in Detroit or Clark's at Blue Island—while our plant is to be gutted?[36]

In fact, Lima's survival was directly correlated with Blue Island's demise. Certainly, the Blue Island plant, near Chicago, had been troubled for years by a series of environmental and safety problems of its own making. Throughout the 1990s, two managers there had filed misleading reports about wastewater discharge into area sewers and neglected to report other violations of pollution codes. In 1995, the plant had been rocked by two explosions, one of which had killed two workers, and emitted a gas leak that had sent nearby high school students to the hospital. After the plant was temporarily closed following another fire in December 1999, Illinois's state attorney general had tried unsuccessfully to keep it from reopening. Six months later, the Blue Island plant had sent out a vast cloud of particle emissions over eight blocks of a nearby residential neighborhood, covering the homes and parks of three thousand people with a noxious chemical dust. Refinery officials insisted it was nontoxic but admitted it could cause respiratory problems and eye burning. Staggered by the fines that the federal and state governments had levied, Clark officials announced the closing of the Blue Island refinery early in 2001. Now local people would no longer have to deal with the explosions, gas leaks, and chemical dust of the refinery next door, but they also faced the exodus of nearly three hundred well-paying jobs from their community. "It's rough, rough to the family too," lamented one newly unemployed maintenance man. "You just wake up with nothing to do, feeling that you are worth nothing." Chicago-area residents and officials pointed their fingers at the larger economic context of the refining industry, and also blamed the plant's series of environmental problems. Farther away, Groman and others at the Lima refinery knew another reason quite well: that Clark's acquisition of Lima had simply rendered the Blue Island plant superfluous to its new corporate owner.[37]

A second reason local stories are important is that they suggest ways to empower such local communities. While the global economy may be a zero-sum game, Lima's story fits into a more recent and expanding narrative suggesting that individual communities do have several effective sociocultural resources for challenging corporate power. The possibility of community agency in corporate affairs appears especially important and worth repeating in the socioeconomic climate of the late twentieth and early twenty-first centuries in the United States because much of the prevailing economic teaching has instead stressed local powerlessness. This is an era, scholars have argued, where the doctrine of "market populism" or "economic liberalism," after a half-century-long march from the ideological wilderness, has finally attained a triumphant pride of place in popular culture, at least until quite recently. This doctrine rests on certain central claims: that, if freed from state regulation, free markets are the best means of maximizing wealth and distributing societal resources, and that market capitalism can accomplish wonders on a global level if left to move freely across national borders without restraints. Economist Milton Friedman, the most celebrated acolyte of such teaching, encapsulates the basic point in his oft-quoted dictum that the only responsibility of business is to maximize profits.[38]

Not only are such arguments morally tenuous at best, as Lima's story suggests, but they also seem to suffer from extreme historical amnesia. Any corporate manager devoting the energies of his or her company toward social ends "thoroughly undermines the very foundation of our society," Friedman asserted. To him, expressions of corporate social responsibility amounted to "pure and unadulterated socialism." But long before Karl Marx, the founders of the American republic had worried about concentrations of power of all kinds, whether they were military, political, or economic, and strictly limited them. This was not socialism at all but rather good, old-fashioned populism, the belief that ordinary citizens, not machines, were masters of American society.[39]

From the beginning of the republic, jurists had weighed two contrasting understandings of the corporate nature. One was that they were natural entities. It was from this legal foundation that the *Santa Clara* and other cases had taken their bearings and laid down the basic framing of corporate personhood. According to the other understanding, however, corporations were artificial beings, temporary in duration and ultimately subject to the sovereign will of the people. And if ever there was a place where such ideas had taken particularly deep root, it was in early Ohio, a state whose creation had taken place under the auspices of radical Jeffersonian principles. The vast numbers of small farmers who made up its early body politic only empowered leaders who spoke in egalitarian language, rejected the aristocratic trappings of federalism, and otherwise celebrated the power of ordinary people. So deeply rooted was Jeffersonian republicanism in early Ohio, in fact, that no sooner had statehood been achieved than some of its key republican leaders, like Thomas Worthington and Edward Tiffin, came under attack for their ostensibly aristocratic bearing. The ideology of revolutionary republicanism to which most of Ohio's voters subscribed taught that power was inherently threatening to liberty. While people needed to contract together to form governments, power of all kinds should be carefully watched and circumscribed.[40]

The governmental structures of the early state thoroughly reflected this ideological heritage. Ohio's first constitution invested all judicial, legislative, and executive power in the legislature, the lower house of which was elected annually. Its governor was a figurehead, with no powers of appointment and no veto. The revised state constitution of 1851, which remains the foundation of Ohio state government today, reaffirmed the supremacy of the legislature; not until 1903 did Ohio governors receive even the power of veto. The stalwart Jeffersonians who gave birth to Ohio, so jealous in their safeguarding of the rights of the people, naturally regarded concentrations of economic power with deep suspicion. "There is a great difference between natural persons and corporations," declared the Ohio Supreme Court in 1838. "Natural persons have the capacity to make and enter into any contracts which are not prohibited by law . . . but it is otherwise for corporations. A corporation is a body created by law . . . and derives all its powers and capabilities from the law of its creation." Nor were such sturdy republican principles confined to Ohio. All across the country, until well past the Civil War, states chartered early corporations—early turnpike and canal companies, for example—only for specific and limited purposes. After they had accomplished their designated purposes, they were routinely dissolved.[41]

To summarize this history is not to somehow deny the social good that large business enterprises have brought. Out of the hard work of risk-taking entrepreneurs emerged business structures that facilitated revolutions in transportation, communication, and even public health, all of which immeasurably enriched the lives of subsequent generations. However, in their beginning, at least, these enterprises were carefully restricted as artificial beings subject to the popular will. Perhaps democracy stands at risk when such restrictions are removed.

The limitations on corporate power imposed in the United States during the revolutionary and antebellum eras did not survive the shift to a burgeoning industrial economy that emerged following the Civil War. New Supreme Court decisions like the *Santa Clara* case ushered in the dominance of the alternate "natural entity" theory of corporate personhood. Yet the legacy of the earlier understanding did not disappear, and left a powerful and important residue in U.S. law that later reformers readily utilized. In fact, with the rise of antimonopoly sentiment during the Gilded Age and Progressive Era, it served as the foundation for a vast legal structure that substantially regulated corporate autonomy in America. This structure built on key court decisions of its own, like the critical 1876 case of *Munn v. Illinois,* which ruled that private property was no longer private when it conflicted with the public interest. Historian Stanley Buder traces two corresponding and interrelated developments: "the change in business organization from the relatively simple to the complex and the loosely parallel growth of the use of the power of government to modify or control market forces when they have harmful consequences." In fact, Buder says, the *Santa Clara* decision actually strengthened the regulatory hand of the state. The growing power and size of corporations shifted the regulatory focus and agency from the state to the federal level, culminating in the political revolution of Roosevelt's New Deal and in the cresting wave of political liberalism of the 1960s. In the words of Supreme Court justice Louis Brandeis, Americans did not have to "accept the evils attendant on the free and unrestricted use of the corporate mechanism as if these evils were the inescapable price of civilized life." A wide number of consumer, environmental, and public protest movements from the 1960s on have engineered the further restriction of corporate power in America. Meanwhile, ethicists have advanced new arguments distinguishing narrowly defined stockholders from wider numbers of stakeholders. Stockholders, business ethicists maintain, are not the only important stakeholders in a company's behavior. Workers, neighbors, and communities are interested and important parties in corporate decisions as well. As a result, business scholar Geoffrey Jones has suggested, state power remains strong and corporate autonomy in the global economy may remain more limited than it was a century ago.[42]

There seems little doubt that the meltdown of Wall Street in the bleak autumn of 2008—a financial crisis caused primarily, thoughtful analysts have written, by a speculative frenzy induced by a lack of adequate governmental oversight—has deepened doubts as to the wisdom of allowing an unhampered "economic liberalism" to work its will. Even before this most recent financial crisis, national poll data have confirmed a deep public distrust in the willingness or ability of corporations to safeguard the public's interest, a lack of confidence that has escalated steadily over the past two decades. Reflective of this climate, global capitalism in recent years has sought to assume a new and pointedly "moral" face. The number of members in a coalition called Businesses for Social Responsibility, for instance, grew from a few at its beginning in 1990 to more than four hundred today, including half the corporations listed in the *Fortune 500*. Business scholar Rosabeth Moss Kanter has recently described in detail the healthy profits accruing to a host of multinational corporations she calls "vanguard companies"—businesses like Procter and Gamble, IBM, the Brazilian megabank Banco Real, and the Mexican cement company Cemex. These corporations, she argues, have managed to flourish while integrating moral behavior and global consciousness into the heart of their business methods, a trend noted and increasingly followed by other corporations. A hundred corporate chief executives, for example, have lined up at the United Nations with nonprofits like Amnesty International and

Greenpeace to sign a pledge mandating their adherence to the Universal Declaration of Human Rights, while more than seventy companies, including such giants as Sunoco, Nike, Bank of America, and Coco-Cola, have signed on to a ten-point code of corporate environmental conduct cobbled together by a group called the Coalition for Environmentally Responsible Companies. The quarterly reporting firm *Business Ethics* issues an annual list of good corporate citizens, and companies pride themselves on making this list.[43]

Foremost among these vanguard companies has been BP. From the very emergence of this most recent movement toward global corporate social responsibility, BP's leaders have moved repeatedly to stress their company's human and responsible side, to carefully burnish its public image as a Corporation That Cares. In moments of extreme exasperation, they would drop the subtleties and trumpet the message. By August 1997, after the expense and the effort he had invested in creating the Lima Integrated Complex, Greve seemed frustrated at local obtuseness—maybe even local ingratitude—regarding BP's magnanimity. "People may not like what we are doing," he told the Lima Rotary Club, "but I doubt they can criticize the way we are doing it. For instance, on E-Day we announced a 10-point plan for our employees that reduces the number of jobs at risk from 447 to less than 90 employees . . . How many other companies who have downsized in Lima or elsewhere have made a similar commitment?" In 1998, BP officially jettisoned its old corporate insignia and launched a corporate marketing campaign centered on a green, white, and yellow sunburst as the corporate sign and a multimillion-dollar PR effort stressing that BP now stood for Beyond Petroleum. "BP can be a friend—listening to consumers, speaking in a human voice," one of its marketing specialists told the *New York Times Magazine*. Browne began making well-received speeches on the dangers of global warming. "If you don't embrace such ethical concerns," he told other corporate CEOs, "you're an anachronism."[44]

Perhaps it would be naïve for individual communities to put too much stock in such corporate declarations of good faith. One reason is just a matter of scale. Certainly in some ways, Greve was right. In its response to partner communities like Lima or Cleveland, BP could point to an unimpeachable and demonstrated record of corporate generosity, especially when compared with those of a great many other companies. It would be erroneous and unfair to conclude that Lima's fate did not matter to BP. Yet on the relative list of BP's global priorities, it surely would be accurate to conclude that Lima did not matter that much. How could it? If for no other reason, it was just too small. This is why Paisley dismisses Berger's theory that BP preferred the refinery's closure to its sale out of concern over competition from the new owner. Having worked for the corporate planning team in London, Paisley was sure that the Ohio retail market simply was not worth that much to BP. With all the other opportunities the company was pursuing, its leaders couldn't possibly be afraid of a little bit of competition in Ohio; for BP, Paisley asserted, "it's a world game."

When he returned to work for BP after his unsuccessful leave in pursuit of a management buyout bid for the Lima refinery, Paisley quickly joined in the all-consuming task at the time: getting all the company's pieces in place for what became the Amoco deal. Yet in response to his few periodic sighs of regret over his quashed bid, his fellow executives would tell him, "Hey, Bob, get over it. You're getting all bent out of shape over $50 million." Money on that level, they told him, was "a friggin' drop in the bucket" to BP. For a small company, an annual profit of $20 million would be decent money. Had he succeeded in buying the Lima refinery, Paisley said, he would have been happy with such returns. But for the executives of a megacompany like BP, used to thinking in the billions, that kind of money was only "rounding error." The attitude of Paisley's BP superiors toward Lima was primarily one of exasperation; they wanted to get rid of that headache, to close the plant and thus get it off their plate. Perhaps this is why Berger's persistent agitation proved such a supreme irritant. "The head of BP is used to talking with kings, presidents, prime ministers," Schaefer said. Who is this little mayor and why is he still stirring things up?[45]

Moreover, as BP's Walpole openly admitted, even if Lima had been big enough to register on BP's list of major issues, perhaps it simply was not in BP's nature—or the nature of any corporation—to significantly alter its behavior because of moral or human concerns. In response to reports of job losses in Lima that a shutdown of the refinery would occasion, a BP spokesperson in London admitted, "Nobody can do anything but sympathize with a community being buffeted in this way. But these decisions have to be made. Companies are multinational and under an obligation to deliver the goods to investors." Because of such differences in scale and because of the immense power of large corporations, some of the most astute and eloquent critics of that power have concluded that, in their very essence, corporations must remain unmoved, on an official level, by any ethical concern whatsoever.[46]

Certainly, corporations may *claim* to care about certain principles or particular communities. People may ascribe human characteristics to a corporation: that it is fundamentally good, or that it somehow imbibes the essential nature of the particular celebrity athlete or jungle animal that its marketing experts have currently associated with it. This is an understandable tendency, given the billions of dollars such entities invest in highly effective advertising designed to implant positive images in the public mind. Yet, argues writer Jerry Mander, such confusion emanates from the "split personality" of the legal status corporations enjoy in U.S. law. By the fantastic legal alchemy of decisions like the 1886 *Santa*

Clara case, corporations have received the rights of living people but none of the social responsibilities that come with them. A corporation enjoys the right to buy and sell property, the right to sue others to protect its reputation, and all the rights to freedom of expression guaranteed regular citizens by the Bill of Rights. At the same time it enjoys protections and expressions denied to ordinary living people. Since it has no physical being—as Mander says, "no corporality"—it cannot be imprisoned or executed by governments, nor in any other way (unlike its owners) reach a natural death. In this manner, "a corporation actually has the possibility of immortality." In its essence a corporation is "a machine, a technological structure, an organization that follows its own principles and morality." It is an entity that cannot care about any person or community, for it cannot express human feelings such as shame, guilt, or regret. Nor—at least according to the 1919 case of *Dodge v. Ford*—can it be answerable to any moral system other than that permitted by its fundamental and sole obligation: the pursuit of profit. A corporation in its very nature could never officially put the welfare of a community above its own profit concerns. If such a conflict of goals should occur, "then corporations are similarly disloyal to the communities they may have been part of for many years."[47]

For a perfect example of the corporate inability to express human feeling, consider the case of Union Carbide in Bhopal, India. In 1986, a Union Carbide chemical plant there accidentally vented a toxic gas that killed more than 6,000 people and injured some 200,000 others. Its board chairman initially took full responsibility for the disaster, and personally pledged he would devote the remainder of his life to making amends. Yet within a year he had reoriented himself to lead Union Carbide's legal fight against paying damages in Bhopal. What had changed his mind? This particular CEO, Mander points out, had "at first reacted as a human being." The very nature of corporate structures can admit no such response.[48]

BP's actions in northwest Ohio were not comparable, of course, to Union Carbide's in Bhopal. BP is a corporation that has stated its commitment to moral action in the world. Its leaders would insist that it stands at the other end of the corporate scale from soulless entities like Union Carbide. Even so, it was prepared to scrap an excellent refinery—and with it, a proud industrial community—just because the plant did not fit its current corporate portfolio. As Atton blandly informed the British press, "Our first responsibility is to our shareholders." Lima's fate simply took a back seat to BP's other options, options that exposed it to less risk and better fit its corporate needs. After the sale of the refinery had been consummated and Lima's mayor and BP officials could finally lower their gloves, Greve assured Berger that BP had never felt any "animus" to him personally; they knew he was merely trying to do his job as his city expected, and he seemed to be doing it well. Yet from their side, Greve confessed, they had been mystified by the mayor's apparent hostility toward them, when, he said—as Berger summarized it in his diary—"all they were doing was conducting business." All BP was doing was threatening to kick away one of the last remaining props from under the local economy, plunging an untold number of people into poverty in a community already hard hit, and a senior-level BP executive could not understand why the mayor took it so personally.[49]

Yet the story of Lima's resistance suggests that Mander and other critics may go too far. First of all, despite the overwhelming preponderance of corporate power, the fact that corporations are made up of human beings can give industrial communities an opening. Significant numbers of corporate employees may routinely come to care deeply about their partner communities in spite of the larger, profit-driven agendas of their employer, while other employees may find their decisions influenced by other emotions. Examples of this are legion in the story of BP in Lima. BP executives in London, for example, apparently let their personal animus against Lima's mayor so cloud their judgment that they were willing to walk away from a quarter-billion-dollar deal for their company if they received any intimation that Berger had had a hand in it. Closer to Lima, there were the several key individuals inside BP, from Deep Well on down, who were moved enough by the city's plight that they secretly fed Berger and others inside information, even when it was detrimental to their employer's interests. There were also individuals like Schaefer, who may have lost his job because he advocated for Lima too vigorously. There were immensely loyal employees like Judy Gilbert, who still treasures her memories of working for BP, regards the company with deep affection, and to this day regards her time with the company as the high point of her professional career. But she had spent her adult life in Lima, and even while she faithfully represented her employer to the press, deep down she believed "that BP was trashing a worthwhile refinery." She wished, she confessed later, that, like Schaefer, she had had the financial wherewithal to tell her bosses, "I don't need this job. You can take this job and shove it. This is such a dishonorable thing you're doing." There is enough fragmentary evidence to suspect that Gilbert's sentiments may have been privately shared high up BP's chain of command. On the day their company finally sold the refinery to Clark/Blackstone, both Gilbert and Kuenzli discerned a mood of almost giddy relief among the high-level BP executives who had come down to Lima that day. In the car on the way to the Lima TV station for an interview, Conn remarked to Gilbert on how great he felt in participating in the events of the day, how BP really was doing the right thing in selling the refinery. The BP executives he witnessed, Kuenzli later remembered, likewise "were impacted emotionally beyond just the event. There was a burden, a certain amount of depression . . . that weighed heavy on BP management who were close to Lima." The sale "lifted the burden off them."[50]

Second, the intimately human dimension of the Lima story uncovered by this study suggests that industrial communities may have the wherewithal to penetrate the cloak of amorality by which large corporations legitimize their actions. It's not personal, it's business, executives insist, "straight moral issues never make it." Industrial communities can assist their corporate partners in making the connection between their actions and acceptable moral behavior. After laying out an exhaustive social history of American business, Stanley Buder was led to conclude that "the free market and capitalism are not moral ideals, and they do not possess internal moral compasses . . . the economy is not an end in itself but a means to other more selective ends. An ethical order must be imposed on business behavior." By highlighting the human dimension of corporate decisions, communities can underscore their fundamental moral dimension.[51]

In the same manner, industrial communities can call into question the oft-repeated corporate insistence that their affairs remain private enterprise and therefore the public has no right to express any agency in them. In fact, argues Nissen, his case studies of community activism in the face of plant closings suggest that "the conventional wisdom counseling strict subservience to the corporation actually *invites* abuse" (emphasis his). Such communities would be better off demanding certain standards of "good corporate citizenship" from their corporate partners. That was part of the fundamental clash that he had had with Jakeway, Berger said. The state development director confined his activities to safe and traditional tasks like encouraging investment in the state. "The idea of chastising business for negative decisions probably isn't in his job description," Berger knew. "And I think that few public officials would say that it's part of theirs. I believe fundamentally that it was part of mine." The mayor continued:

> What the case of Lima demonstrates is that the questioning or the accountability that the community can bring to something. I don't know that I'd want to argue for legal barriers or new laws or more bureaucracy. But there ought to be an expectation of legitimacy that the community can raise and demand, just as we did, interactions that are appropriate, and not be seen as I think BP wanted to see us, as just a wacko group . . . I would argue that it doesn't require bureaucracy. It doesn't even necessarily require legislation. It does require an ethic. It does require community expectations. And it does require a business community that responds in some responsible way.[52]

Of course, "chastising business for negative decisions" may be an easier course to take in light of the degree to which corporations are positioning themselves as legally endowed beings with profound senses of social conscience. Communities have every right to enforce this ethic, with legislation if necessary. They may not find a more appropriate moment than the present for imposing these kinds of regulatory mechanisms. If corporations really are embracing a new role for themselves as creatures of conscience, it may be because similarly oriented consumers are rewarding them for doing so, and penalizing them if they do not, through a mechanism and a language that they instantly understand—that of profits. The value to corporations of a moral stance is evident in the steady consumer market for products ranging from hybrid cars and green buildings to fair-trade products and socially responsible investment portfolios. One observer of business trends has noted that "the values-driven consumer" is a driving force behind a thousand daily corporate decisions across the country. Corporate consciousness of this trend may be only a momentary opening, but it is also a profound one. Lima's story provides just one example of the kind of agency a community may restore to itself simply by seizing it.[53]

Finally, it is important to recognize that, while meeting with happier results than most other communities have achieved, the determined activism displayed in Lima was not all that terribly extraordinary in contemporary America. To be sure, the past half-century has witnessed the accumulation of several sociopolitical trends in America that have worked to significantly undermine community activism, notably the current decay in local political party structures and a greater distrust of governmental policies. Compared with those of a half-century ago, today's market is stronger and corporate power is greater, changes that certainly are fragmenting democratic possibilities. Sociologists like Robert Putnam and Robert Bellah and his team of researchers have documented a pervasive sense of individualism and disintegrating social capital that likewise seems to be dissolving the foundations of American civic life.[54]

However, since the 1960s the nation has also witnessed a number of countervailing trends. Greater levels of higher education across America and the subsequent spread of postindustrial skills like collaboration and problem solving; the information revolution, which has put endless reams of useful data into the hands of ordinary citizens; and shifts in cultural values that have enhanced the civic participation of previously marginalized citizens, like women and people of color: all of these trends have reinforced democratic possibilities. "Although many studies show a decline in *national* citizen participation," writes political analyst Gar Alperovitz, "the United States is in fact in the midst of an extraordinary resurgence of *local* community-building efforts" (emphasis his). For the past four decades, American communities from rural hamlets to metropolitan centers have witnessed an explosion of citizen activist groups and energies, ranging from neighborhood associations to activist congregations to economic entities like community development corporations (CDCs). The number of CDCs alone may now be reaching close to eight thousand, while the total number of Americans involved in such activism on all levels is measured in the millions. Communities across the country have discovered they have a variety of tools and resources at their disposal for exerting agency over their common lives and futures, and for decades have used such resources with increasing and demonstrated effectiveness.[55]

In localities all across the country, moreover, evidence is beginning to accumulate that the vitality of local democracy is increasingly being accompanied by a willingness to limit corporate personhood. If Friedman and his acolytes are taken seriously, then corporations have all the freedom of real persons but none of the responsibilities. They can move about freely, make and dissolve contracts at will, and sue other citizens in the courts. They can engage in the same kinds of political behavior as living, breathing citizens and even contribute to the election campaigns of the particular politicians they favor, now—as the U.S. Supreme Court ruled in January 2010 in its landmark *Citizens United* case—without monetary limit. At the same time, however, unlike real people, their behavior cannot be limited by any kind of moral framework, at least in the reasoning of their free-market defenders. Two of Friedman's law professor devotees, for example, have argued that a corporation is "incapable of having social or moral obligations much in the same way that inanimate objects are incapable of having such obligations."[56]

To defend the vitality of American democracy, perhaps all local activists need to do is suggest to their corporate partners that they cannot have it both ways. Such suggestions are increasingly forthcoming and are being enacted into law. Communities are filing lawsuits against the use of taxpayer dollars to attract corporations, or suing to get back the public's money from companies that have moved away. Several states have begun to experiment with the possibility of revoking corporate charters. Taking corporate personhood seriously, a Pennsylvania township in 1998 tried to hold corporations accountable to the popular "three-strikes-and-you're-out" criminal laws that many states have passed, ruling that any company that had broken any local, state, or federal law over the previous fifteen years would be prohibited from doing local business. Perhaps it is time, as two scholars have argued recently, to "write new rules" that can help transform what remains of America's industrial work sites into "a more humane and responsible place."[57]

A century ago, as corporations such as various railroads and heavy industrial concerns grew to a size and power greater than those of many states, the regulatory momentum of the country shifted from the state to the national level. They could not leave it to Ohio or Indiana, Americans realized, to regulate a national empire the scope of Standard Oil. Since the Second World War and especially since the 1960s, corporate size and power have grown from the national to the multinational level, while regulatory capacities have remained locked at the level of individual nations. The obvious solution to the dilemma would seem to be the creation of a global regulatory apparatus. Until such a mechanism appears, however, perhaps an equally necessary and more achievable intermediate step might be to reject the fundamental framework of company personhood itself. In other words, as corporate legal scholar Carl Mayer argues, we need to return to the older and inherently democratic notion of corporations as artificial beings, subject to the popular will, with only the limited rights and powers that the sovereign people have accorded them.[58]

It is in such formulations that Lima's story could perhaps make its greatest contribution. For Lima's encounter with BP continually revolved around a central basic theme: that the actions of real people matter as much as those of corporate machines and that, simply put, corporations are not persons. The Lima refinery exists and continues to generate wealth today partly because of luck, but also because a whole host of people, both within and outside the plant gates, determined not to let it die. Foremost among these, of course, were the plant employees themselves, salaried and hourly, who still possessed too much of the self-respect and working-class dignity they had inherited from blue-collar forebears to do anything else but continue to run their refinery as efficiently as they could—a determination that existed independently of BP's plans and calculations. There also was the loose coalition of people connected to the refinery task force that Berger set up: individuals like Kenneth Belcher and Chamber of Commerce chief Rockhold. Their efforts were augmented by the considerable resources and skills of Thomas Mullen and his associates at the *Lima News*. The libertarian ideology that the local paper shared with its corporate owner may have lined up, theoretically at least, with the likes of Milton Friedman. Yet for Mullen and others at the paper, all that theory seemed to quickly dissolve when confronted with BP's apparent decision to throw their city away. Legally, the company could do what it wanted with its assets, Mullen reasoned, "but that did not make them immune from second guessing, from criticism, from resistance."[59]

Finally, it is important to recognize the central role of Lima's relentless mayor. At every step he pushed and prodded BP with a dogged determination until, in the end, the company's defenses finally gave way. It was the mayor's "aggressiveness" that had made the Clark deal possible, Belcher concluded. To Payne, the major hero of the entire story "was solely Dave Berger. Everyone else was a coincidental player in the script . . . all along I thought that if it weren't for Berger being so tenacious, and convinced and committed to saving the refinery, it would not have happened." For decades, scholars have tallied up the vast imbalance between the immense clout of massive corporations and the meager resources of industrial communities and concluded that the latter didn't have much of a chance. Even if local officials were inclined to confrontation, political scientist John Portz noted, they rarely possessed the staff, legal skills, or financial skills to compete with top-level corporate management. In this case, however, the training Berger had received from years in Catholic seminary had apparently rendered him more than a match for BP. A "populist brand of politics is possible in urban America," Portz theorized. In Lima, Berger provided a recent and glittering example.[60]

Over the phone one Monday in early December 1998, Berger and Schaefer spent some time looking back on what had transpired between BP, its refinery, and the city of Lima. Schaefer told Berger that he had heard from inside the company that it did not want any more publicity of the episode whatsoever. The Amoco deal had provided BP with a total of fourteen different refineries and BP was looking to close a few of them down. "BP's nightmare," the mayor summarized later in his diary, "is that they will have to deal with a bunch of 'Limas,' communities that believe they can chart their own futures. Big Oil does not want to deal with those kinds of dynamics."[61]

Berger continues to believe today that BP had determined to shut down the Lima refinery because of an anticompetitive strategy he characterized as "scorched earth," insisting that the refinery was too valuable for BP to sell to a competitor. "It's the Napoleonic naval tactic of scuttling ships," he informed London's *Guardian*. "They are not content to leave; they have to scorch the earth, too." The jury may be out on whether or not Berger's analysis is entirely correct, but his phrase still works. For more than a century now, the flat landscape of the old industrial Midwest has been burned by the movements of international capital. Indeed, in the fiery furnaces of the massive steel plants along rivers like the Monongahela and the Mahoning, or in the great cathedral hangar of the old Lima Locomotive Works, that burning occurred quite literally. The rivet guns are silent in Lima now and smoke has cleared away long ago from the river valleys of Braddock and Youngstown. The fires have passed, the earth scorched, and midwestern communities have been left to figure out paths to a different kind of economic future.[62]

As the industrial heritage of the old Midwest demonstrated repeatedly, however, fire can be a creative as well as a destructive force. Long before the arrival of European invaders, various key plants in the natural landscape of the Midwest, such as several species of oak in the savannahs of northwest Ohio, germinated best in the ash left by the great fires that periodically swept across the forest lands before burning themselves out. In this, the fires left another aspect of the midwestern heritage that is worth considering anew. Maybe from the scorched earth of the old industrial Midwest a new growth can spring forth once more. In this flat and creative landscape, fresh political offshoots might be germinating that could reclaim an older democratic heritage. It is an ideology that was held close by the founders of the republic, one that insists that ordinary citizens, not economic machines, are sovereign in America. If such old roots were to sprout forth and blossom once again, they certainly would need to emanate from a great many places across the country. Yet one of their most fertile hotbeds might be said, one day, to have been the still-potent residue left by the Great Black Swamp, the weathered gray streets of Lima, Ohio.[63]

Epilogue

"Nobody Was Defending Us Except Ourselves"

In the happy glow that immediately followed his company's profitable sale of the Lima refinery to Clark Oil, BP senior executive Ian Conn ventured to a *Wall Street Journal* reporter that the sale certainly seemed "the correct final chapter" to the story. Conn may have been an able businessman but he was not much of a historian. For history provides few final chapters to any story and even fewer "correct" ones. A decade later, a number of the key figures in the Lima/BP encounter—Browne and BP, Mayor Berger, the refinery, the city of Lima itself—have been treated both well and ill by the intervening years, some in quite surprising ways.[1]

For many of the story's principals, the subsequent decade brought well-earned retirement: Percy in the Cleveland area, Mullen in Colorado, and Judy Gilbert in Lima. Others resumed career trajectories in various sectors of the oil or financial industries. Daniel Groman and many of his colleagues continue to work at the Lima refinery. Robert Paisley left BP within a few years to take a senior position in the financial services sector. Payne, the Wasserstein Perella broker, today works for an investment firm in Texas. Ohio newspapers continue to periodically run feature stories on various local companies—an aluminum panel business in Akron, a brass fittings manufacturer in Cleveland—that have achieved amazing turnarounds, partly because of the efforts of business consultant Schaefer, who would show up to coax workers into identifying ways they could improve production and then coax management into implementing their suggestions. Others continued on with BP. Kuenzli, BP's manager of the Lima refinery, relocated to the Gulf Coast to head up a BP refinery there, while "idea factory" Paul Monus moved to the Baltimore area to assist in BP's initial ventures into solar energy.[2]

Fate has been less kind to David Stockman. Apparently invigorated by his foray into oil refining, Stockman left Blackstone in fall 1999 to co-found a buyout firm called Heartland Industrial Partners. "I believe we are entering a golden age for the revival of industrial America," he exclaimed. Through his new firm, he planned to raise $2 billion in equity capital to acquire and reenergize older industries throughout the Midwest. Initially the project seemed to go swimmingly. Within several years he had acquired majority ownership of Collins and Aikman, an auto-parts manufacturer, and in 2003 he moved to Troy, Michigan, to function as its CEO. Then things went sour. The American auto industry continued its long spiral into disintegration and took parts suppliers down with it. Stockman frantically tried to keep his company afloat, "juggling creditors and suppliers," wrote journalist Greider sympathetically, "in desperate, impromptu arrangements," but none of the measures succeeded. In May 2005, the Collins and Aikman board demanded Stockman's resignation, and a week later the company filed for bankruptcy. Federal investigators began poking into Stockman's efforts to keep the company alive, and in March 2007 indicted him in a Manhattan courtroom for securities fraud, conspiracy, and obstruction of justice. His case involved no fraud at all, he told the *New York Times,* but instead was merely "a dangerous criminalization of a business failure." In his defense, as Greider pointed out, not only did he not profit personally, but he poured $13 million of his own money and $350 million in Heartland funds into the firm in his efforts to save it. In January 2009, federal prosecutors dropped all charges against him, but, at age 62, his career seemed over.[3]

If guilty of nothing else, Greider noted, Stockman seemed guilty of "overabundant confidence" and "arrogant overreaching." These were qualities that people in Lima would have recognized in several of the corporate executives they had seen come and go over the years, beginning with Benjamin Faurot, whose meteoric rise and fall in the nineteenth century began this story. Now, in the first years of the new century, they would watch the same arcing trajectory occur with one of the biggest players of them all, BP's John Browne. In the end, Browne would not fall as far or as hard as Faurot, but as high as Browne had climbed and as powerful as he had become, Lima's people knew he didn't have to fall nearly as far to make an even bigger mess.[4]

For several years following the sale of the Lima refinery and the mergers with Amoco and Arco, BP in general and Browne in particular continued to rocket upward to unbelievable heights of wealth, power, and fame, an ascent that appeared at times irreversible. The thousands of former Amoco and Arco employees quickly learned what it was to operate by Browne's way. He went after his new acquisitions with a meat-ax, cutting more than six thousand jobs from Amoco alone, explaining, "We have to get through the harvesting of low-hanging fruit" before BP could "go after growth." Meanwhile, bitter jokes percolated through the corridors of the old Amoco headquarters in Chicago:

"What do you call the new CEO?" "Sir John." "Our old CEO?" "Sur-render." Or, "What's the British pronunciation of BP-Amoco?" "BP; the Amoco is silent." However, since Browne's moves saved the combined companies an immediate $2 billion, BP stock shot up still higher as the big chief began to levy his ax at what he thought were two thousand or so excess positions at Arco. Survivors learned they had to produce profits above all else, and the results showed in the company ledgers. By the end of 2002, BP was producing 3.5 billion barrels of gas and oil annually. It trailed only Exxon-Mobil in size among the world's major oil companies and reveled in fantastic profits; in 2006, these profits reached almost $20 billion. In addition to his preeminence within his industry, such accomplishments brought Browne some personal, nonmonetary rewards. Early in 1998, Queen Elizabeth knighted him for his record as a model corporate citizen; three years later, the British government granted the BP chief a life peerage, awarding him the lofty title Lord Browne of Madingley.[5]

Having cemented his reputation in his own country as perhaps its most admired business executive, Browne set out to wield his influence in efforts to solve global problems. In 1997, after he enjoying a conversation over dinner with the head of the activist group Greenpeace, he gave a widely noted speech at Stanford in which he recognized the growing scientific consensus about the human influence on global climate change. Up to that point, BP had been functioning as a leading member of an oil company lobbying group denying such influences, and Browne's admissions came as a startling bombshell. "BP was the first to say that climate change was a problem," an activist admitted, "the first to take responsibility . . . They were pretty brave." Further, Browne acted on his new beliefs. Not only did BP resign from the oil lobbying group and publicly begin supporting the Kyoto Protocols on global warming but Browne announced that BP would dramatically cut its own emissions of carbon dioxide to levels far lower than the Kyoto accords had even specified. On Earth Day, 1999, Browne received an award at the United Nations for what another activist termed his "astonishing" environmental leadership.[6]

At the same time, BP remained an oil company in headlong pursuit of the profits its chief executive demanded. As its oil production in Alaska steadily declined, it lobbied Congress to reopen the Arctic National Wildlife Refuge to oil drilling, gave tens of thousands of dollars to prodevelopment groups, and between 1999 and 2001 paid at least $17 million in fines for illegally dumping hazardous waste in Alaska and for violations of the federal clean air laws in its U.S. refineries, policies that prompted Greenpeace to give Browne a new award—for having provided "the Best Impression of an Environmentalist." Undaunted by the criticism, Browne pressed ahead. In 2002, he gave another speech at Stanford to announce that BP not only had met the lower greenhouse gas emissions levels it had set for itself but had exceeded them eight years early. Such models of environmental consciousness by an oil industry leader began to have an impact. When Browne gave his first climate change speech at Stanford in 1997, fellow oil company executives regarded him as an apostate, but so quickly did his views move into the oil business mainstream that, three years later, he gave the keynote address at the World Petroleum Conference and was widely regarded as the industry's preeminent leader.[7]

Behind the echoing praise, however, deeper problems gnawed at the vitals of Browne's BP empire, problems that later were traced to the hard-charging leadership of the company's chief executive. Early in 2001, 77 of BP's maintenance technicians on Alaska's North Slope sent a letter to an oil company whistleblower named Charles Hamel, which he forwarded to Browne, saying that BP had so ignored health and safety concerns they felt their lives were in danger. Hamel began archiving internal evidence the technicians sent him on a public website. The next year, a BP Alaska health and safety inspector named William Burkett testified before a U.S. Senate subcommittee, charging that BP had so focused on cutting costs that it ignored routine safety inspections and maintenance. "London knew what to do to keep the dollars coming—cut," Burkett told the senators. "Cut the budget, cut the employee numbers, cut wages, cut the spare parts, cut maintenance, cut supervision, just *cut!*"[8]

Such inattention to elemental details like safety in a highly flammable business like oil could have dire results. In March 2005, a massive explosion rocked a BP refinery in Texas City, near Houston, killing 15 workers and injuring upwards of 170 others. Another blast flamed through the same plant in July. Later investigations showed that the company's neglect of safety matters had led to the tragedies. Governmental regulators quickly charged BP with 300 health and safety violations and fined it a record $21 million. Other estimates of the financial costs to the company from lawsuits brought by the injured and the families of the dead ranged as high as $700 million. Stories began appearing in the press documenting how BP led the U.S. in refinery deaths. Over the previous decade alone, 22 people had lost their lives in various accidents at BP plants, double the number of fatalities experienced by Shell Oil, the corporation next-highest on the tragic list. Late in 2005, a government agency created a special Safety Review Panel, headed by former U.S. Secretary of State James Baker, to probe into the company. In August 2006, U.S. investigators began exploring whether BP had engaged in shady trading in oil and gasoline markets, and the company's stock immediately fell by 2 percent. In March, and again in August 2006, hundreds of thousands of gallons of crude broke from BP pipelines and spilled into Prudhoe Bay, leading BP to suspend almost half its production there. Investigations later revealed massive corrosion in the company's pipelines, corrosion it had failed either to notice or correct. The company seemed guilty of "chronic neglect," charged one Republican congressman. In April 2006, BP's refinery near Toledo was hit with a $2 million fine for other safety missteps; workers there had been afraid of reprisals from supervisors if they reported such problems. Fundamentally, one federal investigator declared, BP senior management "has been blind to the safety culture issue." In January 2007, the Baker panel issued its report; as expected, it was profoundly critical of BP's neglect of elemental health and safety concerns, a neglect seemingly endemic throughout the company. The following October, BP agreed to pay a total of $373 million in fines and restitution as a result of the Alaskan crude leaks and Texas refinery fires.[9]

BP certainly was able to ride out the disasters. Fines of $373 million in a company whose profit levels hovered near $20 billion were stings, not mortal wounds. However, the damage inflicted on the company's carefully cultivated reputation was beyond financial measure. Somebody would have to pay. A growing chorus of critics pinned much of the blame for the oil leaks and explosions on Browne's ruthless cost-cutting, which had led to neglect of routine maintenance. The day before Christmas, 2006, the *Sunday Times* of London published a feature story on BP's "annus horribilus," headlined both with a play on BP's name—which now stood for "Battered Petroleum"—and a huge, half-page photo of Browne's face. The photo had been cleverly photo-shopped to look as if he had just emerged from a bar fight, with missing teeth, a cut lip, a black eye, and a forehead wrapped in bandages. Browne's deputies—men he had carefully groomed for leadership and whom he had regarded with apparent affection—sensed a coming change at the top, the story relayed, and had begun to jostle for power, leaking controversial memos critical of the top boss. Through that summer and fall, BP's chief had issued repeated denials of a growing rift between him and the company's chair, Peter Sutherland, but papers reported "bruising" clashes. The two agreed that Browne would leave his post on his sixtieth birthday, at the end of 2008. Then in January 2007—a few days before the Baker commission released its report—BP moved up his departure date to August of that year, when he would be replaced by his longtime lieutenant, Tony Hayward. In fact, however, Browne's resignation came even sooner than that, as the proud and cultured oilman watched his glittering career come to a sudden end in scandal and public disgrace. For the previous four months, he admitted in May 2007, he had been engaged in furious private legal battles to prevent his former lover, a Canadian man named Jeff Chevalier, from selling the intimate story of their four-year relationship to the British tabloid press. Triggered by Browne's confession that he had lied about how he had originally met Chevalier, a British court released relevant documents. All the embarrassing personal details came spilling out, followed by Browne's humiliating public apology and his abrupt resignation from BP. Although it is unclear if the move was related to Browne's departure, by early 2009 BP had begun to cut back its investment in renewable sources of energy. Moreover, it clearly began to quietly deviate from its stated pledge to refrain from making political donations. In the seven years from 2002 through 2009, it pumped at least $4.8 million to partisan American political campaigns. Nearly four-fifths of that total went to two different political action groups in Colorado and California. These groups had emerged to defeat ballot initiatives in those states that could have resulted in higher gas and oil taxes. No more, apparently, was BP "Beyond Petroleum."[10]

Moreover, unfortunately for Browne and his heir-apparent as CEO, Hayward—not to mention much of the American Gulf Coast—BP would soon discover that it could not change the bent-on-profits corporate culture that such leaders had created. Hayward assumed leadership saying all the right things. "BP makes its money by someone, somewhere, every day putting on boots, coveralls, a hard hat, and glasses, and going out and turning valves," he acknowledged. "And we'd sort of lost track of that." From then on, he pledged, BP would focus on safety as its "No. 1 priority." Almost immediately, he sold off the modern art decorating the walls of BP's corporate headquarters in London, replacing it with photos of BP service stations and oil platforms. He issued firm directives down the chain of command that he hoped would reinvigorate the safety culture. Such initial moves were not enough, however, to change the daily decisions of thousands of salaried managers at BP work sites around the world, managers who had for decades absorbed a more basic BP teaching: produce profits or lose your jobs; Lima's "Don't just fix it; improve it" mantra had apparently been just a local exception. So events moved along their ultimately tragic trajectory. The explosion and deaths at Texas City were followed by another huge oil spill of 200,000 gallons on Alaska's North Slope. In 2009, federal inspectors once again toured the Texas City facility and, finding more than 700 violations of safety codes, imposed an additional $87 million in fines on the corporation. In a visit to the refinery in Oregon, Ohio, in March 2010, inspectors located another 62 violations, chalking up another $3 million in fines. The next month came the worst tragedy of all. BP's Deepwater Horizon rig exploded off the Louisiana coast, killing eleven workers and sending a fountain of black oil into the sea. Not until the following August would the corporation finally succeed in plugging the hole, which in the meantime gushed forth uncounted millions of gallons of oil. The spill was soon regarded as possibly the worst environmental catastrophe in the nation's history. The repercussions for BP were severe, although the subsequent sacking of Hayward and the massive fines BP would end up paying (these have ranged recently from $5.4 billion to upwards of $21 billion) paled in significance to the price paid by the BP workers who died. BP blamed its well-drilling partners which in turn pointed the finger back at BP. Whichever corporation bore the bulk of the blame, the ultimate problem was underscored in congressional hearings. "BP cut corner after corner to save a million dollars here and a few hours there," said Congressman Henry Waxman. "And now the whole Gulf Coast is paying the price."[11]

Back in Lima, the contrast between the fortunes of Browne and BP and those of the local refinery could not have been more dramatic or stunning, although the plant's good fortune took half a decade to jell. Lurking behind all the jubilation over the plant's sale to Clark in July 1998 were suspicions that the future of oil refining still looked dark. One financial analyst commented that Lima was very lucky to have sold the plant and doubted it would make any money. Mayor Berger kept a watchful eye on the plant's prospects. Within two years after the purchase of the plant by Clark (which, under Blackstone's management, soon changed its name to Premcor), Berger was regularly consulting his circle of industry experts, worrying about the refinery's future, and discussing how to nudge Premcor to sell the plant to Marathon. Late in 2002, Premcor CEO Thomas O'Malley told the trade press that he thought the Lima plant was "still very much on the fence" and cut thirty local jobs. "I think the threat is quite real" to the refinery, one of Berger's experts told him.[12]

As it turned out, the Lima refinery just needed to hang on. Looking back wistfully years later, Kuenzli realized that if BP had accepted the bid he and Paisley had made, and if they had been able to survive the first few rocky years, "we would have made a pile of money." Paisley put it more simply: "We would be rich." In 2004, gas prices launched into a steady upward cycle because of the great bottleneck in the U.S. gasoline market: the nation's critically short refining capacity. Over the preceding quarter-century, the number of American refineries had dropped by half, from 324 to fewer than 132; the country had not built a new refinery since 1976. Refiners began talking heady talk of a new "golden age" for the industry. Then came Hurricanes Katrina and Rita. In two massive blows in late summer 2005, the twin storms devastated New Orleans and pounded the vulnerable Gulf Coast, home to a third of the nation's refineries. In a single day, Katrina shut down 20 percent of the country's oil refining industry. A new demand for more refineries reverberated across the country. Gas prices shuddered to unprecedented heights nationally and the stock prices of refiners shot through the roof, along with oil company profits.[13]

This kind of climate could bring only good news for any existing U.S. refinery, and Lima prepared to ride the new wave. Late in 2004, Premcor had announced the start of negotiations with a Canadian company, EnCana, to begin a $1 billion upgrade to the refinery to allow it to process massive amounts of sour crude that its partner would pump in, via pipeline, from its fields of tar sands in Alberta. Here was the long-awaited conversion to sour crude that would secure the plant's viability for half a century. In April 2005, the refinery acquired a new owner,

Valero Energy, which had launched into a headlong effort to buy as many refineries as it could ("I want 'em all," declared Valero's CEO Bill Greehey). Acquiring Lima made particular sense for Valero as part of its strategy of expansion into the upper Midwest. Best of all, Valero specialized in sour crude and Greehey assured local people that the EnCana deal and the big upgrade seemed to be on track. So it came as a particular disappointment the following December when Valero decided against the move. The estimated price of the upgrade had doubled from $1 to $2 billion, and the company was reluctant to part with that kind of cash, especially with its many other available sour crude options.[14]

Local people would have been wise to temper their disappointment. In the golden new world of oil refining, a facility as well regarded and well positioned as the Lima plant needed only to wait. Early in 2007, rumors of a possible sale of the refinery once again began to filter through the Lima community. The *Lima News* learned from the trade press that Valero had begun quietly shopping the plant, rumors that the company finally admitted were true. From the beginning, however, it was clear that this would be a very different sale process from the roller-coaster ride of a decade before. The industry had entered an active year for refinery deals, the trade press predicted. In the profit-saturated climate of oil refining, buyers would easily lay down a billion dollars for a plant, particularly for one situated in the upper Midwest that could take advantage of U.S.-Canadian trade dynamics. By the end of March, an eager group of potential buyers for the Lima plant had emerged, which Valero narrowed down to ten. From all he could tell, Berger told the Lima Rotarians, the refinery was enjoying "a dynamic, almost giddy sales process."[15]

One afternoon early in May 2007—ironically, the day after the story broke about Browne's scandal and abrupt resignation—Berger drove down to the refinery for what he thought would be an update on the sales process. There Valero officials told him they'd just sold the facility to a Canadian firm, Husky Energy. Great sighs of relief once again swept through the community. The contrasts between this sales process and the one with BP were stunning, both in terms of the ease and quickness with which the sale to Husky occurred, and in terms of the price the Canadians had paid; the "mediocre" refinery that BP had tried to scrap a decade before had just sold for just short of $2 billion. Moreover, Husky said it planned to immediately invest $2 billion more in order to render its new Lima plant able to process the millions of barrels of sour crude it would pump in from the tar sands underlying its 10,000 acres of Alberta prairie. The reason was immediately clear. Lima's location, a hundred miles from the Canadian border, meant that it was perfectly positioned to process raw crude pumped down from the next major oil boom in North America: the massive quantities (upwards of 100 billion barrels, estimates ranged) discovered under the northern Alberta prairies. This meant the Lima refinery would soon become, Berger said, the major portal for Canadian tar sands crude into the United States, thus securing its profitable future for another half-century or more. As spelled out by environmentalist critics, the ecological implications of pumping out Alberta tar sands could be quite chilling. But for a community in desperate need of manufacturing jobs, those kinds of considerations ranked fairly far down its list of immediate priorities.[16]

For Lima did need the jobs. The refinery itself continued to prosper in the new century, but its surrounding city had not. For midwestern communities and industries linked to the automobile as opposed to the oil industry, the toll of repeated job losses read like casualty lists from a natural disaster. Late in 2005, GM announced plans to slash thirty thousand jobs. Two months later, Ford followed suit, cutting thirty thousand more positions; a year later, Chrysler announced reductions of thirteen thousand additional jobs. Closer to Lima, local people watched the ongoing exodus of well-paid manufacturing jobs from communities whose pain they could feel like their own. Twenty miles to the southwest lay the small city of Celina, home to 10,400 people whose major source of sustenance was the Huffy Bicycle plant. For the past forty years, upwards of 1,000 local people had worked at what for a time was the largest bike plant in the country; to no small degree, Huffy bikes had built Celina. In 1998, Huffy management told local people to accept wage reductions down to $6.10 an hour with no health benefits and no pensions. When the union refused—many area fast-food workers made better wages than that—Huffy's management shuttered the entire plant and moved the center of its operations to Mexico and China. Local unemployment levels immediately shot up from 3 percent to 12 percent. Thirty miles to the north of Lima, the small city of Ottawa reeled to the news in 2000 that Philips Electronics, the longtime economic backbone of that community, planned to lay off 1,500 people, 80 percent of its workforce, and, like Huffy, move production to Mexico.[17]

Contemporary Lima could no more remain immune from such economic dynamics than could the city of Faurot's day. Jobs bled away in spurts. While Ford invested $300 million into its Lima engine plant, rendering the facility's future a bit more secure for the time being, the Dana Corporation, an auto-parts supplier, axed a hundred positions. The most recent big blow came in 2004, with the controversial decision by the State of Ohio to close Lima Correctional Institute. One of the largest poured-concrete structures in the world (second only to the Pentagon), the facility had existed since 1915 and for nearly a century had anchored the economics of North Lima in the same way that the refinery had anchored that of the city's southern edge. A large coalition of Lima-area activists fought the state tooth and nail for more than a year to prevent its closure, yet to save $25 million annully, the state proceeded anyway, throwing five hundred more local people onto the unemployment lines. A California demographer that year listed

Lima as one of the twenty worst-hit places in the country in terms of job losses. From 2000 to 2003, according to these estimates, the city's number of jobs had fallen by almost 23 percent.[18]

Mayor Berger remained as busy as ever fighting such trends. His biggest single new gain for his city came in landing a commitment by the energy firm Global Energy to build a $550 million power plant—to be called Lima Energy—inside city limits on the site of the old locomotive works. Not only would the plant provide between 80 and 120 new jobs but its operation would require a water contract with the city of nearly $1 million; moreover it might even lure in other industries, attracted to the cheap power it would provide. After the excitement wore off, local people had to adjust themselves to the reality that Global Energy would be a long time in coming. It struggled for years to line up the requisite financing and permits, and by spring 2006 had only just started construction. The City of Lima could certainly use the money from an enhanced tax base. By U.S. Census estimates, its poverty rate in 2003 stood at nearly 23 percent (compared with 10.6 percent statewide), while its median household income was at $27,067, compared with the national median household income level of nearly $42,000. In 2000, almost 20 percent of Lima families (or 1,862) lived below the poverty line, again compared with 9.2 percent nationally.[19]

While Berger had personally triumphed in his struggle with BP, and the Lima metropolitan region as a whole benefits from the refinery's continued presence, years later the rejection of his efforts to annex the plant into Lima itself still caused sadness to seep into Berger's voice. The rejection of his annexation effort still stings. "I felt that the city of Lima had been wronged by all parties," Berger said. "In the end, all the townships benefited and we were left without our interests being addressed. Nobody was defending us except ourselves. I'm not ashamed of defending the City of Lima. But I have no illusions about the charity of others."[20]

When Berger ran for his fourth term in 2001, the opposition could not find anyone to run against him. For his record fifth term in 2005, he squared off against a political neophyte named Ned Bushong. In a heavily blue-collar city that depended to great degree on the efforts of volunteers, Bushong, in two months of politicking, insulted volunteerism, claimed unions "protect slackers," and called Berger a snake whose head should be cut off. The incumbent mayor won in a walk. In Berger's bid for a sixth term in the fall election campaign of 2009, he faced a seemingly tough opponent in Dan Beck, a popular Allen County sheriff who had been gearing up for a run against Berger for years. Beck's inability to posit any other solutions to Lima's problems than to get tough on crime, however, alienated voters. Berger won reelection by 11 percentage points. He continues to hold the post today, the longest-serving such official in the history of the City of Lima.[21]

Notes

1. "Local Communities Are No Match for Industrial Corporations"

1. "Bean-Counting as You Look for a House? Try Lima (Ohio)," *Christian Science Monitor*, Aug. 31, 2005; David Berger, oral interview by author, Mar. 18, 2004.

2. Marc Cooper, "A Town Betrayed: Oil and Greed in Lima, Ohio," *Nation*, July 14, 1997, 12; Ted Brown, *Ohio Election Statistics* (Columbus, Ohio: State Printing Office, 1964), 132.

3. Judith Gilbert, oral interview by author, Mar. 10, 2005.

4. M. Cooper, "A Town Betrayed," 11–12; Lynn Oxyer, "Plant Forges Family Ties," *Lima News*, Sept. 27, 1998; Gilbert, interview, Mar. 10, 2005; Judith Gilbert, oral interview by author, June 17, 2005 (quoted).

5. Stanley Buder, *Capitalizing on Change: A Social History of American Business* (Chapel Hill, N.C.: Univ. of North Carolina Press, 2009), 261–62 (quoted), 344–63; Marjorie Kelly, *Divine Right of Capital: Dethroning the Corporate Aristocracy* (San Francisco, Calif.: Berret-Koehler Publishers, 2001), 54–56; Robert Reich, *Supercapitalism: The Transformation of Business, Democracy and Everyday Life* (New York: Knopf, 2007), 75–80 (Fortune 500 study noted, 76).

6. Geoffrey Jones, *Multinationals and Global Capitalism: from the Nineteenth to the Twenty-First Century* (New York: Oxford Univ. Press, 2005), 64; Joseph A. Pratt, *Prelude to a Merger: A History of Amoco Corporation, 1973–1998* (Houston, Tex.: Hart Publications, 2000), 6. For journalists on oil company profits in the 1990s, see M. Cooper, "A Town Betrayed," 12; and Richard Thomas, "Heartbreak in Sundown City," *Guardian* (London), reprinted in the *Lima News*, May 4, 1997.

7. Steven High, *Industrial Sunset: The Making of North America's Rust Belt, 1969–1984* (Toronto, Can.: Univ. of Toronto Press, 2003), 92–93, 109–24 (quoted, 109); Barry Bluestone and Bennett Harrison, *The Deindustrialization of America: Plant Closings, Community Abandonment, and the Dismantling of Basic Industry* (New York: Basic Books, 1982), 3–8, 15–21; Paul Kantor, *The Dependent City: The Changing Political Economy of Urban America* (Glenview, Ill.: Scott, Foresman, 1988), 166–67.

8. James Willard Hurst, *Law and the Conditions of Freedom in the Nineteenth-Century United States* (Madison, Wis.: Univ. of Wisconsin Press, 1964), 48; Kelly, *Divine Right of Capital*, 90–91, 163; Carl J. Mayer, "Personalizing the Impersonal: Corporations and the

Bill of Rights," *The Hastings Law Journal* 41, no. 3 (Mar. 1990); Eric Foner, *A Short History of Reconstruction, 1863–1877* (New York: Harper and Row, 1990), 114–17; Allen Kaufman, Lawrence Zacharias, and Marvin Karson, *Managers vs. Owners: The Struggle for Corporate Control in American Democracy* (New York: Oxford Univ. Press, 1995), 16–21.

9. Kelly, *Divine Right of Capital*, 52–53; Joel Bakan, *The Corporation: The Pathological Pursuit of Profit and Power* (New York: Free Press, 2004), 36–37; Milton Friedman, quoted in Kent Greenfield, "From Rights to Regulation in Corporate Law," in *Perspectives on Company Law*, ed. Fiona McMillan Patfield (Cambridge, Mass.: Kleuver Law International, 1997), 8. For a detailed exploration of the fervor and sway of the new market populism of the 1990s, see Thomas Frank, *One Market under God: Extreme Capitalism, Market Populism, and the End of Economic Democracy* (New York: Anchor Books, 2000).

10. Jerry Mander, "The Rules of Corporate Behavior," in *The Case against the Global Economy: And for a Turn toward the Local*, ed. Jerry Mander and Edward Goldsmith (San Francisco, Calif.: Sierra Club Books, 1996), 309–14; Kelly, *Divine Right of Capital*, 90, 149 (Berle quoted).

11. John Portz, The *Politics of Plant Closings* (Lawrence, Kans.: Univ. Press of Kansas, 1990), 3–4; Kantor, *Dependent City*, 170–72, 226; Lawrence Rothstein, *Plant Closings: Power, Politics, and Workers* (Dover, Mass.: Auburn House, 1986), 170–72.

12. For a summary of such effects on individual workers and communities that have suffered plant closings, see Bluestone and Harrison, *Deindustrialization of America*, 49–81 (U.S. Chamber of Commerce data noted, 69); R. Jeffrey Lustig, "The Politics of Shutdown: Community, Property, Corporatism," *Journal of Economic Issues* 19 (Mar. 1985): 132 (quoted); Sherry Lee Linkon and John Russo, *Steeltown U.S.A.: Work and Memory in Youngstown* (Lawrence, Kans.: Univ. Press of Kansas, 2002), 51; Thomas G. Fuechtmann, *Steeples and Stacks: Religion and Steel Crisis in Youngstown* (Cambridge, UK: Cambridge Univ. Press, 1989), 57–59.

13. High, *Industrial Sunset*, 197 (quoted). For such typologies, see Portz, *Politics of Plant Closings*, 5–12, 170–71; and Bruce Nissen, *Fighting for Jobs: Case-Studies of Labor-Community Coalitions Confronting Plant Closings* (Albany, N.Y.: State Univ. of New York Press, 1995), 13–15. Political scientists who sketch out this activist role concede that while it looks good in theory, they can actually point to very few instances where such a role has emerged victorious. Portz says that while such examples exist, "they are partial and fragmented. Existing local governments often lack either the will or resources that must contend with the hostile business firm." Similarly, while Nissen insists that urban activism against plant closing isn't "hopeless," his survey of the extant literature reinforces a general pessimism. See Portz, *Politics of Plant Closings*, 11; and Nissen, *Fighting for Jobs*, 170.

14. Darcy Frey, "How Green Is BP?" *New York Times Magazine*, Dec. 8, 2002, 3; British Petroleum, Annual Report, "Performance for All Our Futures," 2, in "Amoco, Miscellaneous" folder, David Berger Papers, Office of the Mayor (hereafter, DBP), Lima Municipal Building, Lima, Ohio (hereafter, LMB).

15. Reich, *Supercapitalism*, 21–31; Bakan, *Corporation*, 39–42 (Browne quoted), 44, 144; Frey, "How Green Is BP?" 1–4.

2. Oil Town

1. George Knepper, *Ohio and Its People*, 2nd ed. (Kent, Ohio: Kent State Univ. Press, 1997), 93, 112.

2. Knepper, *Ohio and Its People*, 109; R. Douglas Hurt, *The Ohio Frontier: Crucible of the Old Northwest, 1720–1830* (Bloomington, Ind.: Indiana Univ. Press, 1996), 131–41, 373; Frank

Hackman, "City and County Organization," in *The 1976 History of Allen County, Ohio,* ed. John R. Carnes (Evansville, Ind.: Unigraphic, 1976), 2–3 (legislature quoted, 3).

3. Hackman, "City and County Organization," 3; Mike Lackey, "The Beginning of Lima, Ohio," *Lima News,* Feb. 14, 1999.

4. Hackman, "City and County Organization," 4; Lackey, "The Beginning of Lima, Ohio"; Frank Hackman, "A Stake . . . and THERE Was Lima!" *Lima News,* vertical file (hereafter, v.f.) Lima—History, Allen County Historical Society (hereafter, ACHS) (John quoted).

5. William Rusler, *A Standard History of Allen County, Ohio* (Chicago: American Historical Society, 1921), 200–201; Frank Hackman, "Peruvian Bark Won Lima Its Name," *Lima News,* Dec. 31, 1952.

6. Hackman, "City and County Organization," 5–6.

7. Leslie A. Floyd, "Lima and Manufacturing, 1850–1910," *Allen County Reporter* 33 (1987): 35; Hackman, "City and County Organization," 7–8.

8. Floyd, "Lima and Manufacturing," 55; Hackman, "City and County Organization," 8; "Allen County Regiments of the Civil War," v.f. U.S. History, Civil War—Local, ACHS.

9. M. L. Hunter, "Reminiscences by Mrs. M. L. Hunter, of Rockford, Ohio," Jan. 31, 1917, v.f. Lima, Reminiscences, ACHS.

10. Daniel Nelson, *Farm and Factory: Workers in the Midwest, 1880–1990* (Bloomington, Ind.: Indiana Univ. Press, 1995), 33–35; Alfred D. Chandler Jr., *The Visible Hand: The Managerial Revolution in American Business* (Cambridge, Mass.: Belknap Press, 1977); Robert Heilbroner and Aaron Singer, *The Economic Transformation of America, 1600 to the Present,* 4th ed. (New York: Wadsworth, 1999), 173–91; Thomas McCraw, *Prophets of Regulation: Charles Francis Adams, Louis D. Brandeis, James M. Landis, Alfred E. Kahn* (Cambridge, Mass.: Harvard Univ. Press, 1984), 74–75.

11. Blake McKelvey, "The Emergence of Industrial Cities," in *Urban America in Historical Perspective,* ed. Raymond Mohl and Neil Betten (New York: Weybright and Talley, 1970), 180–92; Constance McLoughlin Green, *The Rise of Urban America* (London, UK: Hutchinson University Library, 1965), 89–94; Floyd, "Lima and Manufacturing," 37–40 (quoted, 37); Ellis L. Armstrong, ed., *History of Public Works in the United States, 1776–1976* (Chicago, Ill.: American Public Works Asso., 1976), 394–95.

12. Floyd, "Lima and Manufacturing," 58–59; John E. Dixon, *Lima-Hamilton: Its Historical Past: 1869, 1845, and Later* (New York: Newcomen Society of England, American Branch, 1948), 13–14; "Census Bureau's Recount Boosts Population by 821," *Lima News,* Aug. 23, 1951.

13. Frank G. Love, "The Discovery of Oil in Allen County," *Allen County Reporter* 37 (1981): 33–34; Lackey, "The Beginning of Lima, Ohio"; Greg Hoersten, "Search for Natural Gas Led to Oil Boom in Lima," *Lima News,* Oct. 28, 1984; "Discovery of Oil in Lima," *Allen County Reporter* 41 (1985): 9 (newspaper quoted).

14. Brian Black, *Petrolia: The Landscape of America's First Oil Boom* (Baltimore, Md.: Johns Hopkins Univ. Press, 2000), 14–17, 22–25; Richard O'Connor, *The Oil Barons* (Boston: Little, Brown and Co., 1971), 12; Hoersten, "Search for Natural Gas"; "Early History of Petroleum," ACHS.

15. Black, *Petrolia,* 28–36; O'Connor, *The Oil Barons,* 13–17 (*Tribune* quoted, 14).

16. O' Connor, *The Oil Barons,* 46–47; Daniel Yergin, *The Prize: The Epic Quest for Oil, Money, and Power* (New York: Simon and Schuster, 1992), 52 (geologist quoted).

17. Harvey S. Ford, "The Faurot Failure at Lima," *Northwest Ohio Quarterly* 23, no. 2 (Spring 1951): 82–84.

18. Helen Marr Hale Edmonds, "Gaslit Era in Lima Recalled," *Lima News,* Dec. 22, 1957;

"Discovery of Oil in Lima," 10–12 (newspaper quoted, 11); "Early History of Petroleum," 31–36; Hoersten, "Search for Natural Gas."

19. Harold F. Williamson and Arnold R. Daum, *The American Petroleum Industry*, vol. 1, *The Age of Illumination, 1859–1899* (Evanston, Ill.: Northwestern Univ. Press, 1959), 590; Floyd, "Lima and Manufacturing," 42–44; "Discovery of Oil in Lima," 14; Edmonds, "Gaslit Era in Lima Recalled"; David Freeman Hawke, *John D.: The Founding Father of the Rockefellers* (New York: Harper and Row, 1980), 181.

20. Harvey S. Ford, "The Life and Times of Golden Rule Jones" (Ph.D. diss., University of Michigan, 1953), 24–26; Floyd, "Lima and Manufacturing," 47.

21. Ron Varland, "In Good Times or Bad, Lima Adapts, Stays Dynamic," *Lima News*, Oct. 28, 1984; Ralph Hidy and Muriel Hidy, *Pioneering in Big Business, 1882–1911* (New York: Harper and Bros., 1955), 159. On the perennial problem of overproduction in the early stages of any new industry, see Marnie Jones, *Holy Toledo: Religion and Politics in the Life of "Golden Rule" Jones* (Lexington, Ky.: Univ. Press of Kentucky, 1998), 61; and McCraw, *Prophets of Regulation*, 65–68.

22. Anthony Sampson, *The Seven Sisters: The Great Oil Companies and the World They Shaped* (New York: Viking Press, 1975), 23–25; O'Connor, *The Oil Barons*, 24, 29 (Rockefeller quoted, 29); Ron Chernow, *Titan: The Life of John D. Rockefeller, Sr.* (New York: Random House, 1998), 283–84; M. Jones, *Holy Toledo*, 61.

23. Chernow, *Titan*, 283 (quoted).

24. Chernow, *Titan*, 284–85 (quoted, 285); Yergin, *The Prize*, 52; Hawke, *John D.*, 181–83, 185–87.

25. Chernow, *Titan*, 284–86; George S. Patterson, "History of Buckeye Pipeline," 12–13 v.f. Lima-Industries—Buckeye Pipeline, ACHS; Williamson and Daum, *The American Petroleum Industry*, vol. 1, 597–98, 602.

26. Thomas F. Stemen, "A Brief History of the Standard/BP Lima Refinery," *Allen County Reporter* 54 (1998): 68–69; Rusler, *Standard History of Allen County*, 341 (Rockefeller quoted).

27. Hope Strong, "Standard Oil's Growing—At 90," *Lima Citizen*, Jan. 1, 1960; Kim Kincaid, "Lima Oil since 1885," *Lima News*, Oct. 12, 1996; Stemen, "A Brief History of the Standard/BP Lima Refinery," 73.

28. Williamson and Daum, *The American Petroleum Industry*, vol. 1, 606–7 (Orton quoted); Floyd, "Lima and Manufacturing," 52.

29. Ford, "Life and Times of Golden Rule Jones," 26–28, 29 (Jones quoted); M. Jones, *Holy Toledo*, 3–7, 61–62 (Jones quoted, 62).

30. Chernow, *Titan*, 284 (newspaper quoted); Williamson and Daum, *The American Petroleum Industry*, vol. 1, 591.

31. Chernow, *Titan*, 285; Hawke, *John D.*, 182–84 (Rockefeller quoted, 182); Hidy and Hidy, *Pioneering in Big Business*, 162.

32. Chernow, *Titan*, 286–87 (quoted, 287); Mari E. W. Williams, "Choices in Oil Refining: The Case of BP, 1900–1960," *Business History* 26 (Nov. 1984): 309; Hidy and Hidy, *Pioneering in Big Business*, 163.

33. Floyd, "Lima and Manufacturing," 47–49.

34. Hoersten, "Search for Natural Gas"; Floyd, "Lima and Manufacturing," 49.

35. Floyd, "Lima and Manufacturing," 49; Chernow, *Titan*, 286–87, 288 (Standard official quoted, 286; Rockefeller quoted, 288); O'Connor, *The Oil Barons*, 49; Hawke, *John D.*, 185 (Rockefeller quoted). On Standard's domination of the U.S. oil market by 1880, see Kevin Phillips, *Wealth and Democracy: A Political History of the American Rich* (New York: Broadway Books, 2002), 254.

36. Hidy and Hidy, *Pioneering in Big Business,* 166; Hoersten, "Search for Natural Gas."

37. Varland, "In Good Times or Bad"; Mike Lackey, "There's Still Oil under Allen County," *Lima News,* Feb. 24, 1980; Robert Snell, "Dirty and Dangerous," *Lima News,* July 26, 1998.

38. Hidy and Hidy, *Pioneering in Big Business,* 161; Floyd, "Lima and Manufacturing," 49–50; "Lima Grows Up," *Lima News,* Aug. 23, 1951.

39. Kincaid, "Lima Oil since 1885"; Snell, "Dirty and Dangerous."

40. Mike Lackey, "Lima Fueled by 'Brains, Energy, Capital,'" *Lima News,* Feb. 19, 1995; Kim Kincaid, "A Novel Mode of Transportation," *Lima News,* Mar. 10, 1999.

41. Jack Keenan, "Electric Street Railways of Lima: The Formative Years," *Allen County Reporter* 48 (1992): L-4–L-6; James H. Bassett, Inc., "Kibby Corners Neighborhood Redevelopment Plan" (unpublished document, 1979), 4–7, v.f. Lima City Planning, ACHS.

42. *Allen County Democrat,* quoted in Ford, "Life and Times of Golden Rule Jones," 29.

43. "Standard Oil Created Buckeye for $100, 000," *Lima News,* Mar. 30, 1986.

44. Hidy and Hidy, *Pioneering in Big Business,* 164–65; Ronald Lederman, "Making What Sells," *Lima News,* July 26, 1998; "The City of Lima and Her Institutions," *Lima Republican Gazette,* Aug. 1, 1903.

45. Ford, "Faurot Failure at Lima," 84–85.

46. Ibid., 85–93 (quoted 90).

47. Ibid., 93.

3. Rust Belt

1. "Council Adopts City Flag," *Lima News,* Dec. 15, 1965.

2. For this contrasting imagery, see High, *Industrial Sunset,* 29–34.

3. D. Nelson, *Farm and Factory,* 32; Eric Hirsimaki, "The Lima Locomotive Works," *Locomotive and Railways Preservation,* Mar.–Apr. 1991, 38–40; Frank M. Hackman, "Ephraim Shay and His Locomotive," *Allen County Reporter* 18 (1962): 22–25; Marilyn Baxter, "Lima Locomotive Sets Pace for Industrial Growth," *Lima News,* Oct. 28, 1984 (quoted); Dixon, *Lima-Hamilton,* 15–17.

4. Hirsimaki, "The Lima Locomotive Works," 42, 46–47; Baxter, "Lima Locomotive"; Hans Houshower, "We Built the Best," *Locomotive and Railways Preservation* 31 (Mar.–Apr. 1991): 11.

5. Hirsimaki, "The Lima Locomotive Works," 48 (quotes, "abundant speed at steam" and "one of the most influential locomotives"); Baxter, "Lima Locomotive"; Andrew Guilliford, "Self-Portrait," in *High Iron: A Series of Exhibits Exploring the Effect of the Railroading Industry on the Lima, Ohio, Community* (Lima, Ohio: American House, 1987), 31; Hans Houshower, *Working at the Lima Loco: The Lima Locomotive Works and Its Workers* (Lima, Ohio: American House, 1988), 13 (quote, "I am going to see"); Albert Churella, *From Steam to Diesel: Managerial Customs and Organizational Capacities in the Twentieth-Century American Locomotive Industry* (Princeton, N.J.: Princeton Univ. Press, 1998), 10–11; Dixon, *Lima-Hamilton,* 23, 27, 118; "Shovels, Cranes Built Here Famous Throughout World," *Lima News,* Feb. 23, 1969.

6. Keith Helmlinger, "Foresight of Galvin Led Steel Company through Adversity," *Lima News,* Oct. 28, 1984; Kim Kincaid, "Remembering Ohio Steel," *Lima News,* Feb. 9, 2000; Anne Beehler, "Present Places and Past People—Part IV," *Allen County Reporter* 36 (1980): 32.

7. Robert M. Reese, "Hospitals," in Carnes, *The 1976 History of Allen County, Ohio,* 478–79; Ron Varland, "In Good Times or Bad"; Jud Shelnutt, "Henry Diesel Rolled First Cigars in Home," *Lima Citizen,* Aug. 11, 1963; Patricia A. Cooper, *Once a Cigar Maker: Men, Women, and Work Culture in American Cigar Factories, 1900–1919* (Chicago, Ill.: Univ. of Illinois Press, 1987), 167.

8. Houshower, *Working at the Lima Loco,* 11; John Keller, oral interview by Andrew Guilliford, Dec. 2, 1986, transcript, Railroad Oral History Collection, ACHS; L. W. Tomlinson, "Superior Coach Division Sheller-Globe Corp," in Carnes, *The 1976 History of Allen County,* 243; "Superior Coach Corp. Grows," *Lima Citizen,* Sept. 17, 1961; Kim Kincaid, "A Sole Man: Lima Puts a Bounce in the World's Step," *Lima News,* June 2, 1999; "L. A. Larsen Holds City Is Thriving," *Lima Star,* Feb. 3, 1926; "Employment in Lima Shows Big Gains above 1926," *Lima Star,* Apr. 26, 1929, v.f. Lima—Employment and Unemployment, ACHS; "Pennsy Group Inspects City Industries," *Lima Star,* Feb. 2, 1931.

9. Furl Williams, oral interview by Andrew Guilliford, Jan. 14, 1987, transcript, Railroad Oral History Collection, ACHS; Mike Lackey, "Hard Work for Low Wages," *Lima News,* Mar. 21, 1999; Mike Lackey, "The Shaping of Lima," *Lima News,* Mar. 21, 1999.

10. Rufus Williamson, oral interview by Hans Houshower, Dec. 11, 1990 (quoted), transcript, Hist. Mss. 10–58, Memory Engines Collection, Ohio Historical Society, Columbus, Ohio (hereafter, OHS); Willie Thompson, oral interview by Hans Houshower, Nov. 11, 1989, transcript, Hist. Mss. 10–58, Memory Engines Collection, OHS; Mike Lackey, "Searching for the American Dream," *Lima News,* Mar. 21, 1999; Red Parker, oral interview by Hans Houshower, Feb. 23, 1990 (quoted), transcript, Hist. Mss. 10–58, Memory Engines Collection, OHS.

11. Eldridge "Bubba" Fields, oral interview by Andrew Guilliford, Nov. 24, 1986, transcript, Hist. Mss. 10–58, Memory Engines Collection, OHS; William K. Davenport, oral interview by Beverly McCoy, Nov. 26, 1990, transcript, Hist. Mss. 10–58, Memory Engines Collection, OHS; American House, Inc., "The Lima Legacy: Railroaders in the Community: An Exhibit Exploring the Historical Experience of Railroading in Lima, Ohio," v.f. "Lima—History," ACHS; Guilliford, "Self-Portrait," 31; June Remley, "Lima Retains Flavor of Miniature Melting Pot," *Lima News,* Oct. 28, 1984; Lackey, "Searching for the American Dream" (quote, "You'd go into a restaurant"); W. Thompson, interview, Nov. 11, 1989; Myrtle Ann Ward Johnson, oral interview by Hans Houshower, Mar. 27, 1989, transcript, Hist. Mss. 10–58, Memory Engines Collection, OHS; Kim Kincaid, "A Different Time for African-Americans," *Lima News,* Feb. 16, 2000.

12. Fields, interview, Nov. 24, 1986; Lackey, "Hard Work for Low Wages."

13. Williams, interview, Jan. 14, 1987.

14. Ibid.; Helmlinger, "Foresight of Galvin"; Williamson, interview, Dec. 11, 1990; Lackey, "Hard Work for Low Wages."

15. Remley, "Lima Retains Flavor"; Spring Quarter History 260 Class, OSU Lima, "The Black History of Lima: A Preliminary Study," June 1971, unpublished mss., Local History Collection, Lima Public Library, 28, 38; Nathzollo Gurley, oral interviews by William Thompson, Nov. 11, 1989, July 7, 1990 (quoted), transcripts, Hist. Mss. 10–58, Memory Engines Collection, OHS.

16. D. Nelson, *Farm and Factory,* 142–45; "Employment Hits High Figure as Plants Hum Day and Night," *Lima News,* June 22, 1941; "Lima Industry Rushed by War Orders," *Lima News,* Jan.1, 1942; "Job Placement in Lima Rises 223 Per Cent," *Lima News,* Jan. 1, 1943; "Drive for 7,000 Workers Opened," *Lima News,* Aug.1, 1943; "Lima Listed as One of Three Critical Labor Areas in Ohio," *Lima News,* Mar. 29, 1944; "One-Fourth of Lima's War Workers Are Women," *Lima News,* Mar. 10, 1943.

17. "85,000 to Get Ration Book," *Lima News,* Nov. 23, 1943; Beehler, "Present Places and Past People," 40; "Victory Village Ready for Occupancy Dec. 15," *Lima News,* Dec. 5, 1943; Helmlinger, "Foresight of Galvin"; "Tank Shop at Lima Loco to Be Enlarged," *Lima News,* May 3, 1942; "Old Marks on Lima Business Upset in 1943," *Lima Sun,* Jan. 2, 1944.

18. Kim Kincaid, "Westinghouse Had Proud History," *Lima News,* Mar. 20, 1996; Helm-

linger, "Foresight of Galvin"; "306th Engine Completed; Employees Hold Celebration," *Lima News*, Dec. 31, 1944; "'Axis Grave Digger' On Way to Front," *Lima News*, Dec.24, 1944; "Lima Loco Arsenal One of First Tank Producers to Change to New Phase of War Production Program—Workers Are Commended," *Lima News*, Apr. 16, 1944; "U.S. Army Tank-Automotive Command, Historical Overview, Lima Army Tank Plant, Lima, Ohio," Apr. 1984, ACHS.

19. "Vast Array of War Goods to Be Displayed," *Lima News*, July 15, 1943; "$700,000 Bond Drive Launched; 50,000 Jam Streets to See Parade," *Lima News*, v.f. Lima—World War—1945, ACHS.

20. John Stover, *The Life and Decline of the American Railroad* (New York: Oxford Univ. Press, 1970), 124, 131–57, 197; Sarah H. Gordon, *Passage to Union: How the Railroads Transformed American Life* (Chicago: Ivan R. Dee, 1996), 339–43; Churella, *From Steam to Diesel*, 58–59, 70–74, 118–21; Thomas G. Marx, "Technological Change and the Theory of the Firm: The American Locomotive Industry, 1920–1955," *Business History Review* 50 (Spring 1976): 6–8, 13–14; Marilyn Baxter, "Lima Locomotive"; George Dunster, "'All Aboard' Still Sounds for 779's Last Trip," *Lima News*, Nov. 15, 1964.

21. Jefferson Cowie and Joseph Heathcott, introduction to *Beyond the Ruins: The Meanings of Industrialization*, ed. Cowie and Heathcott (Ithaca, N.Y.: Cornell Univ. Press, 2003), 14.

22. Bluestone and Harrison, *Deindustrialization of America*, 112–15, 133–34 (quoted, 133); Charles Craypo and Bruce Nissen, introduction to *Grand Designs: The Impact of Corporate Strategies on Workers, Unions, and Communities*, ed. Craypo and Nissen (Ithaca, N.Y.: ILR Press, 1993), 8; Scott Camp, *Worker Response to Plant Closings: Steelworkers in Johnstown and Youngstown* (New York: Garland, 1995), 116–19, 129, 296. Also, on the informal "social contract" between management and labor, see D. Nelson, *Farm and Factory*, 175–77; and Mansel G. Blackford, *The Rise of Modern Business: Great Britain, the United States, Germany, Japan, and China* (Chapel Hill, N.C.: Univ. of North Carolina Press, 2008), 196.

23. Bluestone and Harrison, *Deindustrialization of America*, 133–39; Camp, *Worker Response to Plant Closings;* Bennett Harrison and Barry Bluestone, *The Great U-Turn: Corporate Restructuring and the Polarizing of America* (New York: Basic Books, 1988), 3–4; Wallace Peterson, *Silent Depression: The Fate of the American Dream* (New York: Norton, 1994), 35–42; Robert J. Samuelson, *The Good Life and Its Discontents: The American Dream in the Age of Entitlement, 1945–1995* (New York: Random House, 1995), 3–10, 34–48.

24. Craypo and Nissen, introduction to *Grand Designs*, 8; Jon Teaford, *Cities of the Heartland: The Rise and Fall of the Industrial Midwest* (Bloomington, Ind.: Indiana Univ. Press, 1993), 102–11; High, *Industrial Sunset*, 115.

25. "Ford to Build Giant Lima Plant," *Lima News*, June 9, 1955; James Walpole, "Groundbreakings in Lima Punctuate Company's History," *Lima News*, Mar. 7, 1999; Ohio Department of Development, "Population: Population Series, Table 1: Allen County and Township Population Trends, 1850–1990," v.f. Allen County—Population, ACHS.

26. BP America (copyright 1992), "Employment in the Manufacturing Industry in Allen County, Ohio, 1939–1988," 8, ACHS; Kim Kincaid, "Tanks for the Memories," *Lima News*, Aug. 12, 1998; "U.S. Army Tank-Automotive Command, Historical Overview, Lima Army Tank Plant," Apr. 1984, p. 1, v.f. Tank Plant, ACHS; "Lima's Industrial Front Swings into Defense Work," *Lima News*, Dec. 30, 1951.

27. Paul Janczewski, "Influence of Labor Unions on Lima Felt since Early 1880s," *Lima News*, Oct. 28, 1984 (Williams quoted); Robert Blade, "Organized Labor Constantly Aiming for Better Life," *Lima News*, Feb. 24, 1974; Furl Williams and Thomas P. Thompson, "Labor," in Carnes, *The 1976 History of Allen County, Ohio*, 305–9; Joe Connor, "Lima News Staff Rates Water Leak Top Story in 1956," *Lima News*, Dec. 31, 1955.

28. "Why Lima Feted a Newspaper's Birthday," *Business Week,* July 12, 1958, 31; James A. Maxwell, "One Paper Too Many in Lima, Ohio," *The Reporter* 20 (June 11, 1959): 26–27 (*Lima News* editorial quoted), Van G. Sauter, "According to Hoiles," *New Republic,* Feb. 22, 1964, 5 (businessman quoted).

29. "Ford Workers Earn Record Wages," *Lima News,* Oct. 15, 1961; "Average Allen Worker Chalking Up Gains," *Lima Citizen,* July 3, 1963; Ralph Phelps, "Lima: Progress Report for '58," *Toledo Blade,* Sunday Pictorial, Sept. 14, 1958, 8–9; "City's Population at 57,246," v.f. Lima—Population, ACHS; "Lima Council Annexes Two Subdivisions," *Toledo Blade,* July 19, 1960; "480-Acre Westwood Area Joins Lima Monday Night," *Lima Citizen,* Jan. 22, 1961.

30. Ruth Milkman, *Farewell to the Factory: Auto Workers in the Late Twentieth Century* (Berkeley, Calif.: Univ. of California Press, 1997), 11–12; Blade, "Organized Labor Constantly Aiming" (UAW leader quoted).

31. Pete Stanley, "New Census Report Draws Profile of Lima, Metro Area," v.f. Lima Census, 1973, ACHS; Clarence Roller, oral interview by author, Apr. 28, 2004; Carey English, "Why They Call the Midwest the 'Rust Bowl,'" *U.S. News and World Report,* Jan. 17, 1983, 27 (machinist quoted).

32. Robert Blade, "The Housing Puzzle: War's Temporary Housing Becomes Permanent," *Lima News,* July 3, 1973; Ann Jett, "Negroes Rap Slum Housing," *Lima Citizen,* Aug. 2, 1963; Dennis Henderson, "Stratification of the Black Working Class: Lima, Ohio," student senior honors thesis, Harvard University, 1971, 22, Lima Public Library; Melvin Woodard, oral interview by author, Oct. 31, 2003; Robert Blade, "Racial Discrimination: Laws and Reality," *Lima News,* July 6, 1973.

33. Blade, "The Housing Puzzle," 8; Henderson, "Stratification of the Black Working Class," 49; Jett, "Negroes Rap Slum Housing"; W. Ben Myers and Matt Francis, "Summary of Interview with Alberta Shurelds," Bluffton College student paper, author's possession; Jason Thomas, "Hidden Squalor of Lima Spurs Rumbles of Strife," *Cleveland Plain Dealer,* Oct. 6, 1971 (quote, "I saw these kinds of structures"). Also see John Mecartney, *A Challenge to Poverty in Lima, Ohio* (Lima, Ohio: McDonald Foundation, 1975), 40–52, 60–64, in which Mecartney documents how these south side districts were more than 85 percent black, 47–48.

34. Williamson, interview, Dec. 11, 1990; Spring Quarter History 260 Class, OSU Lima, "The Black History of Lima," 26, 29–30; Woodard, interview, Oct. 31, 2003. Woodard claimed that "token" hiring of minority applicants resulted from that particular effort.

35. Spring Quarter History 260 Class, OSU Lima, "The Black History of Lima," 23, 43, 40, 46–47; Woodard, interview, Oct. 31, 2003; Bart Mills, "Furl Williams Dies," *Lima News,* Aug. 22, 1993. To an entrepreneur like Williamson, the end of Jim Crow was in some ways, ironically, an unfortunate development. In 1959, he was the first African American in Lima to get a motel license, and for four years his business flourished by providing shelter to weary black travelers denied admittance to the bigger, whites-only motels along the highway. Then, as Williamson recalled, "the civil rights came" and they "wiped me completely out." Williamson, interview, Dec. 11, 1990.

36. Woodard, interview, Oct. 31, 2003. Christian Morris, Lima mayor from 1965 to 1973, later said that the previous police chief, Don Miller, "still thought a lot like a motorcycle cop." Christian Morris, oral interview by author, Feb. 5, 2004.

37. Mecartney, *A Challenge to Poverty in Lima, Ohio,* 39, 65–66; Jon Stapleton, "A Citywide Housing Code: Defeated but Not Forgotten," *Lima News,* July 10, 1973; "George Dunster, "HRC Bill Rejected Despite Williams' Plea," *Lima News,* Dec. 14, 1971 (Williams quoted). The opposition to the housing codes was led by the WHY Committee, a Lima coalition. In

addition to realtors, landlords, and businesspeople, its members included factory workers and poor homeowners who had accepted the committee's scare tactics—warning the public, for example, that such codes would lead to widespread evictions or extensive fines levied by the municipal bureaucracy for minor violations of the code. See Mecartney, *A Challenge to Poverty in Lima, Ohio.*

38. Spring Quarter History 260 Class, OSU Lima, "The Black History of Lima," 44; Mecartney, *A Challenge to Poverty in Lima, Ohio,* 20–22, 138–39.

39. Mecartney, *A Challenge to Poverty in Lima, Ohio,* 21–23; Thomas Nelson, oral interview by Hans Houshower, Nov. 29, 1990, transcript, Hist. Mss. 10–58, Memory Engines Collection, OHS; Christian Morris, oral interview by author, Feb. 9, 2004 (FBI informing); "Mayor Rejects Panther Ultimatum," *Lima News,* July 27, 1969; Spring Quarter History 260 Class, OSU Lima, "The Black History of Lima," 31–33, 42, 45–46; "School Head Blames Panthers; Color Line Split Threatens," *Lima News,* Nov. 16, 1969 (McGovern quoted). For examples of national Black Panther rhetoric, see Philip S. Foner, ed., *The Black Panthers Speak* (Philadelphia, Pa.: J. B. Lippincott, 1970).

40. Mecartney, *A Challenge to Poverty in Lima, Ohio,* 22–23, 139; Tom Watkins, "Unruly Pupils Disrupt City Schools," *Lima News,* Nov. 16, 1969; "South Group Seizes Office," *Lima News,* Jan. 6, 1970; Kathy and Larry Oatman, "Court Friday for School's Protest Force," *Lima News,* Jan. 7, 1970; "The Year That Was: Local Mixture of Good, Bad," *Lima News,* Jan. 1, 1971; "Unrest Shuts Lima Senior," *Lima News,* Jan. 11, 1970; Spring Quarter History 260 Class, OSU Lima, "The Black History of Lima," 31–33; "Student Disorders Close High School," *Lima News,* Feb. 11, 1971; "Senior High Shut Down as Racial Fights Erupt," *Lima News,* Feb. 10, 1972; Robert Daniels, "Lima High School Seeks Cause of Its Annual Racial Conflict," *Cleveland Plain Dealer,* Feb. 29, 1972 (Haithcock quoted).

41. Morris, interviews, Feb. 5, Feb. 9, 2004; George Dunster, "Churches Lack Involvement, Morris Says," *Lima News,* undated but c. early or mid-spring 1967. These clippings were in a scrapbook in Christian Morris's possession, which he kindly loaned to the author.

42. "King Day March Confronts Mayor," *Lima News,* Jan. 16, 1970; Morris, interview, Feb. 9, 2004; Nelson, interview, Nov. 29, 1990; Velton Louis Hamilton, oral interview by Willie Thompson and Molly Weis, Nov. 6, 1990, Hist. Mss. 10–58, Memory Engines Collection, OHS; "South-End Youth Blamed for Shot Felling Officer," *Lima News,* Feb. 2, 1970; Melvin Woodard, oral interview by author, Nov. 21, 2003.

43. Morris, interview, Feb. 9, 2004; Tom Watkins and Fred Parker, "One Slain, Five Others Shot; Guardsmen Patrol City," *Lima News,* Aug. 6, 1970; Watkins, "Disorder Subsides, but City Curfew Remains," *Lima News,* Aug. 7, 1970; "The Year That Was: Local Mixture of Good, Bad," *Lima News,* Jan. 1, 1971. Pierce was lucky to have survived; Ricks fired six bullets at him from point-blank range. Later on, a grand jury investigation corroborated the police department's account of Ricks's death.

44. Mecartney, *A Challenge to Poverty in Lima, Ohio,* 155; Bob Snodgrass, "Crime Rate Down for Lima in 1971," *Lima News,* Feb. 4, 1972; Watkins, "Unruly Pupils Disrupt City Schools" (quoted).

45. Kenneth T. Jackson, *Crabgrass Frontier: The Suburbanization of the United States* (New York: Oxford Univ. Press, 1985), 20–86, 113–48, 157–71; David K. Hamilton, *Governing Metropolitan Areas: Response to Growth and Change* (New York: Garland, 1999), 48–51; Teaford, *Cities of the Heartland,* 239–40 (statistics).

46. Teaford, *Cities of the Heartland,* 241–42; Jackson, *Crabgrass Frontier,* 170; Jack Keenan, "Electric Street Railways of Lima: The Formative Years," *Allen County Reporter* 48 (1992): 96–97.

47. Jackson, *Crabgrass Frontier,* 195–207 (quoted, 203); Rosalyn Baxandall and Elizabeth Ewen, *Picture Windows: How the Suburbs Happened* (New York: Basic Books, 2000), 56–57, 122–27.

48. "Move to Suburbs Continues," *Lima Citizen,* Jan. 7, 1962; "Residential Construction Maintaining Torrid Pace," *Lima News,* Aug. 4, 1964; Parker, interview, Feb. 23, 1990; "Expanding Suburbs Highlight Limaland Construction Boom," *Lima News,* Feb. 27, 1966.

49. Kim Kincaid, "Shopping Would Never Be the Same," *Lima News,* Apr. 9, 1997; "Shopping Centers Visitors' Delight" and "Commerce, Trade Bloom; Sales Mushrooming," *Lima News,* Feb. 27, 1966; "Lima Mall Opening Attracts Thousands," *Lima News,* Nov. 18, 1965; "Lima, Allen Trading Center Ranks among Tops in State," *Lima News,* Dec. 6, 1964.

50. "Expanding Suburbs" (quoted); "Work Survey Unveils 5,000 Available Jobs," v.f. Lima—Employment and Unemployment, ACHS; "Residential Building Grows 28 Per Cent" and "Allen Unemployment Falls," both in *Lima News,* Feb. 27, 1972; James Stegall, "Rise Out of Doldrums Puts Lima on Trail of 'All-America' Title," *Toledo Blade,* Nov. 4, 1972.

51. Morris, interview, Feb. 9, 2004 (quoted); Ned Bell, "Most Area Cities Extend Water, Sewer Services," *Toledo Blade,* Oct. 24, 1967; "Lima Mall Expands to New Concourse," *Lima News,* Feb. 27, 1972; "Refurbishing Lima," *Time,* Nov. 4, 1974, 12.

52. Jackson, *Crabgrass Frontier,* 207–18 (quoted, 213); Myron Orfield, *American Metropolitics: The New Suburban Reality* (Washington, D.C.: Brooking Institution Press, 2002), 10–13; Hamilton, *Governing Metropolitan Areas,* 52–54, 61–62; Blade, "Racial Discrimination: Laws and Reality" (Bolden quoted); U.S. Census Bureau, *18th Census of the United States, 1960,* vol. 1, part 37, *Ohio: Characteristics of the Population,* Table 21 (Washington, D.C.: Government Printing Office, 1961), 107; U.S. Census Bureau, *1990 U.S. Census,* Section 1, "Social and Economic Characteristics—Ohio" (Washington, D.C.: Government Printing Office, 1993), 51; U.S. Census Bureau, *1980 U.S. Census,* vol. 1, *Characteristics of the Population,* ch. A, part 37, "Ohio," Table 44 (Washington, D.C.: Government Printing Office, 1993), 318.

53. Robert Blade, "Older Homes Lose Appeal in Rush to Suburban Life," *Lima News,* July 2, 1973; Fr. Norbert Howe, oral interview by author, Sept. 10, 2003; Ohio Department of Development, "Population"; Williamson, interview, Dec. 11, 1990.

54. Orfield, *American Metropolitics,* 133–35; Hamilton, *Governing Metropolitan Areas,* 55–60; Jon Teaford, *City and Suburb: The Political Fragmentation of Metropolitan America, 1850–1970* (Baltimore, Md.: Johns Hopkins Univ. Press, 1979), 171–73, 184–86; Jackson, *Crabgrass Frontier,* 150–53.

55. "Ruling May Halt Perry Anti-Annexation Move," *Lima News,* Apr. 8, 1968; "Annexation Verdict Near," *Lima News,* Sept. 7, 1969; "Arguments Started in Land Transfer," *Lima News,* Sept. 10, 1969; "C of C Reveals Annexation Effort," and "Adjacent to Industries Previously Petitioned," both in *Lima News,* Oct. 31, 1969; Gene Rockwell, "Morris Blames Industry in Annexation No," *Lima News,* Nov. 13, 1969 (quoted); Morris interview, Feb. 5, 2004. Morris saw nothing wrong with such attempts at annexation. Those industries would never have come to Allen County in the first place, he reasoned, had the City of Lima not first wooed them and provided the requisite services that had enabled them to profit. Moreover, the industries stood to gain economically by joining Lima. The refinery and the chemical plant consumed millions of gallons of Lima water, and as corporate citizens of the city they would no longer be subject to the 50 percent surcharge. Morris, interview, Feb. 5, 2004.

56. Chuck Eckstein, "Preliminary Census Results Shock Officials," *Lima News,* June 25, 1980 (Moyer quoted); Chuck Eckstein, "The Census: Townships Increase Population at the Expense of Central Lima Area," *Lima News,* June 26, 1980; Greg Hoersten, "Census Says Lima Lost 11.8%," *Lima News,* June 25, 1980; Jackson, *Crabgrass Frontier,* 285.

57. For example, see Orfield, *American Metropolitics,* 15–17, 23–28.

58. Paul Ryscavage, *Inequality in America: An Analysis of Trends* (Armonk, N.Y.: M. E. Sharpe, 1999), 56–72; Peterson, *Silent Depression,* 93–170; Katharine Newman, *Declining Fortunes: The Withering of the American Dream* (New York: Basic Books, 1993), 40–54; Craypo and Nissen, introduction to *Grand Designs,* 9; Harrison and Bluestone, *The Great U-Turn,* 3–11, 22–23.

59. G. Jones, *Multinationals and Global Capitalism,* 35, 222–23; Bluestone and Harrison, *Deindustrialization of America,* 118–26; Harold C. Livesay, *Andrew Carnegie and the Rise of Big Business* (Boston, Mass.: Little, Brown and Company, 1975), 111–28, 147–66; McCraw, *Prophets of Regulation,* 70–71; Harrison and Bluestone, *The Great U-Turn,* 12–13, 26–27.

60. In many ways, the "new global economy" was not new at all. Geoffrey Jones describes how various forms of a new globalized economy had emerged in the eighteenth, nineteenth, and early twentieth centuries; see G. Jones, *Multinationals and Global Capitalism,* 18–26, 31–33, 285–86.

61. Harrison and Bluestone, *The Great U-Turn,* 12–13, 26–27; Bluestone and Harrison, *Deindustrialization of America,* 112–18; Naomi Lamoreaux, Daniel M. G. Graff, and Peter Temin, "Beyond Markets and Hierarchies: Toward a New Synthesis of American Business History," *American Historical Review* 108 (Apr. 2003): 423–25; Reich, *Supercapitalism,* 50–55, 60–64, 75–78; Tony Clarke, "Mechanisms of Corporate Rule," in Mander and Goldsmith, *The Case against the Global Economy,* 302–3; William Greider, "'Citizen' GE," in Mander and Goldsmith, *The Case against the Global Economy,* 329–30.

62. Mander, "Rules of Corporate Behavior," 315–17, 319; High, *Industrial Sunset,* 98–102; Bluestone and Harrison, *Deindustrialization of America,* 164–71.

63. Bluestone and Harrison, *Deindustrialization of America,* 126–33, 171–72.

64. High, *Industrial Sunset,* 109; Lawrence Rothstein, *Plant Closings,* 43–58, 169–70. Charles Craypo and Bruce Nissen also summarize this myth; see their introduction and "The Impact of Corporate Strategies," both in *Grand Designs,* 4 and 227–28, respectively. For the myth in undiluted form, see Richard McKenzie, "Consequences of Relocation Decisions," in *Deindustrialization and Plant Closure,* ed. Paul D. Staudohar and Holly E. Brown (Lexington, Mass.: D. C. Heath and Co., 1987), 154–58.

65. Lustig, "Politics of Shutdown," 127–28, 130–31 (oil industry acquisitions); High, *Industrial Sunset,* 116–24; Cowie and Heathcott, introduction to *Beyond the Ruins,* 6; Fuechtmann, *Steeples and Stacks,* 34–47; Robert Bruno, *Steelworker Alley: How Class Works in Youngstown* (Ithaca, N.Y.: Cornell Univ. Press, 1999), 112–16; Linkon and Russo, *Steeltown U.S.A.,* 47–49; Bluestone and Harrison, *Deindustrialization of America,* 152–53; Craypo and Nissen, "The Impact of Corporate Strategies," in *Grand Designs,* 226–29, 236–37, 240–41; Benjamin Friedman, quoted in Kevin Phillips, *Bad Money: Reckless Capitalism, Failed Politics, and the Global Crisis of American Capitalism* (New York: Penguin, 2009), 40. On concessions by unions, see D. Nelson, *Farm and Factory,* 192.

66. Archie B. Carroll, "Management's Social Responsibilities," in Staudohar and Brown, *Deindustrialization and Plant Closure,* 172–79; Portz, *Politics of Plant Closings,* 146–47; David Bensman and Roberta Lynch, *Rusted Dreams: Hard Times in a Steel Community* (Berkeley, Calif.: Univ. of California Press, 1988).

67. High, *Industrial Sunset,* 93; Bluestone and Harrison, *Deindustrialization of America,* 25–26, 49–81; Candee S. Harris, "Magnitude of Job Loss," in Staudohar and Brown, *Deindustrialization and Plant Closure,* 89–100; Donald B. Thompson, "The Human Trauma of Steel's Decline," *Industry Week,* Sept. 2, 1985, 39–43; Paul O. Flaim and Ellen Sehgal, "Displaced Workers of 1979–1983: How Well Have They Fared?" *Monthly Labor Review* 108 (June 1985): 3–16.

68. Lustig, "Politics of Shutdown," 13, 138 (quoted, 13); David Fasenfest, "Cui Bono," in Crayo and Nissen, *Grand Designs,* 4, 121–28; Bluestone and Harrison, *Deindustrialization of America,* 184; Camp, *Worker Response to Plant Closings,* 4; Kantor, *Dependent City.* For an example of corporate "whipsawing" between two different communities, see Portz, *Politics of Plant Closings,* 156–57.

69. Harrison and Bluestone, *The Great U-Turn,* 86–94; Christopher Byron, "The Idle Army of the Unemployed," *Time,* Aug. 11, 1980, 44–49; Charles Alexander, "Gathering Gloom for Workers," *Time,* Dec. 14, 1981, 64–65; Steven High, "The Making of the 'Rust Belt' in the Minds of North Americans, 1969–1984," *Canadian Review of American Studies* 27 (1997): 48–59; Byron, "Booms, Busts, and Birth of a Rust Bowl," *Time,* Dec. 27, 1982, 63–64 (quoted); Linkon and Russo, *Steeltown U.S.A.,* 134, 143–46.

4. Resistance

1. Berger, interview, Mar. 18, 2004.

2. James Schaefer, oral interview by author, Mar. 5, 2004; BP Lima, "The Lima Refinery Story," Learning History Document from the Lima Refinery, unpublished mss., June 2003, 2–3, in author's possession.

3. Berger, interview, Mar. 18, 2004.

4. Tom Beyerlin, "Tentacles of Recession: Some Non-Auto Industries Hold Out, But Jobs Scarce," *Lima News,* July 6, 1980.

5. "Clark Expects to Introduce 5th in Series of New Models," *Lima News,* Feb. 24, 1980; Beyerlin, "Tentacles of Recession"; "Discussions Being Held to Sell Lima Clark Facility," *Lima News,* Sept. 25, 1980 (Wall St. insider quoted); Marilyn Baxter, "Clark to Cease New Production Next Month," *Lima News,* Oct. 28, 1980 (Clark managers quoted).

6. Marilyn Baxter, "Tension among Clark Workers," *Lima News,* Nov. 16, 1980 (quote, "I don't know how"); Baxter, "Workers Reveal Feelings about Dying Clark Plant," *Lima News,* July 5, 1981 (quote, "have given half their lives"); Keith Helmlinger, "Auction Ends Era at Clark Facility; Memories Remain," *Lima News,* Oct. 11, 1981.

7. Marilyn Baxter, "Ripple Effect from Clark Closing Expected in Area," *Lima News,* July 12, 1981.

8. Russ Smith, "Despite Employment Dip, Area Has Reasons for Hope," *Lima News,* Apr. 22, 1982; Marilyn Baxter, "Healthy Lima Area Economy Goal of Experts," *Lima News,* Apr. 12, 1982; Michael B. King and Richard B. Schmitt, "Trumpeted Recession, Severe in Lima, Ohio, Spares a Texas Town," *Wall Street Journal,* Mar. 3, 1982; Paul Janczewski, "Although Battered, Labor Optimistic," *Lima News,* Apr. 24, 1982; English, "Why They Call the Midwest the 'Rust Bowl,'" 27 (UAW official quoted); "Ohio's Jobless Rate Up to 14.5%," *Cleveland Plain Dealer,* Jan. 8, 1983; Paul Janczewski, "Unemployment Gets Some Credit for Crime Drop," *Lima News,* May 1, 1983; Todd Halvorson, "Employment on Upswing, But Future Still Uncertain, " *Lima News,* Feb. 26, 1984.

9. Janczewski, "Unemployment Gets Some Credit"; Gerri Willis, "Even Low-Paying Jobs Difficult to Find in Lima Area," *Lima News,* Aug. 2, 1981; Todd Halvorson, "Support Group Gives Frustrated Unemployed Ray of Hope," *Lima News,* May 19, 1983; Gilbert, interview, Mar. 10, 2005; English, "Why They Call the Midwest the 'Rust Bowl'" (McGovern quoted); Howe, interview; Janczewski, "Although Battered, Labor Optimistic" (labor official quoted).

10. Todd Halvorson and Gerri Willis, "Stigma Often Deters Jobless from Seeking Available Aid," *Lima News,* May 20, 1983; Beverly Prueter, oral interview by author, Jan. 20, 2004; Howe, interview, Sept. 10, 2003.

11. English, "Why They Call the Midwest the 'Rust Bowl,'" 26; King and Schmitt, "Trumpeted Recession," 18 (MacDonel quoted); Paul Janczewski, "Home Sales Level as Prices Decline," *Lima News,* May 13, 1984; Marilyn Baxter, "Police, Fire Cutbacks to Follow City Layoffs," *Lima News,* Aug. 13, 1982; "Lima Layoffs Cut Deeply into Safety Forces," *Cleveland Plain Dealer,* Aug. 15, 1982.

12. English, "Why They Call the Midwest the 'Rust Bowl,'" 26; King and Schmitt, "Trumpeted Recession," 1 (Gregg quoted); Timothy Wolfrum, "Bickering Blunted Gains," *Lima News,* v.f. Lima—Economic Development, ACHS; Lori Nims, "'82 Nelson Concert Remembered by Texan, Limaites," *Lima News,* Feb. 26, 1989; Hans Houshower, oral interview by author, Feb. 5, 2004.

13. Houshower, interview, Feb. 5, 2004; Nims, "'82 Nelson Concert Remembered" (MacDonel quoted); King and Schmitt, "Trumpeted Recession," 18; Jerry Hertenstein, "Standard Oil Co. Unveils Gift to City Sunday," *Lima News,* Aug. 4, 1986; Mike Lackey, "Gala Opening Ends One Story, Begins Another," *Lima News,* Oct. 18, 1984; Halvorson, "Employment on Upswing"; Keith Helmlinger, "Defense Spending: General Dynamics Gets Lion's Share of Contracts," *Lima News,* Feb. 26, 1984; Mike Leitz, "Property Transfers' Value Up 18% in '85," *Lima News,* Jan. 26, 1986.

14. Howe, interview, Sept. 10, 2003; King and Schmitt, "Trumpeted Recession," 1 (Merriman quoted).

15. Data for this and the next four paragraphs taken from David Berger, "Autobiographical Reflections," unpublished mss., Jan. 8, 2003, DBP, LMB.

16. Berger, interview, Mar. 18, 2004.

17. Ibid.; Jim Parker, "Inmate's Talk Boosts Impact of Rehab Update," *Lima News,* Oct. 28, 1998; Rita Price, "The Rehab Project," *Columbus Dispatch,* Dec. 8, 1998.

18. William D. Angel, *Not All Politics Is Local: Reflections of a Former County Chairman* (Kent, Ohio: Kent State Univ. Press, 2002), 262–64; Berger, interview, Mar. 18, 2004; Lori Nims, "Rehab's Berger Enters Mayoral Race," *Lima News,* Jan. 6, 1989.

19. Angel, *Not All Politics Is Local,* 259–66, 270; Berger, interview, Mar. 18, 2004.

20. Angel, *Not All Politics Is Local,* 268–70, 272 (quoted, 268); Lori Nims, "Berger, Moyer to Vie for Mayor," *Lima News,* May 3, 1989.

21. Berger, interview, Mar. 18, 2004; Jerry Hertenstein, "Some Train Enthusiasts Steamed over Amtrak Departure," *Lima News,* Feb. 25, 1990 (quoted).

22. Jim Parker, "Manufacturing Remains Strong in Allen," *Lima News,* Feb. 26, 1989; Parker, "Retail Boom Tips Economic Scales in Lima's Favor," *Lima News,* Feb. 26, 1989; "City, County Officials Look Ahead to New Decade," v.f. Lima—Economy, ACHS (Bassitt quoted); Lori Nims, "Lima Regains Economic Strength," *Lima News,* Feb. 26, 1990.

23. Mark Hamilton, "Statistics Show Allen Economy Slowing, Coleson Says," *Lima News,* Jan. 25, 1990; Paul W. Smith, "Lima Plant Chiefs Say More Development Needed," *Lima News,* Feb. 25, 1990.

24. See, for example, John T. Cumbler, *A Social History of Economic Decline: Business, Politics, and Work in Trenton* (New Brunswick, N.J.: Rutgers Univ. Press, 1989), 1–9, 137–49, 160–61 (quoted, 9); Keith Helmlinger, "Foresight of Galvin Led Steel Company through Adversity," *Lima News,* Oct. 28, 1984 (quoted).

25. "The Rocket-Like Pace at Teledyne," *Forbes,* Jan. 16, 1968, 20–22; Eric Schine, "Parting with Henry Singleton: Such Sweet Sorrow for Teledyne?" *Business Week,* Apr. 9, 1990, 81; Phillip C. Pina, "Teledyne Ohio Steel Draws to End," and "Plant Has Long Lima History," both in *Lima News,* Nov. 9, 1990.

26. Phillip C. Pina, "R. G. Dun to End Production of Cigars in Lima Friday," *Lima News,*

Nov. 27, 1990; "Cuts Hurt Older Employees," *Columbus Dispatch*, July 16, 1995; Susan Durant, "Plant Closing, Fears of Recession Drive Up Jobless Rate," *Lima News*, Feb. 24, 1991.

27. Pina, "Plant Has Long Lima History"; Darren J. Waggoner, "Textron Clock Ticks," and Wynne Everett, "Employees React Angrily," both in *Lima News*, Dec. 11, 1993 (Long quoted); Darren J. Waggoner, "Job Loss Fear Pervades Pub Conversation," *Lima News*, Dec. 15, 1993 (worker quoted). For the general contours of this "shutdown pattern," see Lustig, "Politics of Shutdown," 126–30.

28. Darren Waggoner, "Airfoil, Union Local Fail to Compromise," *Lima News*, June 18, 1994; Darren Waggoner, "Weary Workers Face Job Loss," and "Efforts Fall Far Too Short to Save Textron Plant," both in *Lima News*, June 24, 1994 (Beck quoted).

29. Berger, interview, Mar. 18, 2004 (quoted); Waggoner, "Efforts Fall Far Too Short."

30. Phillip C. Pina, "Company a Presence 56 Years," *Lima News*, Jan. 22, 1992; Phillip C. Pina, "Westinghouse Workers React to Plant Sale," *Lima News*, Jan. 23, 1992 (inspector quoted); Jerry Hertenstein, "Sunstrand Settles into Westinghouse," *Lima News*, May 9, 1992 (quote, "celebrating").

31. Timothy R. Wolfrum, "Sunstrand Employees Hope to Cope," *Lima News*, Nov. 14, 1992; Wolfrum, "Sunstrand Slims Workforce," *Lima News*, Aug. 27, 1993; Claire Chapman, "Sunstrand Will Close Lima Site," *Lima News*, Feb. 22, 1992 (Lodermeier quoted); Darren Waggoner, "Stunned Workers Vent Pain, Anger," *Lima News*, Feb. 23, 1995 (worker quoted).

32. Global Security, "Lima Army Tank Plant," 2000, Global Security.org, http://www.globalsecurity.org/military/facility/lima.htm; William Flannery, "Politics, Foreign Sales May Yet Save General Dynamics' Tanks," *St. Louis Post-Dispatch*, Feb. 5, 1990.

33. Flannery, "Politics, Foreign Sales"; James Ellis, "Lima, Ohio: We're All for Peace, but . . . ," *Business Week*, July 2, 1990, 70 (Berger quoted). On the role Oxley routinely played as a loyal servant of the financial services industry, see Gretchen Morgenson, "Pipeline to a Point Man," *New York Times*, Nov. 3, 2002.

34. "In the Gunsights: The Future of an Ohio Town," *Newsweek*, July 15, 1991, 36–37; Roger K. Lowe, "Proposal Is Good News, Bad News for State, City," *Columbus Dispatch*, Jan. 30, 1992; "Lima Tank Plant to Continue Work Even If Contractor Changes," *Columbus Dispatch*, Nov. 4, 1992.

35. Thomas Gerdel, "Lima Copes with Loss of Defense Jobs," *Cleveland Plain Dealer*, Aug. 18, 1996; Mike Mender, "Defense Job Losses Felt Community-Wide," *Lima News*, Aug. 23, 1996; Jon Chavez, "A Little Down, Far From Out: Despite Hits, Lima Is Upbeat," *Toledo Blade*, May 19, 1996 (Wagner quoted); Waggoner, "Stunned Workers" (worker quoted).

36. Dale Hathaway, *Can Workers Have a Voice? The Politics of Deindustrialization in Pittsburgh* (University Park, Pa.: Pennsylvania State Univ. Press, 1993), quoted in Nissen, *Fighting for Jobs*, 170. For a concise summary of studies speaking to the level of corporate hegemony in modern urban affairs, see Nissen, *Fighting for Jobs*, 170. On the community dependency thesis, see Nissen and Craypo, "Impact of Corporate Strategies," 242–43 (quoted, 242); and Portz, *Politics of Plant Closings*, 140–43.

37. Charles Lindblom, "The Market as Prison," *Journal of Politics* 44 (1982): 324–36 (quoted, 326); Keith Knauss and Michael Matuzak, "Relocation of a Torrington Plant," in Crayo and Nissen, *Grand Designs*, 92–118 (Bennett quoted, 107); see also Craypo and Nissen's summary of this case in their introduction to *Grand Designs*, 13–14. For these typologies of municipal political responses to plant closings, see Portz, *Politics of Plant Closings*, 5–10; and Nissen, *Fighting for Jobs*, 13–16.

38. Portz, *Politics of Plant Closings*, 10–12, 169–70; Nissen, *Fighting for Jobs*, 14, 149–50; Rothstein, *Plant Closings*, 170–72.

39. Portz, *Politics of Plant Closings,* 102–21; Bruce Nissen, "Successful Labor-Community Coalition Building," in Craypo and Nissen, *Grand Designs,* 209–23.

40. S. Prakash Sethi, "The Ax Man Cometh: GM Pulls Out of Norwood City," *Business and Society Review* (Spring 1989): 20–25.

41. Berger, interview, Mar. 18, 2004 (quoted).

42. Berger, interview, Mar. 18, 2004; Robert Snell, "Former Defense Plant Bought," *Lima News,* Mar. 4, 1998; David Berger, e-mail letter to author, Apr. 23, 2004, in author's possession.

43. Michael Noe, "Berger Reveals Renewal Ideas," *Lima News,* Dec. 12, 1995; Berger, interview, Mar. 18, 2004 (quoted); Bart Mills, "The 'Win-Win' Formula," *Lima News,* Dec. 28, 1995; Robert Snell, "Annexation Wins Approval," *Lima News,* Aug 22, 1997.

44. Chavez, "A Little Down, Far From Out."

5. Scorched Earth

1. Sampson, *The Seven Sisters,* 26–28; James Bamberg, *British Petroleum and Global Oil, 1950–1975: The Challenge of Nationalism* (Cambridge, UK: Cambridge Univ. Press, 2000), 275; "The Year That Was."

2. Sampson, *The Seven Sisters,* 177–78; R. W. Ferrier, *The History of the British Petroleum Company,* vol. 1, *The Developing Years, 1901–1932* (Cambridge, UK: Cambridge Univ. Press, 1982), 5–104, 158–235; Bamberg, *British Petroleum and Global Oil,* 100–195. On the early roots of BP, also see Alfred D. Chandler Jr., *Scale and Scope: The Dynamics of Industrial Capitalism* (Cambridge, Mass.: Harvard Univ. Press, 1990), 299–303.

3. Bamberg, *British Petroleum and Global Oil,* 272–78; O'Connor, *The Oil Barons,* 425–26; Sampson, *The Seven Sisters,* 178; Thomas Stemen, "A Brief History of the Standard Oil/BP Lima Refinery," *Allen County Reporter* 54 (1998): 86–87; Zach Schiller, "Move Was Only a Matter of Time" *Cleveland Plain Dealer,* Aug. 16, 1998 (initial Sohio enthusiasm for BP merger); "No Immediate Impact on Lima from Standard Restructuring," *Lima News,* July 22, 1987.

4. Roller, interview, Apr. 28, 2004; Paul Monus, oral interview by author, Apr. 8, 2004 (both Monus and Roller referred to the "queen of the fleet" phrasing); Gary Greve, "Oil Spill Overshadows Significance," v.f. Lima—Industries—BP, ACHS; Jim Parker, "Official Predicts Period of Growth at Lima Refinery," *Lima News,* Nov. 12, 1987.

5. Gilbert, interview, Mar. 10, 2005; Ronald Lederman, "Workers Ride the Ups, Downs of Labor Relations," *Lima News,* Sept. 27, 1998 (union official quoted); Roller, interview, Apr. 28, 2004; Monus, interview, Apr. 8, 2004; BP Lima, "The Lima Refinery Story," 3–4.

6. Schaefer, interview, Mar. 5, 2004; "A Timely Perspective: The Refinery and the Community," *Lima News,* Sept. 27, 1998; "Pipeline Emergency City's Top '69 Story," *Lima News,* Jan. 1, 1970; Morris, interview, Feb. 9, 2004.

7. "BP Chemical Pollution Worst in Ohio in 1988," *Lima News,* May 16, 1990; "Lima Plant Chemicals Linked to Birth Defects," *Lima News,* June 6, 1990; Dave Davis and Tom Breckenridge, "Toxic Waste in Wells Tests Faith in Geology," *Cleveland Plain Dealer,* July 14, 1991; Michael B. Lafferty, "Batelle Study Clears Lima's Air, Not Soil," *Columbus Dispatch,* Feb. 12, 1992.

8. Bruce French, oral interview by author, Mar. 29, 2004; Mecartney, *A Challenge to Poverty in Lima, Ohio,* 30–33, 130–31, 143–46, 168. For the ways the Allen County Citizens for the Environment (ACCE) married civic action with environmental activism occurring nationally, see Carmen Sirianni and Lewis Friedland, *Civic Innovation in America: Community Empowerment, Public Policy, and the Movement for Civic Renewal* (Berkeley, Calif.: Univ. of California Press, 2001), 85–86.

9. French, interview, Mar. 29, 2004. Citizen monitoring of corporate pollutants and other kinds of pressure on suspected violators of environmental laws were becoming staple practices among environmental groups nationwide; see Sirianni and Friedland, *Civic Innovation in America,* 99–100, 122.

10. Phillip C. Pina, "BP Chemicals Denies Claims Made in Suit," *Lima News,* Oct. 25, 1991; Pina, "Judge Dismisses Lawsuit Against BP," *Lima News,* Feb. 26, 1991; Tom Breckenridge, "Jury Says BP Waste Disposal Does No Harm," *Cleveland Plain Dealer,* Nov. 19, 1993. According to French, the ACCE was not connected with this second suit. Pina, "BP Refers Requests to Record," *Lima News,* Jan. 28, 1991; Pina, "Emissions Decline Foreseen," *Lima News,* May 9, 1991; Pina, "BP Refinery Wastewater Discharge Permit Approved," *Lima News,* Apr. 9, 1991 (EPA compliance); French, interview, Mar. 29, 2004.

11. Phillip C. Pina, "BP Plan Strengthens Commitment in Lima," *Lima News,* Apr. 24, 1991 (Clean Air Act); Jim Parker, "BP Plants Good Neighbors, Boss Says," *Lima News,* Mar. 14, 1989 (Ross quoted).

12. Davis and Breckenridge, "Toxic Waste in Wells"; Gilbert, interview, Mar. 10, 2005 (quoted); Robin Buckner Price, "BP Chemicals: How to Educate the Public," *Oil and Gas Journal,* Mar. 30, 1992, 15; BP in the Midwest, unpublished pamphlet, "What Is BP Doing to Protect My Family, My Neighborhood, and the Environment?" undated, no page enumeration, in "Other" folder, DBP, LMB.

13. Scott Powers, "Ottawa River Full of Deformed Fish," *Columbus Dispatch,* May 13, 1992 (BP Chemicals manager and Little quoted); French, interview, Mar. 29, 2004; Lafferty, "Batelle Study Clears Lima's Air" (BP spokesperson quoted).

14. Phillip C. Pina, "EPA Hearing Draws Parade of Local Supporters for BP," *Lima News,* Feb. 22, 1991; Jerry Hertenstein, "EPA Wastewater Hearing Draws 300," *Lima News,* Nov. 14, 1992 (Little quoted).

15. Hertenstein, "EPA Wastewater Hearing"; Phillip C. Pina, "BP Official Says Lima Jobs Hinge on Petition Approval," *Lima News,* Feb. 26, 1992; Jerry Hertenstein, "Local Views Split on BP Well Ruling," *Lima News,* May 8, 1992; Hertenstein, "EPA Wastewater Hearing" (Berger quoted); Gilbert, interview, Mar. 10, 2005.

16. French, interview, Mar. 29, 2004.

17. David Bowen, "BP Is Back with a Rush," *London Independent,* May 23, 1993; Bamberg, *British Petroleum and Global Oil,* 58–67. This trend may not have been confined only to BP. According to business historian Mansel Blackford, in these years business management in Britain remained largely "parochial" and "rigid" across the country; see Blackford, *The Rise of Modern Business,* 239–40.

18. Bowen, "BP Is Back with a Rush."

19. "Lord Browne of Madingley—Honorary Graduate—Cranfield Campus Graduation, 2002," Cranfield University Alumni, http://www.cranfield.ac.uk/alumni/graduation02/cranfield1c.htm (accessed Oct. 7, 2002); Roller, interview, Apr. 28, 2004; James Schaefer, oral interview by author, Mar. 17, 2004.

20. Bowen, "BP Is Back with a Rush" (Horton quoted); "BP Marks Progress Toward Strategic Targets," *Oil and Gas Journal,* Sept. 26, 1994, 38; Steven Prokesch, "Now It's Bob Horton's Turn at B.P.," *New York Times,* Sept. 17, 1989; Andrew Freeman, "BP's Debt Strategists Wave the Stars and Stripes over Their British Home," *Financial Times* (London), July 6, 1990; Schaefer, interview, Mar. 17, 2004; G. Jones, *Multinationals and Global Capitalism,* 69; Pratt, *Prelude to a Merger,* 6; Blackford, *The Rise of Modern Business,* 197.

21. Peter Coy, Gary McWilliams, and John Rossant, "The New Economics of Oil," *Business Week,* Nov. 3, 1997, 140; Bowen, "BP Is Back with a Rush"; Paul Roberts, *The End of*

Oil: On the Edge of a Perilous New World (Boston, Mass.: Houghton Mifflin, 2004), 170–71; Prokesch, "Now It's Bob Horton's Turn at B.P."; Steven Percy, oral interview by author, May 13, 2004; Pratt, *Prelude to a Merger,* 3.

22. Bowen, "BP Is Back with a Rush"; "BP Sets Focus on Financial Goals, Core Assets," *Oil and Gas Journal,* Jan. 2, 1995, 24 (quote, "noncore business"); Schaefer, interview, Mar. 17, 2004; Prokesch, "Now It's Bob Horton's Turn at B.P."; Percy, interview, May 13, 2004 (BP executive quoted); Bhushan Bahree, "As Fresh Prospects Dry Up, Petroleum Industry Strikes Deals," *Wall Street Journal,* May 18, 2004; Pratt, *Prelude to a Merger,* 6 (BP shedding of acquisitions); "Popular Shares: BP Pauses for Breath," *Investors Chronicle,* Mar. 24, 1995, 46 (quoted); "Popular Shares: BP Gushes Good News," *Investors Chronicle,* Jan. 5, 1996, 40; "Company Results: British Petroleum," *Investors Chronicle,* Feb. 1, 1996, 61.

23. "Lord Browne of Madingley—Honorary Graduate" (Browne appointment); Jeffrey E. Garten, "Globalism Doesn't Have to Be Cruel," *Business Week,* Feb. 9, 1998, 26 (Browne quoted); Matthew Yeomans, *Oil: Anatomy of an Industry* (New York: New Press, 2004), 199.

24. Becky Yerak, "BP Oil Kicking Its Way to Future: Company's Been in a Rough Match," *Cleveland Plain Dealer,* Mar. 17, 1996. On Browne's at times ruthless management style, also see Robert Frank and Steve Liesman, "While BP Prepares New US Acquisition, Amoco Counts Scars," *Wall Street Journal,* Mar. 31, 1999.

25. Robert Corzine, "BP Launches Refinery Shake-Up," *Financial Times* (London), Nov. 3, 1995, 17; Jennifer Lawson, "BP: A Question of Costs," *Lima News,* Dec. 10, 1995; Percy, interview, May 13, 2004; Schaefer, interview, Mar. 5, 2004.

26. "Dr. R. W. H. Stomberg," in British Petroleum Company, "Annual General Meeting" booklet, 5; "Managing Directors of BP," *Financial Times* (London), July 20, 1991, 15; Percy, interview, May 13, 2004 (quoted); David Berger, "My Chronology," diary entry for May 12, 1997 (Seal study and Greve authorship), DBP, LMB; Schaefer, interview, Mar. 5, 2004; Monus interview, Apr. 8, 2004; Corzine, "BP Launches Refinery Shake-Up"; "Worldwide Energy Giant BP Oil Reveals Corporate Strategy for 1996," *Octane Week,* Apr. 29, 1996. James Walpole, plant manager for Lima BP Chemicals, who had worked throughout the world of BP refining and was in a good position to observe the actions of the high command, agreed that by the late 1980s and through the 1990s, BP clearly wanted to outsource refining. Its heart was in exploration and the acquisition of new fields. James Walpole, oral interview by author, Oct. 7, 2007.

27. Corzine, "BP Launches Refinery Shake-Up," 17 (Stomberg quoted); Percy, interview, May 13, 2004; "Tosco to Acquire BP Oil's Northeast US Assets," *Oil and Gas Journal,* Nov. 13, 1995, 108; "Refining," *Oil and Gas Journal,* Jan. 8, 1996, 26; "Tosco Seeks to Cut 130 Jobs at Refinery," *Philadelphia Inquirer,* Dec. 14, 1995; Reuters, "Company News: Tosco and Union Reach Tentative Agreement," *New York Times,* Aug. 27, 1996; Agis Salpukas, "A Union Gives an Old Refinery a New Lease on Life," *New York Times,* Aug. 31, 1996 (quoted); Agis Salpukas, "Oil, Prices, and Politics: Volatile Blend Fuels a Labor Battle at Shut Refinery," *New York Times,* June 1, 1996.

28. "BP Sells Marcus Hook for $235m in Oil Refinery Restructuring," *Corporate Money,* Nov. 24, 1995, 5; Roller, interview, Apr. 28, 2004; Monus, interview, Apr. 8, 2004 (quote, "slash and burn"); BP Lima, "The Lima Refinery Story," 3; Becky Yerak, "BP Oil Considers Refineries' Fate," *Cleveland Plain Dealer,* Dec. 16, 1995 (quote, "money-losing"); also on this, see Berger, handwritten notes, June 19, 1995, in "BP—My Notes" folder, DBP, LMB; Schaefer, interview, Mar. 5, 2004.

29. Schaefer, interview, Mar. 5, 2004.

30. Thomas Petzinger Jr., "Competent Workers and a Complex Leader Keep Big Oil in Check," *Wall Street Journal,* Dec. 2, 1998; Schaefer, interview, Mar. 5, 2004.

31. Petzinger, "Competent Workers and a Complex Leader"; Schaefer, interview, Mar. 5, 2004.

32. Bradley Jackson, "Reengineering the Sense of Self: The Manager and the Manager Guru," *Journal of Management Studies* 33, no. 5 (Sept. 1996): 575–78 (statistics and surveys); Michael Hammer and James Champy, *Reengineering the Corporation: A Manifesto for Business Revolution* (New York: HarperBusiness, 1993), 1–35, 51–74, 200 (quotes, "yesterday's paradigm," 17; "If American companies," 26; bullet points, 51, 58). For a concise summary of the reengineering paradigm shift, see Buder, *Capitalizing on Change,* 367–68. So complete was the acceptance of Hammer and Champy's new paradigm that their concepts even influenced school and education management; see Brett Davies, "Reengineering and Its Application to Education," *School Leadership and Management* 185 (June 1997): 2.

33. Hammer and Champy, *Reengineering the Corporation,* 70; Gilbert, interview, Mar. 10, 2005; Peter Fingar and Howard Smith, "Business Processes: From Reengineering to Management," *Darwin Magazine,* Mar. 2004, http://www.dorwinmag.com/read/030103/wavehistory.html (accessed Sept. 8, 2006) (quote, "dirty word"); Roller, interview, Apr. 28, 2004.

34. David Streitfeld, "Rank-and-File Style," *Your Turn,* Summer/Fall 1999, 13; Schaefer, interview, Mar. 5, 2004.

35. Schaefer, interview, Mar. 5, 2004; Petzinger, "Competent Workers and a Complex Leader"; Streitfeld, "Rank-and-File Style," 12 (quote, "grassroots-based management"). It is possible, perhaps, to overstate Schaefer's role. Gilbert, for example, saw him as "distant" and "remote," a man many workers "viewed with suspicion," associating him with the more detached management style of BP, as opposed to the easy familiarity allowed by Sohio. Rather than Schaefer, Gilbert credits figures like plant manager Donovan Kuenzli for the success of the Lima plant's revitalization efforts. Roller likewise downplayed Schaefer's role; while personally warm toward Schaefer, Roller saw him as relatively powerless. Gilbert, interview, Mar. 10, 2005; Roller, interview, Apr. 28, 2004.

36. Schaefer, interview, Mar. 5, 2004; Petzinger, "Competent Workers and a Complex Leader."

37. BP Lima, "The Lima Refinery Story," 22–23; Paulette Thomas, "A Town Is Buffeted by Global Crosswinds," *Wall Street Journal,* Mar. 24, 1997; Schaefer, interview, Mar. 5, 2004; Walpole, interview, Oct. 7, 2007.

38. Schaefer, interview, Mar. 5, 2004.

39. Schaefer, interview, Mar. 5, 2004 (quoted); Roller, interview, Apr. 28, 2004 (quoted); BP Lima, "The Lima Refinery Story," 10–17 (Winterstellar quoted, 12); Monus, interview, Apr. 8, 2004; Walpole, interview, Oct. 7, 2007.

40. Schaefer, interviews, Mar. 5 and 17, 2004; Monus, interview, Apr. 8, 2004; James Schaefer, "Should We Close One refinery?" in Insight: An Update for the Ohio System, Mar. 1995, "BP Retention Task Force" folder, DBP, LMB.

41. Schaefer, interview, Mar. 5, 2004.

42. Petzinger, "Competent Workers and a Complex Leader," 1 (quote, "mechanical inventiveness"); Schaefer, interview, Mar. 5, 2004.

43. Percy, interview, May 13, 2004; Schaefer, interview, Mar. 5, 2004.

44. Walpole, interview, Oct. 7, 2007. This encounter was reconstructed in Schaefer, interview, Mar, 5, 2004.

45. Schaefer, interview, Mar. 5, 2004.

46. Percy, interview, May 13, 2004; Schaefer, "Should We Close One Refinery?" 1–2 (in this publication, Schaefer clearly laid out for refinery workers the kinds of arguments he was then aiming at London); BP Lima, "The Lima Refinery Story," 1–2; Schaefer interview, Mar. 5, 2004.

47. Percy, interview, May 13, 2004; Schaefer, interview, Mar. 17, 2004; Berger, "My Chronology," diary entry for Dec. 12, 1997, DBP, LMB. On corporate hierarchies, see Alfred D.

Chandler Jr. and Herman Daems, introduction to *Managerial Hierarchies: Comparative Perspectives on the Rise of the Modern Industrial Enterprise,* ed. Chandler and Daems (Cambridge, Mass.: Harvard Univ. Press, 1980), 1–2, 4, 6; and Gareth Morgan, *Images of Organization,* 2nd ed. (London: Sage, 1997), 325–26, 329; Buder, *Capitalizing on Change,* 366 (quote, "imperial CEO").

48. In fact, in contrast to U.S.-based international corporations, many European multinationals tended to allow their overseas companies a fair degree of autonomy; see G. Jones, *Multinationals and Global Capitalism,* 293. Percy, interview, May 13, 2004; Schaefer, interview, Mar. 5, 2004.

49. Percy, interview, May 13, 2004; Schaefer, interview, Mar. 5, 2004; Walpole, interview, Oct. 7, 2007.

50. Schaefer, interview, Mar. 5, 2004; Percy, interview, May 13, 2004; R. Thomas, "Heartbreak in Sundown City"; Becky Yerak, "BP Selling Rockefeller Legacy: Lima Refinery," *Cleveland Plain Dealer,* Jan. 12, 1996; also see Hans De Jongh, "BP to Slash Over-Capacity," *Daily Telegraph* (Sydney, Australia), Jan. 12, 1996; Patrick Donovan, ""BP to Write off $1BN in Refineries Shake-Up," *Guardian* (London), Jan. 12, 1996. Percy later disagreed with Schaefer's characterization that the sale was a concession that London had made; Percy, interview, May 13, 2004.

51. Phillip C. Pina, "Refinery Looking for Another Successful Year," *Lima News,* Feb. 24, 1991; Bart Mills, "BP Discounts Closing Rumor," *Lima News,* Aug. 30, 1990; Jerry Hertenstein, "BP Workers Feel Safe—For Now," *Lima News,* July 9, 1992; Pina, "BP Official"; Claire Chapman, "BP Holds Steady," *Lima News,* June 6, 1995; Jennifer Lawson, "BP: A Question of Costs," *Lima News,* Dec. 10, 1995; Associated Press, "BP Earnings Spurt Past $2 Billion," *Lima News,* Feb. 15, 1995.

52. P. Thomas, "A Town Is Buffeted by Global Crosswinds" (quote, "spectacular"); Mike Mender, "Industry: BP Officials Remain Dubious Despite Painting a Rosy Picture of the Facility in Their Literature," *Lima News,* Nov. 21, 1996 (Schaefer and Atton quoted).

53. Berger, interview, Mar. 18, 2004 (quoted); Schaefer, interview, Mar. 5, 2004.

54. Berger, interview, Mar. 18, 2004 (quoted); Berger, "My Chronology," diary entry for Aug. 12, 1998, DBP, LMB.

55. Berger, interview, Mar. 18, 2004; Berger, "My Chronology," diary entry for Jan. 10, 1997, DBP, LMB.

56. Berger handwritten notes dated June 19, 1995, and fall 1995, in "BP—My Notes" folder, DBP, LMB; Berger, interview, Mar. 18, 2004; Corzine, "BP Launches Refinery Shake-Up"; Berger to Browne, Nov. 20, 1995, in "BP—My Correspondence" folder, DBP, LMB.

57. Berger, "Meeting Regarding Future of Lima Refinery," Nov. 29, 1995, attachment to Berger to Percy, Dec. 1, 1995, in "BP—Correspondence with Me" folder, DBP, LMB.

58. Berger, "Meeting Regarding Future of Lima Refinery"; Berger, interview, Mar. 18, 2004.

59. Percy, interview, May 13, 2004; Berger to Percy, Jan. 19, 1996, and "BP Announces Outcome of International Refining Study," both in "BP—Correspondence with Me" folder, DBP, LMB.

60. De Jongh, "BP to Slash Over-Capacity" (quote, "three-year over-capacity"); "British Petroleum to Drop 3 Refineries," *New York Times,* Jan. 12, 1996; "BP Takes Huge Charge," *The Gazette* (Montreal), Jan. 12, 1996; Robert Corzine, "BP to Shed Refineries and Cut Capacity by 30 Per Cent," *Financial Times* (London), Jan. 12, 1996 (quote, "the top 25 per cent"); Donovan, "BP to Write Off $1BN" (quote, "was an option"); "Popular Shares: British Petroleum," *Investors Chronicle,* Jan. 26, 1996, 44; P. Thomas, "A Town Is Buffeted by Global Crosswinds."

61. Yerak, "BP Selling Rockefeller Legacy"; George Stein, "Lima's Mayor Thrusts Himself into New Role: Finding a Buyer," *Platt's Oilgram News,* Mar. 26, 1996, 8; Berger, interview,

Mar. 18, 2004; Roller, interview, Apr. 28, 2004; Martie MacDonel, oral interview by author, May 19, 2004; Schaefer interview, Mar. 5, 2004; R. Thomas, "Heartbreak in Sundown City" (workers' view of Schaefer).

62. Berger, interview, Mar. 18, 2004; James Schaefer, "Refinery Should Be Attractive to Potential Buyers," *Lima News,* Feb. 4, 1996; Alan Kovski, "Government Officials Get Behind BP's Effort to Sell 170,000 b/d Refinery in Lima, Ohio," *The Oil Daily,* Feb. 20, 1996.

63. "Article for February Edition of BP Today Regarding Sale of Lima Refinery," attached to Berger to Voinovich, Sept. 29, 1996, in "BP—Correspondence with Me" folder, DBP, LMB; "BP Oil Exec Named CFO of BP America," *Cleveland Plain Dealer,* May 7, 1994; Walpole, interview, Oct. 7, 2007 (on Atton).

64. David Atton and James Schaefer, "Update for Area Media: Lima Refinery Sale," Sept. 12, 1996, in "BP—Correspondence with Me" folder, DBP, LMB; R. Thomas, "Heartbreak in Sundown City"; Berger, interview, Mar. 18, 2004 (quoted).

65. Robert Paisley, oral interview by author, Oct. 29, 2005.

66. Berger, interview, Mar. 18, 2004 (quoted); David Drum, oral interview by author, Apr. 23, 2004.

67. Berger, "My Chronology," diary entry for July 17, 1997, DBP, LMB.

68. Berger to Browne, Apr. 9, 1996, and Browne to Berger, Apr. 16, 1996, both in "BP—Correspondence with Me" folder, DBP, LMB; Berger interview, Mar. 18, 2004 (quote, "If you're selling something").

69. Berger, interview, Mar. 18, 2004.

70. Berger, interview, Mar. 18, 2004; Berger to Percy, Sept. 13, 1996, in "BP—Correspondence with Me" folder, DBP, LMB.

71. Berger to Voinovich, Sept. 20, 1996, in "BP—Correspondence with Me" folder, DBP, LMB.

72. Berger, interview, Mar. 18, 2004; Schaefer, interview, Mar. 17, 2004; Stanley Reed and Gary McWilliams, "BP: A Well-Oiled Machine," *Business Week,* May 26, 1997, 80. I remembered the last line of this paragraph from the old *Los Angeles Times* sports columnist Jim Murray, who wrote it sometime in the early 1970s in reference to the onetime baseball commissioner Bowie Kuhn.

73. Reed and McWilliams, "BP: A Well-Oiled Machine"; "BP Sets Focus on Financial Goals, Core Assets," 24; John R. Brandt, "Level the Playing Field in Politics," *Industry Week,* Oct. 2002, 21; Yerak, "BP Oil Kicking Its Way to Future." I have borrowed the conceptualization of these last three paragraphs from Lawrence Goodwyn, *The Populist Moment: A Short History of the Agrarian Revolt in America* (New York: Oxford Univ. Press, 1978), 212.

74. David Berger, e-mail letter to author, Apr. 23, 2004, in author's possession.

6. "It Was Like a Death—to the Town"

1. High, *Industrial Sunset,* 93.

2. Paisley, interview, Oct. 29, 2005; Don Kuenzli, e-mail to author, July 13, 2005, in author's possession. Also, on the relative advantages of sour versus sweet crude oil, see Mike Mender, "Industry: BP Officials Remain Dubious Despite Painting a Rosy Picture of the Facility in Their Literature," *Lima News,* Nov. 21, 1996.

3. Mender, "Industry: BP Officials Remain Dubious" (quote, Lima as "top quartile"); Mike Mender, "BP Bidder Fell Short in Funding," *Lima News,* Nov. 16, 1996 (Ashland and Marathon interest); Berger, interview, Mar. 18, 2004; Paisley, interview, Oct. 29, 2005; Becky Yerak, "Lima Fuming at BP," *Cleveland Plain Dealer,* May 4, 1997 (Nobile quoted). On the state of the bids by mid-September, also see Atton and Schafer, "Update for Area Media:

Lima Refinery Sale," Sept. 12, 1996, in "BP—Correspondence with Me" folder, DBP, LMB.

4. Senior BP executive, oral interview by author, July 30, 2004; responses from Steven Percy and David Atton in "Letters to BP," *Lima News,* Nov. 19, 1996; Mike Mender, "BP Will Not Delay Plans to Close Plant," *Lima News,* Nov. 19, 1996.

5. Senior BP executive, interview, July 30, 2004; Donovan Kuenzli, oral interview by author, July 13, 2005.

6. Gilbert, interview, June 17, 2005.

7. Voinovich to Percy, Sept. 24, 1996, and Browne to Berger, Oct. 15, 1996, both in "BP—Correspondence with Me" folder, DBP, LMB; Mike Mender, "BP: Tale a Tangled Web; Refinery's Demise: Letters Reveal Oil Giant's Shift in Attitudes Toward Lima Facility," *Lima News,* Feb. 2, 1997 (Browne and Percy quoted); Memo to file, voice mail from Steven Percy, Oct. 15, 1996 (quote, "precipitous"), Berger to Browne, Oct. 24, 1996, Berger to Voinovich, Oct. 25, 1996, and Jakeway to Berger, Oct. 31, 1996, all in "BP—Correspondence with Me" folder, DBP, LMB; Berger, interview, Mar. 18, 2004 (quote, "non-priority status").

8. Berger, "My Chronology," diary entry for Feb. 1, 1997 (Berger's sources), DBP, LMB; Mender, "BP: Tale a Tangled Web" (quote, "playing the part of the good soldier"); David Berger, oral interview by author, July 7, 2005 (quote, "things happened"); Berger, "My Chronology," diary entry for July 19, 1997, DBP, LMB. While Walpole doubted this was the case, Kuenzli also understood that Atton had gone to London preparing to recommend that BP accept the Paisley bid. Walpole, interview, Oct. 7, 2007; Kuenzli, interview, July 13, 2005.

9. Gilbert, interviews, Mar. 10 and June 17, 2005.

10. Paisley, interview, Oct. 29, 2005.

11. Ibid.

12. Ibid.; copy of fax, Paisley to Atton, Nov. 5, 1996 (quote, "shuttle diplomacy"), in "BP—Correspondence with Me" folder, DBP, LMB.

13. Paisley, interview, Oct. 29, 2005; Yerak, "Lima Fuming at BP" (Dove quoted); Drum, interview, Apr. 23, 2004.

14. Berger, interview, Mar. 18, 2004 (Berger quoted); David Berger, e-mail to author, May 30, 2006, in author's possession.

15. Memo to file, "Re: Telephone conversation with Steve Percy, President of B.P. America," Nov. 6, 1996, in "BP—Correspondence with Me" folder, DBP, LMB; Mender, "BP: Tale a Tangled Web."

16. Gilbert, interview, June 17, 2005.

17. James Schaefer, oral interview by author, June 6, 2006.

18. Daniel Groman, oral interview by author, Mar. 9, 2005; Ameet Sachdev, "Ashland Called Likely Buyer of BP Plant," *Lexington (Ky.) Herald Leader,* Oct. 8, 1996; Peter Zipf, "Ashland Wants A 'Role' in Future of BP's Lima Plant," *Platt's Oilgram News,* May 15, 1996, 1; Roller, interview, Apr. 28, 2004.

19. Percy to Lima refinery employee, Nov. 8, 1996, Judy Gilbert Papers, copy in author's possession; Groman, interview, Mar. 9, 2005; Percy, interview, May 13, 2004; Gilbert, interview, Mar. 10, 2005; Roller, interview, Apr. 28, 2004; Hans Houshower, *A Voyage beyond the Horizon and Back: The Heartland Refinery's Continuous Improvement Story* (Cambridge, Mass.: Society for Organizational Learning, 1999), 46–47 (quoted); Mike Mender, "Workers Stunned by Decision," *Lima News,* Nov. 9, 1996.

20. Jennifer Lawson, "The Market: Oil Refiners Face a Host of Problems That Stand in the Way of Profits," *Lima News,* Nov. 9, 1996 (Atton and industry expert quoted); Darren Waggoner, "Company Ditches Possibility of Selling Refinery," *Lima News,* Nov. 9, 1996 (Atton quotes, "hardly any money," "close to zero," and "clean break"); Paisley, interview, Oct.

29, 2005. Walpole also understood that the major problem with Paisley's bid was that it lacked deep enough financial resources to protect BP from future legal liabilities. Walpole, interview, Oct. 7, 2007.

21. Darren Waggoner, "Closing Will Have Far-Reaching Impact," *Lima News*, Nov. 10, 1996 (Rex and retiree quoted).

22. Mender, "BP Will Not Delay Plans" (quote, "make this fair)"; Waggoner, "Company Ditches Possibility" (quote, "lucky to be given"); Atton, "Op-Ed column: BP Has No Choice But to Close Lima Refinery," *Lima News*, Nov. 22, 1996 (quotes, "generous" and "at least"); Bart Mills, "Charities: Oil Giant Has Long Been the Largest Single Contributor to the United Way and Other Groups," *Lima News*, Nov. 9, 1996; Ronald Lederman, "BP Will Pay Tax through 2000," *Lima News*, Feb. 26, 1997; R. Thomas, "Heartbreak in Sundown City" (quote, "bending over backwards").

23. Kenneth Belcher and A. D. MacDonel to Donald Jakeway, Dec. 9, 1996, published in *Lima News*, Dec. 18, 1996 (refinery payroll); Thomas Gerdel, "BP Closing Its Lima Refinery," *Cleveland Plain Dealer*, Nov. 9, 1996; Yerak, "Lima Fuming at BP" (Twining quoted); William Lodermeier to staff, Feb. 20, 1997 (Shawnee statistics), in "BP Task Force" folder, DBP, LMB.

24. Belcher and MacDonel to Jakeway, Dec. 9, 1996 (ripple effects statistics); Response from Lima Utilities Department to Chamber of Commerce Questionnaire, Nov. 22, 1996, in "BP Task Force" folder, DBP, LMB; Mike Mender, "Shellshock Wearing Off," *Lima News*, Nov. 22, 1996 (Buckeye Pipeline); M. Cooper, "A Town Betrayed," 12 (total economic cost of closure).

25. Waggoner, "Closing Will Have Far-Reaching Impact" (resident quoted); Gilbert, interview, Mar. 10, 2005 (quoted).

26. Editorial, "BP Owes Lima Some Answers," *Lima News*, Nov. 12, 1996.

27. Mike Mender, "BP Battle Plan Forming: Task Force Formed to Find Buyer for the Refinery," *Lima News*, Nov. 13, 1996; BP Task Force Meeting minutes, Nov. 12, 1996, in "BP Task Force" folder, DBP, LMB; Kenneth Belcher, oral interview by author, Aug. 17, 2004.

28. Mender, "BP Battle Plan Forming" (Cunningham and union official quoted).

29. BP Task Force Meeting minutes, Nov. 15 (Dove meeting), Nov. 20, Nov. 26, and Dec. 4, 1996, in "BP Task Force" folder, DBP, LMB; Mike Mender, "BP Task Force Gets to Work," *Lima News*, Nov. 14, 1996; Mender, "BP Bidder Fell Short in Funding," *Lima News*, Nov. 16, 1996 (Dove and Berger quoted).

30. Belcher, interview, Aug. 17, 2004; Berger, handwritten notes on Dec. 14, 1996, meeting with Atton at the Chamber of Commerce, and Atton to Belcher and MacDonel, Nov. 29, 1996, both in "BP Task Force" folder, DBP, LMB; Mike Mender, "BP Will Not Delay Plans to Close Plant" (Percy quoted); Mender, "BP Outlines Bidding Criteria," *Lima News*, Nov. 27, 1996 (Atton quoted); Mender, "Group Assesses 'No Sale' Fallout," *Lima News*, Dec. 12, 1996 (quote, "unspoken message").

31. Belcher, interview, Aug. 17, 2004; P. Thomas, "A Town Is Buffeted by Global Crosswinds."

32. Responses from Percy and Atton in "Letters to BP"; Mike Mender, ""BP Will Not Delay Plans to Close Plant" (Percy quoted); Groman, interview, Mar. 9, 2005; Gilbert, interview, Mar. 10, 2005; P. Thomas, "A Town Is Buffeted by Global Crosswinds" (Lima improvements spread worldwide); Belcher, interview, Aug. 17, 2004; Berger, interview, Mar. 18, 2004.

33. Mike Mender, "Berger Says BP Balking at Sale," *Lima News*, Dec. 4, 1996; Belcher and MacDonel to Jakeway, Dec. 9, 1996; Percy, interview, May 13, 2004; David J. Atton, "Editorial: BP Has No Choice But to Close Lima Refinery," *Lima News*, Nov. 22, 1996. BP people like Kuenzli, Paisley, and Schaefer reiterated that BP executives had to abide by the confidentiality agreements they had signed; BP "wasn't that devious," said Kuenzli. Kuenzli, interview, July 13, 2005; Paisley, interview, Oct. 29, 2005; Schaefer, interview, June 6, 2006.

34. Paisley, interview, Oct. 29, 2005. "If you don't want to get something done you can always come up with lots of reasons," Schaefer said. "You can always find company lawyers to tell you why something won't work." Schaefer, interview, June 6, 2006.

35. Belcher and MacDonel to Jakeway, Dec. 9, 1996 (quoted); Belcher, interview, Aug. 17, 2004.

36. Gilbert, interview, June 17, 2005 (quoted); Berger, interview, July 7, 2005; Belcher, interview, Aug. 17, 2004 (quoted); Mike Mender, "Support, Anger Vented," *Lima News*, Dec. 17, 1996 (Berger quoted).

37. Belcher, interview, Aug. 17, 2004; Mender, "Support, Anger Vented" (Berger and signs quoted); Gilbert, interview, June 17, 2005 (quoted); Berger interview, July 7, 2005 (quoted).

38. "Refinery Task Force Community meeting, Dec. 16, 1996, Agenda," draft, Dec. 5, 1996, in "BP Task Force" folder, DBP, LMB; Belcher, interview, Aug. 17, 2004.

39. Gilbert, interview, June 17, 2005; Monus, interview, Apr. 8, 2004; Mender, "Support, Anger Vented."

40. Senior BP executive, interview by author, July 30, 2004; Percy, interview, May 13, 2004; Paisley, interview, Oct. 29, 2005; Walpole, interview, Oct. 7, 2007; Belcher and MacDonel to Jakeway, Dec. 9, 1996 (on Lima refinery percentage of BP gasoline sales).

41. Undated memo, no author, on BP/Teppco relationship, in "BP—Correspondence with Me" folder, DBP, LMB; Berger, interview, Mar. 18, 2004 (quoted).

42. Belcher and MacDonel to Jakeway, Dec. 9, 1996 (quoted); "BP Says $235-mil Toledo Refinery Upgrade on Track," *Platt's Global Alert Service*, Jan 22, 1997, 1 (possible closure of Toledo refinery), in "BP Media Coverage" folder, DBP, LMB.

43. Mike Mender, "Ohio BP Refineries Manager Out of Job," *Lima News*, Nov. 21, 1996 (Percy quoted); Schaefer, interview, Mar. 4, 2004 (Stomberg quoted); Kuenzli, interview, July 13, 2005; R. Thomas, "Heartbreak in Sundown City" (workers' regard for Schaefer); Roller, interview, Apr. 28, 2004 (Schaefer quoted); Streitfeld, "Rank-and-File Style," 13–14.

44. Mender, "Group Assesses 'No Sale' Fallout" (on task force); Belcher, interview, Aug. 17, 2004 (quoted); five-week timetable in BP Task Force Meeting minutes, Dec. 14, 1996, in "BP Task Force" folder, DBP, LMB; Bernie Woodall and Antoine Halff, "BP Bid to Sell Lima Plant Masked Pipeline Plan, Group Says," *Oil Price Information Service*, Dec. 20, 1996, 28187, in "BP Media Coverage" folder, DBP, LMB.

7. "Whether We're for BP or against BP, We All Sound Conspiratorial"

1. Sirianni and Friedland, *Civic Innovation in America*, 13–14 (quoted, 13); Nissen, *Fighting for Jobs*, 170–71. For case studies of these dynamics operating in responses to plant closings in other industrial communities in this era, see the individual case studies in Nissen, *Fighting for Jobs*, and in Craypo and Nissen, *Grand Designs*.

2. Nissen, *Fighting for Jobs*, 166–67, 170–71 (quoted, 171); Craypo and Nissen, *Grand Designs*, 248–50 (quoted, 248); Belcher, interview, Aug. 17, 2004 (quoted).

3. Thomas Mullen, oral interview by author, Sept. 27, 2005 (Mullen quoted); Thomas Lucente, editorial, *Lima News*, Sept. 24, 2000 (quote, "lying crook"); Lucente, editorial, "Time for a Change in the White House," *Lima News*, Nov. 5, 2000 (quote, "cesspool"); Lucente, editorial, "Al Gore a Pathological Liar," *Lima News*, Oct. 8, 2000; Lucente, editorial, "Clinton Was an Embarrassment as President," *Lima News*, Jan. 20, 2001.

4. Mullen, interview, Sept. 27, 2005 (quoted); Mullen's background in "Excerpts from remarks by Tom Mullen at his retirement luncheon in Colorado Springs," Sept. 23, 2004, and letter, Tom Mullen to author, Sept. 16, 2005, copies of both in author's possession.

5. Mullen, interview, Sept. 27, 2005 (quoted); Berger interview, July 7, 2005 (quoted).

6. Mullen, interview, Sept. 27, 2005 (quoted); Berger, interview, July 7, 2005 (quoted). Mullen agreed generally with Berger's account of the events of that meeting, but the specifics of the exchange came mostly from Berger.

7. Mullen, editorial, "BP Owes Lima Some Answers"; Berger, interview, July 7, 2005 (quoted). For "anonymous source" references, see Mender, "BP: Oil Giant Had Idea to Close Site in February," and Mender, "BP: Tale A Tangled Web"; Berger, "My Chronology," diary entries for Jan. 19 and 21, 1997 (quoted), DBP, LMB; Mullen, interview, Sept. 27, 2005; Thomas Mullen to William Thacker, Jan. 23, 1997, in "BP Task Force" folder, DBP, LMB.

8. Mullen to Thacker, Jan. 23, 1997; Berger, interview, July 7, 2005; Belcher, interview, Aug. 17, 2004 (quoted).

9. Antoine Halff, "Ohio Gov. Joins Bid to Block Lima Refinery Closure," *Oil Price Information Service,* Jan. 15, 1997, 2–4, in "BP Phelps" folder, DBP, LMB.

10. Berger, interview, July 7, 2005 (quoted); Mike Mender, "State to Help Seek a Buyer for Lima Site," *Lima News,* Dec. 18, 1996 (Jakeway quoted).

11. Mike Mender, "Development Officer Separates Refinery from Pipeline Issue," *Lima News,* Dec. 20, 1996 (Jakeway and Belcher quoted); Donald Jakeway, Letter to the Editor: "State to Lima: Focus on Future, Let BP Pursue Its Best Interest," *Lima News,* Dec. 22, 1996; Berger, "My Chronology," diary entry for Jan. 9, 1997, DBP, LMB; Clarence Roller, "Viewpoint: Jakeway's Letter Shows State's Inaction over BP's Lima Plans," *Lima News,* Jan. 2, 1997.

12. Berger, interview, July 7, 2005 (lobbyist and Berger quoted).

13. "Voinovich, George V.," in *Current Biography Yearbook* 58 (Bronx, N.Y.: H. W. Wilson), 57–59; Thomas Suddes, "Panorama of Ohio Politics in the Voinovich Era, 1991–1996," in *Ohio Politics,* ed. Alexander P. Lamis (Kent, Ohio: Kent State Univ. Press, 1994), 157–59; Voinovich to Percy, Sept. 24, 1996, and Jan. 7, 1997 (fax), both in "BP—Correspondence with Me" folder, DBP, LMB; BP senior executive, interview, July 30, 2004; J. Kenneth Blackwell, Ohio Secretary of State, Campaign Finance Database, search results for "Voinovich, George," http://serform.sos.state.oh.us/pls/porthope/DEV.RPT_CAND_CONT.show (accessed Apr. 21, 2004) (BP 1990 contributions); Center for Responsive Politics, Detailed Contributor Breakdown, 2000 cycle, for "Voinovich, George V.," http://www.opensecrets.org/politicians/detail.asp?CID=N00003583&cycle=2000 (accessed Apr. 15, 2004) (BP 2000 contributions).

14. Voinovich to Percy, Jan. 7, 1997 (Voinovich quoted); Mike Mender, "Voinovich Weighs In to Save Refinery," *Lima News,* Jan. 10, 1997 (Voinovich quoted).

15. Berger, interview, July 7, 2005 (quoted); Mullen, interview, Sept. 27, 2005 (quoted); Schaefer, interview, June 6, 2006; Mike Mender, "Task Force: Party Interested in BP Refinery," *Lima News,* Jan. 3, 1997; Mike Mender, "BP Buyer Emerges," *Lima News,* Jan. 18, 1997.

16. Berger, "My Chronology," diary entries for Jan. 8 (Phelps and Jakeway quoted), and 9, 1997 (Voinovich quoted), DBP, LMB.

17. Berger, "My Chronology," diary entries for Jan. 10 and 17, 1997 (Berger quoted), DBP, LMB; Berger, interview, July 7, 2005.

18. Berger, "My Chronology," diary entries for Jan. 10, 12, 14 (quote, "the first headline"), 15, and 17, 1997, DBP, LMB; Mender, "BP Buyer Emerges" (Berger quoted).

19. Berger, "My Chronology," diary entries for Jan. 18 (quote, "it was great!"), and 21, 1997 (quote, "We had spent weeks"), DBP, LMB; Mike Mender and Ronald Lederman, "Task Force Gains Time," *Lima News,* Jan. 23, 1997 (effects of bargaining agreement).

20. James Norman, "Corco's Phelps Joins Fray for BP's Lima," *Platt's Oilgram News,* Jan. 22, 1997; Berger, "My Chronology," diary entry for Jan. 23, 1997, DBP, LMB; Schaefer, interview, June 6, 2006 (on Sheperd); Mike Mender, "In a Word: Disappointment," *Lima News,* Jan. 31, 1997 (on Phelps's anger).

21. Berger, "My Chronology," diary entries for Jan. 23 (quote, "insider jargon"), and 27, 1997, DBP, LMB.

22. Mike Mender, "Refinery Offer Revealed," and Mender, "Phelps Defends His Firm Against 'Vulture' Charges" (Berger quoted), both in *Lima News*, Jan. 24, 1997.

23. Berger, "My Chronology," diary entry for Jan. 24, 1997 (Phelps quoted), DBP, LMB; Darren Waggoner, Jennifer Lawson, and Mike Mender, "BP Denies Disparaging Phelps," *Lima News*, Jan. 25, 1997 (Atton quoted). Nearly a decade later, Percy was emphatic in denying that, to his knowledge at least, anyone at BP had anything to do with the "vulture investor" charges. Percy, interview, May 13, 2004.

24. Berger, "My Chronology," diary entries for Jan. 29 (quote, "day is not over"), 30 (Phelps to Berger), and 31, 1997 (on Jakeway), DBP, LMB; Darren Waggoner, "BP Deal Ends," *Lima News*, Jan. 31, 1997; Halff, "Ohio Gov. Joins Bid" (Little quoted).

25. Berger, "My Chronology," diary entries for Jan. 30 (quoted on Shreefer), Feb. 6, 20, Mar. 7, 26, and Jan. 31, 1997 (on Jakeway), DBP, LMB; editorial, "BP Remains the Real Issue," *Lima News*, Jan. 31, 1997.

26. Senior BP executive, interview, July 30, 2004; Associated Press, "BP Did Not Intend to Sell Refinery," *Cleveland Plain Dealer*, Feb. 1, 1997 (too late); Waggoner, "BP Deal Ends."

27. Berger, interview, July 7, 2005.

28. Ibid.; Gilbert, interview, June 17, 2005; Berger, "My Chronology," diary entries for Jan. 31 (quote, "fronting for BP"), and Feb. 1, 1997, DBP, LMB; M. Cooper, "A Town Betrayed," 14 (Mullen quoted).

29. Ronald Lederman and Mike Mender, "BP Task Force Mum," *Lima News*, Feb. 13, 1997; Belcher, interview, Aug. 17, 2004 (quoted); Berger, "My Chronology," diary entry for Feb. 12, 1997, DBP, LMB; Berger, handwritten notes, "BP task force mtg, 3/5/97" (on Atton), in "BP Task Force" folder, DBP, LMB; Lederman, "BP Task Force Turns to Committees," *Lima News*, Mar. 6, 1997 (BP transferring workers).

30. Berger, "My Chronology," diary entries for Jan. 13 (Kaptur meeting, Kaptur quoted), Feb. 13 (fuel boycott), and 14, 1997 (Oxley quoted), DBP, LMB; Berger, interview, July 7, 2005 (antitrust attempt).

31. Roller, interview, Apr. 28, 2004; "A Timely Perspective: The Refinery and the Community," *Lima News*, Sept. 27, 1998; Gilbert, interview, Mar. 10, 2005; Kuenzli, interview, July 13, 2005.

32. Lyn Oxyer, "Plant Forges Family Ties," *Lima News*, Sept. 27, 1998; M. Cooper, "A Town Betrayed," 14 (Winterstellar quoted).

33. Ronald Lederman, "Union: BP Ignoring Pact," *Lima News*, May 13, 1997; M. Cooper, "A Town Betrayed," 14 (Lombardo and refinery task force member quoted); OCAW trips found in Task Force Meeting minutes, May 7, 1997, in "BP Task Force" folder, DBP, LMB; Darren Waggoner, "BP Workers Seek 'Higher Help,'" *Lima News*, May 19, 1997; Ronald Lederman, "Union to Shun Products of BP," *Lima News*, June 5, 1997.

34. Berger, "My Chronology," diary entry for Feb. 15, 1997 (rumors), DBP, LMB; "BP Delays Supply Notice," *Lima News*, Feb. 22, 1997; Task Force Meeting minutes, May 7, 1997; Ronald Lederman, "Petroleum Carrier Says BP Talks Off," *Lima News*, May 30, 1997.

35. "Pipeline Projects Reflect Changing Nature of US Refining," *Octane Week*, Sept. 15, 1997; Senior BP executive, interview, July 30, 2004.

36. Berger, interviews, Mar. 18, 2004, July 7, 2005; Kuenzli, interview, July 13, 2005; Berger, "My Chronology," diary entries for Feb. 15 and June 2, 1997, DBP, LMB. On the other hand, Walpole dismissed the possibility that BP might have overlooked the potential problem of ICC regulations. Walpole, interview, Oct. 7, 2007.

37. Berger, interview, July 7, 2005 (quote, "it needed to be seen"); Mullen, interview, Sept. 27, 2005; Berger, "My Chronology," diary entry for Jan. 24, 1997 (quoted), DBP, LMB. On the full exposé of Berger's correspondence, see Mender, "BP: Tale a Tangled Web."

38. Berger, interview, July 7, 2005; Mullen, interview, Sept. 27, 2005; Berger, "My Chronology," diary entry for Jan. 24, 1997, DBP, LMB; P. Thomas, "A Town Is Buffeted by Global Crosswinds" (Atton and Mosier quoted).

39. Berger, "My Chronology," diary entry for Apr. 18, 1997 (quote, "suitably cynical") DBP, LMB; Yerak, "Lima Fuming at BP."

40. Berger, "My Chronology," diary entry for Mar. 27, 1997 (quote, "Christmas cards"), DBP, LMB; R. Thomas, "Heartbreak in Sundown City" (Berger quoted).

41. Berger, "My Chronology," diary entries for May 15 and June 26, 1997, DBP, LMB; M. Cooper, "A Town Betrayed," 11 (Berger quoted).

42. M. Cooper, "A Town Betrayed," 12 (Belcher and Berger quoted), and 15 (Mullen quoted).

43. BP senior executive, interview, July 30, 2004; Berger, "My Chronology," diary entries for May 15 and June 26, 1997 (*60 Minutes* possibilities), and June 3 and July 15, 1997 (Greve comments), DBP, LMB; Gilbert, interview, June 17, 2005.

44. Berger, "My Chronology," diary entries for Jan. 30 (county commissioner worries), and June 3, 1997 (Greve charges), DBP, LMB; Belcher, interview, Aug. 17, 2004; Mullen, interview, Sept. 27, 2005.

45. Ronald Lederman, "Touched by Downsizing: A Dad's Question," *Lima News,* June 15, 1997; Ronald Lederman, "Lima Refinery Workers Once Stood Tall and Proud, But Waiting for Closure Is Taking a Toll on Morale, Families," *Lima News,* June 15, 1997; Groman, interview, Mar. 9, 2005.

46. Gilbert, interview, June 17, 2005; James W. Walpole, "BP and the Community," BPC Nitriles Management Conference, Aug. 12, 1997, Gilbert Papers, copy in author's possession; "HS&E Communications Tracking—All Sites" (polling data), in "BP Post-Closure Announcement" folder, DBP, LMB; Berger, "My Chronology," diary entry for June 3, 1997 (Greve encounter, Berger quoted), DBP, LMB.

47. Berger, "My Chronology," diary entries for June 3 and July 19, 1997, DBP, LMB; Berger, interview, July 7, 2005; Noreen Warnock, letter to the editor, "More Research Needed about Area's Health" *Lima News,* July 19, 1997; Elizabeth Rogers, "Cleaning Up Superfund Law," *ABA Journal* 83 (Dec. 1997): 91; Hope Whitney, "Cities and Superfund: Encouraging Brownfield Redevelopment," *Ecology Law Review* 30, no. 1 (2003): 68–69; Paisley, interview, Oct. 29, 2005.

48. Percy, interview, May 13, 2004; Becky Yerak, "BP Moving CEO to New York," *Cleveland Plain Dealer,* Feb. 19, 1997; MacDonel, interview, May 19, 2004 (quote, "barracuda"); Kuenzli, interview, July 13, 2005; Gilbert, interview, June 17, 2005; Berger, "My Chronology," diary entries for May 12 (Greve descriptions), and June 3, 1997 (quote, "do more research"), DBP, LMB.

49. Gilbert, interview, June 17, 2005; Kuenzli, interview, July 13, 2005.

50. Gilbert, interview, June 17, 2005. Greve had served in Lima in the 1980s when the refinery and the community, Schaefer said, "just had a wonderful relationship." Because of this previous experience, he would have been uniquely situated among senior BP executives to realize the extent of the community's animus against his company now. Schaefer, interview, June 6, 2006. Walpole remembered the chain of events somewhat differently. They had returned from France, he recalled, and were in a planning meeting at a resort near Cleveland when Greve approached him at a reception, wanting to know, "What's happening in Lima? I can't believe how bad BP is being treated in the media. Everyone's mad at us . . . How did we ever get in a position where the mayor and everyone hates BP?"

Walpole offered to pull together a group of a half-dozen people into a series of separate sessions, where, in two days of furious brainstorming, they produced what became the LIC. Walpole, interview, Oct. 7, 2007.

51. Berger, "My Chronology," diary entries for July 14 (quote, "think positive"), and 15, 1997 (quote, "Go hard"), DBP, LMB; Walpole, interview, Oct. 7, 2007. Although nobody in Lima knew it, the final permission for the Lima Integrated Complex project came from London only because Greve had flown there and argued for it. Senior BP executive, interview, July 30, 2004.

52. Ronald Lederman, "BP Unveils New Future," *Lima News,* July 17, 1997; Roller, interview, Apr. 28, 2004; "BP Notebook," *Lima News,* July 20, 1997 (quote, "Anything But Crude"); Walpole, interview, Oct. 7, 2007.

53. Darren Waggoner, "BP's Decision Tough Pill for Some Who Left Jobs," *Lima News,* July 17, 1997; Lederman, "BP Unveils New Future" (Berger and Winterstellar quoted); Jennifer Lawson, "Announcement Met with Relief, Guarded Optimism," *Lima News,* July 17, 1997 (quotes, "deal with a rattlesnake" and "not much to complain about"); Thomas Gerdel, "Nearby BP Plant Will Give Jobs to Many Lima Workers," *Cleveland Plain Dealer,* July 17, 1997 (United Way official); Jennifer Lawson, "Shawnee Schools Welcomes News," *Lima News,* July 17, 1997 (quote, "ecstatic").

54. Berger, "My Chronology," diary entry for July 16, 1997 (dialogue with Greve), DBP, LMB; Lima Integrated Complex, "BP and the Community: Blueprint for the Future," power-point slides, Aug. 25, 1997 (boilermaker photo), in Gilbert Papers, copy in author's possession; Darren Waggoner, "Upgrade Cost Spelled Lima Refinery's Doom," *Lima News,* July 17, 1997, and Ronald Lederman, "New BP Jobs May Be Much Like the Old," *Lima News,* July 18, 1997 (refinery closure rationales); Lederman, "Refinery Task Force Shifts Focus," *Lima News,* July 24, 1997 (Belcher).

55. Unpublished pamphlet, Lima Integrated Complex, "BP and the Community: A Shared Responsibility," Aug. 25, 1997 (Greve quoted, 1–2), in "BP Post-Closure Announcements" folder, DBP, LMB.

56. Lima Integrated Complex, "BP and the Community," 3–4 (Greve quoted); Jennifer Lawson, "BP Softens Departure," *Lima News,* Aug. 16, 1997 (D'Arcy Fund).

57. Mullen, interview, Sept. 27, 2005; Berger, "My Chronology," diary entries for July 22 and Aug. 25, 1997 (Berger and Sheffield quoted), DBP, LMB; Chad Lerch, "Board Will Work to Bring Business to BP Site," *Lima News,* Sept. 4, 1997; Ronald Lederman, "Refinery Workers' Security Growing, Manager Reports," *Lima News,* Nov. 6, 1997. Also, on other community perceptions that the mayor's efforts functioned as a lever resulting in the D'Arcy Fund, see Charles Fuller, letter to the editor, *Lima News,* Oct. 23, 1997.

58. "Oil Companies Likely to See Windfall from Gas Prices," *Cleveland Plain Dealer,* Sept. 2, 1997; Stanley Reed, "BP: A Well-Oiled Machine," *Business Week,* May 26, 1997, 80; "Company Results: British Petroleum," *Investors Chronicle,* Aug. 8, 1997, 52; Keith Cunningham, letter to the editor, *Lima News,* Aug. 30, 1997; Berger, "My Chronology," diary entry for Sept. 5, 1997 (on Cunningham), DBP, LMB.

59. Kuenzli, e-mail to author, July, 13, 2005 (quote, "great day"); Kuenzli, interview, July 13, 2005; Groman, interview, Mar. 9, 2005; Monus, interview, Apr. 8, 2004; Gilbert, interview, Mar. 10, 2005; Roller, interview, Apr. 28, 2004. Likewise, Berger noted in his diary comments from various officials from the OCAW local, who in September told him that "BP was playing hard ball on a wide variety of topics." Berger, "My Chronology," diary entry for Sept. 3, 1997, DBP, LMB.

60. Kuenzli, interview, July 13, 2005 (Watters quoted); Roller, interview, Apr. 28, 2004.

61. Kuenzli, interview, July 13, 2005; Houshower, *Voyage beyond the Horizon and Back,* 18, 49–50; Lederman, "Lima Refinery Workers Once Stood Tall and Proud, But Waiting for Closure Is Taking Toll on Morale, Families" (safety awards); Task Force Meeting minutes, Sept. 3, 1997 (refinery numbers), in "BP Task Force" folder, DBP, LMB; Berger, "My Chronology," diary entry for June 12, 1997 (BP profits), DBP, LMB; Hans Houshower, oral interview by author, Aug. 16, 2006 (outside observer).

62. Houshower, *Voyage beyond the Horizon and Back,* 49 (quote on gain-sharing), 51 (senior management official quoted); Gilbert, interview, June 17, 2005; Monus, interview, Apr. 8, 2004.

63. Kelly, *Divine Right of Capital,* 107–15 (Smith quoted, 109).

64. Monus, interview, Apr. 8, 2004; Groman, interview, Mar. 9, 2005; Kuenzli, e-mail response.

65. Gilbert, interview, June 17, 2005; Groman, interview, Mar. 9, 2005; Monus, interview, Apr. 8, 2004; Houshower, *Voyage beyond the Horizon and Back,* 48 (maintenance worker quoted).

66. Monus, interview, Apr. 8, 2004; Houshower, interview, Aug. 16, 2006 (quote, "idea factory").

67. Houshower, interview, Aug. 16, 2006; Houshower, introduction to *Voyage beyond the Horizon and Back,* iv; Roller, interview, Apr. 28, 2004.

68. Berger, interview, Mar. 18, 2004; Berger, interview, July 7, 2005 (quote, "I had a problem"); Jennifer Lawson, "Berger Breezes," *Lima News,* Nov. 5, 1997.

69. Ronald Lederman, "Bouncing Back: Economics Key in Construction of BDO Facility," *Lima News,* Nov. 20, 1997 (Greve quoted); editorial, "New BP Plant Backs Promise of Future Here," *Lima News,* Nov. 20, 1997 (Z-Day); Troy Flint, "BP Chemicals Lets Contract for Chemical Plant in Lima," *Cleveland Plain Dealer,* May 27, 1998 (Rockhold quoted); Berger, "My Chronology," diary entry for Dec. 1, 1998 (quote, "BP's toady"), DBP, LMB. Walpole contends that Lima landed the BDO addition not as a way for BP to get back in the community's good graces but instead, simply because, with most of the customers for BDO located in the upper Midwest, the economics made more sense. Walpole, interview, Oct. 7, 2007.

70. Editorial, "New BP Plant Backs Promise"; Lederman, "Bouncing Back" (Greve quoted).

71. Berger, "My Chronology," diary entry for Jan. 19, 1998, DBP, LMB; Schaefer, interview, June 6, 2006.

8. Victory

1. Berger, "My Chronology," diary entry for Jan. 22, 1998, DBP, LMB; Berger, interview, July 7, 2005.

2. David Berger, oral interview by author, Jan. 19, 2007.

3. Robert Payne, oral interview by author, Sept. 14, 2006; Berger, interview, Jan. 19, 2007; Berger, "My Chronology," diary entry for Jan. 23. 1998 (quote, "sham"), DBP, LMB.

4. Payne, interview, Sept. 14, 2006; Berger, interview, July 7, 2005, and Jan. 19, 2007; Berger, "My Chronology," diary entry for Jan. 23, 1998 (quote, "liability"), DBP, LMB.

5. Berger, "My Chronology," diary entries for Feb. 5 and 18, 1998, DBP, LMB; Payne, interview, Sept. 14, 2006 (quoted); Chad Lerch and Ronald Lederman, "Community Had Role in Clark Purchase," *Lima News,* Aug. 17, 1998 (task force involvement).

6. David A Stockman, *The Triumph of Politics: Why the Reagan Revolution Failed* (New York: Harper and Row, 1986), 80–81, 94–95, 135–36; William Greider, "Stockman Returneth,"

Nation, Apr. 2, 2001; Heartland Partners, "David A. Stockman: Founding Partner," http://www.heartlandpartners.com/managemnent/bios/david_stockman.shtml (accessed Jan. 12, 2004); Greider, *The Soul of Capitalism: Opening Paths to a Moral Economy* (New York: Simon and Schuster, 2003), 142–43; Payne, interview, Sept. 14, 2006.

7. Berger, "My Chronology," diary entry for Aug. 14, 1998, DBP, LMB; Berger, interview, Jan. 19, 2007; Payne, interview, Sept. 14, 2006.

8. Berger, "My Chronology," diary entries for Mar. 18 and 23, 1998, DBP, LMB; Payne, interview, Sept. 14, 2006.

9. Berger, "My Chronology," diary entry for Apr. 13, 1998, DBP, LMB; Payne, interview, Sept. 14, 2006; Berger, interview, Jan. 19, 2007; "Clark Attracts New Backing: The Blackstone Group to Fuel Growth," PR Newswire, Nov. 3, 1997; James Norman, "Blackstone Group Buys 65% Stake in US Refiner Clark," *Platt's Oilgram News*, Nov. 4, 1997, 1. "Marginal" is Payne's characterization of Clark's existing refineries. Payne, interview, Sept. 14, 2006. Later on, Stockman handed Berger an internal Blackstone/Clark "White Paper" they had compiled, which laid out the same kind of data Paisley had charted: the decline in refinery profitability through the late 1990s and (as it turned out, accurate) forecasts of increased refining margins that would begin to accelerate in the next decade. Berger, interview, Jan. 19, 2007.

10. Berger, "My Chronology," diary entries for Apr. 16 and 24, 1998, DBP, LMB. For a concise background summary of the entire secret sales process of the Lima refinery, see Thomas Petzinger Jr., "A Mayor's Mission: Tenacity Saves a Plant, a Town and a Future," *Wall Street Journal*, Dec. 11, 1998.

11. Schaefer, interview, June 6, 2006; Petzinger, "A Mayor's Mission." Browne and Wasserstein were apparently personal friends. Senior BP executive, interview, July 30, 2004.

12. Schaefer, interview, June 6, 2006; Berger, "My Chronology," diary entry for Apr. 27, 1998, DBP, LMB.

13. Berger, "My Chronology," diary entries for May 4 and 8, 1998, DBP, LMB; Payne, interview, Sept. 14, 2006 (quoted).

14. Berger, "My Chronology," diary entry for May 7, 1998, DBP, LMB.

15. Berger, "My Chronology," diary entry for May 15, 1998 (Stockman quoted), DBP, LMB.

16. Berger, "My Chronology," diary entries for May 26 (Browne quoted), and June 1, 1998 (Chase's instructions), DBP, LMB; Payne, interview, Sept. 14, 2006; Schaefer, interview, June 6, 2006. Nearly a decade later, Payne remembered Chase's warning about Berger as just that explicit. Payne, interview, Sept. 14, 2006.

17. Ronald Lederman, "Clark's Serious Talk Sped Up Process," *Lima News*, July 2, 1998; Berger, "My Chronology," diary entries for June 10, 19, and 29, 1998, DBP, LMB; Gilbert, interview, June 17, 2005; Berger, interview, Jan. 19, 2007 (quoted); Belcher, interview, Aug. 17, 2004; Mullen, interview, Sept. 27, 2005; Ronald Lederman, "Clark USA Will Keep Oil Flowing, Jobs Growing," *Lima News*, July 2, 1998. All Mullen knew was that Berger was still working frantically behind the scenes to find a buyer before BP demolished the refinery, and he didn't press the mayor for details. Mullen, interview, Sept. 27, 2005.

18. Berger, "My Chronology," diary entry for July 1, 1998 (Kuenzli and Conn quoted), DBP, LMB; Walpole, interview, Oct. 7, 2007; Berger, interview, Jan. 19, 2007.

19. Jennifer Arend, "BP Refinery Workers to Keep Jobs under New Owner," *Cleveland Plain Dealer*, July 2, 1998; Groman, interview, Mar. 9, 2005 (Kuenzli quoted); Roller, interview, Apr. 28, 2004 (quote, "straight out of the blue"); Robert Snell, "Employees Brace for 'Blind Date,'" *Lima News*, July 2, 1998 (quote, "demolishing the place"); Kuenzli, interview, July 13, 2005.

20. Berger, "My Chronology," diary entry for July 1, 1998 (Berger, Kuenzli ["sneaking suspicion"], and Conn ["some insight into your feelings"] quoted), DBP, LMB; Lederman,

Clark USA Will Keep Oil Flowing, Jobs Growing" (Conn ["long-term future" and "market bid"] and Kuenzli quoted). Even though they had been in the dark about the proceedings, plenty of people besides Kuenzli suspected Berger had been up to something. "I can't think of anyone who was not elated when he pulled off that deal with Clark," Gilbert said. "But getting there was stressful because we all knew he was working under the table. Everybody knew it . . . It was like the elephant in the room." Gilbert, interview, June 17, 2005.

21. Lederman, "Clark USA Will Keep Oil Flowing, Jobs Growing"; Berger, "My Chronology," diary entry for July 2, 1998 (WLIO coverage), DBP, LMB; David Johnston and Nicholas Towasser, "Lima Refinery Purchase to Add $1 Bill/Year to Sales: US' Clark," *Platt's Petrochemical Report,* July 9, 1998, 3; Payne, interview, Sept. 14, 2006.

22. Berger, "My Chronology," diary entries for Aug. 11 (quote, "shook my hand"), and Aug. 17, 1998 (quote, "humbling experience"), DBP, LMB; Mullen, interview, Sept. 27, 2005; Gilbert, interview, June 17, 2005; Schaefer, interview, June 6, 2006.

23. Groman, interview, Mar. 9, 2005 (on the crediting of Schaefer inside the refinery); undated power-point, no author but on Clark stationary, "Clark's Purchase of the Lima Refinery," in "Premcor, Misc." folder, DBP, LMB; Snell, "Employees Brace for 'Blind Date'" (Conn comments).

24. Berger, "My Chronology," diary entries for Aug. 11 and 12, 1998, DBP, LMB; "BP, Amoco to Join to Create Third Largest Public Oil Company," *Platt's Oilgram News,* Aug. 12, 1998, 1; John Affleck, "Bad Day for Cleveland," *Columbus Dispatch,* Aug. 12, 1998 (Browne quoted); Zach Miller, "BP to Buy Amoco, Leave Cleveland," *Cleveland Plain Dealer,* Aug. 12, 1998 (financial analyst quoted); Pratt, *Prelude to a Merger,* 1–2, 9–16.

25. Berger, "My Chronology," diary entry for Aug. 12, 1998, DBP, LMB; Berger, interview, Jan. 19, 2007; Bhushan Bahree, "As Fresh Prospects Dry Up, Petroleum Industry Strikes Deals"; Christopher Cooper, Bhushan Bahree, and Steven Liesman, "Why Arco Agreed to BP Merger—Oil Industry's Consolidation Forced Firm into Deal; Holders Get a Premium," *Wall Street Journal,* Apr. 2, 1999. On oil industry mergers in the 1990s, see Pratt, *Prelude to a Merger,* 7–8, 286; G. Jones, *Multinationals and Global Capitalism,* 70; and Roberts, *The End of Oil,* 51–59, 171, 177.

26. Bowen, "BP Is Back with a Rush"; Prokesch, "Now It's Bob Horton's Turn at B.P."; Mike Tobin, "Dead, Gone, and Global," *Inside Business,* Nov. 1998; Schaefer, interview, Mar. 12, 2004.

27. Berger, interview, Jan. 19, 2007 (quoted); senior BP executive, interview, July 30, 2004; Zach Schiller, "Move Was Only a Matter of Time" (Percy's knowledge). Kuenzli and Paisley also realized that the Amoco deal settled the alternate supply question. Kuenzli, interview, July 13, 2005; Paisley, interview, Oct. 29, 2005. Payne later estimated that the longer Blackstone delayed the deal with BP, the higher the price it would ultimately pay for the refinery. Payne estimated that just in the weeks between Stockman's initial "no" and his decision to pursue purchasing the plant, its price escalated by $25 million to $50 million. Payne, interview, Sept. 14, 2006.

28. Zach Schiller, "Bad Day for Cleveland" (quote, "promised that they would stay"); Angela Townsend, "BP to Get Amoco for $48B," *Dayton Daily News,* Aug. 12, 1998 (quote, "they gave us assurances"); Tobin, "Dead, Gone, and Global" (impact on Cleveland charities); Zach Schiller, "BP to Buy Amoco" (BP further contributions).

29. Sarah Livingston, "White, Voinovich Begin Fight to Retain BP Jobs," *Cleveland Plain Dealer,* Aug. 14, 1998; Ronald Lederman, "Was Lima Ignored? State Reacted Much Quicker to Cleveland," *Lima News,* Aug. 30, 1998; Tobin, "Dead, Gone, and Global" (development director quoted). Berger was especially indignant at the contrast between Voinovich's and

White's responses to BP's actions in Lima and in Cleveland. "Mike White wouldn't deal with me when we were in the midst of the crisis. Mike White's whole attitude was that BP is a good corporate citizen in my town and I'm not going to try to leverage that for your benefit." Berger, interview, Jan. 19, 2007.

30. This episode has been reconstructed from the handwritten notes Berger jotted down shortly afterward and from an interview with Berger. "Notes from mtg w/ John Brown," Sept. 30, 1999, in "BP—My Notes" folder, DBP, LMB; Berger, interview, Jan. 19, 2007.

31. Berger, "My Chronology," diary entries for Apr. 27, July 7, 8, 9, and 16, Aug. 12 (quote, "to be able to survive"), and 20, 1998 (quote, "earned their livelihoods"), DBP, LMB; Berger, interview, Jan. 19, 2007; Walpole, interview, Oct. 7, 2007 (quoted).

32. Berger, "My Chronology," diary entries for July 8, Aug. 12, and 20, 1998, DBP, LMB; Berger, e-mail to staff, July 10, 1998 (included in diary), DBP, LMB; Berger, interviews, July 7, 2005, and Jan. 19, 2007; Walpole, interview, Oct. 7, 2007.

33. Berger, "My Chronology," diary entries for Aug. 20, Sept. 3, and 11, 1998, DBP, LMB; Berger, e-mail to staff, July 10, 1998 (quote, "votive candles"); Berger, interview, Jan. 19, 2007.

34. Berger, "My Chronology," diary entry for Apr. 9, 1999 (Winterstellar quoted), DBP, LMB; Berger, interview, Jan. 19, 2007; Groman, interview, Mar. 9, 2005; Gilbert, interview, June 17, 2005 (quoted); Lima OCAW official, interview by author, Apr. 28, 2004 (quoted). Walpole was equally clear about the reasons for the rejection. "We have a thousand employees that aren't paying (Lima) tax right now," he later remembered telling the mayor. "If we put it to a vote, 995 of our employees would say 'no'" to annexation. Walpole, interview, Oct. 7, 2007.

35. Robert Payne, oral interview by author, Oct. 11, 2006; Schaefer, interview, June 6, 2006; Berger, "My Chronology," diary entry for Mar. 18, 1998, DBP, LMB.

36. Monus, interview, Apr. 8, 2004; Gilbert, interview, Mar. 10, 2005.

37. "Refinery Shouldn't Reopen: Official," *Chicago Sun-Times*, Jan. 14, 2000; Steve Warmbir, "Refinery to Pay $2 Million Fine," *Chicago Sun-Times*, Aug. 25, 2000; "State Officials Filing More Charges against Premcor," Associated Press, Sept. 1, 2000; Art Golab, "297 to Lose Jobs in Refinery Closing," *Chicago Sun-Times*, Jan. 18, 2001; Luis Munoz-Oliviera, "Starting Over: Premcor Closing Leaves More Than Jobs Behind," *Chicago Daily Herald*, Feb. 1, 2001 (worker quoted); Groman, interview, Mar. 9, 2005. Payne also recognized this point. Payne, interview, Oct. 11, 2006.

38. David C. Korten, "The Mythic Victory of Market Capitalism," in Mander and Goldsmith, *The Case against the Global Economy*, 184–85; Frank, *One Market Under God*, 1–50; Greenfield, "From Rights to Regulation," 8–9; Buder, *Capitalizing on Change*, 329–30. For a more fully developed elaboration of the glories of unhampered free markets, see Richard B. McKenzie, "Consequences of Relocation Decisions," in Staudohar and Brown, *Deindustrialization and Plant Closure*, 153–66. Such abstract reasoning has, in the past two decades, directly found its way into public policy expression in the waves of tax cuts aimed disproportionately at the upper end of the economic spectrum, justified by a kind of born-again, supply-side religion that dominated the White House in the Reagan-Bush era. On this point, see Norton Garfinkle, *The American Dream vs. the Gospel of Wealth: The Fight for a Productive Middle-Class Economy* (New Haven, Conn.: Yale Univ. Press, 2006), 1–11, 144–62.

39. Greenfield, "From Rights to Regulation," 9 (Friedman quoted); Drew R. McCoy, *The Elusive Republic: Political Economy in Jeffersonian America* (New York: Norton, 1980), 13–23, 105–32. On the ethically shaky nature of Friedman's arguments, see Robert C. Solomon, *The New World of Business: Ethics and Free Enterprise in the Global 1990s* (Lanham, Md.: Rowman and Littlefield, 1994), 213–18.

40. Kaufman, Zacharias, and Karson, *Managers vs. Owners*, 15–16; Andrew R. L. Cayton, *The Frontier Republic: Ideology and Politics in the Ohio Country, 1780–1825* (Kent, Ohio: Kent State Univ. Press, 1986), 52, 68–76; Jeffrey P. Brown, "The Political Culture of Early Ohio," and Andrew R. L. Cayton, "'Language Gives Way to Feelings': Rhetoric, Republicanism, and Religion in Jeffersonian Ohio," both in T*he Pursuit of Public Power: Political Culture in Ohio, 1767–1861*, ed. Brown and Cayton (Kent, Ohio: Kent State Univ. Press, 1994), 4–5, 33–34; Bernard Bailyn, *The Ideological Origins of the American Revolution* (Cambridge, Mass.: Harvard Univ. Press, 1967), 55–93.

41. Cayton, *The Frontier Republic*, 76–77; Knepper, *Ohio and Its People*, 96–97, 212–14, 332; Ohio Committee on Corporations, Law, and Democracy, *Citizens over Corporations: A Brief History of Democracy in Ohio and Challenges to Freedom in the Future* (Akron, Ohio: AFSC, 2000), 11–53 (Ohio Supreme Court quoted, 17–18); Kelly, *Divine Right of Capital*, 129; Greenfield, "From Rights to Regulation," 21; Richard L. Grossman and Frank T. Adams, "Exercising Power over Corporations through State Charters," in Mander and Goldsmith, *The Case against the Global Economy*, 374–85. Buder describes how this resistance toward the early emergence of corporations and deep popular suspicion of corporate powers was shared widely across antebellum America; see Buder, *Capitalizing on Change*, 112–14. Conversely, James Willard Hurst has argued that while the initial granting of a corporate charter was an occasion for significant controversy in the early nineteenth century, such legislative disputes soon settled down into "rather standard demands for the means of reaching rather standard business ends." See Hurst, *Law and the Conditions of Freedom*, 15–18 (quoted, 16).

42. McCraw, *Prophets of Regulation*, 58–61; Garfinkle, *The American Dream vs. the Gospel of Wealth*, 70–79; Kelly, *Divine Right of Capital*, 136–37; Lustig, "Politics of Shutdown," 140 (on *Munn*); Buder, *Capitalizing on Change*, 1–6, 183–87, passim (quoted, 3); Greenfield, "From Rights to Regulation," 21 (Brandeis quoted); Bakan, *Corporation*, 20–21; William F. May, *Beleaguered Rulers: The Public Obligation of the Professional* (Louisville, Ky.: Westminster John Knox Press, 2001), 137–38 (stakeholder analysis); G. Jones, *Multinationals and Global Capitalism*.

43. On economic liberalism and the 2008 Wall Street meltdown, see Phillips, *Bad Money*, xi–lxv, 1–68; and Paul Krugman, *The Return of Depression Economics and the Crisis of 2008* (New York: Norton, 2009), 139–90. For poll data, see Gar Alperovitz, *America beyond Capitalism: Reclaiming Our Wealth, Our Liberty, and Our Democracy* (Hoboken, N.J.: John Wiley and Sons, 2005), 173–74 (poll data). On "moral capitalism," see Rosabeth Moss Kanter, *Supercorp: How Vanguard Companies Create Innovation, Profits, Growth, and Social Good* (New York: Crown Business, 2009), 1–2, 13–25, 57–72, 245–53; and Patricia Aburdene, *Megatrends, 2010: The Rise of Conscious Capitalism* (Charlottesville, Va.: Hampton Roads Publishing, 2005), 22–27; Bakan, *Corporation*, 33, 41.

44. Lima Integrated Complex, "BP and the Community," 3 (Greve quoted); Bakan, *Corporation*, 33, 41; Frey, "How Green Is BP?" (PR expert quoted); Yeomans, *Oil: Anatomy of an Industry*, 200.

45. Paisley, interviews, Oct. 29 and Dec. 22, 2005; Schaefer, interview, June 6, 2006.

46. R. Thomas, "Heartbreak in Sundown City" (BP spokesperson quoted).

47. Mander, "Rules of Corporate Behavior," 310, 312–14, 320–22 (quoted, 314, 321–22); Bakan, *Corporation*, 56–61, 69–70; Greenfield, "From Rights to Regulation," 2–3; Kelly, *Divine Right of Capital*, 52–3, 90–91.

48. Mander, "The Rules of Corporate Behavior," 315.

49. R. Thomas, "Heartbreak in Sundown City," 1 (quote, "responsibility is to our shareholders"); Berger, "My Chronology," diary entry for Aug. 12, 1998 (Greve statement), DBP, LMB. Scholars who have studied the responses of corporate CEOs to plant closings describe a great deal of awareness by executives about the social cost of such economic decisions for their

partner communities. Many accept a sense of obligation. Even so, notes Archie Carroll, such realizations have not always been accompanied by "more positive responses" to these communities. For a summary of these studies, see Carroll, "Management's Social Responsibilities," in Staudohar and Brown, *Deindustrialization and Plant Closure,* 171–72, 180 (Carroll quoted).

50. Gilbert, interview, June 17, 2005; Kuenzli, interview, July 13, 2005.

51. Buder, *Capitalizing on Change,* 464.

52. Nissen, *Fighting for Jobs,* 151; Berger, interview, July 7, 2005.

53. Aburdene, *Megatrends, 2010,* 90–114, 140–60.

54. Sirianni and Friedland, *Civic Innovation in America,* 10–11; Robert Putnam, *Bowling Alone: The Collapse and Revival of American Community* (New York: Simon and Schuster, 2000), see especially 31–64, 277–84; Robert Bellah et al., *Habits of the Heart: Individualism and Commitment in American Life* (New York: Harper and Row, 1985); Harry Boyte, *Everyday Politics: Reconnecting Citizens and Public Life* (Philadelphia, Pa.: Univ. of Pennsylvania Press, 2004), 6–13. Sirianni and Friedland do a fine job of encapsulating both Putnam's analysis and convincing arguments against it; see their *Civic Innovation in America,* 16–20.

55. Sirianni and Friedland, *Civic Innovation in America,* 9, 35–58, 79–85; Alperovitz, *America beyond Capitalism,* 131–46 (quoted, 131); Boyte, *Everyday Politics,* 34–39; Jeffrey Berry, Kent E. Portney, and Ken Thomson, *The Rebirth of Urban Democracy* (Washington, D.C.: Brookings Institution, 1993), 46–70, 159–91.

56. Mayer, "Personalizing the Impersonal"; Greenfield, "From Rights to Regulation," 8 (law professors quoted). On the *Citizens United* case, see Adam Liptak, "Justices, 5–4, Reject Corporate Campaign Spending Limit," *New York Times,* Jan. 22, 2010.

57. "Write new rules," in Cowie and Heathcott, *Beyond the Ruins,* 15. For charter revocation and other efforts at corporate restriction, see Kelly, *Divine Right of Capital,* 167–77; Lustig, "Politics of Shutdown," 144–46; and Grossman and Adams, "Exercising Power over Corporations through State Charters," in Mander and Goldsmith, *The Case against the Global Economy,* 386–89.

58. For early efforts at developing a global corporate regulatory apparatus, see Brian Roach, "A Primer on Multinational Corporations," in *Leviathans: Multinational Corporations and the New Global History,* ed. Alfred D. Chandler Jr. and Bruce Mazlish (Cambridge, UK: Cambridge Univ. Press, 2005), 42–43; G. Jones, *Multinationals and Global Capitalism,* 222–23; and Mayer, "Personalizing the Impersonal."

59. Mullen, interview, Sept. 27, 2005.

60. Belcher, interview, Aug. 17, 2004; Payne, interview, Sept. 14, 2006. Local banker David Drum agreed. "For the record I give Dave Berger all the credit in the world for saving that refinery," Drum claimed. "He's the one who did it, by himself." Drum, interview, Apr. 23, 2004; Portz, *Politics of Plant Closings,* 140 (quoted), 170–71.

61. Berger, "My Chronology," diary entry for Dec. 7, 1998, DBP, LMB.

62. Berger's comments in R. Thomas, "Heartbreak in Sundown City."

63. Mark D. Abrams, "Fire and the Development of Oak Forests," *BioScience* 42 (1992): 346–49, 351–52; Gordon Whitney, "An Ecological History of the Great Lakes Forest of Michigan," *Journal of Ecology* 75 (1987): 672, 688–81.

Epilogue

1. Petzinger, "A Mayor's Mission" (Conn quoted).

2. Jim Mackinnon, "Company Turnaround Lifts Morale," *Akron Beacon Journal,* June 11, 2007; Alison Grant, "Team Approach Inspires Workers," *Cleveland Plain Dealer,* Sept. 28, 2005.

3. "David Stockman Announces Plans for New Firm to Focus on Industrial Buyouts and Buildups," Business Wire, Sept. 16, 1999 (Stockman quoted); "David A. Stockman and Timothy D. Leuliette Establish $2 Billion Equity Fund Focused on Midwest's Industrial Economy," PR Wire, Oct. 11, 1999; "Former Reagan Budget Director Facing 3 Charges," *Toledo Blade,* Mar. 27, 2007, A3; William Greider, "Stockman's Folly," *Nation,* Apr. 16, 2007, 8; Landon Thomas, "Stung by Fraud Indictment, a Power Broker Punches Back," *New York Times,* Apr. 15, 2007; Geraldine Fabrikant, "US Drops Fraud Charges against David Stockman," *New York Times,* Jan. 9, 2009.

4. Greider, "Stockman's Folly," 8.

5. Frank and Liesman, "While BP Prepares New Us Acquisition, Amoco Counts Scars" (Browne and jokes quoted); "BP Amoco Cites Discovery, Reform," *New York Times,* July 15, 1999; Pratt, *Prelude to a Merger,* 286–87; Frey, "How Green Is BP?" (BP statistics); Helene Cooper, "BP's Browne Is 'Green' But with Focus on Profits," *Wall Street Journal,* Aug. 12, 1998; Dominic Rushe, "Battered Petroleum," *Sunday Times* (London), Dec. 24, 2006; Chip Cummins et al., "Scandal, Crises Hasten Exit for British Icon," *Wall Street Journal,* May 2, 2007.

6. H. Cooper, "BP's Browne Is 'Green'"; Frey, "How Green Is BP?" (activist quoted); Bakan, *Corporation,* 39–46 (activist quoted, 40).

7. Frey, "How Green Is BP?"; Bakan, *Corporation,* 40–41.

8. Senate testimony of William Burkett, Mar. 4, 2004, http://anwrnews.com/docs/20020404_Bill_Burkett_Letter.asp (accessed Aug. 15, 2006) (Burkett quoted); Jason Leopold, "Documents Show BP Ignored Pipeline Woes for Years," Aug. 11, 2006, http://www.truthout.org/docs_2006/081106J.shtml (accessed Aug. 15, 2006); Bakan, *Corporation,* 80–84.

9. "Second Blast as BP Refinery This Year Frays Texas City's Nerves," *Houston Chronicle,* July 29, 2005; Anne Belli, "OSHA Slams BP with Record $21 Million Fine," *Houston Chronicle,* Sept. 23, 2005; Anne Belli and Dino Cappiello, "BP Missed Clues to Blast," *Houston Chronicle,* Oct. 28, 2005; "BP Leads Nation in Refinery Deaths," Associated Press State and Local Wire, May 15, 2005; "The Year of the American Nightmare," *Sunday Times* (London), Dec. 24, 2006; Jad Mouawad, "BP Confirms US Inquiry into Its Energy Trading," *New York Times,* Aug. 29, 2006; Barton, quoted in Tom Henry, "Fallout from Oil Leaks in Alaska Reaches BP's Oregon Refinery," *Toledo Blade,* Sept. 11, 2006 (quote, "blind to the safety culture"); Henry, "BP Probe Results Not a Shock Here," *Toledo Blade,* Jan. 8, 2007; Henry, "BP Refinery Suffers "Deep' Problems," *Toledo Blade,* Jan. 17, 2007; Julia Werdigier and Stephen Labaton, "BP, Under New Chief, to Pay a Big Settlement," *New York Times,* Oct. 26, 2007.

10. Rushe, "Battered Petroleum," 5; Bhushran Bahree and Chip Cummins, "BP's CEO Browne Will Give Up Job Early," *Wall Street Journal,* Jan. 13, 2007; Chip Cummins, "BP Now May Feel Heat from Alaska," *Wall Street Journal,* Aug. 8, 2006; Chip Cummins et al., "Scandal, Crises Hasten Exit for British Icon," *Wall Street Journal,* May 2, 2007; Alan Cowell, "John Browne Steps Down Abruptly from BP," *International Herald Tribune,* May 1, 2007, http://www.iht.com/articles/2007/05/01/news/bp.php (accessed Aug. 1, 2007); Jad Mouawad, "Oil Giants Loath to Follow Obama's Green Lead," *New York Times,* Apr. 7, 2009; Carol D. Leonnig, "Despite BP Corporate Code, Firm Has Made Political Contributions," *Washington Post,* June 29, 2010.

11. Sarah Lyall, Clifford Krauss, and Jad Mouawad, "In BP's Record, a History of Boldness and Costly Blunders," *New York Times,* July 12, 2010 (Hayward and Waxman quoted); Jad Mouawad, "For BP, a History of Spills and Blunders," *New York Times,* May 8, 2010; Pierre Thomas et al., "BP's Dismal Safety Record," May 27, 2010, ABC News Online, http://abcnews.go.com/WN/bps-dismal-safety-record/story?id=10763042 (accessed June 7, 2010); "BP Starts Operation to Seal Well for Good," *Toledo Blade,* Aug. 4, 2010.

12. Arend, "BP Refinery Workers to Keep Jobs Under New Owner"; Berger, e-mail to Schaefer and Kevin Hawkley, Aug. 30, 2001; Schaefer, e-mail to Berger et al., Sept. 20, 2001; Brad Hull, e-mail to Berger et al., Sept. 21, 2001; Michael Press, e-mail to Berger et al., Aug. 14, 2002; Hull, e-mail to Berger, Nov. 28, 2001 (quote, "the threat is quite real"), all in "E-mail Misc." folder, DBP, LMB; Joseph Leto, "O'Malley Sees Refining Comeback, But Not until Next Year," *Oil Price Information Service,* Aug. 14, 2002; Jim Sabin, "St. Louis–based Oil Refiner to Cut Jobs from Lima, Ohio, Plant," *Lima News,* Sept. 17, 2002.

13. Kuenzli, interview, July 13, 2005; Paisley, interview, Dec. 22, 2005; Nelson Antosh, "Gasoline Demand and Prices Are Going Up, But Refineries Aren't," *Houston Chronicle,* Mar. 28, 2004 (quote, "golden age"); John Dillin, "How Will This Era End?" *Christian Science Monitor,* Sept. 20, 2005, 10; Russell Gold and Thaddeus Herrick, "Storm's Damage to Energy Plants Appears Limited," *Wall Street Journal,* Sept. 26, 2005; Herrick, "Refiners' Tough Call: Do Fall Maintenance or Pump-Out?" *Wall Street Journal,* Sept. 28, 2006; Russell Gold and Michael M. Phillips, "Gulf Energy Facilities Get Off to a Slow Start After Storms," *Wall Street Journal,* Sept. 30, 2005; Mark Clayton, "A Push to Build New US Refineries," *Christian Science Monitor,* Sept. 21, 2005: 11–12; James Peltz, "Katrina's Aftermath: Energy Profits Likely to Keep Rising," *Los Angeles Times,* Sept. 8, 2005.

14. Jim Sabin, "Premcor Talking $1 Billion Expansion," *Lima News,* Nov. 30, 2004; Jim Sabin, "Premcor Plans Would Vault Lima to Top Tier," *Lima News,* Dec. 1, 2004; James Norman, "Premcor, EnCana Studying Refinery Upgrade," *Platt's Oilgram News,* Nov. 30, 2004; Beth Evans, "Premcor Deal to Further Valero Sour Strategy," *Platt's Oilgram News,* Apr. 26, 2005, 1, 4; "Valero Chief Eager to Buy Refineries," *Houston Chronicle,* Mar. 23, 2004 (quote, "I want 'em all"); Tim Rausch, "Valero Buys Premcor," *Lima News,* Apr. 26, 2005; Julie McKinnon, "Refiner Drops $2 Billion Plan for Lima Site," *Toledo Blade,* Dec. 16, 2005; Jim Sabin, "Refinery Upgrade Project Killed," *Lima News,* Dec. 19, 2005.

15. Heather Rutz, "Valero Won't Comment on Sale Rumors," *Lima News,* Jan. 20, 2007; Tim Rausch, "Signs Point to Refinery Sale," *Lima News,* Jan. 23, 2007; "Special Report: Active Consolidation Likely for Refining in 2007," *Oil Price Information Service,* Feb. 7, 2007; accompanying e-mail, David Berger to author, Feb. 8, 2007, in author's possession; Bart Mills, "Valero Narrows Field for Lima Plant Sale," *Lima News,* Mar. 20, 2007; Rutz, "Rumored Valero Suitors Raise Concern," *Lima News,* Mar. 27, 2007 (quote, "giddy sales process").

16. Heather Rutz, "Big Deal: Husky Acquires Valero Plant," and Rutz and Bart Mills, "Husky Good News for Refinery, Employees, City," both in *Lima News,* May 3, 2007; Gary Pakulski, "Canadian Firm Buys Lima Refinery," *Toledo Blade,* May 3, 2007; Ana Campoy, "Refiners Cash In on High Gasoline Prices," *Wall Street Journal,* May 18, 2007; Berger, interview, July 7, 2005; Yeomans, *Oil: Anatomy of an Industry,* 111. For environmental criticism of tar sands plans, see Naomi Klein, "Baghdad Burns, Calgary Blooms," *Nation,* June 18, 2007, 10.

17. Julie M. McKinnon, "GM to Slash 30,000 Jobs," *Toledo Blade,* Nov. 22, 2005; "Ford to Trim 30,000 Jobs, Shut 14 Sites," *Toledo Blade,* Jan. 24, 2006; Micheline Maynard, "Chrysler to Cut 13,000 Jobs in Overhaul," *New York Times,* Feb. 15, 2007; Mike Wagner, "Bicycle Plant Workers Suffer Setback in Ohio," *Atlanta Journal-Constitution,* May 30, 1998; Sandra Livingston, "Huffy Corp. 'Doing Everything Right,'" *Cleveland Plain Dealer,* July 12, 1998; Kym Liebler, "Huffy Rides Out of Town," *Cincinnati Enquirer,* July 27, 1998; "Philips to Cut 1500 Jobs in Ohio, Moving Work to Mexico," *New York Times,* Apr. 28, 2000; Julie McKinnon, "From High Pay to Uncertainty," *Toledo Blade,* Dec. 7, 2003.

18. Homer Brickey, "Ford to Invest $335 Million in Lima," *Toledo Blade,* July 16, 2003; Tim Rausch, "Dana Cutting 100 Jobs in Lima," *Lima News,* Oct. 21, 2005; Jennifer Feehan, "Doors Locked on Empty Prison Cells," *Toledo Blade,* June 27, 2004; "Welcome to Ohio—and the Heart of the Election Battle," *The Economist,* May 6, 2004 (demographic data).

19. Ronald Lederman, "Global Could Lure in Other Industry," *Lima News,* Nov. 30, 1999; editorial, "Economic Projects Often Happen in Gradual Steps," *Lima News,* Sept. 24, 2003; Jim Sabin, "Global Plans October Start," *Lima News,* Sept. 28, 2005; Jim Sabin, "Global Building Taking Shape," *Lima News,* Apr. 26, 2006; U.S. Census Bureau, "State & County Quickfacts, Lima (city), Ohio," http://quickfacts.census.gov/qfd/states/39/3943554.html; US Census Bureau, HUD State of the Cities Data System: output for Lima Ohio, http://socds.huduser.org/census/incpov.odb (accessed June 19, 2007); US Census Bureau, American Factfinder, "Lima, Ohio: Census 2000 Demographic Profile Highlights, http://factfinder.census.gov/servlet/SAFFFacts?_event=&activeGeoDiv+geoSelect&pctxt (accessed June 19, 2007).

20. Berger, interview, Jan. 19, 2007.

21. Jim Sabin, "Berger Unopposed," *Lima News,* Oct. 22, 2001; Jim Sabin, "Candidates Bombarded: Berger, Bushong at Forum," *Lima News,* Oct. 19, 2005 (quote, "protect slackers"); "Ned Bushong," *Lima News,* Nov. 5, 2005; Jim Sabin, "Berger Sworn In: Mayor's Fifth Term Makes City Record," *Lima News,* Dec. 2, 2005; Heather Rutz, "Berger Wins by a Knockout," *Lima News,* Nov. 4, 2009.

Selected Bibliography

Aburdene, Paticia. *Megatrends, 2010: The Rise of Conscious Capitalism.* Charlottesville, Va.: Hampton Roads Publishing, 2005.

Alperovitz, Gar. *America beyond Capitalism: Reclaiming Our Wealth, Our Liberty, and Our Democracy.* Hoboken, N.J.: John Wiley and Sons, 2005.

Angel, William D., Jr. *Not All Politics Is Local: Reflections of a Former County Chairman.* Kent, Ohio: Kent State Univ. Press, 2002.

Armstrong, Ellis L., ed. *History of Public Works in the United States, 1776–1976.* Chicago, Ill.: American Public Works Association, 1976.

Bailyn, Bernard. *The Ideological Origins of the American Revolution.* Cambridge, Mass.: Harvard Univ. Press, 1967.

Bakan, Joel. *The Corporation: The Pathological Pursuit of Profit and Power.* New York: Free Press, 2004.

Bamberg, James. *British Petroleum and Global Oil, 1950–1975: The Challenge of Nationalism.* Cambridge, UK: Cambridge Univ. Press, 2000.

Baxandall, Rosalyn, and Elizabeth Ewen. *Picture Windows: How the Suburbs Happened.* New York: Basic Books, 2000.

Bensman, David, and Roberta Lynch. *Rusted Dreams: Hard Times in a Steel Community.* Berkeley, Calif.: Univ. of California Press, 1988.

Berry, Jeffrey, Kent E. Portney, and Ken Thomson. *The Rebirth of Urban Democracy.* Washington, D.C.: Brookings Institution, 1993.

Black, Brian. *Petrolia: The Landscape of America's First Oil Boom.* Baltimore, Md.: Johns Hopkins Univ. Press, 2000.

Blackford, Mansel G. *The Rise of Modern Business: Great Britain, the United States, Germany, Japan, and China.* Chapel Hill, N.C.: Univ. of North Carolina Press, 2008.

Bluestone, Barry, and Bennett Harrison. *The Deindustrialization of America: Plant Closings, Community Abandonment, and the Dismantling of Basic Industry.* New York: Basic Books, 1982.

———. *The Great U-Turn: Corporate Restructuring and the Polarizing of America.* New York: Basic Books, 1988.

Boyte, Harry T. *Everyday Politics: Reconnecting Citizens and Public Life.* Philadelphia, Pa.: Univ. of Pennsylvania Press, 2004.

Brown, Jeffrey P. "The Political Culture of Early Ohio." In Brown and Cayton, *The Pursuit of Public Power.*

———, and Andrew R. L. Cayton, eds. *The Pursuit of Public Power: Political Culture in Ohio, 1767–1861.* Kent, Ohio: Kent State Univ. Press, 1994.

Bruno, Robert. *Steelworker Alley: How Class Works in Youngstown.* Ithaca, N.Y.: Cornell Univ. Press, 1999.

Buder, Stanley. *Capitalizing on Change: A Social History of American Business.* Chapel Hill: Univ. of North Carolina Press, 2009.

Camp, Scott. *Worker Response to Plant Closings: Steelworkers in Johnstown and Youngstown.* New York: Garland, 1995.

Carroll, Archie B. "Management's Social Responsibilities." In Staudohar and Brown, *Deindustrialization and Plant Closure.*

Cayton, Andrew R. L. *The Frontier Republic: Ideology and Politics in the Ohio Country, 1780–1825.* Kent, Ohio: Kent State Univ. Press, 1986.

———. "'Language Gives Way to Feelings': Rhetoric, Republicanism, and Religion in Jeffersonian Ohio." In Brown and Cayton, *The Pursuit of Public Power.*

Chandler, Alfred D., Jr. *Scale and Scope: The Dynamics of Industrial Capitalism.* Cambridge, Mass.: Harvard Univ. Press, 1990.

———. *The Visible Hand: The Managerial Revolution in American Business.* Cambridge, Mass.: Belknap Press, 1977.

———, and Herman Daems. Introduction to *Managerial Hierarchies: Comparative Perspectives on the Rise of the Modern Industrial Enterprise,* edited by Chandler and Daems. Cambridge, Mass.: Harvard Univ. Press, 1980.

Chernow, Ronald. *Titan: The Life of John D. Rockefeller, Sr.* New York: Random House, 1998.

Churella, Albert. *From Steam to Diesel: Managerial Customs and Organizational Capacities in the Twentieth-Century American Locomotive Industry.* Princeton, N.J.: Princeton Univ. Press, 1998.

Clarke, Tony. "Mechanisms of Corporate Rule." In Mander and Goldsmith, *The Case against the Global Economy.*

Cooper, Patricia. *Once a Cigar Maker: Men, Women, and Work Culture in American Cigar Factories, 1900–1919.* Chicago, Ill.: Univ. of Illinois Press, 1987.

Cowie, Jefferson, and Joseph Heathcott. Introduction to *Beyond the Ruins: The Meanings of Industrialization,* edited by Cowie and Heathcott. Ithaca, N.Y.: Cornell Univ. Press, 2003.

Craypo, Charles, and Bruce Nissen, eds. *Grand Designs: The Impact of Corporate Strategies on Workers, Unions, and Communities.* Ithaca, N.Y.: ILR Press, 1993.

———. Introduction to Craypo and Nissen, *Grand Designs.*

Cumbler, John T. *A Social History of Economic Decline: Business, Politics, and Work in Trenton.* New Brunswick, N.J.: Rutgers Univ. Press, 1989.

Dixon, John E. *Lima-Hamilton: Its Historical Past, 1869, 1845, and Later.* New York: Newcomen Society of England, American Branch, 1948.

Fasenfest, David. "Cui Bono." In Craypo and Nissen, *Grand Designs.*

Ferrier, R. W. *The History of the British Petroleum Company.* Vol. 1, *The Developing Years, 1901–1932.* Cambridge, UK: Cambridge Univ. Press, 1982.

Flaim, Paul O., and Ellen Sehgal. "Displaced Workers of 1979–1983: How Well Have They Fared?" *Monthly Labor Review* 108 (June 1985): 3–16.

Floyd, Leslie A. "Lima and Manufacturing, 1850–1910." *Allen County Reporter* 33 (1987): 33–79.

Ford, Harvey S. "The Faurot Failure at Lima." *Northwest Ohio Quarterly* 23 (1950–51): 82–95.

Frank, Thomas. *One Market under God: Extreme Capitalism, Market Populism, and the End of Economic Democracy.* New York: Anchor Books, 2000.

Fuechtmann, Thomas G. *Steeples and Stacks: Religion and the Steel Crisis in Youngstown.* Cambridge, UK: Cambridge Univ. Press, 1989.

Garfinkle, Norton. *The American Dream vs. the Gospel of Wealth: The Fight for a Productive Middle-Class Economy.* New Haven, Conn.: Yale Univ. Press, 2006.

Gordon, Sarah H. *Passage to Union: How the Railroads Transformed American Life.* Chicago, Ill.: Ivan R. Dee, 1996.

Green, Constance McLoughlin. *The Rise of Urban America.* London: Hutchinson University Library, 1965.

Greenfield, Kent. "From Rights to Regulation in Corporate Law." In *Perspectives on Company Law 2,* edited by Fiona McMillan Patfield. London: Kluwer Law International, 1997.

Greider, William. "'Citizen' GE." In Mander and Goldsmith, *The Case against the Global Economy.*

———. *The Soul of Capitalism: Opening Paths to a Moral Economy.* New York: Simon and Schuster, 2003.

Grossman, Richard L., and Frank T. Adams. "Exercising Power over Corporations through State Charters." In Mander and Goldsmith, *The Case against the Global Economy.*

Hamilton, David. K. *Governing Metropolitan Areas: Response to Growth and Change.* New York: Garland Publishing, 1999.

Hammer, Michael, and James Champy. *Reengineering the Corporation: A Manifesto for Business Revolution.* New York: HarperBusiness, 1993.

Harris, Candee S. "Magnitude of Job Loss." In Staudohar and Brown, *Deindustrialization and Plant Closure.*

Hawke, David Freeman. *John D.: The Founding Father of the Rockefellers.* New York: Harper and Row, 1980.

Heilbroner, Robert L., and Aaron Singer. *The Economic Transformation of America, 1600 to the Present.* 4th ed. New York: Wadsworth Publishing, 1999.

Hidy, Ralph, and Muriel Hidy. *Pioneering in Big Business, 1882–1911.* New York: Harper and Brothers, 1955.

High, Steven. *Industrial Sunset: The Making of North America's Rust Belt, 1969–1984.* Toronto, Ontario: Univ. of Toronto Press, 2003.

———. "The Making of the 'Rust Belt' in the Minds of North Americans, 1969–1984." *Canadian Review of American Studies* 27 (1997): 48–59.

Hirsimaki, Eric. "The Lima Locomotive Works." *Locomotive and Railways Preservation* 31 (March–April 1991): 38–53.

Houshower, Hans. "We Built the Best." *Locomotive and Railways Preservation* 31 (March–April 1991): 10–32.

Hurst, James Willard. *Law and the Conditions of Freedom in the Nineteenth-Century United States.* Madison, Wis.: Univ. of Wisconsin Press, 1964.

Hurt, R. Douglas. *The Ohio Frontier: Crucible of the Old Northwest, 1720–1830.* Bloomington, Ind.: Indiana Univ. Press, 1996.

Jackson, Bradley G. "Re-engineering the Sense of Self: The Manager and the Manager Guru." *Journal of Management Studies* 33 (Sept. 1996): 571–90.

Jackson, Kenneth T. *Crabgrass Frontier: The Suburbanization of the United States.* New York: Oxford Univ. Press, 1985.

Jones, Geoffrey. *Multinationals and Global Capitalism: From the Nineteenth to the Twenty-first Century.* New York: Oxford Univ. Press, 2005.

Jones, Marnie. *Holy Toledo: Religion and Politics in the Life of "Golden Rule" Jones.* Lexington, Ky.: Univ. Press of Kentucky, 1998.

Kanter, Rosabeth Moss. *Supercorp: How Vanguard Companies Create Innovation, Profits, Growth, and Social Good.* New York: Crown Business, 2009.

Kantor, Paul, with Stephen David. *The Dependent City: The Changing Political Economy of Urban America.* Glenview, Ill: Scott, Foresman, 1988.

Karson, Marvin, Allen Kaufman, and Lawrence Zacharias. *Managers vs. Owners: The Struggle for Corporate Control in American Democracy.* New York: Oxford Univ. Press, 1995.

Keenan, Jack. "Electric Street Railways of Lima: The Formative Years." *Allen County Reporter* 48 (1992): 1–106.

Kelly, Marjorie. *The Divine Right of Capital: Dethroning the Corporate Aristocracy.* San Francisco, Calif.: Berret-Koehler Publishers, 2001.

Knepper, George. *Ohio and Its People.* 2nd ed. Kent, Ohio: Kent State Univ. Press, 1997.

Korten, David C. "The Mythic Victory of Market Capitalism." In Mander and Goldsmith, *The Case against the Global Economy.*

Lamoreaux, Naomi, Daniel M. G. Graff, and Peter Temin. "Beyond Markets and Hierarchies: Toward a New Synthesis of American Business History." *American Historical Review* 108 (April 2003): 404–32.

Lindblom, Charles. "The Market as Prison." *Journal of Politics* 44 (1982): 324–36.

Linkon, Sherry Lee, and John Russo. *Steeltown USA: Work and Memory in Youngstown.* Lawrence, Kans.: Univ. Press of Kansas, 2002.

Livesay, Harold C. *Andrew Carnegie and the Rise of Big Business.* Boston, Mass.: Little, Brown and Co., 1975.

Love, Frank G. "The Discovery of Oil in Allen County." *Allen County Reporter* 37 (1981): 29–39.

Lustig, R. Jeffrey. "The Politics of Shutdown: Community, Property, Corporatism." *Journal of Economic Issues* 19 (March 1985): 123–52.

Mander, Jerry. "The Rules of Corporate Behavior." In Mander and Goldsmith, *The Case against the Global Economy.*

———, and Edward Goldsmith, eds. *The Case against the Global Economy: And for a Turn toward the Local.* San Francisco, Calif.: Sierra Club Books, 1996.

Marx, Thomas G. "Technological Change and the Theory of the Firm: The American Locomotive Industry, 1920–1955." *Business History Review* 50 (Spring 1976): 1–24.

May, William F. *Beleaguered Rulers: The Public Obligation of the Professional.* Louisville, Ky.: Westminster John Knox Press, 2001.

Mayer, Carl J. "Personalizing the Impersonal: Corporations and the Bill of Rights." *The Hastings Law Journal* 41 (March 1990): 577–688.

McCoy, Drew R. *The Elusive Republic: Political Economy in Jeffersonian America.* New York: Norton, 1980.

McCraw, Thomas. *Prophets of Regulation: Charles Francis Adams, Louis D. Brandeis, James M. Landis, Alfred E. Kahn.* Cambridge, Mass.: Harvard Univ. Press, 1984.

McKelvey, Blake. "The Emergence of Industrial Cities." In *Urban America in Historical Perspective,* edited by Raymond Mohl and Neil Betten. New York: Weybright and Talley, 1970.

McKenzie, Richard M. "Consequences of Relocation Decisions." In Staudohar and Brown, *Deindustrialization and Plant Closure.*

Milkman, Ruth. *Farewell to the Factory: Auto Workers in the Late Twentieth Century.* Berkeley, Calif.: Univ. of California Press, 1997.

Morgan, Gareth. *Images of Organization.* 2nd ed. London: Sage Publications, 1997.

Nelson, Daniel. *Farm and Factory: Workers in the Midwest, 1880–1990*. Bloomington, Ind.: Indiana Univ. Press, 1995.

Newman, Katharine. *Declining Fortunes: The Withering of the American Dream*. New York: Basic Books, 1993.

Nissen, Bruce. *Fighting for Jobs: Case-Studies of Labor-Community Coalitions Confronting Plant Closings*. Albany, N.Y.: State Univ. of New York Press, 1995.

O'Connor, Richard. *The Oil Barons*. Boston: Little, Brown and Co., 1971.

Orfield, Myron. *American Metropolitics: The New Suburban Reality*. Washington, D.C.: Brookings Institution Press, 2002.

Peterson, Wallace C. *Silent Depression: The Fate of the American Dream*. New York: W. W. Norton and Co., 1994.

Phillips, Kevin. *Bad Money: Reckless Capitalism, Failed Politics, and the Global Crisis of American Capitalism*. New York: Penguin, 2009.

———. *Wealth and Democracy: A Political History of the American Rich*. New York: Broadway Books, 2002.

Portz, John. *The Politics of Plant Closings*. Lawrence, Kans.: Univ. Press of Kansas, 1990.

Pratt, Joseph A. *Prelude to Merger: A History of Amoco Corporation, 1973–1998*. Houston, Tex.: Hart Publications, 2000.

Putnam, Robert. *Bowling Alone: The Collapse and Revival of American Community*. New York: Simon and Schuster, 2000.

Reich, Robert. *Supercapitalism: The Transformation of Business, Democracy, and Everyday Life*. New York: Alfred A. Knopf, 2007.

Roach, Brian. "A Primer on Multinational Corporations." In *Leviathans: Multinational Corporations and the New Global History*, edited by Alfred D. Chandler Jr. and Bruce Mazlish. Cambridge, UK: Cambridge Univ. Press, 2005.

Roberts, Paul. *The End of Oil: On the Edge of a Perilous New World*. Boston, Mass.: Houghton Mifflin, 2004.

Rogers, Elizabeth. "Cleaning Up Superfund Law: Controversy over Liability Provisions Stalls Reauthorization Drive." *ABA Journal* 83 (Dec. 1997): 91.

Rothstein, Lawrence E. *Plant Closings: Power, Politics, and Workers*. Dover, Mass.: Auburn House Publishing, 1986.

Rusler, William. *A Standard History of Allen County, Ohio*. Chicago, Ill.: American Historical Society, 1921.

Ryscavage, Paul. *Income Inequality in America: An Analysis of Trends*. Armonk, N.Y.: M. E. Sharpe, 1999.

Sampson, Anthony. *The Seven Sisters: The Great Oil Companies and the World They Shaped*. New York: Viking Press, 1975.

Samuelson, Robert J. *The Good Life and Its Discontents: The American Dream in the Age of Entitlement, 1945–1995*. New York: Random House, 1995.

Sethi, S. Prakash. "The Ax Man Cometh: GM Pulls out of Norwood City." *Business and Society Review* 69 (Spring 1989): 20–25.

Sirianni, Carmen, and Lewis Friedland. *Civic Innovation in America: Community Empowerment, Public Policy, and the Movement for Civic Renewal*. Berkeley, Calif.: Univ. of California Press, 2001.

Solomon, Robert C. *The New World of Business: Ethics and Free Enterprise in the Global 1990s*. Lanham, Md.: Rowman and Littlefield, 1994.

Staudohar, Paul D., and Holly E. Brown, eds. *Deindustrialization and Plant Closure*. Lexington, Ky.: D. C. Heath and Co., 1987.

Stemen, Thomas F. "A Brief History of the Standard/BP Lima Refinery." *Allen County Reporter* LIV (1998): 66–93.

Stockman, David A. *The Triumph of Politics: Why the Reagan Revolution Failed.* New York: Harper and Row, 1986.

Stover, John. *The Life and Decline of the American Railroad.* New York: Oxford Univ. Press, 1970.

Suddes, Thomas. "Panorama of Ohio Politics in the Voinovich Era, 1991–96." In *Ohio Politics,* edited by Alexander P. Lamis. Kent, Ohio: Kent State Univ. Press, 1994.

Teaford, Jon. *Cities of the Heartland: The Rise and Fall of the Industrial Midwest.* Bloomington, Ind.: Indiana Univ. Press, 1993.

———. *City and Suburb: The Political Fragmentation of Metropolitan America, 1850–1970.* Baltimore, Md.: Johns Hopkins Univ. Press, 1979.

Whitney, Hope. "Cities and Superfund: Encouraging Brownfield Redevelopment." *Ecology Law Quarterly* 30, no. 1 (2003): 59–112.

Williams, Mari E. W. "Choices in Oil Refining: The Case of BP, 1900–1960." *Business History* 26 (Nov. 1984): 307–28.

Williamson, Harold F., and Arnold R. Daum. *The American Petroleum Industry: The Age of Illumination, 1859–1899.* Evanston, Ill.: Northwestern Univ. Press, 1959.

Yeomans, Matthew. *Oil: Anatomy of an Industry.* New York: New Press, 2004.

Yergin, Daniel. *The Prize: The Epic Quest for Oil, Money, and Power.* New York: Simon and Schuster, 1992.

Index